Pre-Occupied Spaces

Critical Studies in Italian America
Nancy C. Carnevale and Laura E. Ruberto, *series editors*

This series publishes works on the history and culture of Italian Americans by emerging as well as established scholars in fields such as anthropology, cultural studies, folklore, history, and media studies. While focusing on the United States, it also includes comparative studies with other areas of the Italian diaspora. The books in this series engage with broader questions of identity pertinent to the fields of ethnic studies, gender studies, and migration studies, among others.

Series Board
Simone Cinotto
Thomas J. Ferraro
Donna Gabaccia
Edvige Giunta
Joseph Sciorra
Pasquale Verdicchio

Pre-Occupied Spaces

Remapping Italy's Transnational Migrations and Colonial Legacies

Teresa Fiore

FORDHAM UNIVERSITY PRESS
NEW YORK 2017

Copyright © 2017 Fordham University Press

All rights reserved. No part of this publication may be reproduced, stored in a retrieval system, or transmitted in any form or by any means—electronic, mechanical, photocopy, recording, or any other—except for brief quotations in printed reviews, without the prior permission of the publisher.

Fordham University Press has no responsibility for the persistence or accuracy of URLs for external or third-party Internet websites referred to in this publication and does not guarantee that any content on such websites is, or will remain, accurate or appropriate.

Fordham University Press also publishes its books in a variety of electronic formats. Some content that appears in print may not be available in electronic books.

Visit us online at www.fordhampress.com.

Library of Congress Cataloging-in-Publication Data available online at http://catalog.loc.gov.

Printed in the United States of America

19 18 17   5 4 3 2 1

First edition

CONTENTS

Preface   vii

Introduction. All at One Point: The Unlikely Connections between Italy's Emigration, Immigration, and (Post)Colonialism   1

Part I. Waters: Migrant Voyages and Ships from and to Italy

Aperture I: An O*sea*n of Pre-Occupation and Possibilities: *L'orda*   23

1. Crossing the Atlantic to Meet the Nation: The Emigration Ship in Mignonette's Songs and Crialese's *Nuovomondo*   31

2. Overlapping Mediterranean Routes in Marra's *Sailing Home*, Ragusa's *The Skin Between Us*, and Tekle's *Libera*   50

Part II. Houses: Multiethnic Residential Spaces as Living Archives of Pre-Occupation and Invention

Aperture II. A Multicultural Project in a National Square: The Orchestra of Piazza Vittorio   75

3. Displaced Italies and Immigrant "Delinquent" Spaces in Pariani's Argentinian *Conventillos* and Lakhous's Roman *Palazzo*   83

4. Writing the Pasta Factory and the Boardinghouse as Transnational Homes: Public and Private Acts in Melliti's *Pantanella* and Mazzucco's *Vita*   104

Part III. Workplaces: A Creative Re-Occupation of Labor Spaces against Exploitation

Aperture III. Labor on the Move: Rodari's Construction Workers and Kuruvilla's Babysitter   131

5. Edification between Nation and Migration in Cavanna's *Les Ritals* and Adascalitei's "Il giorno di San Nicola"   137

6. The Circular Routes of Colonial and Postcolonial Domestic Work:
   Però's and Ciaravino's *Alexandria* and Ghermandi's
   "The Story of Woizero Bekelech and Signor Antonio" — 161

Conclusion. Italy as a Laboratory for Imagi-Nation:
The Citizenship Law between Inbound and Outbound Flows — 183

Notes — 197
Works Cited — 227
Index — 241
Image Credits — 249

PREFACE

This book was born more than a decade ago, when issues of migration concerned me at a scholarly and personal level in inextricable ways. As I navigated my way through work and study visas as an Italian "legal alien," to use the official language of the immigration service bureaus, and eventually the green card and U.S. citizenship process, my personal concern diminished while the scholarly, and hence cultural and political, concerns have remained high. In fact, these issues have only become increasingly more relevant (and alas, tragic) globally, and my interest in reading them simultaneously in terms of space and time has, if anything, gained in meaning and scope.

In its final form, the book reflects a thematic organization and a sectional division that I had envisioned from the start. Yet, over this arc of time, many specific aspects have changed, and I found myself updating and adding to the project as over time new texts became available for analysis and inclusion and I felt compelled or inspired to embrace them. Given the long period over which this manuscript was composed, it was perhaps inevitable that several other articles and book chapters would take me temporarily away from it: In the process I could only joke at the fact that the book itself had come to embody a source of preoccupation. Fortunately, the decision by Fordham University Press to publish the book allowed me to end that preoccupation. Writing a book is a form of migration, and for the time being the journey related to this book of mine is over.

This extended and multifaceted project has been possible thanks to the patience and encouragement of a special group of people who have supported my efforts despite the complications born out of many relocations on my part for both work and family reasons. Since I started writing this book, I have changed my address roughly fifteen times and lived in two countries (Italy and the United States) and three states within the United States (California, Massachusetts, and New York), while regularly traveling to four continents (Europe, Asia, North America, and now South America). While usually one's partner is thanked at the end of the acknowledgments, I would be remiss in relegating my life companion Sharad Chaudhary to the bottom of the list. More than anybody else he has read, edited, and provided critical commentary on this book and the complex and fascinating world it explores. There are no words to express a deeply felt *grazie* to him for co-existing for such a long time with a project that spoke so much to our trajectories as migrants, and that enriched our fruitful conversations about belonging, and especially linguistic belonging. Laura Ruberto has known about my research project since we were

PhD students at the University of California San Diego in the early 2000s; as fate would have it she became the coeditor of the "Critical Studies in Italian America" series at Fordham University Press. I am grateful to her for unfailingly reminding me about the importance of bringing a project to a close at a manageable pace, while also inspiring me to consider new sources and new approaches year after year. Her coeditor, Nancy Carnevale, has repeatedly rekindled my interest in the project, while Fred Nachbaur and William Cerbone, respectively director and editorial associate at Fordham University Press, have provided professional guidance with a warm and professional approach. My thanks also go to the copy editor, Gregory McNamee, and, in particular, to the Press's managing editor, Eric Newman, who shepherded the project to completion.

The project stems from years of reading, writing, and discussing works on the subject in the Department of Literature at the University of California San Diego, where professors such as Stephanie Jed, Winifred Woodhull, and George Lipsitz exposed me to theories that profoundly shaped my views of the subject. It is to Pasquale Verdicchio that I owe the early formation of an interconnected way of looking at the subject of migration and nationhood, as well as the cross-pollination of creative work and criticism. And it is to William Boelhower, former Professor at the University of Trieste, Italy, that I owe my very first and yet long-lasting theoretical understanding of the relationships between history, culture, and space, and more specifically textual space. Since my graduate-school days, Clarissa Clò has been involved in this fascinating laboratory of reflections about Italy within a transnational perspective: I feel fortunate that she has continued to be part of intense exchanges about Italy (and its captivating contents and unnerving discontents).

Like any project of this duration, the book has grown thanks to the input, direct and indirect alike, of many colleagues and students where I have worked: My academic migrations from California State University Long Beach to Harvard, Rutgers, NYU, and Montclair State University have been too numerous to acknowledge them individually. Some of these institutions have provided precious support for the advancement of the project: from the De Bosis Fellowship at Harvard to the CEMS (Center for European and Mediterranean Studies) Fellowship at NYU; various intramural funds in Long Beach; release time at Montclair State University; and a Rockefeller Foundation grant for an early stay in Bellagio, Italy.

In particular, this book has benefited from the close reviews and enthusiastic support of two colleagues whose work I have been inspired by over the years: Robert Viscusi for his transnational view of Italian America, and Cristina Lombardi-Diop for her global view of colonial and postcolonial Italy. Forms of support ranging from invitations to give talks, moderate panels, or publish work related to this book have been offered over two decades by some of the founders and/or most committed proponents of the fields I am active in: Anthony J. Tamburri, Fred Gardaphé, Peter Carravetta, Joseph Sciorra, Stanislao Pugliese, Edvige Giunta, Caterina Romeo, Stefano Albertini, Anna De Fina, and Luciana Fellin. Among my colleagues in the department where I work, a special position is held by Marisa Trubiano at Montclair State University for her constant presence in projects that, while not strictly connected to this book, have made writing it possible thanks to shared tasks on special initiatives. I have also benefited from conversations with current or former graduate students committed to research on topics of migration whom I have had the pleasure of mentoring over the years: Anita Pinzi at NYU, Arianna Fognani at Rutgers University, and in particular Eveljn Ferraro at Brown University.

I am immensely indebted to all the artists and scholars who have written on the subject in ways that have proven so inspiring, but mostly to those artists and scholars who accepted to present their work as part of the cultural programs and initiatives I coordinate at Montclair State University: La Compagnia delle Acque and Gian Antonio Stella, the Teatro delle Albe and the Fratelli Mancuso, Amara Lakhous, and Simone Cinotto and Donna Gabaccia have brought theory, art, and history to campus in very meaningful and in many cases unforgettable ways. I would also like to express my specific *grazie* to scholars and artists who shared their unpublished or out-of-print works so that this book could take new routes: Gualtiero Bertelli for the DVD of the show *L'orda*; Robert Viscusi for select handmade booklets of the early limited edition of *Ellis Island*; Eric Byron for the copies of Mignonette's songs from his private collection; Gabriella Bellorio for the transcript of her interview with Vincenzo Amato; Annika Lems and Christine Moderbacher for the DVD of their documentary *Harraga*; Franco Baldasso for allowing me to quote from his unpublished interview with Mazzucco in Italian; Mariana Adascalitei for sharing the manuscript of "Il giorno di San Nicola"; and Franco Però and Renata Ciaravino for providing a DVD copy of the performance of *Alexandria* and a range of related materials. Additionally, the maps in the Introduction were developed by Anthony Bevacqua at the Center for Mapping and GeoSpatial Analysis, Montclair State University in New Jersey. A heartfelt thank you goes to Angelo Pitrone, whose photograph is reproduced on the book cover: It is a shot of the one-room home of Filippo Bentivegna, a Sicilian outsider artist who became known for sculpting heads from rocks for decades in his garden and turning it into his Castello Incantato (enchanted castle). Filippo of the Heads, as he was informally known, had emigrated to the United States and then returned to Sicily under mysterious circumstances. The frescoes he painted in his home are a poignant personal representation of that experience of dislocation and discovery. Pitrone's picture captures a detail of the painted wall that combines the sea journey (a fish pregnant with fishes like a migrant ship) and the built environment of the modern metropolis (American skyscrapers oddly resembling medieval Italian towers). Located in the domestic environment of the artist, the frescoes interweave waters, houses and workplaces, like this book of mine.

Last, but certainly not least, my family (Gianna, Nicolò, Ignazio, Elvira, Gabriele, and Evelina) is to be deeply thanked for believing in the personal as well as intellectual importance of my own migration while they remained put at home, unable to read what I write (including this very book) in a language that is not theirs. The very final edits of the book happened while my family became larger: Daniela, my adoptive Colombian daughter, has unwittingly turned into a migrant herself in order to be with us, bringing with her new questions about the significance of borders and belonging. It is in this tension between abroad and home, foreign and familiar, that this work has continued to acquire depth for me and I hope meaning for its readers. This book is dedicated to all migrants, of yesterday and today, for the ways in which they constantly prompt a vital remapping of our concrete and mental worlds.

Pre-Occupied Spaces

INTRODUCTION

All at One Point: The Unlikely Connections between Italy's Emigration, Immigration, and (Post)Colonialism

> But there were those who insisted that the concept "immigrant" could be conceived in the abstract. . . . It was . . . a narrow-minded attitude . . . that, basically, has remained with all of us, mind you: it keeps cropping up even today.
>
> —ITALO CALVINO

This book is above all a space for the analysis of stories. I will therefore begin with a story as a starting point for my discussion. The resistance exercised against the arrival and presence of immigrants, reductively perceived as subaltern subjects from a supposedly uncivilized area of the world, and the related conviction that certain people belong to one place more than others has been arguably best represented in Italo Calvino's short story "All at One Point," thanks to its hyperbolic flavor. A brilliant exploration of the absurdity and hypocrisy of this resistance and conviction, the story confirms Calvino's unique ability to intervene in the political arena as a storyteller by deploying inventive mechanisms of analogic shifts rather than the more common strategy of direct denunciation adopted by *engagé* literature. Included in *Cosmicomics* (1965), a collection entirely devoted to the imbrications of scientific theories in our daily lives, "All at One Point" addresses models of the development of the universe such as the Big Bang in order to analyze social conflicts and to gesture toward a not-too-utopian space of fruitful coexistence beyond the traditional distinction between the "inside" and "outside" spheres.

Calvino's "One Point" as a Departure Toward Pre-Occupied Spaces

In the story, Calvino invites the readers to picture an impossible space, one point: in an imaginary pre–Big Bang era. Before space was created, everything and everybody was concentrated in that one point. The inhabitants of this non-space obviously lived a quite claustrophobic life, although they were not aware of it since space did not yet exist, and time even less so. Nonetheless, they had a quite clear idea of what an immigrant was: The narrator himself—the story is told by the old Qfwfq as a historical account—distinguishes the local immigrant family, the Z'zus, from the rest of the inhabitants, by marking their cultural habits. A numerous family with too many mattresses and baskets in the yard and with the peculiar habit of hanging laundry on a rope stretching from one point to another . . . of the "one point," the Z'zus seem to be named after the Zulus, a term that in Italian has lost its actual reference to a South African ethnic group and has acquired the import of a generic offense against people considered as "boorish" and "ignorant" (Garzantilinguistica.it). For being different, these immigrants were automatically marked as aliens in the one-point world. The narrator clearly denounces the nonsensical nature of such racist attitudes in a space that cannot be pre-occupied because it never existed previously. In an environment with no time before or after, and "no other place to migrate from or to," it should be impossible to mark the difference between those who are allowed to stay and those who are rejected. Yet, this ancestral preoccupation over difference was pervasive. The narrator comments: "This was mere unfounded prejudice . . . but there were those who insisted that the concept 'immigrant' could be conceived in the abstract." Among those is the unfriendly Pber^t Pber^d, whom the narrator meets one day in the post–Big Bang era only to see his anti-immigrant sentiments confirmed with the same embittered preoccupation. Here is the narrator again: "It was . . . a narrow-minded attitude . . . that, basically, has remained with all of us, mind you: it keeps cropping up even today" (44). During a chat with Qfwfq at a café, Pber^t Pber^d remembers the good old days in the one point. While envisioning a possible return to that time, or rather non-time, he also remarks: "When we go back there . . . the thing we have to make sure of this time, is [that] certain people remain out. . . . You know whom I mean: those Z'zus" (45). This desire to cleanse even a prototypical space and to posit it as an ideal place to return to is criticized by a narrator who effectively conveys the author's perspective. Annoyed by the insinuations of Pber^t Pber^d against the immigrant family, Qfwfq criticizes this sense of superiority by recalling and celebrating the infinite generosity and abundance of another inhabitant of the one-point world, Mrs. Ph(i)Nk$_o$, a Felliniesque character whose desire to feed tagliatelle to the world results in the Big Bang, thus making her a mythic generator of space and time.

This fantastic tale, characterized by a comic and yet serious spirit, provides a set of considerations on the meaning of belonging to a space and by extension to a culture. To question forms of racism, Calvino does not resort to abstract intellectualism or simplistic morality. He does not intend to claim that people are undifferentiated, either; all his characters are indeed very peculiar in their idiosyncratic ways, and as such they are part of the one point, where everything and everybody has to share. The one-point metaphor allows Calvino not only to ponder on and condemn the forms of discrimination effected against immigrants, but to also hint at the genealogy of such discrimination in the colonial enterprise through referencing Z'zus/Zulus, who historically embodied resistance against colonial aggression as well as apartheid in South Africa. That this process of analysis of practices and this proposal of alternatives took place in the mid-1960s, when Italy was experiencing a decline in emigration and was not yet affected by the arrival of immigrants, makes this short story particularly representative of one of the functions of literature, namely, examining society in its historical developments and current mores, but also rethinking it imaginatively at a more universal level, thus sometimes anticipating future manifestations. As a witty and surreal piece demonstrating the absurdity of any territorial demand whether set in migratory or colonial spaces, this brilliant story sets the tone for a book like mine, preoccupied with space.

The Geostatistics of Italy's Migrations and Colonialism

Since migrations are perceived and described via geography, whether physical, social, or imagined, space is the central preoccupation of this book on migrations and, in particular, migrations from and to Italy. The book's main aim is to explore space in its complex forms and implications, embracing time within it. Migrations have to do with statistics as well: Migrants are constantly counted and assessed based on numbers. Thus, this book also looks at numbers, mostly to understand what stories cannot be told by numbers alone. However, numbers can play an important role in revealing flaws in most of the trite attacks leveled against migrants and demonstrate how the "preoccupation" around migrants can be dissipated by looking at past histories of migration and their effects, what I term as "pre-occupation." While the hyphenated word—"pre-occupation"—indicates the presence of prior experiences of relocation in space, the distinction, yet even more so, the intersection with the unhyphenated word—"preoccupation"—is what lies at the core of this book which, in order to identify and in the attempt to dissipate the reasons behind the concern over migrants, explores the linkages between the past and the present of human relocations. If we look at numbers, for example, this linkage becomes apparent. At the end of 2013 there are 4,636,647 Italian citizens registered in the list of Italians abroad (AIRE), that is, people who have moved to a new country and retained Italian citizenship or acquired dual citizenship, as well as descendants of Italians who recently acquired citizenship through the 1992 law.[1] These people are the result of contemporary migrations or the effect of past migrations originating from Italy, a departure point for worldwide migrations par excellence. Interestingly, according to the ISTAT data of January 1, 2014, there are 4,922,085 immigrants in Italy.[2] Their countries of origin practically span the entire globe, including, albeit in small part, former Italian colonies in the Horn of Africa and the Mediterranean region. The numerical comparison offered here—practically the same number of Italians live abroad as the number of foreigners living in Italy—dissolves the myth of "invasion" by showing that space cannot be represented one-dimensionally as overcrowded by new arrivals when its occupation is decreased by the absence of (previous or potential) residents whose entitlement to protection would entail high commitment and expenses for the state.[3]

Inscribed within a deeper and broader investigation of the country's historical outbound flows due to economic emigration and colonial expansion as well as its more recent inbound flows due to economic and political pressure, these statistics function as a starting point for a critical reading of Italy's intricate national formation project and its position in the present scenario of international exchanges as a result of its role as a sending country until the post–World War II era up to the 1970s. That Italy has since the mid- to late 2000s been one of the most active proponents and supporters of surveillance, discipline, and punishment for "Fortress Europe" is thus quite ironic. While one could argue that this controller's task is also forced on the country by its crucial geographical position and configuration as one of the main Mediterranean points of entry into the EU, it still seems paradoxical in light of the historical role played by Italy as a major point of departure for emigrants in the nineteenth and twentieth centuries, as a colonial power, and today as a prominent sending country despite its presence in the G7. The current (as of this writing) government, which came into office in 2014, is adopting a markedly different approach to the arrival of migrants, and in particular political refugees. Albeit not without contradictions, it is showing a deeper awareness of the interconnected nature of transnational relations and the value of solidarity, in part as a response to Pope Francis's call to a politics of support and welcome; in his words, "the migrants are not a danger: they are in danger" ("Papa").

The fundamental premise of this book is that the contemporary history of Italian civilization cannot be understood without a rigorous reconsideration of the influence of its outbound and inbound migrations as well as its colonial and imperial experience, all of which I view as phenomena that are not marginal with respect to the country's national formation, but that rather are congenital to its complicated birth and development. A foundational tale of unified Italy is the long and hard process of stitching together over decades (from the first half of the 1800s all the way to World War I) territories that belonged to foreign powers or the Church, and which have in turn produced a diverse regional texture in the country (Figs. 1 and 2).

There is another powerful story that unraveled outside the national borders, even when they were still newly formed. From 1876, shortly after the unification of Italy, to 1976, approximately 27 million Italians left the country and emigrated to practically all continents (Franzina, *Gli Italiani* 145). According to the *Rapporto Italiani nel mondo 2012*, that number increases to 30 million if we count up to our decade (ibid., 1). Considering that in 1871 Italy had 27 million inhabitants (Golini 48), the outbound "flow" is probably more accurately described as a hemorrhage. Despite the high rate of return, about 50 percent,[4] Italy's diaspora constitutes the largest emigration from any country (Vecoli 114) with peaks in the 1880–1920 period and after World War II.[5] Italians emigrated virtually everywhere, giving priority to different continents and countries at different times for specific economic and political reasons (Fig. 3).

Because of their strong regional affiliations (North vs. South), they were treated differently in different places, but overall integration was never easy, not even in places where the Italian community, or colony as it was called back then, was large and mixed. On the contrary, their substantial numerical presence prompted more rooted prejudices that were only somewhat surmounted over time in some countries such as the United States, for example. Primary destinations initially included Argentina and Brazil (starting in the 1870s), especially from the northern regions of Italy, while with the mass emigration of 1880–1920, the United States became a major receiving country for Italian immigrants,[6]

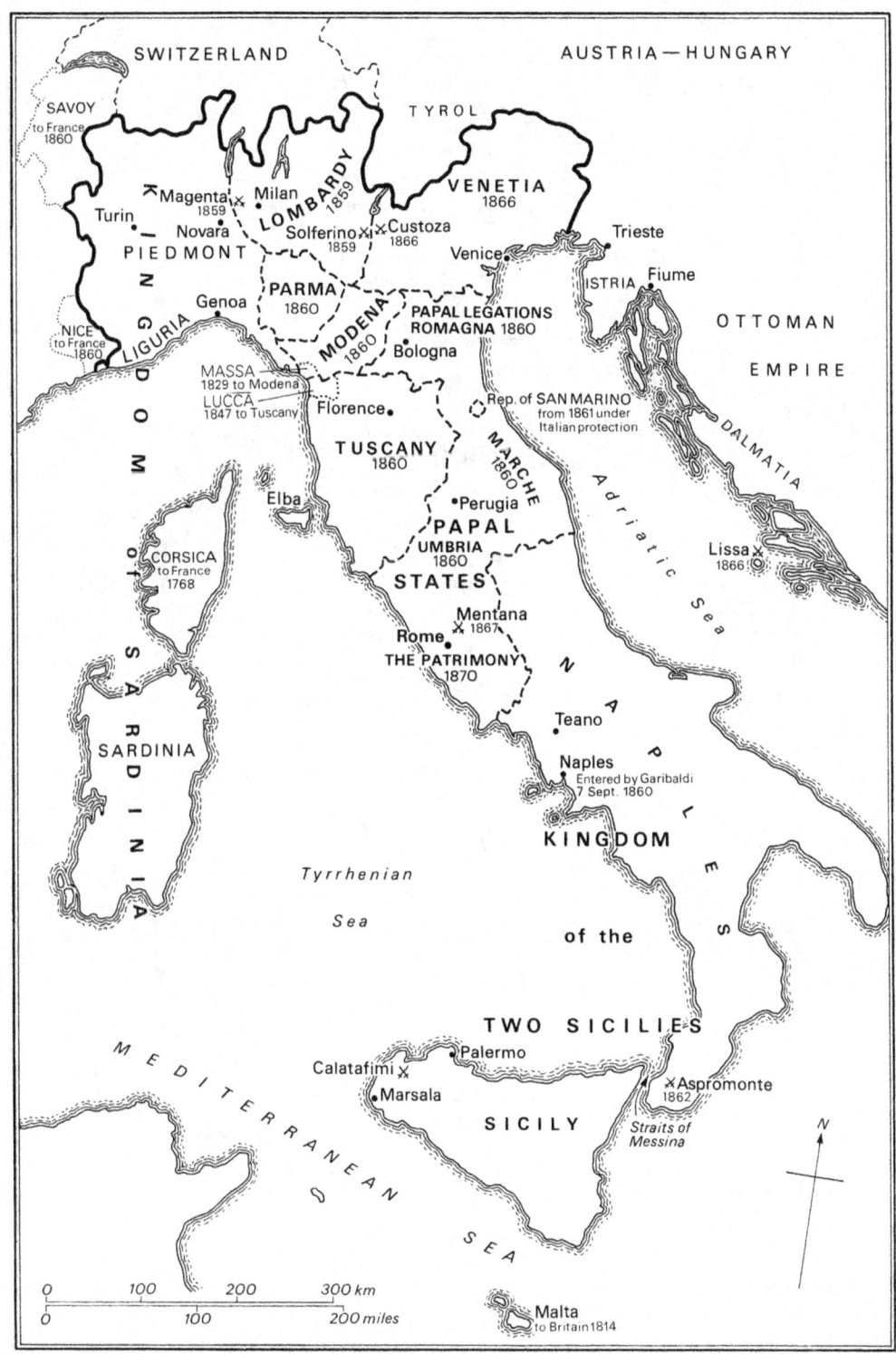

Figure 1. Italy's unification process, 1859–70.

FIGURE 2. Italy's regions.

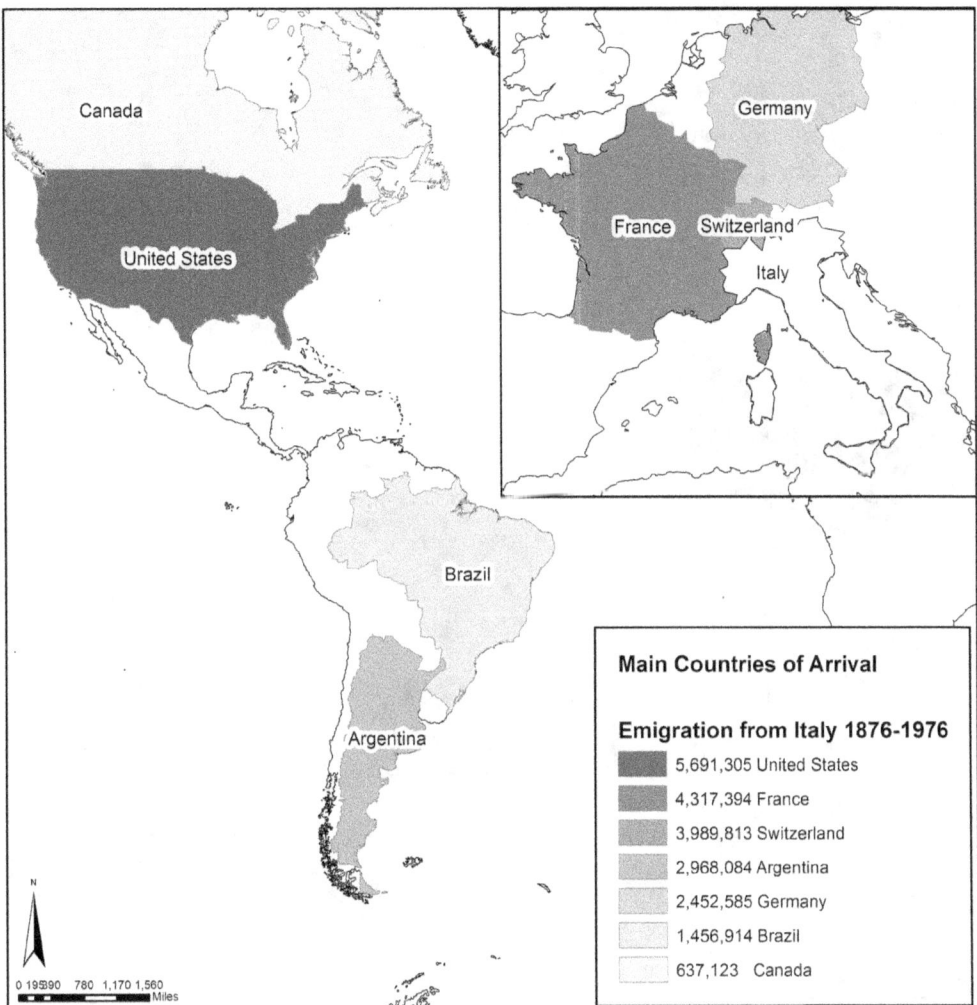

FIGURE 3. Italy's main emigration flows, 1876–1976.

especially from Italy's South. While Italian emigration is strongly linked to "America" in the common perception, in reality, Italians emigrated predominantly to Europe over the century under discussion, and added Canada and Australia to their routes mainly after World War II. This book travels to several countries of destination (Argentina, the United States, France, Tunisia) through the analysis of significant cultural texts that investigate the impact of the Italian presence abroad as well as the faint trace it has ironically left in Italy's collective imaginary, due perhaps to a shortage of public educational projects (emigration is often a subject of academic research).

Shortly after the official unification in 1861 and coterminous with the diaspora described above, Italy embarked on the colonial enterprise. Over the decades, this economic and military process created an offshore empire, known as Empire of Oriental Africa in the mid-1930s, comprising the Horn of Africa, Libya, the Dodecanese Islands, and Albania. The majority of the colonies were lost during and after World War II (Fig. 4).[7]

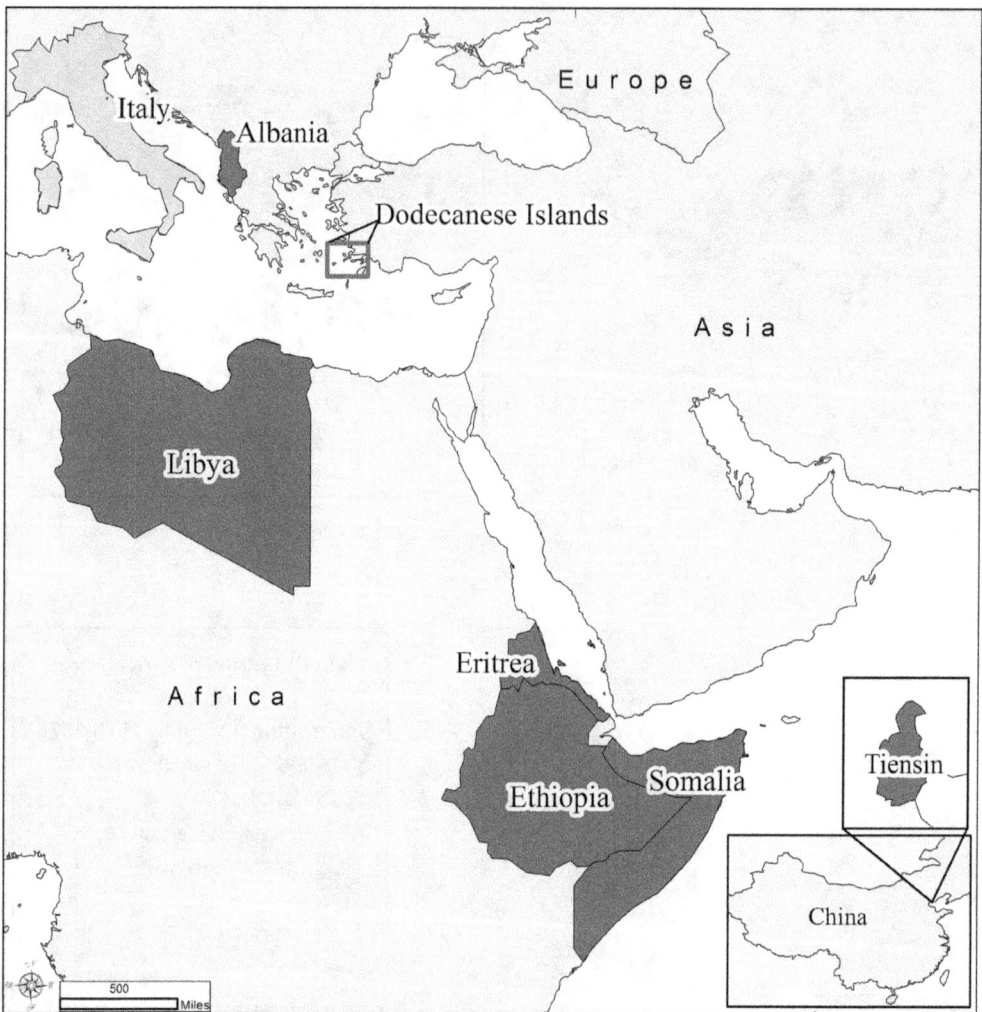

Figure 4. Italian colonies.

Italian colonialism is a complex mosaic of both brief and extended forms of control of territories, which owing to its fragmentation has often been dismissed as secondary or harmless. Fraught with contradictions and omissions that the country has too slowly uncovered through historical studies of the records, Italy's colonialism/imperialism overlapped with emigration. Together, the two projects fundamentally contributed to the atypical formation of national identity outside the country, characterized as both these initiatives were by demographic relocations.[8] The apparently small percentage of Italians who moved to the colonies between the end of the nineteenth century and the first half of the twentieth century—2 percent of the total Italian emigrants in the world, as reported by historian Labanca, citing Sori ("History" 31)—indicates a multidirectional demographic flow that along with emigration shaped the modern nation of Italy away from its centuries-long fragmentation into small states and regions often subject to foreign powers. The nationalist propaganda accompanying both emigration and the colonial/imperial enter-

FIGURE 5. Italian descendants in the world, 1994.

prise functioned as cultural connective tissue for Italy and also Italians outside the country, while forming a model of a nation in motion variously characterized by brief seasonal and long-term definitive relocations of people for economic, military, and political reasons. This demographic dispersion has over time produced a population of an estimated 60 million descendants (*Rapporto 2012*, 2) scattered around the globe, a number curiously close to that of the residents of Italy in 2014 (almost 60 million) (Fig. 5).[9]

In an interesting reversal, Italy since the mid-1970s has become a country of destination, virtually as soon as it stopped sending emigrants abroad in large quantities. In reality, the Tunisian community in Sicily had been forming since the 1960s, and early cases of Chinese presence date back to the interwar period (Giustiniani 20). After the first arrivals of domestic helpers from Catholic countries such as the Philippines in the 1970s, the 1980s mark the more visible presence of immigrants from Africa; yet, it is with the following decade that the phenomenon becomes even more tangible, variegated, and

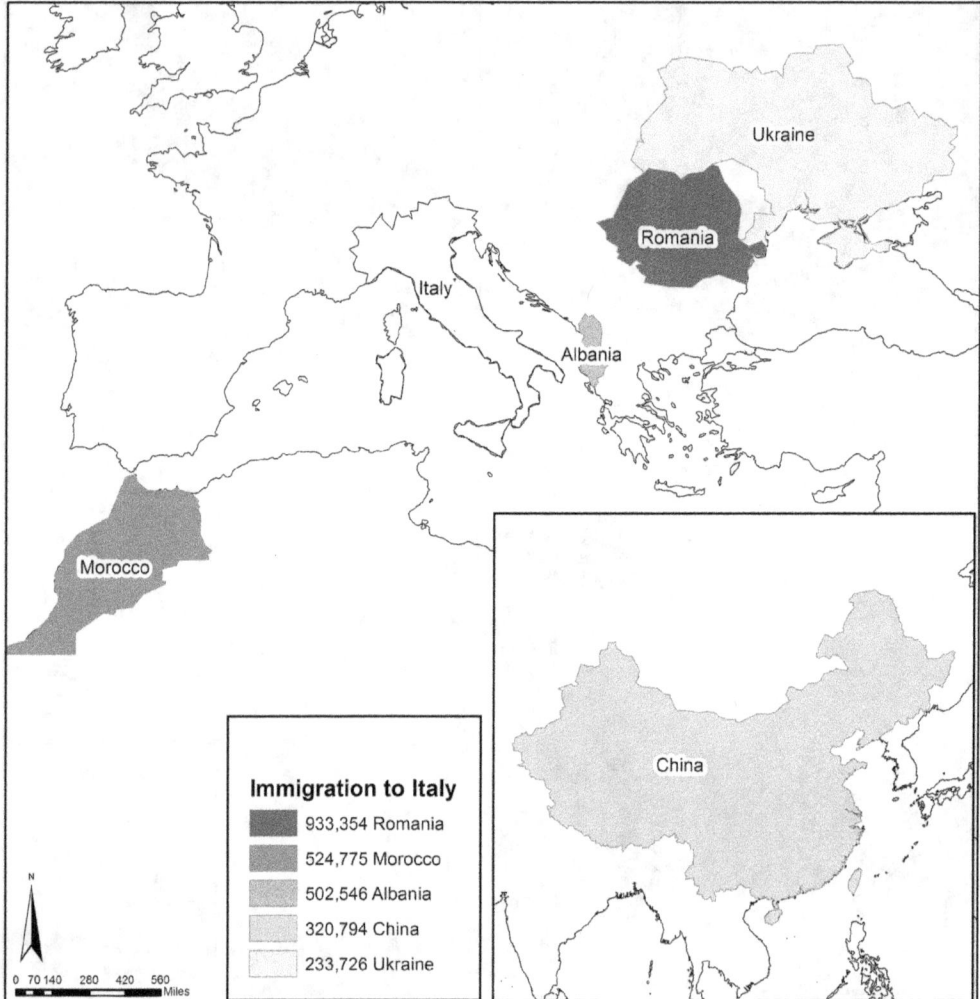

FIGURE 6. Immigration in Italy, 2014.

rooted. As we have seen, today Italy is home to a large and growing[10] foreign population, which is younger than the existing population of citizens ("La Popolazione" 3), thus more active in the economy, and more prolific (15 percent of newborns are of immigrant parents). Scattered throughout Italy in both urban and rural areas, with population densities reaching 11 percent of the local populace in some regions of the North ("La Popolazione" 6), immigrants come from a really wide range of countries, which has created a cultural, religious, and linguistic population of unprecedented diversity in Europe. In order, their primary areas of origin are Eastern Europe—especially Albania, Romania (a EU member), and Ukraine; Africa—particularly Morocco, Tunisia, Egypt, and Senegal; and Asia—mostly China, the Philippines, and India (*Dossier* 2013, 4) (Fig. 6).[11]

Despite imbalances between men and women internal to the national groups, as a whole the immigrant population represents both genders rather equally ("La Popolazione" 1). Mixed marriages with Italians have been steadily growing, and the population of Italy-born children of immigrants now constitutes a solid group of "new Italians" whose presence is openly challenging enclosed perceptions of Italianness, as the Conclusion will show. Indeed, as the demographic and sociological studies have demonstrated for years, immigration to Italy is not a temporary or circumstantial phenomenon but an intrinsic fact in the current and future development of the country. Immigrants should exist in a space of the collective consciousness occupied by memory, as they are a contemporary reincarnation of Italians looking for economic opportunities, political freedom, and personal discovery until the 1970s (and even today, given the current exodus of Italians looking for jobs abroad).[12] Contemporary immigrants in Italy are just more educated, more connected and informed thanks to technology, and in some ways even more adventurous than those Italian emigrants who in some cases traveled to countries with open-door immigration policies (Giustiniani 30–32).

When the numerical coincidence observed between the number of foreign immigrants in Italy, and Italians registered in AIRE is seen in percentage form, the presence of immigrants, takes on a different meaning. As of January 2014, 8.1 percent of the Italian population consists of immigrants, while Italians abroad are equal to 7.6 percent of the resident population in Italy, based on ISTAT data. These coincidental numerical correspondences are mentioned here not just for anecdotal purposes or to fall prey to an empty numerology, but to actually expose the unfounded nature of invasion myths and to also prompt more careful readings of the country's past in order to contain certain anti-immigrant drives identifiable in the current national landscape, with the openly racist comments against former Italo-Congolese Minister of Integration Cécile Kyenge on the part of the Northern League Senator Roberto Calderoli being the tip of the iceberg.[13] As a country occupied by a multilayered history of migrations, today's Italy appears to be in large part preoccupied with safeguarding a national uniformity that in reality openly clashes with its pride in regionalism; its cultural role in the Mediterranean; uninterrupted North- and Rome-bound internal migratory flows since unification; the unsolved economic distance between North and South; the country's dramatically low birth rate;[14] the homogenizing forces of the EU supranational project; the current exodus of Italians due to the economic and political crisis; and the forces of financial and informational globalization affecting Italy as well as the entire world. Italy's shorter and less culturally impacting colonial enterprise, along with its unique postcoloniality (for the most part, immigrant flows are not linked to the country's colonial past), further complicate its position in the international scenario as a G7 country with this peculiar set of experiences.

Thus far, studies in Italian and English on the subjects of emigration and immigration have looked at these two phenomena as separate,[15] or only loosely connected them.[16] Relatively recent publications address the process of national formation and/or belonging in relation with the discrete areas of immigration, transnational diaspora, colonialism, or paired areas of only emigration/colonialism and colonialism/postcolonialism.[17] As I will explain in detail later, in the field of social history, sustained comparative analyses of both emigration and immigration exist but do not address culture, while those volumes that do so in the areas of literature and film set each subject as independent from the other in the single essays anthologized. In contrast, *Pre-Occupied Spaces* integrates Italy's two-way migratory movements in a systematic way and within a colonial and postcolonial context, as part of a study on national identity that, in embracing the precious contributions of historical, economic, and sociological studies, places the cultural text at its core. If Italian society at large has never fully given voice to its own experience of leaving, much less to that of its colonial enterprise, and is resisting dealing comprehensively with the lives of its new immigrants, what do its cultural products—writing, film, visual art, and even urban architecture—have to say about these experiences? More generally, what does it mean to be "Italian" in a culture defined by boundary crossing, movements, displacements, and differences, especially not long after the sesquicentennial of Italy's unification in 2011? Various scholars have investigated all these questions in different ways. What I am instead proposing in *Pre-Occupied Spaces* is to either connect the analysis of texts on emigration from and immigration to Italy that address similar issues despite their spatial and temporal distance, or to analyze texts that directly address the unlikely connections that I have discussed in this introduction.

Space, Pre-Occupation, and Culture

By positing space, and in particular what I call "pre-occupied space" as the focus of my investigation into these issues, I consider the layered forms of both material and intangible occupation encountered by migrants, but also affected by them. Immigrants arrive in spaces (neighborhoods, workplaces, etc.) that are already occupied by others and start interacting with these spaces by borrowing fragments of past traditions and leaving new signs. This is the first definition of the term *preoccupied*, according to Merriam-Webster: Like the verb "to preoccupy," this adjective finds its etymological root in the Latin *praeoccupare* (to seize in advance) and means "already occupied," "taken possession of," "filled beforehand or by others." The use of the hyphen for this term in my book signals this temporal connotation.

At the same time, the impact of the immigrants' arrival and settlement in local environments is a source of concern: These spaces are therefore "preoccupied"—the second definition of the term, this time without the hyphen, is "absorbed in some preoccupation"—in the sense that they host worries among both newcomers and locals, who perceive each other respectively as defensive occupants of and illegitimate intruders into natural, urban, and domestic spaces.[18] The resulting emotional landscape in Italian society is a "geography of preoccupation" (227), to use sociologist Corrado Bonifazi's term, which is a source of tension but, as I argue, also holds a potential transformative power. This preoccupation not only has bearing on the question of control over physical space, but also implies a necessary theoretical rethinking of the forms of being in space and of possibly changing it. Being preoccupied with space—the more abstract meaning of the word, being lost in thought, absorbed, *impensierito*—opens a new cognitive route into people's movements from, to, and around Italy that, I suggest, is eventually characterized by recognition of shared stories among people beyond space- and time-based separations. As unexpected parallels between the experiences of Italian emigrants and immigrants are revealed along the diachronic and synchronic axes at once and within post/colonial contexts, Italy is remapped on a larger space, preoccupied with, rather than by, the richness of human experiences in motion. My use of the hyphenated version of the term in the title of the book brings attention to the type of philosophical and political quarrying that I am engaged with in order to link history and consciousness: Somewhat paradoxically, the hyphen functions as a sort of cognitive caesura that allows me to activate connections.

The concept of pre-occupation and preoccupation I am proposing effectively intertwines notions of space and time, which are normally seen as separate. Migrations are usually read historically, that is to say according to a temporal paradigm that sanctions its beginning, development, and, if applicable, end. This is the reason why Italian emigration has been officially considered a concluded phenomenon of dispersion: In the mid-1970s, ISTAT net flows for migration became positive, meaning that more people entered rather than left Italy. The apparent sense of historical completion that characterizes the emigration experience as well as the colonial one in the general perception is at odds with the presence, in reality, of epiphenomena or legacies of these experiences. Whereas it is often claimed that Italians do not emigrate anymore, as a matter of fact work-related relocation, seasonal emigration, and even "illegal" emigration from Italy continue to occur, and not only occasionally, as a plethora of books on the subject are revealing.[19] Additionally, in 2012, the migration net flows turned negative again for the first time in decades, due to the precarious political, economic and social situation in Italy, as well as the easy mobility granted by the EU, which have prompted a surge in outbound flows, reaching over 100,000 in 2014 (Nava, "La Fuga"). By the same token, while it is believed that Italy's colonialism is a closed historical chapter, its knowledge and analysis is essential to understanding race relations in Italy today.[20] The visibility of epiphenomena and legacies of emigration and colonialism—which belong to the time trajectory—can indeed be traced in the space of today's immigration in Italy.

In setting the question "where" at the core of human existence in my cultural analysis (Derrida 52), I embrace Foucault's proposal that "the present epoch will perhaps be above all the epoch of space" and his belief that "the anxiety of our era has to do fundamentally with space, no doubt a great deal more than with time" (22–23).[21] I thus consider space as a crucial paradigm to examine the links between old and new forms of migration. Concepts such as "heterotopia" (Foucault), "thirdspace" (Soja), "delinquent space" (de Certeau, *Practice*), "dissemiNation" (Bhabha), "imagination" (Cassano), "imagining planetarity" (Spivak), along with Lefebvre's critique of urban space in the direction of "the possible . . . elsewhere" (182), and Sassen's reflections on the socioeconomic modalities of globalization and postmodernism have then been adopted and rechanneled in this book toward the issues of migration and nationhood within the Italian transnational context. In reality, space descriptors are never absent from studies of migration, but they tend to define other spaces (destinations), external to the departure point, and thus make the experience of migrants alien to the space discussed. So, for example, on the map of Italian emigration, Argentina, one of the main destinations for Italian emigrants up to World War I, is an elsewhere with respect to Italy and by the same token, on the immigration map Albania is not Italy. I am instead interested in showing how such seemingly disconnected places have affected Italy and were affected by it over time through the experiences of emigration and colonialism and how these connections become obvious in specific pre-occupied spaces at specific historical moments. Space, in other words, hosts time in my definition of pre-occupied spaces, as I consider concrete, metaphorical, forgotten, recuperated, and (re)invented realities.

In particular, I analyze three types of pre-occupied spaces that correspond to the three parts of the book: oceans/seas, and metonymically boats and ships, as spaces of the crossing, where emigrants turn into immigrants; houses, or more generally places of residence, where migrants live (sometimes work) and interact with other migrants and/or so-called locals; and workplaces, those sites where immigration is partially more visible, but also simplistically flattened to an economic issue. Directly and indirectly, many other spaces such as neighborhoods, schools, as well as worship and entertainment sites are also considered, but these three spaces are crucial in terms of being able to look at emigration, immigration, and (post)colonial experiences in a connected way, as they pertain to the fundamental acts of traveling, living, and working.

In disrupting linearity and opening up to the coexistence of migration experiences that history sees as discrete, these pre-occupied spaces simultaneously allow for a remapping of Italian culture and identity which challenges fixed forms of belonging in a fast developing multiethnic country like Italy. At the center of this remapping lies the cultural text, because of its simultaneous powers of documentation, evocation, and imagination at the crossroads of the local, the national, and the transnational. How do human experiences of relocation and their translation into cultural production complicate and mediate migrations? What new paradigms do they suggest to conceive and effect intercultural coexistence? In my view, culture constitutes an integral part rather than just an epiphenomenon of migrant experiences: If culture is seen as involving "simultaneously work, pleasure, consumption, spirituality, 'aesthetic production,' and reproduction" (Lowe and Lloyd 26), it then represents a complex foray into migratory phenomena otherwise often treated exclusively from socioeconomic perspectives in the media and policymaking.[22] The challenge, embraced by my study, remains that of seeing in the cultural text the presentation of concrete realities with socioeconomic purport, but also the representation, in the sense of invention and imagination, of new possibilities for the coexistence, creation, and exchange of ideas. Analyzed for their aesthetic quality as well as their sociopolitical impact and anthropological meaning at once, cultural texts—a term that I apply interchangeably to visual, written, oral, filmic, and architectural works—function as spaces in themselves, in which the artistic moment is both the result and the source of new theories and practices of living across borders.

The Book's Pre-Occupied Spaces

Within a framework conceptually shaped by the humanities, my reading of spaces is therefore mediated by specific cultural texts that are by definition spatial. In ranging from novels to short stories, nursery rhymes, memoirs, *testimonios*, films, songs, and documentaries, they account for that which is not immediately observable, like memories, desires, and motivations, and tackle the meaning and consequences of relocations from the perspective of both the places of departure and those of arrival. In this respect, the texts foreground a notion by Abdelmalek Sayad that an emigrant is also an immigrant and vice versa, that is, s/he embodies a double location often reflecting a double form of erasure, what he calls "double absence," both in the country of origin and in the new one.[23] Yet, this condition can also provide a "double vision," an enriching and unconventional view of the world.

In each of the book's three sections, I aim for a thematically focused composite of migrant and nonmigrant authors in order to reveal the unlikely connections of their subjects, spaces, and aesthetic modes. Each part is introduced by what I call an Aperture, a term in photography that refers to the opening of a camera lens to control the amount of light that passes in. Apertures in this book open the section by using a text (or several short texts) able to capture the theme at hand. By highlighting the analytical and propositive quality of the notion of the pre-occupied space in that specific text (or texts), this overture paves the way for the reflections offered in the chapters of the single parts. The individual chapters address two or three authors/artists in tandem and critically analyze their different media, often created in different languages (Arabic, English, French, etc.). While some authors are from and reside in Italy and write or make films about either emigration or immigration (in a number of cases their personal stories are in one way or another linked to these experiences), the majority of them are originally from countries other than Italy (among them Eritrea, Algeria, Ethiopia, Tunisia, and India) and reside in Italy today, or are from the countries of destination of their family's migratory routes (the United States, France). As for works on emigration by emigrants or their descendants, the book attempts at least partially to reflect the vast range of destinations Italians reached and contributed to culturally. The predominance of the United States is somewhat counteracted by the inclusion of works on emigration to three important countries of destination for Italians in three different continents: Argentina for South America, France for Europe, and Egypt for Africa, while several references to Tunisia are made as both a country of destination for Italian emigrants and of departure for contemporary immigrants. Finally, in light of the international nature of immigration in Italy, the works analyzed comprise stories pertaining to a much wider palette of provenances, including Eastern Europe and Asia.[24]

Following this architecture, Part I opens with an Aperture on the multimedia show *L'orda*, based on Gian Antonio Stella's book of the same title and adapted to a music and storytelling performance featuring Gualtiero Bertelli and the Compagnia delle Acque along with Stella himself. The stories of perilous voyages and shipwrecks that have silently punctuated the more than 150-year-long history of Italian emigration are used as a platform to reread Italian history at large, especially in light of the current arrivals of immigrants from all over the world. The two chapters of Part I embrace this same parallel between emigration and immigration by focusing on the pre-occupied/preoccupied space of the Atlantic Ocean and the Mediterranean Sea respectively. I look at the songs of Gilda Mignonette, diva of Naples and New York in the first half of the twentieth century, who was cast within an iconography of nationalism connecting emigration and colonialism, and Emanuele Crialese's 2006 film *Nuovomondo*, which offers a nuanced reading of the "nationalizing" and "transnationalizing" function of the voyage. Also considered are three texts that more clearly point to the sea as a palimpsest of stories of people's relocations: Vincenzo Marra's 2001 film *Sailing Home* links contemporary emigration from and immigration to Italy in a tale about shifting identities in the waters between Sicily and Tunisia; Kym Ragusa's 2006 memoir *The Skin Between Us: A Memoir of Race, Beauty and Belonging* connects emigration and slavery to the United States in a woman's tale of reconciliation unraveling in fluid spaces; and Feven Abreha Tekle's 2005 *Libera* describes a postcolonial flight from Eritrea, comparable to the middle passage, that finds in the Mediterranean the golden door to a world that the protagonist perceives as free. The Mediterranean and the Atlantic are thus spaces whose pre-occupations and preoccupations can be turned into an occasion to forge new linkages. In their waters, these texts design a thick tapestry of forced and chosen migratory routes, and of the cultural connections that they have woven over the centuries.

Part II as a whole is a cultural recognition of the spaces where immigrants reside or resided, that is, residential *loci* that have been or are intrinsically linked to the migration experiences from/to Italy as well as so-called ethnic neighborhoods. The Aperture focuses on an area of Rome which has come to represent the immigrant section of the capital: Through Agostino Ferrente's documusical *L'orchestra di Piazza Vittorio*, the square at the center of the Esquilino neighborhood is explored for its several layers of immigrant occupation. The creative project Ferrente's work portrays is an interesting example of how preoccupations over the presence of immigrants can be substituted by new visions, especially in an area where the very meaning of "ethnic neighborhood" has been taken to a transnational level (multi-multiethnic) given the diversity of the immigrants' origin. The two chapters address more specifically the residential spaces inhabited by the immigrants and the galaxy of experiences, emotions and values that these sites have prompted due to the highly mixed presence of tenants inside them. Chapter 3 looks at the *conventillos* as described by Laura Pariani in her novel *Dio non ama i bambini* (2007) and at a residential building (*palazzo*) inhabited by locals and immigrants in the same Vittorio Square, as depicted by Amara Lakhous in his novel *Clash of Civilizations Over an Elevator in Piazza Vittorio* (2006). Despite the different locations of these buildings and the different time periods of the stories (turn-of-the-century Buenos Aires vs. contemporary Rome), the two novels successfully render the challenges and possibilities presented by the coexistence of people from different backgrounds, in part for their captivating employment of the detective genre, in part for their innovative narrative structure, suggesting the need to investigate immigrant societies with new questions in order to find new answers. In looking at yet another two immigrant residential spaces, Chapter 4 stays in Rome for the first half and then moves to New York through the analysis of Mohsen Melliti's 1992 novel *Pantanella: Canto lungo la strada* and Melania Mazzucco's 2003 novel *Vita*, respectively. In the process, the chapter switches from the 1990s to the early 1900s, yet stays focused on the dynamics of tension and cooperation among immigrants living in desperate conditions. Both novels are characterized by a unique combination of domestic and economic activities that complicate the reading of a residential space inhabited by immigrants, and in the case of *Pantanella* postcolonial immigrants from colonies other than the Italian ones in what I call the phenomenon of "indirect" postcolonialism in Italy.[25] The time shift of these two chapters, which was reversed to heighten the connections between the past of emigration from and colonialism on the part of Italy and the present of immigration to Italy, is an occasion to examine the echoes of these three experiences in the intimate and yet transnational space of immigrant living places where layers of human occupation preoccupy the local governments and yet create unique occasions for invention.

Part III shifts attention to the theme of occupation, not in terms of claiming a space as it was for example in the novel *Pantanella* in Chapter 4, but in terms of working in a space. Of all the numerous job sectors that one could analyze in connection to Italian emigrants abroad and foreign immigrants in Italy, two were chosen for their specific relevance in the historical and contemporary scenario: construction labor and domestic help. The Aperture introduces the topic through texts that focus on bricklayers (Gianni Rodari's nursery rhymes from *Favole al telefono*) and babysitters (Gabriella Kuruvilla's children's story *Questa non è una baby-sitter*). The superficially light tone of these texts written for a young readership conceals a very subtle discussion of the abusive work conditions and prejudices that migrants face, complemented by a recognition of their ability to endure and react. Such themes are addressed in Chapters 5 and 6 through texts that, by relying on different genres ranging from theater to fiction, create a galaxy of constant reverberations between the occupations of emigrants and immigrants. Chapter 5 shows how the current exploitation of foreign immigrant workers in the construction sector in Italy today is not dissimilar from the experiences that Italian emigrants encountered some years ago: Mariana Adascalitei's Romanian protagonists in her "Il giorno di San Nicola" are quite reminiscent of François Cavanna's Italian bricklayers in France, as recounted in his 1978 novel *Les Ritals*. The connection between emigration and immigration offered by these two texts through a combined reading can also be traced in Chapter 6 where demographic movements are additionally defined by the colonial routes. In particular, Renata Ciaravino's script for the 2005 play *Alexandria* about adventurous women from the Friuli region who emigrated to Egypt in the 1920s to work as wet nurses and maids anticipates the silent yet profoundly important role of today's domestic helpers and caretakers in Italy as portrayed by Gabriella Ghermandi's colonial/postcolonial "The Story of Woizero Bekelech and Signor Antonio," included in her 2007 novel *Queen of Flowers and Pearls*. In this sense, Part III is concerned with giving visibility to some of the most invisible or anonymous jobs. By foregrounding the preoccupation of the protagonists of all four texts over housing, health, safety, emotional well-being, and personal gratification, Part III attempts to show how these two job sectors are occupied by the memories of similar preoccupations among Italians abroad. In the process, this part of the book moves preoccupation away from the locals, normally concerned about the danger and threat posed by the immigrants, and suggests forms of empathy that can be developed even within unlikely spaces such as a construction site or a private kitchen.

The Conclusion opens a space of discussion over a thorny and pressing issue that Italy is currently dealing with: the reform of the citizenship law (n. 91) toward the inclusion of a mild *jus soli* that would recognize the presence of hundreds of thousand of young people who were born from immigrant parents and have no access to citizenship until the age of eighteen, if not longer. In attempting to define Italy as a potentially unique laboratory in migration matters, perhaps conducive to Franco Cassano's "imagination," the proposal is to read current immigration through the experience of past migrations and colonial legacies, painful and contradictory as they may be. In lieu of sterile or nostalgic forms of national identity spurred by territorial defense and economic insecurity, Italy can use its transnational archive "to update interpretive and practical tools in the new reality of the phenomenon" (Bonifazi 82).

Recollections and Connections toward Empathy

The concept of pre-occupation and the interpretive practices it offers across space and time are meant therefore to dispel preoccupations by actively linking the phenomena of emigration and immigration, as well as colonialism, in the overall reading of Italy's modern and contemporary history. This operation is virtually absent in the current collective discourse, where the separation is instead heightened by the usual trite considerations: "we as emigrants worked hard and pulled ourselves up by our own bootstraps," or "we went to countries that were openly seeking a foreign labor force and were consequently willing to provide services and support in return," or "we were not illegal/clandestine." Stories of struggle and discrimination experienced by Italians abroad are erased by this approach. While it is true that many communities abroad eventually reached a high level of integration if not success, the price that had to be paid for many Italians was equally high. In any case, this often unchallenged and revisionist view of the history of Italian emigration achieved national and international attention with the publication of Oriana Fallaci's *La rabbia e l'orgoglio* (2001).[26] Her supercilious invective against the immigrants, in particular Muslim immigrants, and eulogy of Italian emigrants sealed a dichotomy between "foreign invaders" and "successful" Italians abroad that was as much incorrect as it was widely accepted. In her book, the once progressive feminist journalist Fallaci went as far as stating that "those who associate the migratory waves hitting Italy and Europe with the ones that hit America in the second half of the nineteenth century are wrong" (127). My book rejects this conclusion and attempts to illustrate the unlikely connections between the two migrations in order both to recover Italian emigration's uncomfortable history (made up of destitution, social threats, political extremism, and so on) and to recognize the ways in which current immigrants in Italy are able to defy through their hard work the common depictions of poverty, marginalization, and the like associated with them.

Fallaci's dichotomy has been challenged by other works that in connecting the past and present of Italy's migrations create a different public awareness based on empathy. Stella's bestselling *L'orda*, published two years after Fallaci's book in 2003, was a clear response to such simplistic readings of Italy's past and espoused an uncompromising thesis advocating the need to see in contemporary immigration a space pre-occupied by emigration: Similarly, Italians were once criminals, prostitutes, street vendors, undocumented, illiterate, naïve, and on and on. With its effective subtitle, "When we were the Albanians," which has by now become a commonly used phrase in Italy, the book offered a new way of looking at the two phenomena by prompting a reconsideration of emigration via a closer look at history and immigration via empathy. While Stella's *L'orda*, similar to his following book *Odissee*, remains anchored in the history of emigration and lets the reader develop connections to the present through an implicit mirroring technique, the general parallelism set up by the author offered useful tools to the general public for a more nuanced reading. The adaptation of the two books for the stage discussed in Aperture I has further emphasized this view of emigration as a cognitive premise for today's immigration. The most notable among the works that offer an integrated look at Italy's migrations is Amelio's *Lamerica* (1994), which brilliantly embraced the connections among the outbound and inbound flows, as well as post/colonialism, and effectively constitutes the implicit matrix of *Pre-Occupied Spaces*.[27]

Even though to this day the three phenomena are generally kept separate in scholarly and nonscholarly publications for reasons related to the areas of specialization of the authors, they are almost always connected by way of a mention in the prologue (books on immigration refer to emigration at the outset, as is the case for Parati's *Migration Italy*) or the epilogue (books on emigration refer to immigration in the conclusions, as in the case of the comprehensive two-volume work *Storia dell'emigrazione italiana*, edited by Bevilacqua, Franzina, and de Clementi in 2001 and 2002). To put it succinctly, emigration precedes immigration, and immigration follows emigration, with colonialism being intermittently addressed. These are the two trajectories acting as the scaffold to the three fields, which remain for the most part independent from each other, except for occasions such as the Oxford University series of conferences and similar initiatives.[28]

A number of books have distinctively adopted a connected reading, but they have usually focused on only two of the three phenomena.[29] A few scholarly volumes have instead opened up to all of them but these are for the most part collections of essays in which the three phenomena are still treated separately by individual authors (Burns and Polezzi's 2003 *Borderlines: Migrazioni e identità nel Novecento*, and Parati and Tamburri's 2011 *The Cultures of Italian Migration*). Pasquale Verdicchio's *Bound by Distance* (1997) is the only single-author work that embraces all these phenomena and actually addresses internal migrations within Italy as well, yet it does so through the specific lens of the Southern subaltern, in Gramscian terms.[30] Inspired by Verdicchio's encompassing view but also eager to make the dialogue across spaces and times more intimate, my book brings events, people, and experiences linked to the three phenomena even closer within an empathic vision of the humanities.[31]

This integrated reading of emigration and immigration, which in addition regularly incorporates the experience of colonialism and the resulting postcolonial condition, breaks traditional boundaries and calls for a more porous disciplinary approach.[32] While aware of the cautionary tales coming from scholars active in disciplines that are less prone to favor boundary-crossing approaches,[33] I am interested in emphasizing the cultural value of these unlikely connections for the form of empathy they can engender (see in particular Aperture I for the striking parallel between migrant voyages of yesterday and today). It is precisely this function that historian Paola Corti signals in her analysis of emigration and immigration in which she coincidentally uses a pivotal adjective for my work: "What one reads by comparing that experience with the more recent experiences allows to assess the recent phenomena in a less preoccupied way" (*Storia* 133).[34] *Pre-Occupied Spaces* embraces this view as a working premise: In the process, it shares useful tools aimed at avoiding the risks of collective amnesia over Italy's past of emigration and colonialism, of manufactured celebratory discourses on Italian emigrants' success abroad, and of discriminatory rhetoric against current immigrants in Italy. Whether through visual correlations, linguistic parallelisms, philosophical correspondences or political analogies, the connection of the three phenomena are based on and in turn foster a fundamental empathy that can only be constructive and ultimately necessary from a pragmatic point of view. Concluding that immigrants are less than we were may provide a temporary sense of social and political control but eventually creates a two-tier society that is intrinsically unstable over time because of its us-versus-them paradigm.[35] *Pre-Occupied Spaces* is instead concerned with conjunctions such as "like" or "as if" ushering a similarity, a metaphor, or even a hypothetical relation. The forms of empathy offered in this book signals the necessity of cognition that rests on recognition via memory and imagination and rethinks the national in the transnational dimension. In revolving around specific spaces, the cultural texts addressed incorporate the macro and micro levels of human pre-occupations and preoccupations.

PART ONE

Waters: Migrant Voyages and Ships from and to Italy

APERTURE I

An Osean of Pre-Occupation and Possibilities: *L'orda*

> There are voyages that make us look at the world in a new way [and] voyages that make us look at our past in a new way.
>
> —PREDRAG MATVEJEVIĆ

This first Aperture is a snapshot of the Italian performance piece *L'orda: Storie, canti e immagini di emigranti* (The Horde: Stories, songs, and images of the emigrants) set in an intermittent dialogue with a variety of texts that illuminate the richness and topicality of its content from different perspectives. *L'orda* brings together stories of emigration and in some small part immigration: Through musical pieces accompanied by oral narrations and projected photographs and illustrations, the show places special emphasis on voyages.[1] It is thus an ideal text to introduce Part I of the book, devoted to voyages, ships, boats, and sea and ocean routes as represented in a variety of texts ranging from film (Marra, Crialese) to memoir (Ragusa, Tekle) and songs (Mignonette) belonging to the vast *corpus* of cultural texts on Italian emigration, immigration, and post/colonialism. Like *L'orda*, these texts address and consequently constitute pre-occupied as well as preoccupied spaces. In exploring the layered quality of the stories of their characters and places, these texts function as palimpsests in which the concern over migratory movements can be turned into an opportunity to transform old views, introduce new perspectives, and offer alternative actions, as Mediterranianist Predrag Matvejević dynamically suggests in the epigraph of this Aperture. Despite their differences in contexts, premises, and audiences, what connects all these stories as a *fil rouge* is the liquid space of the ocean and the sea, along with the boat/ship traversing it.[2]

Directed by veteran ethnomusicologist, composer, performer, and activist Gualtiero Bertelli and presented with his socially engaged Compagnia delle Acque, the show *L'orda* takes its name from famed journalist Gian Antonio Stella's first book (2003), but it also combines its content with that of another book penned by him in 2004, *Odissee* (Odysseys).[3] Both publications aimed at documenting and denouncing the hardships experienced by Italian emigrants as workers of the global diaspora, and as travelers on the perilous journeys taking them abroad. The two books, and in particular the first one, create a parallel between these hardships and those faced by the current immigrants in Italy today, and undercut the stereotypes ironically affecting both the emigrants from and the immigrants to Italy in very similar if not fully overlapping ways.

An explicit reference to this goal is present in the by now widely recycled subtitle of the book *L'orda*—"When We Were the Albanians"—pointing to the fact that Italians in the past have been marked with the same negative labels that they themselves use against immigrants today—such labels include "criminal," "dirty," "tribal," "ignorant," "disloyal," "terrorist," and "backward," and often rework the grammar of racism from the slavery and colonial eras.[4] In *Odissee*, the parallel remains more implicit, but works just as powerfully. Encompassing heartrending stories of tragic voyages across the Atlantic to reach such countries as Brazil, Argentina, and the United States, this book echoes today's Mediterranean crossings whose protagonists, like Italians one hundred years or so ago, look at and beyond a large expanse of water to identify a new life opportunity and are ready to brave that hazardous space. Both seas and oceans become in these stories a topos of preoccupation for not only the current threats they pose to the migrant but also the stories of dramatic struggles and death that they silently hold. In his *Mamadou va a morire: La strage dei clandestini nel Mediterraneo* (Mamadou goes to death: The slaughter of illegals in the Mediterranean, 2009), a powerful contrapuntal work to Stella's *Odissee* focusing on the tragedies of contemporary postcolonial migration, journalist Gabriele Del Grande captures the core of these submerged tales when he writes: "Only the fish could relate the stories of a carnivorous sea" (50). Like Del Grande's current reportage, Stella's research untiringly fishes for these migrant stories on/in the water as well as on related coasts in order to do justice to the migrants' tragedies at sea and to connect the micro and macro levels of migration history.

The show *L'orda*, whose leading narrating voice is that of Stella himself, opens with the account of Bortolo Rosolen's 1889 migrant voyage to Brazil, reported in a letter of his that was included in Franzina's *Merica! Merica!* The letter focuses on the overcrowded ship traveling in tropical temperatures and through stormy waters—"tribulations that not even my dog in Italy would experience," as Rosolen tearfully notes (150). The frailty and desperation produced by this voyage are made more acute by the conditions at arrival on the other side of the ocean. Once in Brazil, Italian immigrants are received like herds of sheep, thousands of them sleeping on wood benches and soon being afflicted by various illnesses, or by intensifications of ones contracted during the voyage. Rosolen, who had left with his family to embrace the American Dream in Brazil,[5] eventually lost six of his eleven children. In this incisive opening of the show, the opportunity for a new life sadly turns into a devastating experience of death.

Mostly centered on the materials included in *L'orda*, namely the stories of Italians who like today's immigrants in Italy struggled to make a living and be accepted in every continent of the world, the show also embraces stories taken from *Odissee*. Even though the latter book has a limited presence in the show, I am interested in its inclusion for the particular light it sheds on ship-related disasters due to medical complications (especially cholera and typhus on the "lazarets on the ocean"),[6] stormy weather, accidents,[7] and technical failures,[8] which uncannily resonate with contemporary tragedies. The tribulations of these "*Titanics* of the poor" were often made worse by expedient decisions on the part of companies and captains who in disregarding the official safety rules privileged profits over the security and health of the passengers.[9] Despite skirting these protective measures, they were protected by lax legal systems, which by the same token did not protect the passengers.

While in some cases the long voyages were characterized by forced returns producing at times a two-month-long snakes and ladders type of situation, the worst disasters involved tragic shipwrecks. The most famous of them remains the *Sirio*, both for the mechanics of the accident and for the powerful figuration of it in the well-known song "Il tragico naufragio del vapore Sirio" (The tragic voyage of the steamship Sirio).[10] Repurposed as part of a folk song revival led by singer-songwriters Francesco De Gregori and Giovanna Marini, this popular song commemorates "*la misera fin*" (the sad ending) of 292 Italian lives (up to 500, according to some sources) in the 1906 shipwreck off the coast of southeastern Spain, at a spot notorious for its treacherous rocks. The fact that the crew was not properly equipped with detailed maps to traverse that area or to provide adequate emergency support created an uproar, to which, in a surreal twist of the story, the ship company owners responded by accusing some passengers of abandoning a ship that took sixteen days to finally submerge in the water (Stella, *Odissee* 139).

The series of dramas out at sea reaches its zenith in the show in the intense song "Figlia benedetta,"[11] which recounts the death of a young girl on a ship that for her mother Amalia Pasin turns into a funeral parlor, while the vast expanse of ocean around her becomes her daughter's tomb. A similar experience is delicately captured in a fleeting scene of *Nuovomondo*, Crialese's film, analyzed in Chapter 1. In the song, the story is told from the point of view of the mother who witnesses her daughter's corpse being hurled into the waters with a stone tied around her neck. Initially devastated by this view and the thought of her daughter alone in the abyss, she reaches a new level of awareness—"*Non ho più dentro la paura del mare*" (I am not afraid of the ocean anymore)—and eventually wishes she could soon join her daughter in the dark waters of the ocean, where she hopes to find "a green place full of toys, children, and abundance."

Such "liquid" deaths permeate the entire history of Italian emigration[12] with thousands upon thousands of people disappearing, people who in many cases were seeing the sea and the ocean for the first time in their lives when they boarded these ships, as is the case for a large number of contemporary migrants.[13] The voyage was at once an exhilarating and dreadful experience. As Leonardo Sciascia put it in his brilliant story about an absurd migrant trip, "Il lungo viaggio" (The long crossing 1973), "the idea of the sea was like the green surface of the fields rippled by the wind, but the actual sea terrified the [migrants]" (22), for they were often people anchored to the land, as the story of Amalia Pasin shows.[14] Accounts of these tragic voyages were shared by emigrants themselves via letters or orally upon their return; they were also reported in newspapers and visually rendered in graphic ex-voto tablets[15] displayed in churches (today such information exchanges usually take place via cellular phone or email). Yet, emigrants yielded to the pressing need for economic survival and improvement as well as to a desire for adventure. Whether driven by a rational plan to improve their lives or a folly imbued with the myth of the American Dream artfully manufactured by the so-called businessmen of emigration, including Italian smugglers,[16] Italians continued to leave despite the dangers.[17]

In a telling reversal, the same emigration business reigns—*mutatis mutandis*—in today's countries of departure, as *Mamadou va a morire* shows in its documentation of the astonishing stories of clandestine migrants first crossing deserts, and then the Mediterranean or the Atlantic (northward) in order to reach Europe, often with no success.[18] Investigative journalism has shown that the contemporary migration business is a structure that similarly relies on police corruption, partial government approval, and the ruthless activity of *passeurs* (the equivalent of the *coyotes*). Most of all, it relies on the power of a dream, which in today's context also has a colonial imprint. Romeo, a migrant from Cameroon trapped in Mali for years with no documents, elucidates the point with disarming simplicity: "Isn't the white man the one who taught us that Europe is the El Dorado?" (84). Del Grande explains how in the face of the colonial legacy of structural disempowerment in the countries of departure and of postcolonial individual determination, the awareness of a likely death during these unthinkable, and yet real, trips is not a deterrent. On the contrary, embracing the slogan "leave or die" (150), young people try several times and rarely give up completely, even after imprisonment and/or torture: "if you have to die, it is better to keep on traveling" toward your destination (127).

The same way Del Grande openly refers to Stella's work in his book (151), a sign of the importance of synchronic and diachronic work in the analysis of migrations from/to Italy within post/colonial frameworks, Stella and the Compagnia delle Acque hint at the present in the show *L'orda*. As Stella walks us through the old stories of risky emigrant voyages, which made illness and death an "immanent presence" in the lives of Italian migrants at that time (*Odissee* 37), the echo of contemporary stories of migration to Italy gains volume until, toward the end of the show, it is clearly heard. To quote the equivalent words from the book, "those voyages were highly risky on those ships often truly old tubs, similar to those in which migrants reach the coasts of Calabria or Lampedusa as clandestines" (62). The parallel between the chilling stories reported by Del Grande after his trips to many countries bordering with the Mediterranean or the Sahara desert and the tales included by Stella in his books and in the show is often astoundingly direct: the financial sacrifices made by the migrants before the trip; the lure of the West and the frequent lack of preparation in facing it; the courage and naiveté of the migrants; the stories (and evidence) of success of the migrants returning home for temporary visits; the high level of political and socioeconomic dissatisfaction at home; the sophisticated scams of the recruiters and the smugglers; the conditions of poverty before leaving and that of deprivation (malnutrition, dehydration) during the trip; the particular vulnerability of women as physical, sexual, and political bodies, and yet their bold decision to embark on these voyages; the conflicting emotions toward the migrant project and the lies surrounding it; the myths and false illusions of the families left behind; and the physical and psychological struggles even after making it to the other side. By referring to the "illegal" nature of the arrivals, Stella, like Del Grande, is not embracing the establishment view; if anything, he is interested in showing how "clandestinity" is a condition and not a crime, one that many Italians (Stella quotes four million without mentioning his source) shared as they crossed the Alps to reach France and Switzerland,[19] but also as they boarded ships heading across the ocean.[20] In reversing the common perception that Italians left as part of safe, well-planned, and secure migration projects, funded by foreign countries and sustained by the Italian government, Stella deconstructs the officially sanctioned stories of success about Italian emigration.

In the end, Stella's goal, along with that of the Compagnia delle Acque's in this show, is of spurring "pride" in the general epics of Italian emigration, since success also characterized this experience. Yet, in so doing, Stella also spearheads a revisitation of history with the purpose of reaching a wider audience. Aware of the important academic work produced globally about Italian migration, Stella and the Compagnia opt for a simplified, but nonetheless rich canvas of events, stories, characters, and emotions that, with a rhetorical style lying somewhere between the magnifying glass of Carlo Ginzburg's microhistory and the visual impact of the Mexican muralists' encompassing works, has perhaps reached a broader public than Stella's books—and certainly more than many scholarly publications on the subject—have so far.

In particular, Stella unearths or reemploys a vast array of Titanic-style stories that for several reasons have not found a visible place in Italy's historical records and collective consciousness. Their omission is not coincidental: They serve as reminders of pain and poverty, memories that are better conveniently removed because it is easier to build a history of hard work and success rather than one of loss. Yet, this has also inevitably created a deficit of memory and collective identity in Italy. As he claims in *Odissee*, the country "has not been able to understand a question that other peoples and nations have embraced: A national identity can be built also on pain. On the sharing of mourning. On the collective elaboration of a common history in which we have mixed dreams and tears together" (20). If Stella's proposition is provocative, the semantic paradox is lost in his articulation: The formation of a national identity based on the losses and suffering produced by global emigration posits not a stronger national identity but instead a stronger transnational Italian identity as a premise and a result. Despite this oversight, his message remains incisive, not only for the archeological operation that he embraces and invites us to expand on and share but also for its vital quality, so different from so many works about Italian emigration. The pedagogical intent of this anti-amnesia project, effective in both his books and the show, is enriched by a dynamic call to rethink the present along with the past.

The closing song, "Noi,"[21] performed by the Compagnia delle Acque to a background of images of emigrants who left Italy and immigrants who are now in Italy, is particularly eloquent in this sense. It philologically rebuilds Italy's mobile genealogy and its iconography of fear, pain, discrimination, violence, and hopes—"we, on the docks for one hundred years" the song recites—and completes it with the images of multiethnic Italy in the third millennium. In pointing to the usually unspoken analogy between the two phenomena, at least in these terms, the final indictment comes across as particularly commanding: "Now from our tables replete with food/With a short and sleepy memory/We rush to start afresh from the other side of the barricade." This barricade has become increasingly more real since the EU has opted for the militarization of borders with both defensive and offensive instruments and strategies. Del Grande's list of burgeoning securitization operations (154), all ironically bearing the names of figures of that very ancient Greek mythology that united numerous Mediterranean places (*Hera, Argonauts, Poseidon*) speaks of how the EU has replaced rational management of legal flows and solidarity with high-tech control and closed borders. While in the post-Berlusconi era several rescue operations have been successfully completed by Italian military forces (*Mare Nostrum*), and the recent Syrian crisis has produced to some degree an acceptance of refugees, the flows continue to be handled in an emergency mode and in the midst of political controversies at the expense of human lives. The public discourse, even the one characterized by a progressive ethos, rarely historicizes the phenomenon of migration, and often invokes a generic goodheartedness that inflames the centrist and right-wing groups in particular, thus preventing the engineering of systematic and effective policies.

In the grand finale, the show *L'orda* presents instead a multicultural call to solidarity through fruitful exchanges of new songs, gestures, games, rhythms, prayers, and dances, despite differences and distances among cultural groups. This ecumenical message ironically resorts to the homogenizing view of the entire humanity as a community of "men different and yet the same," thus bypassing crucial gender inflections that the show nonetheless intermittently addresses in the scenes covering stories of labor exploitation. In spite of this generalization, as seen in the last quote, the show persuasively invites Italy to recognize its hasty desire for modernity and its related blindness to a present a little too similar to its near past.[22] The song that functions as a soundtrack to this Aperture, and to Part I of the book at large, is contained in another show by Compagnia delle Acque, *Bilal* (2009), inspired by the reportage bearing the same name and published by journalist Fabrizio Gatti (2008) after his trip to North Africa designed to follow today's migrant routes.[23] Composed and performed in Italian by Bertelli, "Navi"[24] is a eulogy and elegy of the ship, metonymy of past and present migrant trips. The refrain condenses the mythic attraction of the ship as a conduit of opportunities for a new life, as a vessel of adventures and dreams, and as a source of pain and loss:

maledette navi	damned ships
navi desiderate	desired ships
navi sofferte	suffered ships
navi disperate	desperate ships
navi spezzate	broken ships
navi danzate	danced ships
navi baciate	kissed ships
maledette navi	damned ships
navi amate	loved ships

In the litany-like anaphoric enumeration of the refrain, customary adjectives such as "broken" or "damned," which can be normally associated to structures like ships, are mixed with both emotional adjectives ("desperate") that would not usually be linked to them and made-passive adjectives ("danced") that are syntactically inappropriate in the string, except by way of poetic license. With their defamiliarizing effect, the latter two types of constructions anthropomorphize the ship and transform it into the object of human actions respectively. In both cases, the ship and the unnamed passengers become an organic whole in a give and take of affection, care, and grief. The overall effect is a juxtaposition of sentiments ranging from desperation to love, a sign of the complex role of the ship, a much-needed means toward a new life and an unconscious carrier of pain that is woven into Italy's historical fabric. Now forgotten in the national collective imaginary,[25] migrant ships and boats return in a new and yet familiar form: "Quotidian presences within ourselves," they are represented in the song as "sorrowful ships . . . [full] of faces bringing back other faces, [full] of life bringing back other life." "Navi"'s powerful contrasts and combinations offer a visual rendition of written stories of past and present tragic migrations. On the one hand, it explodes fossilized perceptions of migrant ships such as those coming from a classic of the genre, Edmondo De Amicis's 1889 *Sull'Oceano* (*On Blue Water*). This travel reportage had the merit of documenting for the first time and in epic terms the Italian voyage to South America, yet it fell prey to a populist and chauvinistic ethos by which the Atlantic was actually a rite of passage for these children of the motherland trapped within an inescapable fate of national dispersion but yet enjoying benevolent prospects for future growth.[26] On the other hand, "Navi" is an uncompromising reminder of the present tragedy of a neighboring sea, the Mediterranean, which "on the world maps looks like a pond [yet], at times, becomes more violent and insidious than the ocean," as Giovanni Maria Bellu's 2004 book *I fantasmi di Portopalo* (The ghosts of Portopalo) on the 1996 tragedy off the coasts of Sicily reminds us (91).

These past and present figurations of contact between and superimposition of ocean and sea spaces have prompted my forging of the concept that I am here tentatively calling o*sea*n. In this portmanteau word I identify a pre-occupied space. It is a space that through its history of voyages—the stories of the innumerable migrant ships and boats that have traversed it—can offer new ways of connecting outbound and inbound migrations on broader cultural maps. The global nature of Italian diaspora, represented in the show *L'orda* along with Stella's books, effectively disrupts a purely national model for the study of emigration the same way that the geographical scope of Del Grande's book, covering North and Sub-Saharan Africa as well as various parts of Southern Europe, excludes any traditional national paradigm to address contemporary migration. Ultimately, o*sea*n is a hybrid space in which to envision new possibilities for understanding identity and action both within and beyond national and colonial belonging, as the following chapters will illustrate.

ONE

Crossing the Atlantic to Meet the Nation: The Emigration Ship in Mignonette's Songs and Crialese's *Nuovomondo*

> The voyage was a nightmare with moments of strange brilliance.
> —PASCAL D'ANGELO

The topic of voyages and ships is explored in this first chapter through visual and oral materials in which the emigrants' regional affiliations espouse an in-progress national formation project during transnational travels to "America," at once a real and imaginary place. Songs made popular by the "Queen of the Emigrants," the diva Gilda Mignonette, who mixed a traditional Neapolitan repertoire with dramatic songs on emigration and colonial anthems, are read next to Emanuele Crialese's film *Nuovomondo* (*Golden Door* 2006), which foregrounds the role of the ship for the leaving, traveling, and arriving migrants at the turn of the century. In these texts, the pre-occupied space under discussion is the ship, a floating social microcosm in which national fractures and international dreams coexist on a simultaneously dividing and uniting ocean. The preoccupation over the condition of the emigrants that the ship hosts prompts in these authors different reactions, in turn defining different perceptions and figurations of emigration and consequently of nation formation.

These oral and filmic texts allow us to respectively consider the representation of the historical migrant voyages produced at the time of the voyages themselves and those developed in our times, roughly one century later, when other boats and other immigrants are at the heart of the collective consciousness. Many other texts could have been chosen instead of Mignonette's songs to offer images and tales of ships authored by Italians transplanted in the United States in the late 1800s and early to mid-1900s, notably Pascal D'Angelo's 1924 autobiography *Son of Italy* (see Chapter 4 of his book), or the letters and memoirs of the emigrants themselves (see, for example, the Second Part of Tommaso

Bordonaro's 1991 *La spartenza*, about a 1947 voyage to America).[1] Yet, the success of Mignonette's songs and the specific cultural milieu they mirrored, coupled with the surprisingly marginal role she still has in the literature on Italian emigration, prompted me to explore her songs, and in particular some rare ones on the migrant voyage. Crialese's film does not have any direct antecedent, and certainly not in the realm of contemporary Italian cinema, with the closing scene of Amelio's film *Lamerica* constituting a possible exception.[2] Films such as the silent *L'emigrante* (The Emigrant) by Febo Mari (1915) or *Passaporto rosso* (Red Passport) by Guido Brignone (1936) focused on emigration to South America and moved the action to the "New World" primarily. By contrast, Giuseppe Tornatore's *La leggenda del pianista sull'oceano* (The Legend of 1900, 1998) is exclusively centered on the ship, an unanchored space where worldwide immigration and travel stories cross the life of the rootless protagonist, literally born on the ocean.[3] Silent filmmaker Paradisi devoted some intense scenes to the voyage in his 1916 *Dagli Appennini alle Ande* (an adaptation of De Amicis's short story): They focus on a largely isolated protagonist and adopt an oneiric register that psychologizes the voyage rather than documenting it. *Nuovomondo* thus arguably constitutes the only comprehensive view of Italian emigration to the United States (or the "New World," in general) on screen, and the only one in which the voyage is investigated so closely, along with the material milieu and impalpable dreams that drove emigrants abroad.

The representation of the ship, and by extension of the migrant as a floating identity, produces differing results in Mignonette's songs and Crialese's film, which mostly reflect their different approaches to the mythopoesis of emigration. Both coming from artists whose personal and artistic experiences unraveled in the United States and in Italy, the two representations reveal the degrees to which these cultural productions negotiated and reinvented a collective experience, and in the process created a certain figuration of the nation. Mignonette's songs were the product of a conscious, yet not uncomplicated, alignment with the ideological establishment of the time, while Crialese, assisted by the flexibility of historical distance, freed himself from the canon and spoke for rather than substituting the mythopoesis of the emigrants themselves.

Gilda Mignonette's Postcard Ships: From the New Polis to the New World

> we were facing the water and thinking ten thousand nights
> awaiting a single dawn (Viscusi).[4]

In a very brief but meaningful scene contained in Francesco Rosi's *I magliari* (The cloth sellers), a 1959 film about postwar Italian emigration to Germany, an old man from Naples now living in Hannover is having a solitary bowl of warm milk in a dark room in the company of a tiny cat, while in the background a jukebox plays Gilda Mignonette's "'A Cartulina 'e Napule." In the midst of a crisis for the cloth selling business he and his Italian buddies work for, the old man is in a melancholy reverie. When a co-worker (Mario, played by Renato Salvatori) interrupts him to inquire about their friend Totonno (Alberto Sordi), the old man uses the evergreen myth of Mignonette to displace the conversation away from contingent problems and to place their immigrant struggles within the more abstract context of nostalgia for home.

> "La senti a questa? Questa quann' veniva in terr' i Brucculin faceva piangere i megliu gangster a tant 'i lacrime. Gilda Mignonette: la conosci?"
> "No."
> "E chi ci campi affà?"

> "Do you hear her? This one, when she went to Brooklyn, she would have the toughest gangsters melt down in tears. Gilda Mignonette: do you know her?"
> "No."
> "Why live then?"

The mythic stature of Mignonette is condensed in the incisive last question, whose apparently humorous quality also contains a melodramatic tone. For large numbers of Italian emigrants, whether to the United States or to the many other destinations they reached in the world, Mignonette became the embodiment of home: She healed, while capturing to a high degree, the sense of "homelessness" experienced by the deracinated emigrants of the Italian diaspora. Her music was a success for decades in her native Naples, in her adoptive city of New York, and in all the places that she visited on tour or where her popular 78 rpm recordings were distributed.[5] Mignonette (Naples, 1886–1953),[6] whose real name was Griselda Andreatini, essentially crafted her artistic persona in that complex international space between Italy and the emigrant communities abroad. She began her career in Sicily when her young soprano voice was discovered. Later in Naples, she worked as an actress with writer and performer Raffaele Viviani, whose comedic play *Scalo Marittimo ('Nterr' 'a 'Mmaculatella*, 1918) about the emigrants ready to board the ship at the port of Naples can be considered as one of the ur-sources for many works on emigration, including Crialese's *Nuovomondo*. After a timid start in the comedic genre as a *sciantosa*, a singer at the *cafè chantant*, which mostly revealed her feisty personality and elegant dress style, in 1919 Mignonette was invited to perform some classic songs from Naples for the Lega Italiana Musicale (Italian Musical League) of New York. The association was aimed at fostering both local Italian music production and the circulation of Italian music as part of a program of intellectual and political growth for the "colony," effectively seen as an extension of the nation.[7]

The transnational dimension of Mignonette's career hinged on this concept of Italy beyond its borders, which embraced both the emigrant colonies and the territorial colonies in Africa. Not surprisingly, Mignonette's introduction to the New York scene, where the industry of consumption, leisure, and entertainment was well developed,[8] happened thanks to singer Roberto Ciaramella. Known as "the Christopher Columbus of Neapolitan song," as reported in Sciotti's biography of Mignonette (45), Ciaramella was particularly well known in Tripoli, back then part of the Italian colonies in Africa. That Mignonette owes the first steps of her U.S. success to a figure so entangled with the expanded form of the Italian nation is quite a telling element in the reading of the country's formation vis-à-vis emigration and colonialism that I am proposing in this book. The life and artistic vicissitudes of Mignonette are equally relevant to understand this scenario of transnational entanglements, which did not simply act as a background to Mignonette's career, but was also indirectly built by the cultural content and political message of her songs and shows.

From the performance for the Lega Italiana Musicale on, Mignonette's regular repertoire was characterized by a set of established songs designed to appeal to the emigrants' nostalgia for home: "Santa Lucia luntana" (Distant St. Lucy),[9] "A canzone 'e Napule" (The song of Naples), "Core napulitan" (Neapolitan heart), "A luna 'e Napule" (The moon of Naples), and "Canzone americana" (American song) are representative of a Naples-centered genre that offered in music "views" of the city and its environs, which the film industry had also introduced.[10] During her visit to New York in 1924, under the sponsorship of Feliciano Acierno (whose son Frank she eventually married), she presented these songs, along with some Neapolitan *sceneggiate*, and added to her list the famous "Mandulinata 'e l'emigrante" (The mandolin piece of the emigrant). Mignonette was immediately successful and her popularity placed her next, and eventually beyond, the star of the Italian immigrants in New York at that time, Teresa De Matienzo. In the mid-1920s she started her back-and-forth traveling between Italy and the United States, recording her pieces both in New York and Naples[11] and presenting shows strongly characterized by both her ability to change several dresses over the course of a show and to mix oral narration and songs.

Even in Italy, Mignonette's success is in part attributable to her emigration-centered songs. Typical compositions include "Nterra all'America" (On American soil), "Figliu nun mannà dollare" (Son, do not send any money), "Te ne si ghiut'America" (You moved to America), with the last two addressing such opposing themes as that of the emigrants' willingness to send remittances home and the emigrants' tendency to keep money stingily to themselves. Her success was sealed in 1928 by a song that, in becoming popular worldwide, turned Mignonette into an international star: "'A cartulina 'e Napule" (Postcard from Naples), which Rosi in his film *I magliari* chooses to feature as profoundly expressive of the emigrants' angst. Known as "the musical manifesto of Italian immigrants in America" (Frasca 44),[12] this song is the most obvious exemplification of the "invention of Naples" that Mignonette and the composers and musicians she worked with had forged in these years. It rested on an iconography that froze the picturesque image of the city both in the emigrants' collective imaginary and in the wider audiences of the countries where Italian communities had been formed.[13] Yet, the strong sentimentalism of the songs of the Neapolitan genre in general did not simply respond to an actual sentiment of nostalgia. Mignonette and several of her contemporary artists actually proposed the "crystallization of a largely metabolized experience" of distance (Durante 118), effectively manufacturing in the transnational space of the diaspora a long-lived "national" tradition of regional matrix by which Naples equals Italy.

Among the numerous songs Mignonette made famous both in Italy and the United States, two in particular focus on the emigrant voyage: "Partenza degli emigranti per l'America" (Departure of the emigrants to America), also known as "Partenza da Napoli" (Departure from Naples), and "La dura traversata" (The tough voyage), both recorded in 1936 in Italy for Phonotype and gathered in one supplement of the Phonotype/Phonoelectro catalogue along with other two songs: "Rimpatrio dei napoletani" (Repatriation of the Neapolitans) and "Il festoso arrivo" (The joyous arrival).[14] All together, they represent a cycle of songs devoted to the voyage and design a looplike trajectory from departure to the voyage and arrival and then return home. Whereas the titles of the first two songs suggest a strong reference to the ship and the voyage that are the central topic of this chapter, the actual content reveals the sentimental sublimation of the experience characteristic of the genre. The concrete representation of emigration with its sociopolitical causes, material implications and cultural import is obliterated in favor of a hyperconcentration on the feelings connected to the moment of leaving and the resulting sense of nostalgia for home in the process of traveling and arriving.

The first recording, "Partenza degli emigranti per l'America,"[15] opens with a recited part reproducing the good-byes at the port. Next to the cries of the boarding staff, the running thread is that of emotional exchanges from the very outset:

Un bacio, un bacio ancora, mamma,	One kiss, one more kiss, mother,
e non piangere	oh don't cry!
V'nit, Ciro, bell'e mamma	Come here, Ciro, light of my eyes

The song starts out with a famous first line in a verse that shortly after coalesces singing and being Neapolitan:

Partono 'e bastimente	The ships are leaving
p' 'e terre assaje luntane,	Toward faraway lands,
cantano a buordo, so' napulitane!	People on board are singing: they are Neapolitans!

The environment around the ship could be taken out of a painting: A slice of Naples is still visible, and the moonlight shines on the sea in the gulf; the emotional link between the moonlight and Naples is also established in the following strophes. In alternating between Mignonette's solo voice, that of the chorus, and that of several anonymous characters in recited sections, the song continues to interweave geographical references to the coast of Naples (Posillipo, Marechiaro) with images of amatory exchanges in idyllic scenarios such as a pristine beach along crystalline waters, close to a grotto with fishing boats.

There is no trace here of the financial and physical sacrifices of the emigrants, of the challenges encountered on the way to the port, on the docks or the ship, or of the actual procedures and complications experienced as third-class ship passengers. With a swift metanarrative twist, supported by Mignonette's enchanting voice, the emigrants actually become singers in a song ultimately more concerned with a celebration of the art of singing rather than the documentation or denunciation of the actual conditions experienced by emigrants.[16] In this sense, it is not surprising that the piece consists of a medley of quotations from popular songs, notably "Santa Lucia luntana" (1916), "A Canzona 'e Pusilleco" (1919) and "Torna a Marechiaro" (1922), all written by E. A. Mario, with the last one based on the verses of popular dialect poet Salvatore Di Giacomo. "La partenza" closes with a crescendo of intensity over two verses that could be associated with all themes but that of the emigrant voyage: "If Sunday the weather is good we will go to Marechiaro," a quite improbable scenario for the migrants who had just embarked on a voyage to America that lasted a few weeks.

The central part of the song captures the tone of the composition and by extension the genre:

Se gira 'o munno sano,	One travels around the whole world,
se va a cercà furtuna,	trying to improve one's fate,
ma quanno sponta 'a luna	But when the moon comes out
luntan' a Napule	Away from Naples
nun se po' sta!	One cannot take it!

Regardless of the peregrinations of the emigrants—Mignonette reminded the listeners—a Neapolitan will always look for and essentially see Naples as part of the visual concretization of a dream, a memory, and a desire. Rather than being a space of preoccupation for the migrants over their material situation or occupied with a realistic or fantastically revisited representation of the emigrants' departure as in Crialese's *Nuovomondo*, Mignonette's first part of the voyage is more preoccupied with the panoramic views of Naples from the deck. Even the depiction of emigrants, and in this case Neapolitans, as singers occurs in a sublimated melodramatic context, which removes the emigrants' agency and makes them part of a staged scene. As Franzina explains in his essay "Le canzoni dell'emigrazione," emigration had a soundtrack made up of three clusters of songs: familiar folk songs on various themes that the emigrants entertained themselves with during the travel and relocation experience; folk songs developed by them about the experience itself (emigration songs, strictly speaking); and the songs on that experience that were written by formal composers, performed by professional singers, and circulated through official channels. Mignonette's songs clearly belonged to this last category: As "elite" songs for the masses, they eventually forged a canon.

Unlike *Nuovomondo* which uses Sicilian folk songs to accompany small gestures such as getting ready in the ship's dormitory for the arrival to Ellis Island, or looking out to the sea from the deck in a sort of collective prayer, or giving vent to accumulated grief in a *tarantata* moment punctuated by frantic percussive movements, Mignonette's repertoire includes songs that stem from and reinforce a more canonical genre. Even though the repertoire and the single songs remain strongly linked to the dialect, they define a nonantagonistic, pathos-imbued approach to the vast and complex phenomenon of Italian emigration. The second song under analysis here reflects this same stylization. In "La dura traversata," also known as "In mare doloroso distacco: La burrasca e i napoletani" (A painful separation at sea: The storm and the Neapolitans),[17] the main theme of the song—the storm that makes the voyage so hard—is barely mentioned in the opening recitation and soon turned into an occasion to sing for the traveling Neapolitans. Prompted again by the presence of the moon, the singing this time is addressed to Fortune, a sort of divinity invoked as "bella 'mbriana."[18] The fears and challenges connected to the voyage are translated into a prayer that puts into the hands of fate the future of the emigrants:

Bella 'mbriana scetate po' coro	Bella 'mbriana wake up for this chorus
E cincucientu voci so' una voce	It is five hundred voices into one
Ma 'sta canzun c'a scrittu uno e 'lloro	This song was written by one of them
So cincuciente e portan' una croce	It is five hundred carrying only one cross

Ma state all'aria, è doce	Stay in the open air, it is sweet
Bella 'mbriana scetate po' coro	Bella 'mbriana, wake up for the chorus

While the sense of struggle is articulated in the image of the cross, interestingly opposing a Christian iconography to the initial pagan one, the general atmosphere remains one of a fatalistic wait. Its zenith is reached in the insertion of another anthem of emigration, "Santa Lucia" (or "Partono i Bastimenti," The ships are leaving), which with its Catholic inflection and lyrics in dialect constitutes the epitome of what Franzina has called "a recording market of nostalgia, often victimistic, tear-ridden, and most of all southernized to the nth degree" ("Le canzoni" 560). Not surprisingly, in "La dura traversata," the drive to sing for these emigrants looking for another chance in life is prompted by a glance at the moon and the memory of Naples. In the process, Mignonette once again stitches lyrics from different songs together as part of her typical pattern of recycling for the purpose of easy recognition, especially those verses as famous as the closing ones in the following section of the song:

Santa Lucia[19]	Saint Lucy
Luntan' 'a te	Away from you
quanta malincunia!	Such sorrow!
Se gira 'o munno sano,	One travels around the world,
se va a cerca' furtuna,	trying to improve one's lot,
ma quanno sponta 'a luna	But when the moon comes out
luntan' 'a Napule	Away from Naples
nun se po' sta!	One cannot take it

As "Mamma, Naples, and Saint Lucy" are called for in sobs at the very end of the song, the proposed rhetorics appear strongly anchored to a "Neapolitanized" national discourse that recognizes in the family, the saints and the place of origin the pillars of a collective identity as emigrants. Yet, Mignonette herself did not stand for such values in uncomplicated ways, since her personal and professional choices even reversed the apparent meekness of such rhetoric by defying conventional standards. She was among the first women to wear pants on stage (Sciotti 164), and she cleverly understood the mechanisms of an international entertainment market whose commercial rules she plied to her needs and skills as an artist.[20] Nonetheless, in her songs, it is the glance backward that allows the emigrants to move forward: It points to a paradoxical paradigm that the poet Viscusi turns around in the epigraph of this chapter where dawn at the destination is what propels the voyage. For Mignonette, it is a set of ossified national/local paraphernalia that apparently equips the emigrants for the transnational experience in the form of endurance and fatalism: In her songs, the new polis (Neapolis/Naples) occupies a central role technically overpowering the new world (United States/the Americas).

Painted as an experience of disappointment in Mignonette's "La dura traversata," the arrival to America is already configured as another occasion to "sing nostalgically" and "with a heavy heart" to withstand the difficulties. De Amicis's representation of the emigrants in his well-known book *On Blue Water* (1889) belongs to the same national discourse, albeit developed a few decades earlier, when the impulse to build a national identity was still animated by a pride of Risorgimento roots and the emigration phenomenon was experiencing its first phase of massive outbound flux. In De Amicis's text, a significant image of singing passengers on the boat coincides with a joyous moment—the crossing over the Equator—but also precedes a section focusing on the less than joyous condition of the destitution of the emigrants, within his typical frame of tearful patriotism. In addressing the migrants as "my ragged brothers, my breadless sisters, sons and fathers of soldiers who fought and will fight for a land that they were not and will not be able to inhabit" (137), De Amicis is nonetheless registering the demographic hemorrhage, its causes and its consequences. A few decades later, Mignonette takes this national discourse to a higher level of formalization within the melodramatic register, as the nation at the height of its Fascist development approaches the imperial enterprise, and soon afterward World War II.

Indeed, it is in the mid-1930s that Mignonette's repertoire began to mix emigration songs with those about the contemporary colonial enterprises. Her collaboration with, among others, Carlo Buti, the pop Caruso of Italy during the Fascist era, solidified this new course for Mignonette: The most successful theme of this period is "Faccetta nera."[21] Written by Giuseppe Micheli as a semi-satirical text on the Abyssinian enterprise, the song was composed by Mario Ruccione in 1935 and made famous by Buti. Considered the anthem of Fascism, and in particular Imperial Fascism, "Faccetta nera" in reality was not supported by the Fascist regime, which approved of it only after several change, meant to obfuscate the Italian defeat at Adua as well as any reference to friendly relationships with the Abyssinians. In presenting the justness of the Italian intervention as part of an antislavery operation, the song set the premise for a military operation ostensibly characterized by a civilizing mission. In this scenario, the ship acquires a liberating meaning for the "little black face," that is, the subjugated Abyssinian woman being addressed in the lyrics:

Se tu dall'altipiano guardi il mare	If you look at the sea from the hills
Moretta che sei schiava fra gli schiavi	Cute darky, you are a slave among slaves
Vedrai come in un sogno tante navi	As in a dream you will see many ships
E un tricolore sventolar per te	And a tricolor flag waving for you

The song predicts that the "little black face" will be rescued by Italy, symbolized by the three-colored flag. Infused with an imperialist ethos, the song was one of many written during these years that were added to the more traditional Neapolitan genre and the repertoire of emigrant songs.

This unique convergence between the inventory of emigration songs and colonial/imperial anthems, but most of all, the political quality that Mignonette's art acquired in combining them, are evidence of an Italian identity that through social, military, and cultural movements took shape in the transborder space of the diaspora and colonialism. Mignonette's support of the imperial enterprise in Abyssinia, a historical moment that also prompted tensions in the spaces of the diaspora,[22] reached its pinnacle when she presented herself on stage wrapped in an Italian flag, or dressed as an officer, or set off a background representing Addis Ababa. While her success continued—she was by now known as "La Carusiana" for her voice, even though her repertoire was not operatic like that of Enrico Caruso—the controversy around her political affiliations grew quickly, and right at the beginning of the war she went back to Italy. Upon her return to the United States in 1941, she found a changed environment: The American stance against Fascism made her into a dangerous presence because of her open support of Mussolini and her resistance against the war bonds campaign in the United States. Framed circumstantially by accusations of fiscal evasion, she defended herself in court by claiming her legitimate Italian patriotism, but in reality her career was derailed up until the Cold War: Her concerts were boycotted and her ability to record hindered. Argentina became her new adoptive country, while she continued to go back to Naples for regular shows.

Her final return to Italy is worth mentioning for the almost surreal twist it gave to Mignonette's life. After an existence dedicated to songs about the difficulties of leaving and returning, and in particular about the unreachable distance of the mythical Gulf of Naples for the emigrants, she died of liver disease on a ship a short distance from the port of Naples in 1953. Naples reduced to a framed postcard next to her cabin's bed reflected the sublimated Naples of her songs. Those who were waiting for her at the port welcomed back her corpse, an eerie materialization of the experiences of disease and death on emigrant ships that she only rarely recorded in her songs. She has since remained the "Carusiana" for the emigrants and the "Queen of Emigrants" for Italians at home (Sciotti 155).

Taken as a whole, her song production, and in particular the production focused on emigration, was impressive. Despite the congealing cultural operation offered and maintained by her lyrics and interpretations, she contributed to a lively entertainment scene that involved emigrants actively and made them objects and subjects of the discourse on emigration both in Italy and abroad, within their ethnic communities as well as in the broader scenarios of the countries they had moved to. The songs about the ship analyzed here provide clear evidence of her calculated distancing from documentary intent and her alignment with an abstract regional image of Italy, which not coincidentally the Fascist regime was supportive of in order to replace the depiction of poor and struggling Italians that damaged the nation's respectability. Other contemporary songs (such as those included in Franzina's studies or the show *L'orda*),[23] or the short plays by actor Eduardo Migliaccio (Farfariello) whose "dialect usage did not reflect pride so much as linguistic reality" (Carnevale 132) offered a wide palette of topics related to the life of transplanted Italians, including criticism of the country of origin and the clash/encounter with the new environment. Mignonette's contamination of Italian and dialect, traditional songs and new popular motives, served instead the purpose of creating what eventually became a long-standing canon for the Italian emigrant/immigrant, which effectively hindered a real investigation into such a fundamental aspect of Italian history and culture as the country's diaspora.

Only decades afterward, under the pressure of the new sociocultural scenario designed by the arrival of immigrants in the 1990s, does Italy revisit its past of emigration and with it the figuration of the migrant ship. The arrivals of boats from the other sides of the Mediterranean bring preoccupation about the impact of immigrants in Italy, but ultimately bring with them an implicit history of people's movements from and back to Italy. Pre-occupied by the tales of these past voyages, these boats have prompted a cultural production on Italian emigration at large that finds in the film *Nuovomondo* one of its highest expressions, especially for the role played by the ship in it, a space of constant tension between expectations and reality as well as between tradition and modernity.

Realist and Magical Realist Emigration Voyages in Crialese's Nuovomondo

> A whole nation walked out of the middle ages,/slept in the ocean, and awakened in New York in the twentieth century (Viscusi).

Crialese's 2006 film *Nuovomondo* offers instead a unique opportunity to reflect on the conscious questioning of, or the alternative to, the privileged space of the Italian nation. Crialese has fundamentally crafted a transnational film in which the figurative condensation of the diaspora in the microcosm of the transoceanic ship allows him to address the peculiar transnational formation of a country of regions like Italy within a dynamic framework of demographic movements. From his early playful musings while still a student in New York about recent "undocumented" Italian emigration to the United States (*Once We Were Strangers*, 1997),[24] to his nuanced investigations of hyperregional life in the southernmost periphery of Italy, Lampedusa (*Respiro/Grazia's Island*, 2002), Crialese has constantly explored the forms in which the Italian nation collides against its own purportedly homogeneous identity in and outside itself. Yet, it is with *Nuovomondo* that the director embraces the theme of a nation that truly exceeds its own boundaries in the course of over a century of emigration.[25]

By focusing on the story of one family, the Mancusos, *Nuovomondo* recounts on the screen the tragic and yet exhilarating voyage of a group of Italian emigrants across the Atlantic and their arrival at Ellis Island in the early 1900s. Crialese has thus powerfully intervened through the filmic medium in a collective imaginary otherwise devoid of a shared memory of this colossal exodus. A memory that can only function as a paradoxical pillar for Italy, since it created a nation out of regions in the transnational space of emigration.[26] In other words, in following the vicissitudes of the different members of a Sicilian family as they encounter "America" before, during, and after the voyage, *Nuovomondo* traces the complex map of departures, arrivals, and returns that have made Italy into a circularly diasporic place.

The first part of the film is set in Sicily, par excellence a not fully belonging space vis-à-vis the nation not only in geographical terms, as an island, but also historically. On the one hand, Sicily has been a region with a strong separate and at some point separatist culture and, on the other, it represents an area strongly connected to transnational contexts such as the Mediterranean as well as the Atlantic area and in particular the United States.[27] The choice of Sicily as the place of origin and departure of the protagonists is also dictated by the peculiar migration history of the island: The region, along with Veneto and Campania, is among those that contributed the most to the exodus over the decades (Favero 16).[28]

The main characters of the film are members of a closed family comprised of a young, determined, and gentle widower, Salvatore Mancuso, who lives in a small rural village with his two children, Angelo and Pietro—the latter is hearing- and speech-impaired—and his old mother, Fortunata, who functions as the local sorceress, "*la medica*." It is off the clash and overlapping of the disappointments, delusions, and desires of these characters that Crialese spins a tale of reactions to and decisions about the magnetic allure of what provides the title to the film in the Italian version, the "new world." Interestingly, the term is rendered as one word (technically "neworld" in translation), melding adjective and noun so as to create a new term altogether, which epitomizes the encounter of two elements and the creation of something different and novel. Regrettably, not only does the English title *Golden Door* lose this nuance, but it also restricts the semantic sphere of the term to the very arrival (the door) by making explicit reference to the closing line of Emma Lazarus's 1883 poem "The New Colossus," inscribed at the bottom of the Statue of Liberty. The subtlety of Crialese's original title therefore dissolves in English, leaving no trace of the remapping of spaces that his film suggests in each of its three parts. The same way Sicily is profoundly changed by emigration to a new land, the ocean condenses the migrants' desire/fear to arrive in a new place, and Ellis Island/the United States offers a new social model in the immigrants' country.

Set in an astoundingly beautiful and yet hardly generous natural environment for these poor Southern peasants, the early scenes already reveal the narrative and visual style that Crialese adopts throughout the movie. Supported by attentive research in the field of the *questione meridionale* and Italian emigration as part of the background preparation for the film,[29] Crialese resorts to an apparently realist, almost *verista*, rendition. Yet, he intentionally transcends any documentary drive and repeatedly adopts an explosively surrealist mode in some of the most at once beloved and criticized scenes of the movie. It is this switch in register that marks Crialese's distinctive take: He incorporates the literary legacy left by Pirandello's "The Other Son" and Maria Messina's short stories about the dramatic emptiness produced by emigration at the turn of the century, but also sublimates it.[30] Indeed, the very dreamlike atmosphere and symbolic language that the Tavianis used in their adaptation of "The Other Son" for one of the episodes of *Kaos* (1984) is taken by Crialese to another level. He decides to not only indirectly hint at the oneiric world of the emigrants-to-be, but to actually film their dreamscape. After all, this sphere of desire was so powerful in the heads and hearts of the fleeing emigrants that it became visible and tangible; ultimately, it made the emigration adventure possible.

At the beginning of the film, the camera lingers on two black and white postcards sent from the United States bringing news from "*a terra nova*" (the new land, or new world). One depicts a man carrying a gigantic onion on a wooden cart, and the other catches two men picking huge coins from a bush. While the postcards are taken as material evidence of the existence of the "*paese della cuccagna*" (land of Cockaigne, or country of abundance)[31] by the village youth—"these are true things," one of the local young women firmly states—this visualization of unreal abundance makes the old mother, Fortunata, skeptical. She promptly orders the burning of this "evidence" in the attempt of extinguishing the burning desire to leave, which like an epidemic is taking over the locals, including her own family. But the attempt is in vain. Not only are the postcards not burnt, but her grandson Pietro also takes them to a holy spot on top of the nearby mountains where his father and brother await God's direction on the family's next steps. Salvatore's aspiration to emigrate seeks corroboration. Pietro's unexpected delivery of the postcards is thus interpreted as a proof of divine backing, and Salvatore's desire to leave is further strengthened.

In another famous scene of *Nuovomondo*, Salvatore experiences visions of abundance embodied by mammoth carrots and olives that women and children carry around in the fields. Shortly afterward, in order to protest his mother's refusal to leave for the United States, Salvatore buries himself in the soil, thus "performing" the condition of death that her stubborn position is forcing onto the family. It is a ritualized entombment that he also designs in order to test fate for a second time. Once a rain of coins starts beating down on him as he lies in the soil at night, he takes it as the final, and most concrete, indication that a regeneration is close: The coins of the postcard have materialized on his inert body. The increasing tangibility of these signs (from images to visions and experiences) convinces him of the justness of his resolution to take the family to the United States.

In Crialese's reading, these forms of reification of the desire to join the "*paese della cuccagna*" are necessary to embark on the voyage, which, as actor Vincenzo Amato indicated in an interview,[32] was for the emigrants like a spaceship voyage would be for us today, if we were to consider a massive relocation to another planet. Crialese succeeds in making these magical-realism moments into a reflection of the awe-producing desire for America as the El Dorado and a manifestation of a folk religion where the unseen and the imagined are equally relevant tools for one's understanding of the world. Similarly, contemporary migrants perceive Europe as the New America. In Del Grande's reportage *Mamadou va a morire*, the places of departure in Morocco are dotted by "signs" of today's El Dorado. Soccer T-shirts with player Francesco Totti's name and team number along with Dolce and Gabbana knock offs are the simulacra of a wished-for world which finds its concrete instantiation in the cars driven by returned or visiting emigrants, or in the vacation houses they can now afford to build in the town's new neighborhoods (18–21). The lure of the destination is as powerful across decades and centuries: It simply takes on different forms. The epistemological collapse of what is desired/imagined with what is seen and possibly or reductively taken as a reality accessible to all, is a crucial mechanism in migration experiences and consequently in the stories about them. Whether in the form of reportage or written/filmic text, these stories often focus on this collapse in order to identify the drive that pushes people to leave and to enter an in-between space. Experienced both before the departure as a distancing from reality and reexperienced after the relocation as a condition of bicultural belonging, this in-between space is epitomized by the trip, as the parenthesis between two worlds that embraces both while suspending them.

Crialese convincingly captures this tension in the middle part of his tripartite *Nuovomondo*, placed between the departure from Sicily and the arrival at Ellis Island. He sets this central section on the migrant ship and skillfully shapes it as a space of fear, discovery, and cultural negotiations, all at once. The ship therefore emerges as a quintessential preoccupied space where hyponational and hypernational issues intersect. While studies on ports, ships, corollary activities around the voyage, namely the emigration industry, have carefully reconstructed the history and cultural impact of the voyage in all its components, as we have seen in the Aperture, it is Crialese's ship that has furnished a visual and "moving" rendition of Italy's early emigration experience to a large (and international) audience. In the obvious absence of a direct memory of the Italian migrant voyage via film footage, this particularly hidden aspect of migration—much more inaccessible than the departure and arrival experiences that are shared by nonmigrants as well on the docks of departure and arrival docks—seems to defy representation. During the emigration era, government inspectors and doctors documented the experience for administrative and law implementation purposes in publications of only limited circulation, while De Amicis's *On Blue Water*, despite being written as an accessible travel diary for a larger readership, never became a popular classic in Italy. Today, Stella's and La Compagnia delle Acque's shows analyzed in the preceding Aperture rely on these materials as well as on the letters of the migrants as a rich source of information, and illustrate the readings and commentary with compelling vintage photographs. Still, it is *Nuovomondo* that, by reworking the legacy of such diverse directors as Chaplin, Kazan, and Amelio (as well as Fellini),[33] has provided a visual kinetic tableau of both the outside and inside of the Italian emigrant ship for the first time and for large distribution. (Interestingly, it took up to 2006 for Italy to reflect on this fundamental theme in such comprehensive and accessible terms.)

The ship first appears in the film in a scene of strong pictorial quality that, by hinging on Crialese's characteristic play between reality and perception, emphasizes the role of the ship as a threshold, a point of connection between the regional space of departure and the transnational space of the ocean. In marking the transition between the first part set in Sicily and the second set on the ocean, the scene masterfully incorporates two intrinsic qualities of the departure of millions and millions of emigrants: the caesura from and the in-builtness into a country whose very identity can ultimately be described only in terms of drifting. A camera placed on the ship films the boarding passengers from above first and then cutting to a bird's-eye shot shows a large crowd of people that the spectator mistakenly takes as the passengers themselves. Suddenly, an almost imperceptible motion slowly creates a separation in the middle of the crowd, dividing it between the leaving passengers, on one side, and the families, friends, and workers staying put at the dock, on the other (Fig. 7). The skillful surprise effect has a visual as well as an epistemological impact: What crowd is actually moving? From where to where? After the eye is initially tricked into creating a whole, which stands metaphorically for the nation, the whole gets split, partially drifts away, as the ship, until then part of the land, parts from it and . . . departs.

The Italian nation—still very young back then, still unable to articulate a homogenous discourse out of its regional fragmentation and only partially completed unification process—leaves and goes abroad traveling through space and time at once, as Viscusi lyrically suggests in the epigraph *(Astoria 17)*. The caesura in the film is also marked at the auditory level: The drifting is accompanied by a deep drone, a percussive sound somewhere between a dirge and the slow beating of a melancholy heart. It is the ship's horn that interrupts the face-to-face link between the people on land and those on the ship: The intense whistle turns the emigrants' attention from the shore—a space of preoccupation over survival and social improvement—toward the sky and by extension to the new

FIGURE 7. Emigrant ship leaving the dock in Sicily. Still from *Nuovomondo*, 2006.

world, functioning as a call to adventure and change (Fig. 8). Perceived by some critics as "a self-defeating act of virtuosity" (Bonsaver), this scene is instead an occasion for the effective artistic intervention of the *auteur*. By challenging realist paradigms and privileging theatrical compositions to fully render the coexistence of various space and time levels, Crialese captures one of the quintessential moments of the migratory experience—the departure—in a solemn yet not bombastic style.

Once the ship is on the water, it functions as a floating social microcosm in which class, linguistic, religious, and gender-based forms of identification are inevitably questioned and partially redefined vis-à-vis the encounter with the people in exodus as well as the new space overseas. Unlike De Amicis, Crialese is not invested on the melodramatic articulation of the national loss implicit in the outbound flow or in a grandiloquent celebration of the emigrant colonies as extensions of the nation,[34] nor does he sublimate the voyage experience into a nostalgic song as Mignonette did. Instead, he is intent on representing the social complexity of the ship and the culture it expresses and produces. As a contact zone, the ship is primarily a space in which identities and affiliations are reshaped and newly forged.

A clear exemplification of this process of renegotiation in *Nuovomondo* is the initial conversation among men coming from different regions and suddenly locating a previously unknown common denominator in both the qualifier "Italian" and the space of the ocean, which, as we have seen in the Aperture was often, even until the postwar era, a first-time discovery for the emigrants—"The sea! That must be what they call the sea!" exclaims Pascal D'Angelo in his 1924 autobiography (55). In the film, as they take hold of their berths in the third-class sleeping area, the Italian men introduce themselves to each other by

Figure 8. Emigrants traveling on transatlantic ship. Still from *Nuovomondo*, 2006.

indicating their village of origin. The resulting web of provenances and dialects prompts Vincenzo's candid, and thus exhilarating, comment: "Who's ever slept with so many foreigners before?" A seemingly knowledgeable man among them observes that they are not foreigners but "all Italians." His claim—effectively an act of invention of the Italian community for that time—corroborates the reading of emigration as an experience that created Italians outside of Italy. In this case, the invention occurs in the hybrid space of the ocean, which Vincenzo within the same conversation calls "Il Grande Luciano." In melding the Sicilian word for "*oceano*" with its article (*lu uciano=luciano*), he forges a new term, Luciano, sounding like the name Lucien (meaning light in Latin). He practically anthropomorphizes the large expanse of water, which still unknown to him acquires the status of a gigantic godlike figure. In traversing it, the ship turns into a nationalizing space, preoccupied by the regional stories of single individuals and communities simultaneously entering a transnational cultural sphere.

By the same token, on the ship traditional gender roles come to a halt vis-à-vis the mysterious presence of Lucy/Luce (another name signifying "light" and thus "change"), the upper-class woman who joins the Mancusos and counteracts/complements the mother figure of Fortunata. Despite the practically unanimous criticism on her insertion into the plot,[35] Lucy clearly embodies the new female paradigm of the learned critical woman foreshadowing the different cultural values that the New World will expose the migrants to. Indeed, her alleged allegiance to her social class dissolves in the hybrid spaces of the ship and the ocean, and cannot remain impermeable to contact. On the contrary, it is so porous that it is finally incorporated into the working-class space in the final scenes where Lucy and Salvatore help each other and fundamentally design a "neworld" of sort.

Rather than the non-space and non-time qualifiers often used to describe Crialese's ship (see Borroni), I argue that it is the excess of space and time that characterizes it. The by-now obsolete Italian term used to refer to the ship—"*bastimento*"—is a word interestingly coming from the same Germanic root for "being" and "building." In other words, edification and movement embodied by the ship and the voyage are parts of the same process. This is why Foucault's suggestive notion of "heterotopia" proves in my view to be much more effective than Marc Augé's non-place,[36] to convey the function of the ship as a laboratory of culture. In his 1983 essay, "Of Other Spaces," Foucault defines heterotopias as concrete utopias in which reality is inverted but in a real rather than an imaginary space, which is instead what usually characterizes utopias. He provides several examples of heterotopias, spaces able to include more than one space (and time) within themselves, and to produce meaning for reality by exclusion, alternation, antithesis, etc. Foucault's taxonomy of these apparently nonproductive yet hyperregulated spaces (old people's homes, hospitals, cemeteries, etc.) interestingly culminates in the analysis of the boat, described as the heterotopia par excellence, especially for its ability to contain socioeconomic drives as well as the desires that produce stories and histories. As he writes: "The boat has not only been for our civilization, from the sixteenth century until the present, the great instrument of economic development, but has been simultaneously the greatest reserve of the imagination" (27).[37]

Nuovomondo's ship is a figuration of Foucault's heterotopic ship, a real place acting as a countersite, in which all real sites of a culture are represented, contested, and inverted, as the scenes about the reconfiguration of national/regional affiliations, gender roles, and class belonging point to. Like all other heterotopias according to Foucault, the ship has "the curious property of being in relation with all the other sites, but in such a way as to suspect, neutralize, or invert the set of relations that they happen to designate, mirror, or reflect" (24). In *Nuovomondo*'s ship, the deck is used as the village's main street or square to stroll, kill time, eye a woman; sleeping areas are transformed into communal barbershops or dressing rooms; and after a tragedy, the ship becomes a funeral parlor and the ocean a tomb, as depicted in a somber blue-tinted scene on the deck where a woman mourns her dead child and eventually throws it in the water, like Amalia Pasin in the show *L'orda* examined in Aperture I.

The scene in the film that best reflect this kind of reshuffling of paradigms is the storm at sea, which Crialese decided to set within the interiors of the ship as opposed to the natural environment. Tall waves and high winds are therefore left to the imagination and the focus is on the effects that the storm has upon the third-class passengers. The realistic quality of the scene makes room for a staged *chiaroscuro*-imbued choreography of turning and rolling bodies meshing in slow motion into a whole new creature. As distinctions of gender, provenance, work, and even class (with the presence of Lucy) are erased in the course of this dramatic moment, the ship emerges as a heterotopia insofar as it contests the nation by representing it not as a land-bound entity but as a liquid and frail body whose cohesion is thus challenged and redefined.

It is worth noting that Crialese has inflected this reformulated notion of the national not only at the level of the content, but also at the level of the film production. *Nuovo-*

mondo is the result of a border-crossing operation: Coproduced with Italian and French funds, the film counted on the international experience of French cinematographer Agnès Godard who had worked with Peter Greenway as well as Wim Wenders, and that of set and production designer Carlos Conti from Argentina, who was part of the crew of Walter Salles's *Motorcycles Diaries* and Sally Potter's *The Tango Lessons*. Shot partly in Sicily and partly in Argentina (the scenes on the ship and at Ellis Island were filmed in Buenos Aires), *Nuovomondo* gathered an international cast ranging from Italian actors Vincenzo Amato—a Sicilian artist transplanted in New York—and Aurora Quattrocchi to the late Sicilian-American Vincent Schiavelli and French-British Charlotte Gainsbourg. Regardless of this complex border crossing, the film was the official Italian entry at the Oscar Awards, where despite the strong American component of the film, it did not gather the support of the jurors. In the more favorable Italian context, a special prize (a second Silver Lion) was instead created in order to recognize *Nuovomondo* at the Venice Film Festival, a prize that helped its circulation in the United States, aided in part by the official patronage of Martin Scorsese.

At the level of content, as we have seen, Crialese effectively captures the mechanism by which new worlds are envisioned on an island like Sicily, bound to the United States, in the first part, a separating and connecting ocean in the second, and on a liminal nation-forging space like Ellis Island in the third part. If considered as a voyage from one island to another, the film's space is by definition fluid, only partially anchored, open to dispersion as well as access. The section devoted to the process of checking, examining, and evaluating the bodies and minds of the emigrants in order to assess their suitability to another national project, that of the United States, is once again a first time occurrence for the Italian big screen and serves an educational purpose that perhaps went beyond even Crialese's goals. Not even a visit to the Ellis Island Museum, where some of these scenes are re-created in short-play format, can provide such a wide and rich tableau of emotions and practices (physical exams, intelligence tests, couple matching, family separation, and so on).

In the film, Ellis Island is the site where the magical visions of the emigrants about the "*paese della cuccagna*" are intensified by the proximity of it.[38] Yet, simultaneously, a scientific project of human selection supported by medical research denies the enchanted quality of the immigrants' dreams. The country of abundance is only accessible to healthy bodies, healthy minds, and average and above-average IQs. When lectured on this project designed to avoid contaminating American society with diseases and low intelligence, Lucy scornfully says: "What a modern vision!" She casts a serious doubt on the "twentieth century" culture that immigrants were encountering after leaving the Middle Ages behind, to refer to Viscusi's sentence in the epigraph (Lucy's comment further complicates Viscusi's linear, albeit powerful, vision). Her critique of the system is complemented by the Mancusos' replies to the tests: Their inventiveness defies the very goal of these exams (Salvatore builds a house with the pieces of the matching puzzle game), and their answers question the very nature of the abstract queries, which to them sound utterly absurd. This resistance reaches its zenith when old Fortunata refuses to take the so-called intelligence test and indirectly elaborates a powerful critique of the Ellis Island philosophy through her worldview. With her simple observation, she gets to the heart of the U.S. nationalist project. "What do you want from us . . . folks coming from the Old World?" she calmly but sternly inquires. When told that the officers want to make sure that they are all fit for the New World, she retorts vigorously: "And who are you—Almighty God?—to decide if we are fit or not to enter this land of yours, the outer world?" That comment paradoxically makes her world of healing practices and magic beliefs much more balanced than the one informed by New World science.

A space of preoccupation by definition, for the condensed fears harbored by the emigrants waiting to be given the green light to the United States, Ellis Island appears as another topos of excess: Occupied by the stories, beliefs, and views of individuals coming from all over the world, Ellis Island is a laboratory for the international nation. It is on this small island that people were branded by their national origins in order to become part of a country eventually known as a country of immigrants: It is where Sicilians, Campanians, Piedmontese, and people from other regions were labeled as Italians (either Southern or Northern, according to the distinctions used at that time). It is also where something had to be lost so that something else could be created.

Reduced to silence out of surprise toward and rejection from the New World, Fortunata eventually decides to go back to Sicily. By the time she loses her desire/ability to speak, her grandson Filippo finds his voice, pushed by the need to survive and embrace the adventure. The implicit rebalancing suggests an osmotic transmigration of the voice from one body to another. Even when the decision is to split the family with Fortunata returning home, the last image of the family is one of union and the absence of the actual American world beyond Ellis Island, as in Kazan's 1963 film *America America*, prevents the depiction of the actual separation. In fact, *Nuovomondo* brings together two imaginaries: Subnational (the region) and national (Italian and American) rhetoric and values are ultimately melded in a transnational space. This melding is powerfully conveyed in the conclusive scene of the movie, where the emigrants, now immigrants, literally dissolve into a new space, the "neworld" of the title.

After the Ellis Island verdict, they reemerge in a space at once vast, liquid, rich, and complex: It is the milk river of the "*paese della cuccagna*" that in an early scene Salvatore first imagines ("I don't know how to swim, but I would not mind taking a bath in a milk river") and then in one of his visions briefly experiences with Lucy as they meet and float together in this environment. The gigantic white river, almost an ocean, shown in the final credits is an experimental space in which new forms of "*stare al mondo*" (being in the world) together will have to be tested, starting from the new "light/*luce*" now present in the Mancuso family. This choral film proposes the productive tension between the crowd and the family repeatedly throughout, for instance when the family faces timidly emerge from the crowd on the departing ship; or when their bodies can be spotted in the storm scene. This porous nucleus, distinguishable for its uniqueness and expandable in new directions, reappears in the closing utopia-made-real canvas of the film's conclusion, where the camera slowly zooms out from the close-up-level shots of the family to the vibrant pointillist pattern of a mixed world: the migrants.[39]

It is in this scene that the Italian and the American nations come to coexist, as archaic magical perceptions of culture and modern rational social architectures flow together, or rather fly together—the Mancusos and the migrants around them can be alternately seen as birds flapping their wings in a white sky. By interrogating the birth of a nation (Italian and American) on water, Crialese is simultaneously tackling three topics of crucial importance. First, he is in revolutionary ways suggesting the reading of migrants as emigrants and immigrants at once. He thus does away with reductive views of them as either fleeing or arriving people, two conditions that deprive them of a personal and cultural dimension, as they lose their past from the perspective of the new place or their present from the perspective of their place of origin. In order to counteract the risk of what Algerian sociologist and activist Abdelmalek Sayad has called "the double absence" of the migrant at home and abroad, Crialese opts for "presence" and "representation," if not hyperrepresentation with his magic realism. Second, this indistinct image of people moving in a liquid space is reminiscent of contemporary immigration in the Mediterranean; not only are migrants both emigrants and immigrants, but also countries can be lands of migratory departures and arrivals. With its dynamic interplay between shores and ships, Crialese suggests that the Italian nation is to be read as a circularly diasporic place. Third, he takes a conscious step toward the collective elaboration of a "common history of dreams and tears," called for by Stella in *Odissee* (20), by focusing on the simultaneous tale of mourning and potential regeneration that any emigration entails. Crialese's intent is to form and perform an otherwise unavailable collective memory at the visual level by consciously and inadvertently informing his film with a wide palette of texts ranging from Viviani's play *Scalo Marittimo ('Nterr' 'a 'Mmaculatella)* (1918), to Stieglitz' famous photograph *The Steerage* (1907), Hines's Ellis Island photographs and Gambogi's macchiaioli-style painting "Gli emigranti" (ca. 1895). In his palimpsest-like film, Crialese thus offers the possibility of seeing that experience and hence of "remembering" it in a condensed way, perhaps in a more dynamic and accessible form than a museum could provide.[40] Pre-occupied by several representations of emigration, *Nuovomondo* nonetheless remains an original work for its complexity and scope. Ultimately, it visualizes Gabaccia's intuition that diaspora "made the Italian nation and made it what is—plural, fragile, and debated" (175), fundamentally positing the paradox of finding a "national" trait of cohesion in the transnational dispersion of the nation. In this sense, *Nuovomondo* acts not simply as a cultural antidote against amnesia over a past of emigration, but also as an occasion for an epistemological shift in understanding the porosity of the Italian nation.

TWO

Overlapping Mediterranean Routes in Marra's *Sailing Home*, Ragusa's *The Skin Between Us*, and Tekle's *Libera*

> eppure lo sapevamo anche noi
> l'odore delle stive
> l'amaro del partire
> lo sapevamo anche noi
>
> —GIAN MARIA TESTA, "Ritals"

In adopting a more overt emigration-immigration parallel, this chapter connects cultural texts attentive to the eloquent historical reverberations of Italy somewhere else and of "somewhere elses" in Italy.[1] The liquid space occupied by these reverberations shifts from the Atlantic Ocean of the first chapter to the Mediterranean Sea. In the same way the Mediterranean was the prologue to the transatlantic voyage for the Italian emigrants, the Atlantic Ocean remains an echo or a possibility in almost all the texts analyzed here. Yet, the central focus remains on the Mediterranean, and in particular the Channel of Sicily for its bridging and dividing function between the European and the African continents. In the cross-pollinated space of the Mediterranean basin, iconically a melting pot of cultures, this chapter identifies less an easy place of encounters and exchanges than one of tensions, struggled-for opportunities, and even mortal dangers. The blurring of emigrant and immigrant desires and failures in Vincenzo Marra's 2001 film *Sailing Home* (*Tornando a casa*), the coexistence of painful legacies of emigration and slavery in Kym Ragusa's 2006 memoir *The Skin Between Us: A Memoir of Race, Beauty and Belonging*, and the survival-driven urge to flee North Africa for the postcolonial subject in Feven Abreha Tekle's 2005 *Libera* are all staged, either partially or fully, in a Mediterranean that functions as a preoccupied space. Occupied by previous stories of demographic relocations and cultural movements, this sea now hosts new concerns over economic stability, protection of human rights, and racial tolerance. Yet, each text also elaborates a concept of preoccupation that dynamically points to possibilities in the midst of these worries. Geographer Edward Soja's concept of "Thirdspace," developed off Henri Lefebvre's famous space trialectics (perceived-conceived-lived space), will prove useful in reconciling the different tensions enacted in the Mediterranean as well as in recognizing the transformative power of international waters over national identities. In inviting a reading of space that goes beyond the analysis of perceived space in its socioeconomic practices (Firstspace) and of conceived space in its abstract mapping controlled from above (Secondspace), Soja sets out to regain the creative potentials of a lived-and-imagined space (Thirdspace), a "space of inclusive simultaneities" and "radical openness" (68).

A large array of texts potentially lends itself to a relevant reading within this type of framework, but Marra's film, Ragusa's memoir, and Tekle's self-narrative are able to create an ideal conversation between an Italian filmmaker sensitive to migration and class issues in a mobile contemporary world, an Italian American writer of African descent interested in returning to her emigrant family's place of origin, and an African immigrant narrator carrying implicit stories of colonialism as she seeks a shelter away from a dictatorial regime. Fundamentally, their stories make a stratified reading of the Mediterranean possible. Among the films offering other forays into the topic at hand, one could certainly include Marco Tullio Giordana's 2005 *Quando sei nato non puoi più nasconderti* (Once You're Born, You Can No Longer Hide) and Mohsen Melliti's 2006 *Io, l'altro* (I, the Other)—with the latter being arguably the first feature film by an immigrant in Italy. The two films stage random encounters and the formation of solid relationships between migrants and nonmigrants in the Mediterranean, but without making its waters into a theater of possible transformation.[2] Stories of return among Italian American writers are quite common (see, for example, Jerre Mangione, Ben Morreale, Mario Puzo, and Nat Scamacca's literary writings, to mention just a few), but they rarely focus on the Mediterranean as a space of individual and collective redefinition, even less as a locus of racial formations and relations. Written accounts of the Mediterranean crossing by immigrants themselves are available in the reportages published by Italian journalists such as Gabriele Del Grande's *Mamadou va a morire* and Stefano Liberti's *A sud di Lampedusa*, or in collaborative documentaries such as the collaborative interview-based project *Come un uomo sulla terra*.[3] Compared with these texts, Marra's, Ragusa's, and Tekle's aesthetic and narrative choices address the Mediterranean as a topos-turned-topic, while interpellating Italian and American audiences on issues of collective memory and private routes with specific gender declensions. The legacy of the past—what singer Testa poignantly condenses in the first phrase of the epigraph: "After all we ourselves knew"—reemerges directly and indirectly in the attempt to understand the present and the future. Albeit in not uncomplicated ways, all the texts examined in this chapter offer a convincing and inspiring platform to develop reflections on experiences as well as possibilities.

Going Back Home: Marra's Migratory Loops and Circular Identities

>ch'è meglio non far rumore quando si arriva
>forestieri al caso di un'altra sponda
>
>>(*Testa*, "Il passo e l'incanto")[4]

As has been the case for Crialese's *Nuovomondo*, the translation of Marra's film title into English loses some of the subtle implications of his project. Rendered as *Sailing Home* for the foreign distribution market, the film is actually entitled "Going Back Home," a more accurate expression that emphasizes the circular nature of acts of departure and return. It is in the Mediterranean that Marra's film unravels a tale of real and desired escapes across borders. Accordingly, he opens the film with a shot of the seawaters at night and the images of the Sicilian channel moving on a digital screen connected to a radar. This is the liquid space in which Marra reveals various contradictory identities by following the vicissitudes of a group of fishermen trying to fight against the competition in the Gulf of Naples by regularly entering the extraterritorial waters between Italy and Tunisia in search of greater profits. The crew of the boat, emblematically called *Marilibera* (a slight distortion of the expression "free sea") is made up of Salvatore, a rough Neapolitan who is ready to take risks in order to pull himself out of the local Mafia-controlled market's pressures; Giovanni, the elder of the group, a man resistant to developing friendships; Samir, a graceful Tunisian immigrant with no visa and a perpetual fear of being deported; and Franco, who dreams of emigrating to the United States with his beloved Rosa. With its neorealist style (on-location shooting, diegetic sound, nonprofessional actors), the film follows the fears and aspirations of a series of characters who beyond their individual differences share the same class belonging and the same aspiration to break away from it and find a better life possibly somewhere else (Italy for Tunisians, the United States for Italians, etc.).

The film is set in a transnational scenario that embraces different and yet connected experiences: The immigrant condition is followed not only through the personal trajectory of Samir but also through the encounter with boats of immigrants crossing the Mediterranean as "clandestines," an epic inevitability of the postcolonial globalized era. By the same token, emigration is not just a calcified story from the past, but is also a contemporary phenomenon, especially in Southern Italy, among young people hoping for a different future.[5] Finally, illegality is problematized by placing in the same waters not only the migrants attempting to enter Europe for better opportunities, but also Italians who break national and international laws in order to give themselves an economic alternative. The indirect suggestion here is that the indictment against the immigrants as elements of disturbance in the country should be accompanied by a general revision of social and economic practices within and across borders.

The threads of the film are twined together into an intense narrative knot toward the end of the film. When Rosa is inadvertently killed by one of her young pupils carrying a gun, Franco finds no reason to stay and endure, and at some point considers suicide. Even though the visas for the United States have been approved, his escape from the local environment, almost unconsciously, moves him in a different direction, now that his life's companion is not with him anymore. During his night shift on the boat, he notices a drowning immigrant: As he tries to help him, he ends up holding to the life vest and drifting away with him until they are both rescued, fished out of the waters, by other migrants crossing the Mediterranean. While the anonymous immigrant dies soon after, Franco survives and retreats in a condition of radical silence. Taken by the "clandestine" migrants as "one of them," he voyages toward Italy but his "going back home" takes place in a condition of hybrid identity. His Southern physical features do not separate him from the migrants coming from North Africa: The Mediterranean as a topos of exchanges and encounters has created a similarity of look among people of different national origins.[6] Having hidden his Italian ID card in the clothes of his companion's corpse as they travel toward Europe, Franco becomes "one of them." His act of identity-effacement and obliteration of his past makes him into a *harraga* (or *harrag*, meaning burner), a very common Arabic term among the emigrants from North Africa who are seen both as heroic adventurers burning national borders in the process of crossing frontiers and seas (Del Grande 28) and as astute strategists burning their ID cards so as not to be identified and repatriated after reaching Europe (Liberti 154), as the 2009 documentary *Harraga* also explains.[7] The novelty in Marra's film lies in the fact that it is an Italian that opts for the "burning" of identity and borders within a framework of subtle denunciation of the system and of radical rethinking of categories. Taken as a "clandestine" by the Italian coastal guards who intercept the boat, Franco experiences the humiliating and abusive process at the checkpoint: Eventually, he is sent to Tunisia with the rest of the migrants. With Tunisia considered to be his place of origin by the officers, Franco—unidentifiable to them—is sent there as well as if he were . . . "going back home."

His experience thus acts as a foil to Samir's condition in the film: Having left his country of origin without any papers, Samir is particularly critical of the boat's captain's decision to fish in African waters, since any reported irregularity could result in his repatriation. Besides, the gunfire aimed at them by African coastal guards when they trespass the borders is not just dangerous for their lives, but also generates open outbursts of racism, as it is wrongly imputed, by Giovanni at least, to "evil" black people from Africa like Samir. When Franco sincerely tries to comfort Samir by saying that after all a repatriation would be like "going back home," Samir brusquely replies: *"Vado quando voglio io"* (I go when I want to go), confessing that he does not want to/cannot return to Tunisia since his migration project did not turn out to be the success his family expects and he has to hide the truth. He then inquires into Franco's plans to move to the United States and, as they share concern over their conditions as people in between worlds, they jokingly imagine a return to Tunisia with Franco playing the rich Italian: a utopian projection vis-à-vis their current status.

In the course of this intimate conversation between Samir and Franco, tellingly sitting on a rocking boat, the story of current foreign immigration to Italy literally overlaps with that of contemporary Italian emigration abroad. Not just a fact of the past as the statistics officially state, the emigration of Italians continues as a silent phenomenon investing the younger generation, in particular, with an American Dream that extends into the third millennium and comprises several destinations.[8] In debunking the idea of Italy as a one-dimensional G7 country, turned smoothly from a place of departure into one of destination, *Sailing* subtly interweaves a reflection on the Southern Question and the postcolonial condition. The pressures to leave experienced by people like Samir, abandoning places that, despite the end of colonialism, have not been able to grow autonomously, is directly related to the forms of limitation and control imposed by a neoimperialist system which increases the distance between the rich West/North and the poor elsewhere, to put it in crude terms. Yet, instead of simplifying the dichotomy Africa-Europe, *Sailing* shows that the European destination is equally embedded in forms of underdevelopment as part of internal forms of colonization dating back to the unification, by which the South is still struggling to achieve economic solidity and civic legality.[9] Postcoloniality, in other words, is not a static condition in *Sailing*; it dynamically links historical experiences and economic geographies that in turn complicate individual choices. Rather than marking the end of oppression (signaled by the prefix "post"), it emphasizes the reverberations and extensions of it, while also including the forms of agency that individuals claim in response to it. Marra weaves this complex fabric in the Channel between Sicily and Tunisia in order to make the points of contact and distance even more visible in their material and immaterial impact.

Furthermore, the place of origin of Samir, Tunisia, is presented as a "home" not just because of Franco's decision to reshuffle his life's geographies at the film's conclusion, but also because of the historical role played by Tunisia as both a seasonal and permanent destination for Italian workers, traders, religious exiles, as well as political refugees from the sixteenth century up to World War II.[10] The reversal of flows from Tunisia to Italy (Sicily in particular) started in the 1960s, grew in the midst of the fishing wars of the 1990s, and has continued in different forms to this day. With Tunisia representing one of the prominent countries of origin for immigrants in Italy,[11] Marra's clever choice of the Italy-Tunisia axis prompts, even beyond the confines of the film's plot, a meaningful reflection on the stratified relationships between the two coasts of the Mediterranean and of the channel between Sicily and the African coasts as "a frontier, a barrier between the two worlds" as well as a "road of communication and exchange" (Consolo 242) built on shared experiences.

In the closing scene, Franco is filmed standing between two North African men who look like him. When he greets one of them in Arabic with a salute learned from Samir, he is greeted back in Arabic. The moment signifies his choice to become "one of them," a choice floating between an instinct and a necessity in the same way he floats in the Channel of Sicily. The spectator is left with no sense of what the future holds for Franco—inadvertently mirroring the media coverage of the arrivals of boats to the European coasts that focus obsessively on the boats and the bodies, yet leave the future unseen. Marra's narrative turn is by necessity one of indefinition and openness as he is questioning the purported solidity of Italian identity in the porous space of the Mediterranean. The shift happens in the fluid space of the sea, where at this point "going back home" can be taken as an impossibility if home is Italy or a possibility if home is a new place belonging to a common home, the Mediterranean. As Gregory Pell has noted, Franco "become[s] the other with little effort for he [is] 'a terrone di mezzo'" (an in-between Southerner), an expression that effectively captures the dynamics of internal colonialism and external postcolonialism by reversing the negative connotation of "*terrone*" and opening new spaces for a South otherwise seen only as a remote appendix. It is not coincidental that the identity crisis is a process corresponding with the voyage: The fishing boat turns from a space of economic preoccupation to a vehicle involved in an adventure. The migrant boat, a space of similar concern coupled with the preoccupation to survive, presents itself as a means to a radical redirecting of one's life route. Finally, the coast guard boat, full of preoccupation over the security of borders for the officers and of shame and disappointment for the failed crossing from the migrants' perspective, becomes, for Franco at least, the occasion for an alternative.

The voyage is predicated as a cognitive path that, in rereading the world from dynamic perspectives, offers new epistemologies and ontologies, namely, it defines a "Thirdspace" more complex than the home that one starts from as well as the new coast one reaches. According to geographer Soja, Firstspaces reflect sociality, and in particular the economic practices they contain. The Mediterranean in the film works as such insofar as it is a space of exchanges, profit, and competition over resources for the fishermen. At the same time, the Mediterranean is a Secondspace in its abstract rendition: Mapped on the screens of the boat, it is a space scanned from above. For the sake of growth and security, both the fishermen and the coastal guards control it via detailed charts. Yet, *Sailing* clearly posits the Mediterranean also as a Thirdspace, namely a space "filled with illusions and allusions, a space that is common to all of us yet never able to be completely seen and understood, an 'unimaginable universe'" (Soja 56). Thirdspace entails knowledge able to subsume existential being and becoming as well as historicality and sociality in space. This knowledge "is not obtained in permanent constructions built around formalized and closed epistemologies, but through an endless series of theoretical and practical approximations, a critical and inquisitive nomadism in which the journey to new ground never ceases" (82). *Sailing* designs a Thirdspace by bringing together the concrete space analyzed (the sea as a commercial space—fishing, migrating labor force) and the mental construct related to it (the sea as escape). As a result, it questions the categories of place of departure and arrival and redefines "home" in the process.

As with Amelio's *Lamerica*, *Sailing* offers a rethinking of Italian identity in the direction of a heterogeneity explained on the basis of overlapping historical facts and present phenomena. Their connection remains attentive to the macro context of collective destinies as well as to the specificity of individual trajectories, and ultimately points to the cyclical nature of migratory waves, to the need for a discourse of empathy in confronting them, and to the artificiality of the discourse that distinguishes, even opposes between, "us and them." Compared to Amelio's epic breadth and complex filmic language interweaving old footage, plainly realist shots and strongly choreographed portraits, Marra opts for a rougher take, a less controlled camera, an often incomprehensible language due to his use of local dialects that takes us back to the neorealist tradition.[12] Marra was not new to the topic of immigration when he embarked on *Sailing*: He had filmed a short called *Una rosa prego* (A rose, please), inspired by the life of two young street vendors of Rom origin. *Sailing* was his first feature film, after he had worked as an assistant to Marco Bechis (*Garage Olimpo*) in Argentina and Mario Martone in Naples, his native city. Distributed by Nanni Moretti's Sacher, *Sailing* was voted at the Venice Film Festival as Best Film of the International Critics Week and has often been read vis-à-vis *Lamerica*, generally seen as one the most representative films on immigration/emigration in Italy, for the transformation undergone by the protagonist in the mobile context of migration.[13]

Similar to Gino, *Lamerica*'s protagonist, Franco looks like an immigrant at the end of the film: The mechanisms of passing, traditionally addressed in the field of African American studies, find an interesting application in the Mediterranean case as power relations are assessed and reconstituted. Unlike Gino who is forced into traveling as an undocumented immigrant (once the Albanian government unmasks his corrupt schemes) and undergoes a process of "Albanianization," Franco in *Sailing* chooses to do so, and simulates a "Tunisianization." He thus reveals an agency that immigrant Samir cannot resort too since Samir's non-Western condition would make an escape or a return to Africa a much more complicated, if not dangerous, enterprise. The same way that Gino was traveling to an Italy that Albanians on the ship saw as their America (for his amnesiac travel companion, Michele, it really *was* America), Franco travels toward Tunisia as his potential America, and does it delicately, without being "noisy," which is the image suggested by Testa in the epigraph. His only words for a large portion of the film in the concluding part are emblematically just "Peace be with you," highlighting the discourse of solidarity supported by Marra (and Consolo). Seen as a whole, *Lamerica* and *Tornando* encapsulate the unlikely connections of emigration, immigration, colonialism (*Lamerica* addresses the invasion of Albania), and postcolonialism. Yet, *Sailing* does not show the mythic and nostalgic tendency that O'Healy identifies in *Lamerica* (253).[14] By giving voice to struggling migration-bound Italians and struggling Tunisian migrants, the film employs an unsentimental style to address the complications of the Mediterranean as frontier and crossing point at once (Fig. 9).

FIGURE 9. Rescue of immigrants in the Mediterranean Sea, early 2000s. Photo by Francesco Cocco.

Emigration, Immigration, and Slavery Routes in Ragusa's *The Skin Between Us*

> ma sono già stato qui
> forse in un altro incanto
> sono già stato qui
> mi riconosco il passo
> (*Testa*, "Il passo e l'incanto")[15]

The rethinking of space, identity, and power dynamics in the Mediterranean offered by Marra's *Tornando* rests on a male bond that closely follows Amelio's *Lamerica*.[16] Whether by alliance or opposition, the refractions of the male roles are essential to the film project. Marra certainly privileges a male perspective in choosing the fishing industry and characters whose families are marginal, nonexistent, or distant. Rosa, the only woman in the cast, eventually dies, thus indirectly giving Franco the chance to occupy the Mediterranean in a reimagined form. In her 2006 book *The Skin Between Us: A Memoir of Race, Beauty and Belonging*, Ragusa turns this gender configuration on its head and places women at the center of her story, and in particular the two grandmothers who raised her separately and whose recent deaths trigger her narrative quest. In the process of articulating her complex identity as the daughter of a black woman and an Italian American man—and as such white among blacks, and black among whites, to simplify the opposition—she digs into her family's past. Her investigation aims at understanding the reasons for the distance lying between the two sides of the family, epitomized by her parents' separation and her hidden existence in the eyes of her Italian grandparents for years. The intimate recounting of her family life is constructed around women's stories,[17] since, as Ragusa states, in the end women are the ones who have left her a heritage made up of "the loss, the search, the story" (237). In understanding the loss and trying to compensate for it by embarking on a family search that produces the story we read, Ragusa spins a geographic tale that due to its multiperspectival nature collapses various histories of mobility and innovatively links them.[18]

My reading of *The Skin Between Us* only partially addresses the central issues of the memoir that other scholars have concentrated on (marginalization of the protagonist/writer as black, Italian, and female; the richness of culturally and racially mixed heritage; the cognitive and political function of the memoir; etc.).[19] My focus is instead on the treatment of space in the book, not just as an internal narrative thread but also as a call to experience space as a silent (or silenced) palimpsest of stories. The narrative center of the memoir is located in the United States—and in particular initially Harlem and the Bronx (two working-class areas shared, not without tensions, by blacks and Italians, among other groups), and then later New Jersey (one of the destinations of the "white flight" for upwardly mobile ethnics).[20] Yet, the center of gravity lies in Sicily, which Ragusa visited for the first time in 1999 at the symbolic age of thirty-three from a Christian perspective. Far from representing a restricted geographical reality, in both Ragusa's life and writing, Sicily becomes a privileged observatory to rewrite the national biographies of Italy and the United States through their complex transnational formations and relations. Simultaneously an isolated spot and a crucial crossing point, both physically and historically, Sicily in Ragusa's book becomes the core of endless East-West and South-North linkages, and even of the axis connecting the underground and ground-level worlds, epitomized by the myth of Persephone that she embraces in her journey toward a new form of belonging.

Even though Sicily is directly dealt with only in the prologue and epilogue of the book, I am particularly interested in the role it plays in the writer's experience and the book she writes about it. The prologue opens with a clear spatialization of the tale and the self, a mechanism that characterizes the entire memoir:

> I stood on the deck of a ferry crossing the Straits of Messina, the narrow tongue of water that separates mainland Italy from Sicily.... Behind me lay Calabria, the toe of the Italian boot.... Long ago—the dates are unclear and those family members who could remember the details are long gone—my paternal grandfather's family migrated from Sicily to Calabria. By the beginning of the 20th century most of the family had left Calabria for New York. But I have another connection to this part of the world: Sicily is the crossroads between Europe and Africa, the continent from which my maternal ancestors were stolen and brought to slavery in Maryland, West Virginia, and North Carolina. Two sets of migration, one forced, one barely voluntary. Two homelands left far behind. Two bloodlines meeting in me. (17–18)

With an original turn, Ragusa knots her family's historical ties to Africa through slavery and to Southern Europe through emigration, two demographic movements that despite some profound differences the reader is asked to read in parallel ways for the forced or semi-forced deracination that they impose and the economic struggles and forms of discrimination that they both entailed.[21] While the reader may perceive Ragusa's association as a strained one, in reality these movements did intersect, albeit indirectly, on the boats destined for the transatlantic voyage. In his book on Italian shipwrecks, *Odissee*, Gian Antonio Stella refers to an 1898 report on the condition of the early Italian emigrant ships produced by Nicola Malnate, Inspector of the Port of Genoa, and mentioned in Rosoli's and Grossi's study *Il pane duro* (1976). In the document, Malnate states that often the transportation of emigration "happened on the same ships that were used for the slave traffic," very slow machines with minimal room for the passengers (74, my translation). Interestingly, Ragusa comes to the realization of this connection, when she travels on a boat herself. Ragusa's family palimpsest finds here a little known piece of history to reinforce an unlikely tie that is a concrete part of her individual story as much as it is in the history of emigration.[22] (Uncannily, the connection between migration and slavery will reappear in Tekle's text.) Conceivable as foundational movements for the two nations of Italy and the United States, emigration and slavery are thus presented as histories that can foster a more profound awareness of the present, including the racial conflicts characterizing a multiracial society like the United States or prompted by recent immigration as in the case of Italy.[23]

This awareness is developed in the highly charged topos of the Strait. A narrow, and yet highly strategic and symbolic stretch of water, between the mainland and the island of Sicily, the Strait becomes a Thirdspace in Ragusa's memoir. As a Firstspace in the personal experience of her family, the Strait is a material practice of connection and separation of personal lives for economic reasons. As a Secondspace, the Strait is mapped figuratively and functions as a commonly shared chart with no apparent personal declension, as the ferryboat crosses from Calabria to Sicily. Yet, in *The Skin Between Us*, the Strait is primarily a lived-and-imagined Thirdspace for Ragusa, a space that allows for both historical understanding and personal reappropriation, even though in the midst of contradictions and approximations of closure. In a not surprisingly interrogative mode, Ragusa wonders: "What home was I searching for that chilly morning on my way to Sicily? Death had propelled me there, an ocean away from Harlem. But it was Harlem I was thinking of, longing for. . . . I had to come this far to know that I needed to find my own way back" (19). The circularity of the narrative does not intend to offer a Hegelian synthesis between opposite poles, but rather a possibility for belonging. The Strait appearing at the opening of the memoir is thus a pre-occupied/preoccupied space in both meanings of the term, occupied by stories and concerns, but also by potential new realizations.

In Ragusa's personal map, emigration and slavery, the main movements that pre-occupy "her" Strait and by extension Sicily and the Mediterranean, meet powerfully in her own body: Her birth is the micromanifestation of these two macrophenomena in history. *The Skin Between Us* unravels along these two lines, reductively identifiable as white and black, yet made up of infinite shades, since they were never pure in the first place. The analysis of these shades on the body makes the skin into the *topoi* of sociocultural self-positioning, an operation forced by society that Ragusa claims as an individual path of cognition and recognition. After the prologue, the book opens with a telling snapshot, the first of many in a memoir that could be read as a narrated family photo album.[24] In the picture, materially reproduced in the book, Kym sits with her two grandmothers, Gilda the Italian American from Sicily and Miriam the African American. Using the act of writing as if it were the same as shooting a film, Ragusa registers their skin colors and describes three main chromatic variations (ivory, yellow, and olive).[25] The "skin between us" of the title is what kept them separate throughout her life, functioning as "a border, a map, a blank page" (25) in the sociocultural "locations" of these three women.

Yet, the skin that divides can also be the starting point for a process of reminiscing, storytelling, and discovery. The overlapping of the body with the page—and synecdochically of the veins with the writing—embodies from the very outset the crucial narrative and conceptual question in the text by which "history and biology" (25) intersect. History is uncovered through the analysis of the body and of blood relations, which have initially constituted the very source of separation: Through the introspection made possible by memoir writing, small and grand narratives constantly traverse each other. The same inquiry about history and biology is central to Marra's *Tornando* since the filmmaker deconstructs clear categories of racial belonging and defines spaces in between, although he does it impersonally. To Marra's transformative message Ragusa adds a much wider context of reference by embracing the American continent in more explicit ways, and an even wider historical span in her Mediterranean-based rethinking of paradigms.

Slavery and its legacy of racism and discrimination are investigated by Ragusa through the black side of the family by reconstructing a gyno-genealogy that starting from her mother, and in particular her grandmother Miriam who raised her, reaches many generations back in time all the way to the plantation era. In ascending order, there is Kym's mother, the university clerk who turned to modeling after a failed marriage to an Italian in the days in which such interracial unions were considered unacceptable. And then we find Kym's maternal grandmother Miriam, a talented young actress, a rape victim, and a journalist with ties to the elite society, who worked as an activist for low-income housing in New York's black communities. And then there are Kym's great-grandmother, Mae, who performed as a dancer in the 1920s, and finally Sybela, the black slave who in the mid-1800s fled with her master and started "whitening" the family's blood.

Emigration is probed through the "white" side of the family, which Kym discovered as a young adolescent when she was finally introduced to her grandparents, and eventually moved in with them. In a typical rhetorical move based on juxtaposition, Kym contrasts the legacy coming from the black part of the family to that of the Italian one: "My black inheritance: defiant, desired, conflicted, provisional. My Italian inheritance: a mythic landscape and a family I barely knew" (108), where "the art of sustenance and survival" comes (113). This side of the family, the "white" Sicilian one, is then much more linked to domestic roles, and inevitably to food (cooking, growing herbs, etc.), while the black family is identified with art, political activism, and physical beauty.[26] Yet, both sides shared suffering, abuse, and struggle as disenfranchised groups. With her characteristic spatializing technique, Ragusa pinpoints the place where these two legacies met: "I do not know where I was conceived but I was made in Harlem. Its topography is mapped on my body: the borderlines enforced by fear and anger, and transgressed by desire. The streets crossing east to west, north to south, like the web of veins beneath my skin" (26). Once again the body, family, and politics intersect on abstract yet lived-through maps: Harlem is the place where her parents met, desired each other, and "made" Kym, but also the place where her mother's family frowned upon a working-class Italian son-in-law as much as her father's family frowned upon a black daughter-in-law.

Another physical space that Kym concentrates on in the book is the Bronx, where the Italian family moves as a first step toward social upper mobility. The Bronx is also a space of segregation, where the safety of the Italian section is an artificial result produced by separation from blacks (and other groups). In a powerful scene set in this tense atmosphere, Kym's identity is once again defined spatially, but this time in the tension between the inside and the outside. Seen as "the nigger" by the neighborhood's children, Kym is defended by her Italian cousin Marie who claims that Kym is dark only on the outside (179) and can thus play with them. While Marie's gesture shows her sense of protection toward her cousin across racial and ethnic lines and allows Kym to feel as if she belonged for a while, the assumption remains that Kym's acceptability rests on the fact that she is white inside, that is, "normal."

The other important space of her adolescence is Maplewood, New Jersey, where she moves in with her Italian grandparents as a young girl. In this highly segregated area in which Italians aspire to be whiter than ever, Kym becomes even more painfully aware of her "difference" (188–89). As is common in ethnic memoirs, the definition of the self passes through one's body and one's name: "Most likely my classmates didn't know what to make of me at all, with my dark-but-not-too-dark skin and my long straightened hair, my 'Chinese' first name and my Italian last name" (195). Kym's hybrid identity and her Italian family's problematic relation to it become apparent in one of the most troubling moments in the memoir, when Gilda tells Kym that she hopes their new neighbors who are about to move into their area will be white (223). Gilda's general cultural attitude toward race couples with her unresolved relation to her own black granddaughter (initially introduced to her as the daughter of her son's new partner from Puerto Rico). These incidents, Ragusa suggests, are written on the skin, since they point to the unsolved conflict of skin color and the painful experience of implicit exclusion, even within one's own family.

The Italian family's racist attitudes are difficult to forget and forgive for the writer, mostly because they exclude a self-analytical path about one's racial perception. Effectively, Ragusa problematizes the Italian category, superficially seen as homogeneous even in the third millennium. In portraying what Ferraro has called the "racial liminality" (152) of the memoir's Italian characters, Ragusa unveils the forms of racialization that Southern Italians were subject to. (She is equally interested in tracing the "whitening" of the black side of the family and thus their own "racial liminality" through her ancestor Sybela's escape with her master, but also her grandmother's mixed lineage and the ambiguity it produces in Ragusa's video *Passing*.) The "othering" mechanisms commenced in Italy, at the hands of theorists of the South's "otherness," and then continued within the American system as part of the selection process so attentively portrayed in the Ellis Island section of Crialese's *Nuovomondo*. Ultimately, Ragusa offers in a stream-of-consciousness narrative the concrete manifestation and internalization of this "othering" process by which "Italians were not always white, and the loss of this memory is one of the tragedies of American racism" (J. Guglielmo, "Introduction" 1). With an even subtler move, Ragusa shows how the Italians' official "Whiteness," according to the taxonomies of the early immigration era, became "their single most powerful asset" (T. Guglielmo 43) which brought them to naturalize the sense of superiority of Italians over blacks or justify it via successful social mobility, when in reality Italians were also excluded racially. As Thomas Guglielmo explains, Italians were marked racially as either Northern or Southern Italians, but white in terms of color, according to the early official categories of the immigration bureau. As a result, Italians, and especially Italians from the South, once in the United States, entered an odd social space in which opportunities were never officially denied but the system never made them automatically available either. The closeness to excluded blacks, which was the reason for so much discrimination (including the lynchings in the Southern United States in the late 1800s and early 1900s), therefore pushed them into assimilation in more forceful ways. But the amnesia about this process of distinction from blacks has affected Italians' ability to comprehend the processes of racial formation and the mechanisms of social emancipation, which do not rely exclusively on hard work but color- and race-based access to opportunities.

Not coincidentally, Ragusa devotes several pages to the sociopolitical activism of her black family members. In fact, *The Skin Between Us* is not just a personal or family memoir, but a subtle investigation into the mechanisms of marginalization and erasure generated by the system (in this case against both blacks and Italians) as well as internalized by the very disenfranchised groups to the point of hindering the relationship between a black woman and an Italian man in the late 1960s and in keeping apart the two sides of the family for years.

Pre-occupied by the two historical strands of slavery and emigration, in turn carrying stories and theories of difference and discrimination, Kym's body and by metonymy her memoir is preoccupied with self-positioning. Despite her intermittent desire to solve these complications provocatively by becoming raceless (195), it is the constant self-questioning that allows her to knot together the different strands of her life. These strands start forming a connected fabric in the religious practices of her original neighborhood where the procession of the Madonna of Mount Carmel in East Harlem is an occasion for both black and Italian women to bond as they pay homage to a common Catholic figure.[27] The procession brings them all together through the streets of the neighborhood, which to Ragusa looks like "an almost geological formation, stratified by waves of migration, years of occupation and contestation, different communities who have all called it home" (145). Once again Ragusa reads the body (here the religious body) through history and history through space: The process of identity formation becomes public in the course of a collective moment like a procession and in a space of layered occupations, as she directly suggests with her choice of words.

In the memoir, the most significant spatializing move that continues her relentless search for overlapping stories of race, beauty, and belonging can be found in the epilogue which, along with the prologue, provides a Sicilian frame to an American tale, thus pointing to the fruitfulness of distancing perspectives in the process of cognition. It is this physical outside—a place new to Ragusa who can finally experience it directly and not just in its inscription on her body, skin, and family ties—that opens up a possible resolution. In bringing the narration back to Sicily, where the book had started, Ragusa privileges once again spatial categories with the intent of reshuffling them. As the writer anticipated to Livia Tenzer in an interview published when the memoir had not yet been completed, her goal was to "juxtapose ideas of Sicily as an unchanging, timeless place with the realities of Sicilian life in the twenty-first century" (219).

In particular, Ragusa decides to close her book with a snapshot of her visit to Palermo, described with her usual language of "pre-occupation" as "a site of thousands of years of invasion and violation, accommodation and amalgamation" (234). During her visit, she is invited to a party in the neighborhood called La Kalsa: This "Arab quarter" further enriches the already complex web of historical and personal associations suggested in her story. What strikes Ragusa in walking through it is how the space speaks of early forms of migration from Africa and in particular from Arabic-speaking North Africa. The very name of the neighborhood is Arabic in origin and means, ironically, "the pure." Founded by the emirs, it was designed as the "elected" place for the rulers, yet over time it became a poor working-class area, identified with the destruction brought by the war during the Allies' bombardments that pockmarked the area with broken-down buildings, an odd reminder of the multiple and contradictory declensions of the U.S.-Sicily relationship.

Yet, Africa is not just a faraway echo or a trace hidden in a name: "along with the poor and working-class Sicilians, immigrants from Africa and Asia now called the neighborhood their home" (235). It is in the Kalsa, as she rhapsodically strolls around, that Kym's story comes full circle in the small random encounters with unpredicted migrations: the sight of two Bengali girls wearing traditional attire and yet speaking Sicilian to each other; the brief image of an African prostitute adopting a "white" look to appear more attractive to Sicilian men; or a long chat with a Palermo-based Portuguese woman of Angolan origin who like Kym brings two heritages together. Pre-occupied by stories of century-long emigrations as well as historical arrivals of people from the Norths and Souths of the world, Palermo—along with Sicily and the South by extension—has turned into a destination for immigrants, occupied by a racial landscape similar to the one her home place had exposed her to. As a local woman tells her: "*Palermo is like your Harlem—we are the blacks of Italy. And La Kalsa is the Harlem of Palermo*" (235). At the end of her walk, she is drawn toward a field where young black boys play soccer with olive-skinned Sicilian boys. She sits down and, baffled by the copresence of so many different places in one place, simply wonders: "Was this Palermo, or Cairo, or Lagos, or Harlem?" (237). While in the memoir these multiracial and multicultural encounters are of an ephemeral nature, and would certainly require the type of closer and more nuanced analysis and representation that such Italian immigrant authors as Melliti and Lakhous offer in their writings (see Part II of this book), Ragusa effectively "blends a familial history of marginalization with a global vision of marginalized Souths" (E. Ferraro 171) during her visit to Palermo.

It is in this powerful ability to write across the borders of time and space and to link commonalities in unexpected ways in and outside her body that distinguishes Ragusa's narrative style. Her trip to Palermo is not the discovery of a new place but a meeting with previously known situations. Her puzzlement in Palermo makes Testa's words from the epigraph into a lived, and then renarrated experience: "I have already been here/maybe in another enchantment/I have already been here/I recognize the step." The reverberations of familiar, defamiliarized, and refamiliarized spaces are also reminiscent of Marra's *Tornando* insofar as they define a space of hybrid belonging in opposition to the sense of alienation that home can produce due a crisis of positioning and purpose. The identification of a gravitational point in Sicily is further confirmed at the very conclusion of the book by Kym's connection to the myth of Persephone, which acquires importance both for its content and for the ways in which it circulated in the family. Indeed, quite ironically, this "ancient story of troubled ties between mothers and daughters" (107) was told to young Kym by her black grandmother Miriam so that Kym could stay in touch with her father's legacy. In other words, Sicily first reached Kym through the African American side of her family. The myth, and especially the version in which Persephone is not only the victim of an abduction but the woman who brings regeneration to the world out of choice, eventually offers Ragusa a positive model to rethink generational ties in a creative way along the vertical axis of the underground and ground-level spheres that she locates in Sicily.

The inclusion of the myth of Persephone—a classic element in the memoir of the ethnic female self—proposes a vertical mapping of linkages next to the transcontinental horizontal ones within the spatialization process privileged by the memoir. Yet, in itself, partially because of its brief appearance, it is not as convincing as the kind of spatial experiences and rethinking of space that Ragusa offers in other occasions in *The Skin Between Us*. In this sense, it is the opposition but ultimately constructive complementation of the U.S. experience and the Sicilian trip that provides the genesis of as well as a sense of purpose to the author's quest. It allows her to come to terms with the conflict of two legacies and somehow embrace them both, yet with a "radical openness" (Soja 68). It is in the watery space of the Mediterranean, and in particular the fluid spaces it takes her to in Sicily, that Ragusa turns pre-occupations and preoccupations into a creative tension, poetically.

The Sicilian Channel as Postcolonial Danger Zone and Golden Door in Tekle's Libera

> ma non era così
> che mi credevo di andare
> no non era così
> come ladri, di notte
> in mano a un ladro di mare
> (*Testa*, "Rock")[28]

Ragusa's lyrical recovery project addresses the problematic space of class, race, and gender boundaries and approximates an intersection of these demarcations as part of a voyage in time as well as in space. While aware of the impossibility of a conflict-free condition at the end of this journey, Ragusa presents this personal-as-political trajectory of exploration as a necessary and useful one. Yet, her Mediterranean route is cast as an individual journey in which her destiny, although linked to many threads of collective experiences and official histories, is recovered/discovered in personal terms within a solitary search, especially in the sections devoted to the trip to Sicily. Even in the wide scope of her reflections about the Souths of the world, the global dimension is more projected than experienced. Feven Abreha Tekle's 2005 *Libera: L'odissea di una donna eritrea in fuga dalla guerra* (Free: The odyssey of an Eritrean woman fleeing from war) is instead posited as the story of a forced trajectory shared by large portions of populations escaping from dictatorial regimes and armed conflicts. Even though Tekle goes through parts of her escape as a one-woman experience, the network of family ties, old-time and newly developed friendships, and migration-related connections makes Tekle's story into a mirror, albeit partial, of a contemporary epic in which men's and women's individual fates as well as various historical legacies powerfully intersect (Fig. 10).

Feven Abreha Tekle is the fictitious name of an Eritrean woman, born around 1980, whose identity is kept anonymous in *Libera* for fear of possible repercussions against a political fugitive and, technically, a deserter in the eyes of the Eritrean regime. The book follows Feven's courageous and complicated route of escape from her country of origin to Italy, where she now resides, away from an Eritrea that is still in the grip of social unrest. The story recounted in this memoir was not written directly by Tekle, but told to a Radio Popolare foreign correspondent, Raffaele Masto, who is not new to journalism projects aimed at denouncing the consequences of globalization, the political role of the media,

FIGURE 10. *Mediterranean Sea. Desperate Crossing of Bourbon Argos Boat*, 2015. Photo by Paolo Pellegrin.

and indeed immigration.[29] Masto has explored the *testimonio* genre, that is, that of the as-told-to narrative, on other occasions.[30] The effects of this genre on the migratory story described will be explored in the closing section. What is of relevance for the purpose of this chapter is that, similar to Ragusa's book, *Libera* is framed by a prologue and an epilogue, respectively set in the Mediterranean waters and on land, signifying the in-between phase and the arrival point of the voyage (and a temporary sense of closure). After shedding light on key moments of Feven's life and escape, my analysis will focus on the prologue and on the last two chapters of the book, all devoted to the crossing. These sections offer a reading of the Mediterranean migrant routes from the point of view of an immigrant that indirectly dialogues with the reportages of Liberti and Del Grande, as we will see. Effectively though, Tekle's represents not only a rare detailed written self-testimony of the crossing at the end of a long trajectory of escape, but also a unique female account of it (Liberti and Del Grande mention women migrants only intermittently). The stratified image of the Mediterranean crossing that emerges from Tekle's story warrants a subtler understanding of the migrant escape's drives and mechanisms, fundamentally implying a Copernican turn in the European view of these flights.

Feven undertakes two trips in the attempt to avoid her country's harsh restrictions. A dictatorship under the one-party-only, no-constitution regime of Isaias Afworki, in power since 1993, Eritrea imposes mandatory military service on both male and female youth for eighteen months between the ages of eighteen and forty.[31] Thanks to the financial and logistic support of her progressive middle-class family, Feven attempts a first escape from Asmara probably around the late 1990s (precise dates are not provided in the text, but later references to the 2000 war with Ethiopia help in inferring a rough chronology). In order to avoid conscription, she illegally crosses the border and lives in Ethiopia with some family members for a while. Discouraged by the scanty opportunities to build a better future for herself in the peaceful but poor neighboring country, she decides to return to Asmara. Homesickness drives her home, despite the risks she exposes herself to once back in Eritrea and the substantial money ($800) gathered by her family to pay the *passeur*—as her father puts it, "running away is a luxury" (29). As a result, Feven is overwhelmed by a sense of failure, a common feeling among emigrants whose escape project is interrupted. Yet, this initial feeling produces the impetus to try again and again, even given high levels of risk, as reported in many of the interviews gathered in North Africa by Liberti (31) and Del Grande ("nobody goes home with the burden of shame" 55). Unfortunately, while Feven is planning her next flight, this time toward Europe, she is drafted into the Eritrean army in the course of a *giffa*, a roundup that involves house searches by local officials to forcibly conscript service-eligible citizens. The account of the military service, which takes up almost one third of the book, is replete with an endless array of unfathomable abuses, ranging from heavy discipline and political brainwashing to psychological and physical violence, which become particularly severe for young women, subject to machismo and nepotism within the camp. Luckily, thanks to her position as a secretary for the main officer of the camp, Feven is eventually able to obtain a fake leave and runs away from the camp.

The detailed description of the military abuses illustrates the main push factor for the outbound flow of emigration from Eritrea. Notwithstanding the fairly steady economic condition of the family of origin and the closeness of its members, the exodus of young people is inexorable and actually supported by older generations. The political matrix of these departures introduces another element to the scenario of global migrations considered so far in the chapter. While the emigrants from and the immigrants to Italy described in *Sailing Home* and *The Skin Between Us* are driven by economic need, Tekle's story is cast as a political flight, and in this sense is in dialogue with *Come un uomo sulla terra*, the documentary about Ethiopian asylum seekers. While Feven never refers to political asylum as an option for entry into Europe and eventually takes the route favored by economic migrants, the violation of human rights in the country triggers her escape. Eritrea is then clearly cast as a space of preoccupation due to the absolutist nature of the government, its deep economic crisis, and its war-ridden political agenda. This is the same preoccupation of many postcolonial countries in Africa, yet in the *testimonio* the present chaos of internal and external tensions is not actively linked to the colonial legacy (Eritrea was territorially "invented" by Italian colonialism; constituted in 1890 as Italy's first colony, it was definitively lost in 1947).[32] Surprisingly, Tekle's account never provides—and neither does a note by Masto—a map of the complex colonial entanglements between Eritrea and Italy: The presence of Italians in the African Horn remains a vague reference in the text, thus contributing to the national amnesia over Italy's past, or even worse to the "noncontroversial" memory of this history (Ottaviano 11). In Tekle/Masto's reading, countries are instead represented as post–World War II independent nation-states, an approach partially justified by the young age of the storyteller. The desirability of Italy as a migrant destination can thus coexist with an idealization of Eritrea while the deep-rooted effects of colonialism, such as the Ethiopia-Eritrea conflict, are erased. As a matter of fact, the strong nationalist pride of the protagonist creates a patriotic tale that easily slips into anti-Islamic sentiments.

This mechanism becomes particularly apparent during Feven's second flight from Eritrea (probably around 2000 or 2001), when she embarks on an eighteen-month-long trip through deserts, villages and cities and eventually the Mediterranean as an undocumented migrant. Regardless of her physical strength, granite-like determination, and cleverness in hiding, finding allies, and securing protection, the risks posed by the adventure are endless. Unscrupulous *passeurs* who set harsh rules, let weak travelers die along the way in the desert for not being respectful, provoke competition among the migrants, and extort money from them at every turn are coupled with greedy locals collaborating with them. As she puts it, "anybody trying to leave is in the hands of the trip organizers" (88). But, the risks are exceptionally high for a woman, and in particular for a non-Muslim woman traveling through Sudan and Libya. Her straightforward account of the threats and abuses perpetrated in Sudan ranging from segregation to physical punishment reveals her anger against this reduction of women to nonpersons (127, 137, 143). The antidote to this belittling and violence is the call upon an Eritrean tradition of respect for women that functions as a source of strength. Feven resorts to the memory of her mother's pragmatism and warmth—emblematic of all Eritrean women's dignity and determination—and the support she receives from an Eritrean young man, Tesfalem, for whom she develops a sentiment of love in environments that suppress the freedom of romantic attraction. Yet, in the process, she forges a patriotic tale that claims separation from Muslim culture, tout court labeled as machismo-ridden and violent. Her desire for inclusion and protection paradoxically hinges on exclusion on the basis of a nationalistic ethos.

Feven's peregrinations on foot and by bus and truck first through Ethiopia and then later Sudan are interrupted by her decision to accept her brother's money (he lives in Italy already) and avoid the risks of the Libyan desert, namely the harsh climate and the brutal police repression. While her travel companion Tesfalem goes on to Canada as planned by the family—"for all of them I am an investment" he claims (129)—Feven takes a flight to Tripoli and enters the *bolgia*-like world of the migrant trafficking business. Here, Tekle knows how to navigate the underworld of the business, showing how the phenomenon is by now so complex that it has created a transnational network of services along the migrant routes, what Liberti calls "the topography of transit" (76). Libya is a particularly tough environment for "candidates for Europe" (Liberti 33) due to local anti-immigrant racism. This is where, as a "traveler forced to immobility" (Liberti 74), Feven realizes in even more concrete ways than in Sudan that the status/role of "*clandestino*" starts before crossing the Mediterranean. In Libya she looks for a famous go-between, an Eritrean woman called Gennette, whose job entails the collection of dues for the trip, the assignment of migrants to departing boats as well as the provision of fake work during the wait. Life in the camps where migrants are temporarily placed is difficult and expensive, another extortion-based source of profit for the business people of the migration industry. Yet, Feven seems to admire and trust Genette (175) both because of her origin, as part of the aforementioned nationalist frame of the story, and because of what she offers in reality: the opportunity to escape.

This reading of the migration experience is crucial to understand the kind of epistemological shift proposed by the text, and echoed in many stories collected by Liberti and Del Grande. In particular, Liberti emphasizes the need to look at the migration flows with a double lens able to identify both sides of the coin. For example, the migration business, tout court condemned (and justifiably) by the media, politicians, and nonprofit organizations, is not just a system of corrupt individuals and gullible migrants but also a necessary network of service support in the escape project in which from "opportunistic premises" "unexpected alchemies . . ." are born (Liberti 178–79), as in the case of Genette's special treatment of Feven (185). By the same token, and in even more evident forms, the Mediterranean crossing is perceived as difficult but not impossible—as a matter of fact preferable to the desert or a prison. Del Grande's report of the view of an Eritrean refugee in Italy speaking about his family waiting in Libya—"if they have to die, better that they die in the sea" (115)—is complementary to Feven's view of the voyage when she is finally assigned to a boat. Although she realizes how frightening the sea looks now that for the first time she will be on it, at night and as an irregular migrant, she does not feel like a thief, as suggested in the delicate image of disorientation and guilt proposed by Testa's West-centered song lines from the incipit. She instead remarks: "I was pervaded by a certain euphoria. . . . Free, this is how I felt" (183).

It is the first time that the title's adjective appears, and not too unexpectedly, in front of the water. A closer look at this self-definition, which appears preposterous in view of the mortal risks that Feven is actually about to face (141) in this Mediterranean danger zone, reveals the complex web of pull and push factors characterizing migrant projects as a whole: the inevitability of the political or conflict-related escape, the magnetic attraction to Europe, the failure of First World incentives in the countries of origin, the power of the neoimperial economies in the postcolonies and the global market, and even the resentment against the master Europe. While no single story embraces all of these characteristics, the overall picture that forms in the end is one that Liberti and Del Grande describe with two cogent images. On the one hand, there is that of the silent anti-European revolution (Liberti 120) or "war" (94–95) of migrants fighting through the obstacles directly and indirectly posed by the Fortress Europe restrictions and the unscrupulous traffickers, and too often "falling" into the sea (or in the desert) like dead soldiers. On the other, there is the image of the adventure. Here, Liberti is worth quoting at length:

> Theirs were not "voyages of hope" or "desperation." They were expeditions. These were not "doomed people" but "adventurers" . . . [who] never conceded their defeat. At times they developed a challenge mechanism . . . : the bigger the obstacles standing between them and the final destination, the more extraordinary the final success. The adventure towards Europe thus acquired the meaning of a rite of passage. (199)

If Feven's story about the voyage itself does not express this overt revolutionary drive, it is the stoic attitude she displays toward its multiple challenges that almost "normalizes" the experience, especially at the beginning. For example, boat engine problems are not seen as exceptional, since migrants (at least around those years) traveled exclusively in old tubs, unfit size-wise (181) and often driven by a reckless and intoxicated migrant who played pilot with no knowledge of the sea, just to travel at no cost (183). Similarly, the voyage is initially experienced as a trip with the friends made in the camp and those made on the boat itself: Together, they form a new family in ways comparable to *Nuovomondo*, since people from different classes intersect their destinies (even the wife of a fleeing minister from Eritrea travels with them), although their common denominator remains the nation of provenance. Finally, the fact that the voyage is interrupted due to interception by the coast guard is not seen as tragic, since it is part of a predictable development. The unlucky *refoulement* (push) back to Tunisia ends a voyage that interestingly reverberates with the fate of the migrants in *Sailing Home*; in *Libera*, though, it is more evidently a random "repatriation," since the boat had originally left from Libya.[33] Nonetheless, these detours never discourage the migrants: the more desperate the situation the higher the number of attempts at crossing, since the Mediterranean is seen as the Golden Door to Europe. This has been the case for Feven as well. Once back in Tripoli, Feven looked for Genette again and was able to successfully cross over and reach Lampedusa. After a period of detention in Crotone, she eventually joined her brother (a street market seller) and since then she has been staying with him, working as a house cleaner. Her "odyssey" (207) was almost two years long.

The odyssey quality of her voyage is particularly evident in the prologue, which constitutes a full excerpt of the last chapter "Drifting," but printed in italics, perhaps to mark its more introspective quality. This style also embeds a dramatic intensity, since it represents the zenith of her fears and her encounter with death. The stories reported by Stella in the book *Odissee* are eerily similar to Feven's voyage experience more than a century later, characterized as hers is by terrible travel conditions, hunger, dehydration, stormy weather, engine failures, illness, not to mention grief and toil. As Feven puts it: "How many stories of suffering and sacrifice did that boat contain?" (186). The sense of tragedy is so intense that Tekle uses a powerful description for the boat, here inserted in the middle passage narrative: "Somewhere I had read that the slavery ships two centuries ago, those used to carry African slaves to America, would soak up a distinctive stink that could not be gotten rid of and was felt dozens of feet away. On that boat it was the same" (203). The description puts Tekle's *testimonio* in dialogue with Ragusa's memoir as part of a complex network of historical echoes. While for Ragusa, it is Italian emigration from the South that is inscribed in the iconography of the middle passage, Tekle creates a linkage between immigration and slavery in the Mediterranean. Both implicitly draw a connection with colonialism and postcolonialism; both "keep alive a process of remembering and mourning" in their drive to "transform the experience of bondage into a promise of emancipation," to use Lombardi-Diop's reading of *Libera* ("Ghosts" 164, 167). Ultimately, Ragusa and Tekle configure these waters as a pre-occupied space par excellence.

The preoccupation of the voyage so deeply expressed in the prologue of *Libera* is eventually dissipated. The final chapter speaks of the rescue, the second attempt, the arrival in Italy, and finally the individual success of the travel trajectory: in a word, what could be termed as freedom. Yet, Tekle cannot but admit the partial nature of this freedom in Italy when she mentions that her permit needs to be renewed on a yearly basis and that there is a sense of distance from the locals, at times even an atmosphere of intolerance around her. In the sincere-sounding, yet rhetorically constructed ending, Tekle identifies sharing information and growing awareness as the implicit goals of her storytelling project. The audience is a mix of real and abstract people ranging from immigration office workers to neighbors in Italy, all those that ignore her past as well as her desires for the future. Where her interpellation reveals some incisiveness in reality is in the normativization of the non-migrant citizen and the implicit, unspoken even, marginalization of the nonbelonging migrant. The simple, yet, profound truth that she conveys is that human, economic, and civic rights continue to be primarily linked to the space of birth, even in the globalized world of today. And that until the time when mobility is considered a given right for everybody unrelated to the countries of origins and those of arrival, mobility will be sought after in underground forms, replete with preoccupations. It is the denial of what Mezzadra calls "*diritto di fuga*" (right to flee) that effectively makes Feven anonymous, even after telling her story, for the risk of repercussions against her as well as her family, still in Eritrea.

Despite her attempt to reach out to readers as part of an educational project, the work's genre (*testimonio*) keeps a certain distance between the reader and this anonymous protagonist/narrator. Existing in a hybrid space between literature and political document, the *testimonio* was originally aimed, since its birth in Latin America in the 1960s, at denouncing abuse and inspiring collective resistance, but eventually lost its radical quality and was included in the canon. It has been subject to close scrutiny for two main reasons: its reliability as a "true" account (and hence its representative function for larger groups of people) and its development as a collaborative project between an eyewitness and the collector of the story, whose mechanisms often remain undisclosed. This latter question surfaces strongly in the case of *Libera*. As Masto writes in the Preface, the idea of the project was born in response to the massive influx of young Eritreans in Italy around the early 2000s, as they were fleeing conscription and the war with Ethiopia. In the role of city ethnographer, Masto started searching for firsthand stories among the Eritrean immigrants in order to find one that would effectively denounce the "hideous multinational business thriving off human trafficking" (x), and the silent shared responsibility of the West. When he listened to Tekle's story, he decided to select it as exemplary, since she openly shared her desire to inform with her story, unlike other immigrants. Masto's act of militant journalism was aimed at counterweighing the silence of the press on stories that can become uncomfortable and are therefore dropped in a "black hole" (xii). Yet, in describing his and Tekle's collaborative project—Masto refers to the book the two wrote together (ix) and amply thanks Tekle and her brother (xii)—he also slips into a telling statement related to the selection process: "she was my story" (x), a not too subtle shift along class and gender power lines. While the book is told in the typical first-person of the *testimonio*, Tekle's voice, and by extension her own self, remain hidden in a partial agency: Coupled with her need to remain anonymous for security reasons, she does not have any visibility as a speaking/writing immigrant. *Libera* is therefore Masto's book slightly more than Tekle's by circumstance and choice; as such, it risks transforming

"Thirdworld salvation discourse . . . into cultural capital" (Gugelberger 6), even despite the original goals of the project.

Masto's intentions were certainly animated by a spirit of denunciation and faith in *engagé* writing, but the silence over the modes of production of the text seems inexplicable at best. Despite the wave of essays produced by literary critics on the genre of the *testimonio*, around the world as well as in Italy, Masto simply takes the conversations with Tekle as a source of truth to be told for a higher cause and does not share any detail about the nature of the collaboration.[34] He does not seem interested in addressing such mechanisms as "the controversial influence of a native speaker" (Parati *Mediterranean* 17), or "the constant negotiation between fiction and autobiography" (Meneghelli 45), or the nonimmigrant artist's self-analysis that this experiment should trigger, which is so evident in the works of Agostino Ferrente, for example (see Aperture to Part II). Masto's level of unrecognized interference can be found in the fact that the story in *Libera* is narrated in the simple past, which is a highly literary verbal tense in Italy, rare in common speech as well as in journalism. Here Masto falls prey to a syndrome that in his essay "Fingertips Stained with Ink," Sandro Portelli identifies about immigrant writings. Due to the editorial intervention of native speakers or for the pressure the immigrants themselves feel to sound Italian, "there is a neat separation between the character's native language . . . and the Italian of the narrative voice" (477). The result is therefore an accessible text that easily conforms to the standard while never questioning its genesis and development.[35]

Despite this structural simplification, which blocks the deeper epistemological rethinking that writing and film on immigration can offer, *Libera* remains relevant for several reasons, especially within the scope of this book on space and especially pre-occupied space. It is a "map biography" with "a cartographic vocation" (Boelhower 113) that functions as a palimpsest. Along with forms of historical pre-occupation (slavery and colonialism), the book points to the political preoccupation engendered by postcolonial dictatorial regimes and by the forced escape from them. Yet, the preoccupation generates a tension toward new awareness, both for the subject who eventually fights for freedom and for the reader who is invited into a story still rarely told by the mainstream media, with the exception of the recent attention paid to Syrian refugees and their odyssey. Mansour, one of Feven's travel companions on the boat, articulates this absence of stories, when he admits with desperate clarity: "If we sink nobody will notice. We do not exist. That's the reality, Feven" (190). Today, after the Syrian crisis, stories are more common, but they are seldom as extensive and deep. Also, due to a widespread tendency to highlight tragedies, the media do not usually feature stories with fairly positive outcomes. *Libera* in this sense compensates for this silence through the tale of a person who "made it." Her story, and in particular the detailed rendition of the trafficking business around and on the Mediterranean, is of crucial importance to understand the First- and Secondspace quality of this sea, but also the Thirdspace potential it holds and delivers. On the one hand, the Mediterranean is a space of migrant economic and social practices ranging from the high-profit travel arrangements—Feven's boat carries 150 people who then paid $1,000 each (190) for a trip that today can cost up to $2,500—to the exchanges of money, medicines, food, and care among the travelers (200). On the other hand, it is a space mapped from above, not only in the chart that the boat should, but fails to, follow, thus drifting for days out at sea, but also in the national and international agreements that regulate migrant arrivals and expulsions (different European countries treat immigrants of differing nationalities in idiosyncratic ways, so Eritreans on the boat fear Malta for its repatriation law, while Somalis hope to reach it in order to be sent to Canada as part of a binational agreement; 195–96). Between these two sets of dynamics, migrants experience the boat as the microreproduction of sectarian national differences: While in *Nuovomondo* the ship becomes a "nationalizing" space that brings together Italians despite their regional differences, the boat in *Libera* is an assemblage of African subgroups. Solidarity and discord are defined by national belonging: Feven, like in the rest of the book, relies on Eritrean friends who do not consider transnational alliances on the boat, and instead witness the thriving of separate interests and even physical violence between the groups (198). Despite these tensions and failures, the Mediterranean is in the book the Thirdspace of "radical openness" (Soja 68) for the protagonist (and her friends) insofar as it functions as a sphere of passage toward new possibilities.

Clearly cast as danger zone and Golden Door at once, the Mediterranean delivers a life opportunity in the conclusion of *Libera*, in ways comparable to Ragusa's and Marra's depictions of migration-related trips. Seen as a cluster within a topological hermeneutic (Boelhower 113), these three texts shed new light on the Mediterranean compared to the meaning it has acquired for Italy (and the European Union) in the last half-decade as part of obsessive general effort to control its waters, even in the repeated efforts to save lives. These stories foreground the human experience and design a geography of desires and sacrifices that effectively counteract the images of migrants otherwise created by an official discourse engulfed by the increasing criminalization of immigration, especially in connection to the string of terrorist acts in Europe since the mid-2000s; the securitization of borders against the so-called immigrant invasion; and its related business of technology (satellite radars, defense barriers), human resources (navy officers, agency employees, dissuaders), and especially allocated budgets (directly used by the European Union members or offered to collaborating countries in Africa and Western Asia as part of official agreements that are externalizing the EU borders).[36] These texts—especially because of their hybrid quality (documentary-like film, visual memoir, literary/nonliterary *testimonio*) function as maps of human movements in time and space that challenge the supposed homogeneity of national cultures. By shifting attention toward the often invisible and unheard stories of migrant subjects on the move in space and by inserting them in the larger historical and socioeconomic contexts they interact with, self-contained national, international, and supranational rhetoric are thus revisited with the aim of identifying forms of pre-occupation in space and thus of dispelling contemporary preoccupations via new alliances and potential dialogues across differences.

PART TWO

Houses: Multiethnic Residential Spaces as Living Archives of Pre-Occupation and Invention

APERTURE II

A Multicultural Project in a National Square: The Orchestra of Piazza Vittorio

> *Immigrati perfavore non lasciateci soli con gli italiani.*
> Immigrants please do not leave us alone with the Italians.
>
> —ITALIAN GRAFFITO

The multiple occupations of stories of migration and relocation explored in Part I with reference to the liquid spaces of the Atlantic Ocean and the Mediterranean Sea become even more evident in concrete residential spaces. This second Aperture introduces this new type of preoccupied/pre-occupied space in relation to the theme of Part II at large. The succeeding chapters will specifically concentrate on tenement houses, buildings (*palazzi*), and squatted-in, abandoned industrial edifices, in which different cultures and stories of relocation coexist. Traveling from Rome to Buenos Aires and New York, Part II will explore novels by Laura Pariani, Amara Lakhous, Melania Mazzucco, and Mohsen Melliti with the goal of identifying the constant echoes between the experience of Italians abroad and foreigners in Italy, despite the geographical and historical distances. Residential spaces, whether intimate or publicly shared, central or peripheral, reflect the intersection of migration stories with inter/national narratives since broader social forces shape family and individual life in these spaces. This Aperture provides instead a look at the larger spaces in which these living structures are located: multiethnic neighborhoods. Immigrant residential buildings are often found in urban areas that have received immigrant flows to one degree or another, and that are characterized by a variety of manifestations ranging from food stores to religious sites and street signage. Traditional forms and views of such neighborhoods have tended to reveal a certain internal homogeneity, thus producing the familiar Chinatowns and Little Havanas in the United States as well as around the world. In reality, studies have not only emphasized the internal diversity of "national" neighborhoods reflecting a wide variety of regional dialects and customs but have also shown how the national and ethnic composition of these urban areas was much more mixed than assumed, as in the case of Italian and Jewish families in New York living in the same Orchard Street building.[1]

A similar and actually even more marked heterogeneity characterizes immigrant neighborhoods in Italy today, mostly because the immigration phenomenon in Italy is characterized by great internal diversity. Immigrants come from practically every continent, and only a few communities show substantial numbers (Romanians, Moroccans, Albanians, Chinese). In other words, immigrants do not cluster together in highly dense formations, even though specific neighborhoods offer targeted services to specific ethnic groups—Little Bucharest near the Tiburtina Station in Rome is in reality a mall by the name of La Strada that sells a wide array of Romanian products—or host a number of ethnic commercial activities next door to others—for example, Milan's Chinatown in the area of Canonica Sarpi, dating back to the first half of the twentieth century. Generally attracted to low-income areas that make rents more affordable, immigrants have settled, albeit often precariously, in the so-called historical centers of many Italian cities.[2] They have thus made them into multiethnic spaces rather than "little" reproductions of faraway nations.

This Aperture will focus on the case of Piazza Vittorio in Rome, a neighborhood that offers an interesting occasion to look at the international composition of a contemporary immigrant area, effectively complicating the square's original "national" spirit. The specific analysis of Agostino Ferrente's documusical *L'orchestra di Piazza Vittorio* (2006) as an indirect remake of Fellini's *Prova d'orchestra* (1978) will explore the complex dynamics of nation building and transnationalization of a quintessential Italian space such as the piazza, and in particular Piazza Vittorio located at the center of the Esquilino area.[3]

The piazza—a word coming from the Latin *platea*, meaning broad street, and over time referring to an "open" area—is by definition a space of "juxtapositions and discontinuities," (Caniffe 11): Its openness makes it into a container of visible and invisible stories often layered with no overall plan. This is even more manifest in Rome, a city that in functioning as "urban exemplar and source of archetypes" (15) produces languages of design and practices of everyday life that constantly combine the most diverse elements along the diachronic axis. A piazza in Rome acquires a particularly layered meaning. The definitive *Urbs*, Rome is an interesting hybrid case: While a city of international standing for its cultural, religious, political, and artistic roles at different moments in history, it is not a huge metropolis by European or world standards, in terms of either size or population, and neither is it the financial center of the country.[4] Within the perspective of this book, and with particular reference to the spatializing operation offered by Ferrente's film (and by Lakhous's novel, as we will see in Chapter 3), Rome, even before Piazza Vittorio, can be read as a migratory site. A point of connection of several demographic movements within and outside the capital and, by extension, the nation, Rome has fundamentally been an immigrant city since the inception of the nation. Its first burst of growth as the Italian state capital dates back to the post-1871 period, when the development of the State's bureaucratic infrastructure, along with the service and commercial industries related to it, attracted many immigrants from the North (an unusual case on the map of Italian internal migrations which were and are generally northbound). Subsequent population growth in the city took place under Fascist rule and in the post–World War II era, with a preponderance of arrivals from the center and the south of Italy.[5] The result was a melting pot of people from different regional backgrounds that made it impossible for Rome to be exclusively identified as Northern or Southern and effectively made the city into a unique hybrid, since immigrants profoundly affected the sociocultural fabric of the city.

The recent substantial increase in the local population is due to the arrival of foreign immigrants since the 1980s, which coincided with the slow abandonment of the historical areas of the city on the part of traditional inhabitants.[6] In the past as well as today, Rome appears as a "city constantly fed from outside" (Golini 135), and ultimately, as sociologist Franco Ferrarotti maintains, it "can legitimately be defined as 'the capital of immigration'" (242). As of January 2014, Rome is the largest immigrant center in Italy with a foreign population of approximately 363,563.[7] The lack of effective political and legislative interventions on immigration has been compounded by the absence of systematic urban planning, thus generating strong concentrations of immigrants in specific areas, characterized today by a large number of lower-income households and precarious housing conditions.

Among them, Piazza Vittorio in the Esquilino neighborhood, near the main railroad station, strongly captures these different migration patterns, while it also harbors vestiges of crucial past eras in the city's history. Both the square and the neighborhood effectively represent an archive of stories characterized by movement, channeling, and transition. The presence of Rome's cathedral, Santa Maria Maggiore, in the square practically adjacent to Piazza Vittorio identifies the Esquilino as the other pulsating religious heart of the city, after the area of Saint Peter's basilica. The vestiges of the ancient fountain Trofei di Mario stand as a symbol of the fluid movement of waters from the outside to the inside of the city walls. The by now destroyed seventeenth-century Villa Palombara was a meeting point for lovers of esoteric arts, as witnessed in the inscriptions on the so-called Magic Door, still placed at the center of Piazza Vittorio's garden. At the turn of the last century, the introduction of the produce market and of the city milk plant (Cerchiai 976) marks the neighborhood as an official place for trade. Furthermore, the building of the national mint in 1911 epitomizes the state-related role of an area that used to function as a large receptacle of bureaucrats who migrated from the north. Finally, the main train station, Stazione Termini, is the epitome of circulation and today also represents the typical gathering point for immigrants. The presence of immigrants in the area seems to fit smoothly into this little-known history of change and exchange, which highlights the porous and dynamic nature of the square.

In Piazza Vittorio, the imperial, hence transborder, legacy—visible in the imposing remnants of the Trofei di Mario fountain—rests at the heart of an otherwise national space. Expressions of the Roman "*umbertina*" or "*sabauda*," the square and the neighborhood around it were developed as part of the "building 'fever'" (Agnew 37) aimed at accommodating the new bureaucratic class after Rome was chosen in 1871 as the capital of the recently unified country.[8] The Esquilino thus became a residential area, whose architecture interestingly mimicked the style of the Northern city. In the Piazza Vittorio area in particular, Gaetano Koch, a Roman architect of Tyrolean origin, introduced the element of "*portici*," which projected "a confident image of modernity" (Caniffe 8), made up of the belief in efficiency and in the liberal constitutional monarchy (169). The name given to the square further solidified its national quality: Its full-length version is actually Piazza Vittorio Emanuele II, after the first king of unified Italy. Regardless of the extraneous quality of the aesthetics of its space, probably as alien as Piedmontese residents in Rome after 1871, Piazza Vittorio, at its center, is a Roman piazza by definition. The square is the largest in town. Romans identify it as the "feeder" of the capital for its renowned outdoor produce market, since moved indoors.[9] The beloved square is also increasingly recognized as an area in which a large number of immigrants reside, or, to quote Ferrente's provocative statement in the documentary, where "Italians are an ethnic minority."

Ferrente's documusical *L'orchestra di Piazza Vittorio* reflects this postnational scenario of multiethnic coexistence within an ethical vision that interestingly offers, especially in its final climax, a "success" story. Despite the hurdles and challenges encountered by the protagonists in creating the orchestra of the title, the documentary is intent on showing how the effort toward building projects across cultures is worth entertaining, and is eventually gratifying both artistically and socially. The film documents the real-life story of a multiethnic orchestra assembled by Mario Tronco, a member of the Avion Travel band, with the goal of translating new forms of coexistence in his neighborhood, Piazza Vittorio, into a musical project also known as "a stable orchestra made up of unstable musicians" (Marino). Ferrente filmed the different phases of this ambitious idea (or rather filmed the re-creation of these phases) and recorded the toil involved in finding immigrant musicians and making them work together within the ensemble. Part documentary and part musical (hence "documusical"), the film follows the making of the orchestra.[10] It also captures, albeit in fragments, the lives of the artists offstage, thus bringing to the surface the otherwise invisible or partially visible stories of these immigrants.

Based in Piazza Vittorio, and eventually in the Apollo 11 Theater, the orchestra is the neighborhood and, by extension, today's Italy.[11] The director explores this synecdochical function in all its facets as he shuttles between the intimate spaces of domesticity, the public sites of the capital, and the globalized world in his own backyard. In questioning the purported homogeneity of the local space and culture, this diary-film presents itself as a possible utopia, with its body of sixteen musicians coming from eleven different countries. The end credits are in this sense very eloquent. The fast montage of close-ups of the musicians to the sound of "Ena Andi," the hit song of the 2004 album *L'orchestra di Piazza Vittorio*, is accompanied by the appearance of their names and country of origin: Mohammed Bilal (India); Leandro Piccioni and Peppe D'Argenzio (Italia); Omar Lopez Valle (Cuba); Marian Serban (Romania); Abdel Majid Karam (Morocco); Mohammed Adbdalla (Egypt); Evandro Cesar Dos Reis (Brazil); and many others.

The complex diagram of countries of origin includes some Italian trajectories of crucial relevance for the purpose of this study. First of all, there is evidently a wide array of postcolonial immigrants coming from non-Italian former colonies whose presence confers Italy an unusual postcolonial metropole status, as mentioned in the Introduction. Second, the routes of the Italian diaspora can be identified in the descendants of Italian emigrants to Argentina, Raul Scebba and Javier Girotto, who close the loop of the Italian diaspora with their return "home." These routes also emerge in the story of John Maida, the son of an Italian man and an American woman, who decides to live in Italy to explore his father's roots, and ironically does it by joining a multicultural orchestra. Finally, in less explicit ways, one can make out the Mediterranean connections sketched in Chapter 2 (as seen in the analysis of Marra's film): Houcine Ataa and Zias Trabelsi, two Tunisian artists, are Italy's "guests" from the Mediterranean country that has "hosted" so many Italian immigrants over the centuries for political and economic reasons. Unexpectedly, the credits in the concluding part of the film also include the "origins" of the orchestra director, the documusical's director, and the main female activist of the Apollo 11 association supporting the project. Marked by town, their origin is Southern; hence, they are immigrants in Rome themselves. In other words, Mario Tronco, Agostino Ferrente, and Dina Capuzio are originally from someplace else, like all the other artists of the orchestra, only closer (respectively, Caserta in the region of Campania, and Cerignola and Carlantino in the province of Foggia in the region of Apulia). The musical map of the documentary is thus mobile in practically all its forms, yet its intrinsic sense of "displacement" is an occasion to find common spaces of communication.

Traveling, studying or working abroad, and emigrating along the routes of the Italian diaspora and international colonialism, are all issues at the center of Ferrente's film, which, I maintain, does not simply "stop talking about the nation, and starts thinking again about people" (Piccolo 8), but also offers the possibility of questioning the nation from inside and outside at once, interlacing historical threads in dynamic ways. The very aesthetics that Ferrente adopts is congruous with the artistic project in its content and unraveling. His Vespa rides around Rome—so reminiscent of Nanni Moretti's musings on two wheels in his 1993 film *Dear Diary*—offer a new cognitive mapping of the city. In this "hermeneutic geography" (Carravetta 21), monuments are read through the eyes of visitors from India, and the square becomes a site of redefinition of culture and identity. In the visual of the DVD's main menu, Piazza Vittorio is adapted into a dance floor on which an Asian couple perpetually swirls in a sober Argentinian tango. Rethinking, overlapping, improvising, and reconnecting are all central operations in *L'orchestra di Piazza Vittorio*, whether applied to music performance, travel plans, or human relations. While this internationalization of the "domestic" space tends to remain anchored to national parameters and is orchestrated by two Italian "directors," the shifting in spatial perception signals a different cultural geography that two experimental Italian artists feel compelled to register in music and cinema.[12]

Approximations guide this process of rereading the national space. As a result, incertitude and doubts, comings and goings are actual stages in the making of the orchestra as well as the expression of the kinesis of its form; after all, *errare* in Italian (and Latin) means both "moving around" and "making mistakes." The vagrancies of Ferrente and Bharti around Rome, first on foot and then by Vespa, are followed by a brief scene in which the delicate yet powerful conversation between Tronco and Bharti shows how the transcription in Italian of a song from India proves particularly challenging. The experience is marked throughout by attempts—"*dolaghi* or *dolagi*?" Tronco asks Bharti and concludes "Are you sure about this?"—as well as by small errors in the music and lyric sheets made as the national and international "immigrants" of Rome wander around the city and on the screen. It is this interactive effort across differences along with the constant questioning entailed by it that makes the transcription, and ultimately both the orchestra and the film possible.

Ferrente's film does not simply depict the immigrants as artists (just a few of them make a living through music, and if so only partially); it also registers, albeit sparsely, the pragmatic aspects of living as an immigrant in Rome. In denouncing the lack of housing (Scebba lives in a garage), the precarious nature of jobs, and the administrative delays in obtaining visas, the film adopts a double perspective showing the immigrants' point of view as well as the reactions of Roman residents and institutions to the changed social fabric of the city (this alternation becomes more structural in Lakhous's novel, as we will see in Chapter 3).[13] Interestingly then, the documentary is not a musical just because it focuses on the orchestra project, but because it adopts music as a lens on life, and as a commentary on specific sociocultural dynamics. Fellini embarked on a similar project almost thirty years earlier with *Prova d'orchestra*, an interrogation on the Italian nation from a regional perspective. Directly inspired by this film, Ferrente dialogues with a canonical auteur, but he fundamentally reshapes the terms of Fellini's project. Fellini could only focus on the regional diversity of Italy to question the country's abstract homogeneity and show its chaotic nature at that time. In *Prova d'orchestra*, a group of musicians with dialect accents reflecting the internal "Tower of Babel" of the Italian country tries to play a concert in its entirety under the authoritarian guide of a German director, while a TV crew films the scene. Yet, the ensemble constantly gives priority to "exorbitant individualism" (Liehm 300), thus causing disorder. Generational clashes, political conflicts, petty concerns mingle with small acts of solidarity, love, and sex, so that the general atmosphere is primarily one of dissonance. Only after the general disorder reaches its zenith through destruction and physical violence is the German director able to lead the orchestra through the concert, although he remains skeptical about the fate of music and humanity in the contemporary world.

Read as "a metaphor of the Italian sociopolitical situation in the mid-1970s" (Brunetta, *Cent'Anni* 274), and often considered a secondary film, especially for its ambiguous message, *Prova d'orchestra* is for Ferrente an occasion to step into a film tradition but also to distance himself from it both in its intentions and formal solutions. Unlike Fellini's film, claustrophobically shot in an old oratory-turned-auditorium, Ferrente's film travels the city and highlights both indoor (apartments, the rehearsal basement, an airport, stores) and outdoor spaces (streets, squares, gardens) through fluid transitions. Most importantly, Ferrente's view of the dynamics of an orchestra takes home Fellini's lesson on the risk of anarchy and foregrounds the need for an organizational mechanism by which roles are defined and respected. In reality, as the documusical demonstrates, Ferrente and Tronco deal with tensions similar to those experienced by Fellini's director, but accept them as part of the interactive and creative process, and hence depict them matter-of-factly. The arrogance of a musician who finds the orchestra members too dilettantish, disappointment at the poor performance of one of the singers, and the open anger of Tronco himself over the orchestra's lack of motivation along with its logistical and financial challenges are not expunged from the film because they are integral to the project. What emerges is the tendency to avoid political correctness à la multiculturalism and to interact with the immigrants as musicians from an artistic point of view (Clò, "Orchestrating" 217).

Unlike Fellini, Ferrente and Tronco do not let the orchestra degenerate into a Tower of Babel: Differences and distances are mainly expressed in terms of artistic perceptions rather than cultural or ideological distances. The scene in which the Tunisian singer ridicules the Ecuadorian musician's scatting technique (the Spanish title of his song, "Tarateando," refers to the act of coming up with mere sounds in the absence of lyrics) for its "meaninglessness" brilliantly mingles criticism and humor. The effect is a hilarious moment, included in the album as a track, that does not detract from the appreciation of both singing styles, and does not hinder the collaborations of the musicians in the course of the project. In other words, music and its related acts, practices, and movements—contributing original compositions to the concert, sharing a drumming technique, teaching the pronunciation of foreign lyrics without understanding their meaning—come to embody forms of politics. Politics in *L'orchestra di Piazza Vittorio* signifies participation from below and not action from above, with the clear goal of expressing multiculturalism rather than degenerating into abstract rhetoric. At the same time, interactions with official political institutions are not discarded since they make the project relevant: The visionary dream of all these musicians was turned into a public concert in 2002 at the Rome Europe Festival, where the orchestra debuted and offered a highly successful show. The audience's interest arose from an understanding of both the musical and social drives behind the project. Orchestra Piazza Vittorio is not a mere ensemble of immigrant musicians, it is a musical experiment that functions as a piazza, a meeting and mingling point, for musical traditions and instruments. In this new vision, a Rajasthani-style song is slowed down and is unusually accompanied by brass instruments ("Ao Gi"), and a Tunisian-style song acquires a bluesy flavor ("Cherie"). Often rendered as transcriptions of foreign words recognizable in other familiar languages, whether French or Italian, the titles of the songs themselves reflect the polyglossia of the project.

Since then, the Orchestra has undergone different forms of internal mutation, due to its transitory nature, but has undoubtedly grown in visibility, thus providing opportunities for all people involved, migrants and nonmigrants.[14] Ferrente's film climaxes in the public concert of the final scene but actually closes with a line from a letter by Pier Paolo Pasolini, "If only you knew what Rome is," and the footage of a pro-immigrant rights gathering in Piazza Vittorio led by the late activist Dino Frisullo. In weaving together music and sociopolitical work in innovative ways, Ferrente acts as a "documentarist-composer" (De Lazzaris 27) in the sense that he (re)composes and reorders reality. In the process he creates what he himself calls a "cinema of relation," that is, a cinema that does not simply represent a reality in order to compensate for a loss, as in the case of the "cinema of reparation" but attempts to modify it through relationships (Clò, "Orchestrating" 213). The space of Piazza Vittorio, pre-occupied by a composite of migratory routes at the diachronic and synchronic levels, and generally preoccupied by what is seen today as an uncomfortable foreign occupation in the country, has been turned into a laboratory of shared practices and theories by this trailblazing music and film project. Pre-occupations of past migrations and preoccupations over current migrations are channeled into a collective experience located in a dynamic urban space. Through a visual and aural experience that triggers an experimental self-analysis on the role of seeing, the documusical effectively offers new tools for a remapping of Italy in which "locals" are called to embrace active participation while immigrants are given new spaces of involvement, even though the project is still largely managed by Italians.[15] The possibilities opened up by these artistic and in part social experiments respond to the need for new voices in a country that is aging demographically and thus culturally and economically. The by now famous graffiti found on an Italian street wall (perhaps in Bologna), which appears in the epigraph of this Aperture and is visually reproduced in Figure 22, provocatively remarks, "Immigrants, please do not leave us alone with the Italians." It is an ironic (or desperate) invitation to interact within a changed society in creative and transformative ways.

THREE

Displaced Italies and Immigrant "Delinquent" Spaces in Pariani's Argentinian *Conventillos* and Lakhous's Roman *Palazzo*

> We are all immigrants, that is to say, socio-cultural travelers caught in transitional situations where the real immigrants are the first victims, the most lucid witnesses, and the inventors and the experimenters of solutions. From this point of view, immigrants are the pioneers of a civilization based on the mixture of cultures.
>
> —MICHEL DE CERTEAU

The analysis of immigrant residential space in this chapter focuses on two varieties of spaces: those designed for and thus inhabited by immigrants, and those in which immigrants have come to settle gradually, mixing with long-term residents. The former type is here examined in the form of the Argentinian *conventillo*, a residential structure specifically built to host low-income immigrants in large urban areas, and as such comparable to the U.S. tenement house.[1] The latter is identified in the *palazzi* of the historic downtowns of Italian cities where immigrants have fairly recently moved in, either as tenants themselves or as caretakers of Italian tenants.[2] The two varieties are effectively represented in two fairly recent novels published in Italy by two writers whose lives are linked to Italy as much as they are to migrations from and to Italy, Laura Pariani and Amara Lakhous. Pariani, the granddaughter of an Italian political exile who relocated to Argentina, lives between Piedmont and Buenos Aires as part of a voluntary binational shuttling that has vastly influenced her artistic output as novelist, scenarist, and theater writer. Lakhous is a former Algerian refugee who has lived in Italy, a country he became a naturalized citizen of, has recently moved to the United States, and occasionally returns to Algeria for professional reasons. His novels travel metaphorically between the various regions of Italy and the countries of departure of the immigrants he chooses as protagonists.

This chapter examines two of their novels that purposefully "displace" Italy along the routes of emigration and immigration via the analysis of living spaces. Pariani's 2007 novel *Dio non ama i bambini* (God does not love children) provides an occasion to investigate the form and role of *conventillos* in Buenos Aires in the early 1900s, through a powerful narrative on the struggles of Italian immigrants in South America.³ Lakhous's 2006 novel *Clash of Civilizations Over an Elevator in Piazza Vittorio* focuses on the reversed migrant flow of foreign immigrants to today's Italy, and specifically to Rome in the early 2000s. In order to probe issues of economic and cultural challenges among immigrants, Lakhous uses a palazzo as the central locus of his plot, but also by reduced metonymy the space of the palazzo's elevator and by extended metonymy the surrounding neighborhood of Piazza Vittorio, which Ferrente depicts in depth in the documusical analyzed in Aperture II.

Despite their distance in space and time, both Pariani's *conventillo* and Lakhous's palazzo are occupied and reoccupied by migrants and their stories, and as such they produce preoccupation among them as well as among nonmigrants. Yet the tensions internal to these buildings and the fears surrounding them in the view of residents of other areas as well as of the official institutions (police, press) give these two writers an opportunity to complicate an otherwise simplistic perception of immigrants as aliens or invaders. Through a very original use of the detective/noir genre, which in their hands is hybridized "migrant-style," both writers offer a multiperspectival narrative that forces the reader to question received truths and consider alternative cognitive paths to understand reality. Instead of focusing solely on the intuitively "delinquent" quality of their immigrant residences, as crime sites functional to the investigative plot, they repurpose them as "delinquent spaces" à la Michel de Certeau, as spaces that can be rethought and reimagined in creative ways despite the violence and frictions they contain.

De Certeau's theory of space will prove useful in the course of analyzing the two novels, and in particular his reading of space through the practices of everyday life, such as walking in the city or experiencing a living space, that are able to rewrite space in transformative ways. In recuperating and opening up to "unofficial" ways of seeing, experiencing, and interpreting, in the 1980s de Certeau became particularly sensitive to issues related to migration. For him, the migrant was not simply a new element in an old system but a subject bound to reshuffle the coordinates of the system altogether. Based on that premise, the migrant became the occasion to reread power structures and to oppose them in nontraditional forms, for instance via mobile acts in space characterized by dynamism, lack of traditional anchors, and unorganized, even inadvertent, resistance. It is in this mobility, especially when applied to urban environments, that de Certeau recognizes the "migrational" quality of the invisible city, namely the city that "slips into the clear text of the planned and readable city" (de Certeau, *Practice* 93). He terms these almost unobservable interventions "delinquencies" (from the Latin verb "to abandon"). For him, they are transgressions of the institutional code and possess a wild creative quality since they open interstices privileging routes over status (129–30). Interestingly, for de Certeau, narrating is in itself a delinquent practice vis-à-vis the map, which he sees as the expression of a centralized visual representation: A narration becomes delinquent precisely when it transgresses the canon and its tenets (129). Beyond some formal differences that set their two novels apart, at a metaliterary level Pariani and Lakhous make the very detective/noir genre into a "delinquent space" by reconceptualizing its nature in the service of a migration-based view. They adopt the genre to shed light on oft-invisible subjects. In the process, they forge an extraordinary perspective in order to reverse ingrained opinions on "who belongs to where"—Calvino's question, analyzed in the Introduction—or at least problematize biases, and open more flexible spaces of real and imaginary habitation. At the same time, Pariani and Lakhous do not discard the map: They rather redesign it by reclaiming a "pedestrian" usage of space in which preoccupations turn into culturally mixed pioneering inventions, as de Certeau suggests in the epigraph ("Idéologie" 231–32).

The Conventillos *of Immigrant Buenos Aires Retold by Pariani's "Delinquent" Children*

'Cause our little steps take possession of Buenos Aires lightly (Pariani 22).

Pariani's *Dio non ama i bambini* is a choral detective novel that interlaces three main themes: the macrohistory of Argentina at the time of mass immigration with particular reference to the era of anarchist movements and the related anti-Italian sentiment they both produced; the microhistory of the *conventillos*, a paradigmatic space for the immigrant urban experience; and the micro-microhistory of the children living in/around these *conventillos*. The three thematic threads are knitted together by the primary plot: a series of horrific killings targeting Italian children in a poor neighborhood between San Cristobal and Boedo, informally known (in the novel) as Villa Basura, the "trash villa," for being made up of poor *conventillos* located next to the city's slaughterhouses and garbage dump.[4] The novel presents a mosaic structure composed of approximately sixty sections focusing on individual characters and offering their points of view through a clever blend of first- and third-person narration modes coexisting elbow to elbow (at times even with monologue and direct speech joining together, 122–27). Like an album of photos with titles or perhaps like a police archive with individual files, the novel is marked by sections starting with laconic tags: "Catterina Puletta, 28, laundry washer," "Don Vincenzo Fortis, 32, priest," "Adela Massi, 12, prostitute," "Rogelia Testa, 9, factory worker," "Nicanora Korn, 40, brothel owner," "Pà Renzo, 69, ragpicker," "Herminio Pascale, known as Skinny, 39, police vice chief," "Adamo Libermann, 10, carousel operator's assistant." As graphic snapshots of these people, in one telegraphic line the captions register: the name and hence the gender, language, and country of origin of the individual; occasionally their physical or personality traits via their nicknames; and their age and profession, thus indirectly pointing out their class belonging and life opportunities, as well as the general conditions of the city plagued by many social ills (prostitution, children's exploitation) what in the novel is termed "*il mal di città*" (city sickness, 90–91).

This multiperspectival architecture allows for the insertion of voices often erased or relegated to a secondary position such as that of children, women and old people, which in the end actually prevail over the voices of male adults: family members (husbands, sons, fathers-in-law) and officers in the institutions (policemen, schoolteachers, priests). By devoting so much room to multiple points of view, Pariani accomplishes not only the goal of providing a more complete account of the crime story but also lets these people share intimate views of and secrets about their existence. Next to the description of their daily lives as workers, housewives, or children playing in the streets, their desires, disappointments, and fears all emerge powerfully even within the brief space of two or three pages, the average length of each section. The unique quality of the novel lies in the fact that these sections, which never repeat (except in four cases) are not simply detours into private lives away from the central story of the novel. They are actually integral parts of the plot whose central thread—the identification of the murderer—constantly unravels as its substance grows in size while picking up details, anecdotes, and information along the way, contributing to both the micro and macro levels of the narration. To this spiral structure, the author adds in between a plethora of short texts that give a multimedia quality to the novel. They range from tango lyrics (36) to certificates (10), excerpts from newspaper articles (46) and books (111), personal letters (99–101), official documents signed by immigrants (102), announcement ads (212), and a glossary of local scatology (203–204). From the statement that Pariani includes at the end of the book the reader is led to conclude that these interpolated textual fragments are real, or maybe they have just been slightly modified to preserve the privacy of the actual people involved. Purposefully titled "Fiction/reality," the quasi-epilogue points to the archival research buttressing the book as well as to the nondocumentary quality of the novel. In willingly avoiding the label "historical" for *Dio non ama i bambini*, Pariani nevertheless reappropriates history from a different perspective and ultimately posits her immigrant novel as a historiographic operation from below, reminiscent of Melania Mazzucco's writing project addressed in Chapter 4.

While remaining central to the book, the murder plot is essentially subservient to the macro- and microhistory that it intersects and is contextualized in. The graphic violence of the numerous murders that Pariani meticulously illustrates with little self-censorship is in reality the more public face of the physical, emotional, psychic, and economic abuse that more or less visibly characterizes the lives of all the immigrant protagonists, and in particular that of women and children. The novel is in this sense an epic fresco of immigrant life, and especially Italian immigrant life, as well as working-class life in Buenos Aires around the first decade of the twentieth century. Divided in two sections respectively set roughly in the first week of December 1908 and the month between early November and early December 1912 (summer season in Argentina), *Dio non ama i bambini* offers a vibrant Zolaesque study of what could be considered the crucial years of immigration in Argentina both for the large size of inbound flows and the unrest that the socioeconomic conditions prompted. Even though the immigration history of Italians in Argentina covers a much longer period (1830–1950), what is relevant for the book's analysis is that the primarily urban settlements of Italian immigrants formed in the capital city since the outset, and in particular at the turn of the century as "the highest peak for Italian immigration was reached in 1907" (Devoto 34), the year before the novel's plot starts.[5] While initially originating from the North of Italy—not coincidentally, Pariani focuses on many immigrants from Lombardy like the Goletti family, which constitutes the most substantial nucleus—arrivals in the early 1900s included considerable flows from the South, in particular Sicily and Calabria. As was the case in North America, this latter group was perceived as more problematic in terms of public order, decorum, and productivity, and was less favored compared to Italians from the North in both formal and informal settings.

Regardless of their provenance, the massive demographic incidence of Italian immigrants accompanied by their relatives, which means that the gender ratio was quite balanced due to family reunions, implied their capillary presence in many areas of society, and primarily working-class environments.[6] As a consequence, "within the Argentinian elite this mass of Italians initially generated some preoccupation, later a real alarmism" (Devoto 34), even though Italians were considered more "prestigious" than indigenous groups and over time than the Jews and the Middle Easterners (38). Pariani provides an effective portrayal of this anti-Italian sentiment by offering, with her usual prismatic narration, a variety of points of view. She makes references to the negative portrayals offered by the press, representing Italians as godless and unruly (101); the officers' open bias against them, embodied by the police vice chief who attributes anything negative in life—"dirtiness, vagrancy, ignorance" (103)—to Italians; and the interregional frictions among Italians: "The entire world knows that all Sicilians are affiliated with the Black Hand," an Italian character bluntly states (82).[7] At the same time, Pariani persistently gives voice to characters who either explain the reasons for these biases or even more importantly their consequences on innocent individuals. In one of ten passages in the novel in which children speak in unison as if they were a Greek chorus singing ballads pregnant with Gothic fairytale and magical-realist nuances, the collective voice of the *canzone* describes how since their birth children have heard that Italians crowd the prisons and the *conventillos*, and their children fill the reform schools. The "*tanos*," as Italians were nicknamed in Argentina, "cannot but get angry and fight among themselves and end up behind bars."[8] It is a question of race, according to the voice quoted by the children, supposedly that of the police or the teachers, and they start believing that if you grow up amid poverty and violence, this is your inevitable fate (138). As some children internalize their inferior position in the social hierarchy, others resist this destiny by questioning God's will and expressing the desire of being Argentinian. Rosa's brother Peppino wonders: "Why ain't I an Argentinian kid? . . . I am not the one who asked God to be born Italian. . . . If he can do anything, why is it that he did not make us all Argentines?" (121).[9]

The space that is mostly connected to the life of Italian immigrants in the novel is of course their neighborhood. As part of the zoom-in method that Pariani adopts in her writing and by which the larger city practically disappears around the highly in-focus immigrant neighborhood, the *conventillo* acquires a central role.[10] It is simultaneously a living space—hence the space of domestic and house work, children's play, informal acculturation, and family reproduction—and a site of political activity, besides representing the topos of violence ranging from harassment to abuse and murder.[11] As such, it functions as a microcity, and a hellish city at that, which was often described as a murky gut by the press and the local writers. Pariani's spatialization of the narrative becomes particularly clear from the outset when the *conventillo* is carefully described in its architectural nature and social function (Fig. 11). Arnalda, the janitor, is designated by the author to be the expert illustrator of its map:

88 Houses

Figure 11. Conventillo, Buenos Aires, early 1900s.

> There are fifteen units both in the first and second patio, ten in the third one. They are all the same, made up of a single room with a narrow little window and a door marked by a progressive number, which looks out to the yard. For washing and cooking there are three washing tubs and eight grills under which one can light small fires. A life in which nothing can be hidden . . . in the *conventillo* Epifania it's as if the walls were made of glass. . . . Everybody knows everything about everybody else and what they do not know, they imagine it or make it up: squabbles between husband and wife, betrayals, incest, beatings . . . 'cause there are few happy stories among the poor. And when there are, they end in an Amen. (30)

As spaces characterized by physical proximity, limited availability of rooms, intense mutual monitoring, and enforced discipline, the *conventillos* are evidently filled with preoccupation and embody the sense of entrapment felt by immigrants in the society at large (an 11 PM–5 AM curfew is imposed daily by the owner, who lives in a larger separate apartment with a Panopticon view of the street and the entrance to the compound). As the very first character Fiore Goletti notes with deep anger, the resources are so scanty that fighting is intrinsic to survival and the eyes of the residents are on you so constantly that there is no freedom of action (a quite ironic comment considering that he regularly beats his wife and children and sexually abuses his daughters). He concedes that life in Italy was even more sacrificed in terms of space, but at least it was more homogeneous: "here instead there is a hell of families of all sorts: Gallegos, Neapolitans, Turkish, polenta and tigernut eaters, even those big whores, the Polish" (6). Through his offensive remarks, Fiore reveals the highly mixed composition of the *conventillo*, both in terms of multiregional and multinational origin (82).

Precise census data on the *conventillos* was difficult to gather at that time due to the constant relocation of tenants caused by rising rents and to the "*cama caliente*" (hot bed, 70) formula by which beds were rented by the hour to night-shift workers.[12] What the *conventillo* shows though is how not only was Italy "displaced" spatially to another location in the process of emigrating so massively to Argentina, but it was also "placed" within a complex society of immigrants characterized by a mixture of cultures so that the village-based cluster was an important but not sole component of living patterns (Baily 165–171). In commenting on *Dio non ama i bambini*, Pariani has stated that with this book she "had the intention of writing an epic story about Italian emigration to Argentina . . . a novel attempting to understand what happened overseas—the crumbling down of a rural mentality in the process of forced urban integration, the transformation of Italians into Argentines" (Lupo). Yet, she also probes that unique transnationalizing and cross-nationalizing rather than nationalizing process that a country like Argentina offered to immigrants. In a country populated by immigrants by definition, also due to the brutal extermination of indigenous populations by the Spanish colonizers, and in a country populated by Italian immigrants in particular, Italians became Argentinian as much as Argentina became Italian.[13] In reality, the relationship between the two countries and peoples was always ambiguous: Argentina feared the Italian ethnic predominance for the fact that Italy's economic and cultural expansionism at the international level relied largely on its emigrant colonies. At the same time as the colonization of Libya in 1911, Italy's official discourse depicted Argentina as a country of enslavement for Italians, who according to the new colonialist nationalist agenda were supposed to predominate instead of being relegated to a problematic ethnic group.[14] In any case, the multiregional and multinational coexistence of immigrants in Argentina was crucial in deconstructing rigid national paradigms and exploring the porosity of forms of affiliation despite organized attempts at conceiving, forming, and promoting cultures as homogeneous.

Pariani's linguistic inventiveness exemplifies this point: The idiom of her characters is a patois generated by the very protagonists of this hybrid experience, a true "Babel of dialects" (65). In bringing together her knowledge of her mother's native Lombard dialect and other Italian dialects, Argentinian Castillan and, of course, standard Italian, she creates her own *cocoliche*, an Italian language influenced by Spanish syntax and phraseology.[15] This linguistic hodgepodge never hinders comprehension but rather forces the reader to infer meaning from the interstices of the writing, to migrate between one language and another, or to look for translations and definitions outside the space of the novel. Dialect expressions ("*Signur dei puaritti*"—God of the poor, 6) and Spanish words and expressions such as the constantly used "*zaguán*" (the entranceway to the *conventillo*) or "*matadero*" (slaughterhouse) or "*claro que*" (obviously) punctuate the entire novel whereas in some cases languages exist next to each other in a fluid flow and end up creating unlikely words mirroring the fast pace of oral language. For example, in the long string of offenses against an extremely violent child nicknamed Orecchia (Ear)—"*Stronzo di porquerìa, hijo de puta, Orecchia, ésta me la pagás, lo giuro, Padrenuestrosqueestasenloscielos*" (236)—"*stronzo di porquería*" mixes an Italian curse word ("*stronzo*" for bastard) with the Spanish expression ("*di porquería*" meaning "filthy") followed by "son of bitch" in Spanish ("*hijo de puta*") at the outset, then addresses the character Orecchia both in Spanish and Italian ("*ésta me la pagás*," "you will pay for this," precedes "*lo giuro*," "I swear"), and concludes with a long word coming from the incipit of the Lord's prayer in Spanish gluing together the opening invocation and the subsequent relative clause ("*Padrenuestroqueestásenloscielos*," "Ourfatherwhoartinheaven").

Despite the potentially liberating quality of this *métissage*, there is very little trace of *jouissance* in these multinational *conventillos*, which ultimately appear like international prisons. The cross-fertilization of the linguistic codes does not affect the rigid categorization of different nationalities on the part of a central government that identifies in certain groups the generators of social degradation and the fomenters of public unrest. The period in which Pariani sets her novel corresponds with the growth of anarchism in Argentina, with immigrants playing a crucial role. As historian José Moya has shown, next to Spaniards, "Italians continued to play a key role in Buenos Aires' anarchist movement during the first decade of the twentieth century, as it became one of the largest and most active in the world" (194). Pariani's novel contains a substantive political theme reflecting the impact of anarchism among the immigrants. Besides the descriptions of actual strikes attributed to immigrant actions (in particular the strike of the breadmakers in the first part of the book; 46–47), the reference to laws that entailed expulsion from the country for political reasons (9), and the precedence that anarchist insurrections take over the killings of the Italian children (77), Pariani pays specific attention to two aspects of the movement in its positive impact on the Italian community: the education-driven and thus socializing process it comprised and the rethinking of gender roles it proposed.

The former aspect is embodied in two unusual characters who surprisingly reside in the *conventillo*, even though they have an affluent lifestyle. Riscatto (Redemption) and Bonifica (Reclamation) Maine are two siblings whose names tell a story in themselves and whose lives are devoted to reading and writing. Yet, their education does not set them apart from the rest of their neighbors, even though they are considered different (or disliked, since their educational status is seen as dangerous, 6). They instead offer their time to the community by reading the newspaper aloud, in itself a "delinquent act" that threatens the establishment as it raises self-awareness. Riscatto and Bonifica also read entire stories by De Amicis and Verne to their neighbors, and entertain the *conventillo* by playing and singing popular Italian songs. They represent the milder face of anarchism, the one that appealed to so many immigrants and in particular women, because it analyzed the roots of oppression and exploitation from within (ignorance, overcrowded living spaces, violence, lack of opportunity for children, injustice, 78) and offered a new language to think about family and work relationships.

The need for a deeper improvement of living standards spoke to women in effective ways since "gender equality appeared as part and parcel of the anarchist notion of social justice and personal freedom rather than a separate issue" (Moya 202). In the novel, "Clara Carenzi, 25, factory worker" is sensitive to the propaganda of the anarchists: "they say that things will change, that women have to be paid like men" (35). The novelty of their ideas, obviously ridiculed by her conservative and fatalistic mother-in-law ("you will never succeed in changing people's destiny," 35), allow Clara to dream not just of better economic conditions for her family—she is the breadwinner for her two young children and her late husband's mother—but of occasions for personal pleasures such as buying a dress and going to the amusement park. In the context of immigrant life, such simple acts, even when merely dreamt of, became "delinquent" tactics against the predominant view, which employs control-driven strategies instead, to use de Certeau's idiom.[16]

The redefinition of gender roles that the factory prompted had to go hand in hand with a social emancipation of women, otherwise reduced to workers both in the factory and at home and unable to enjoy their supposed economic autonomy. Albeit seen as a "sinful" or "capitalistic" insertion of women into consumerism by detractors, the shift from domestic to factory work also implied a different conceptualization of sexuality and definition of individual decisional power. It is not surprising that 50,000 women participated in the general strike of 1909 (Moya 210): Pariani records this participation with reference to another strike, that of the laundry washers in 1912, which the press condemned as indecorous (169–70). For the readers who have up until this section of the novel's Part II witnessed the most dreadful forms of violence perpetrated against women—often compelled to remain passive to the patriarchal system whether at home (see the Prologue of the book) or in the workplace (148)—this form of rebellion can only be interpreted as a sign of necessary reaction. But for the police it was further evidence of the corrupting force of anarchism exerted by and on immigrants, and the need to close national borders (169–70).

That the anarchist movement was appealing precisely because it addressed the causes of the oppression of immigrants and offered new horizons, did not seem a plausible reading to the police officers, who were only intent on eliminating what they perceived as a terrorist movement.[17] Those immigrants who became interested in anarchism (or other forms of labor organization) reacted to the unbearable conditions they encountered in Argentina.[18] As one of the *tanos* claims, the (South) American Dream is short-lived: "They told me that here in Merica you can find money on the trees and silly person that I am, I believed it was true" (76), where the powerful image offered in Crialese's *Nuovomondo* (see Chapter 1) returns in this other New World. The sense of disappointment of these "displaced" Italians is even more evident in the women's reports in other sections of the novel. Lucia Tomasi in Goletti describes the departure as a brutal severance from her land (13–14); while Clara Carenzi experiences for the first time in Argentina the effects of prostitution on family life and health as her husband eventually dies of a venereal disease after infecting her (32). The country hardly comes across as paradise in the intense words of Pariani's immigrants who think of themselves as the incarnation of the "*tano senza avvenire*" ("futureless Italian," 113).[19] Yet, the painful memories of Italy as a destitute place imposing military conscription still prompted many to cling on to their (South) American Dream, or rather to embrace new ways of dreaming through anarchism, which gives immigrants the "imagination to start afresh" (100). The very *conventillo* that trapped large numbers of Italians was also the space that introduced them to new ideas. As a place blurring the public and the domestic spheres (Moya 202), the *conventillo* became an ideal site for the anarchist movement to be truly international. Its slogan—"the nation is a mystification" (78)—found in the multinational environment of the *conventillo* a natural home.

Despite this air of revolution, in Pariani's novel the economic and social preoccupations of the *conventillo*, and specifically of the adults living in it, remain generally unchanged.

Conversely, outside the *conventillo*, the neighborhood provides more opportunities to perform change, but this ability resides in those who combine freshness of mind, street smarts, and the willingness to take risks. In a novel built mostly around children and adolescents (all of Part II is composed of sections devoted exclusively to young people between the age of five and fifteen), this role is naturally assigned to the new generation. This age group convincingly turns preoccupations into possibilities by gathering information irrelevant to adults, and developing tactics against the murderer that could potentially kill more of them. While the reader is provided with plentiful clues to identify the killer quite early in the novel, the adult characters in it are privy only to partial details. But, even when they witness revelatory occurrences (violent acts on the part of the murderer) or gather data (as is the case of the police officers and security guards), they do not act: Paradoxically they resort to justifications, fatalism, incredulity, or biases instead. Whenever a child can help in the investigation, s/he is discarded for not being credible, although his/her help can save a young life: Indeed, in this place, not even God loves children.

In reality, out of self-defense as well as a visceral sense of justice, the children pursue the case with much more clarity than the adults, and eventually act in lieu of them to resolve the case. Organized in a multiethnic gang (*banda*), these Argentinian-born Italian, Spanish, and Jewish children "walk" the city, which in de Certeau's parlance means substituting the bird's eye view of the institutions (the police, the school) with a concrete experience that offers information hidden in the interstices and provides space for interventions otherwise denied, if not feared. As de Certeau himself put it, "the proliferation of [a] challenging mobility that does not respect places is alternately playful and threatening" (*Practice* 130). Maurilio, the big boy that cleans the boxing gym and dreams of fighting in it himself one day, leads a group of children that without Pariani's attentive categorization by age, we would consider as highly skilled adults already beaten by life. They work, smoke, drink, eye the Blue House of the prostitutes, as well as witness, receive, and dispense violence on a regular basis in the nightmarish neighborhood where they live, which literary critics of Pariani's novel have compared to Dante's Inferno, Serao's Naples, and even Gomorrah. Nevertheless, these children care about and often provide for each other, but most of all they are driven by a sense of justice that the adults numbed by desperation or meanness have lost. Their investigative methods and tactics, even though driven by instinct, prove to be effective and catch the murderer without even imposing on him the fatal violence he inflicted on his victims. In the process, though, the children lose their innocence, as the last words suggest: "It is hard not to be a light kid anymore [and] be left with this bag of flesh, subject to the indifferent and mute force of gravity" (293). While the preoccupation caused by the murderer dissolves, and Italian immigrant parents are finally relieved after his identification, the street children are left with an existential preoccupation: This brutal truth has made them into adults.

In remapping the city through the eyes and acts of the immigrant children and mostly via their linguistic and cultural patois, Pariani proposes a radical shift in cognition by placing children and their hybrid experience as immigrants at the center of the story. Yet, she never falls into the traps of sentimentality or romanticization that a child-focused topic might easily produce. In part, the tightness of her writing is due to her conception of literature, which is not cathartic or dryly documentary but carves out a unique niche for itself. As she told an interviewer: "I mainly believe in a type of writing (and hence reading) that communicates and, if it cannot console us or heal us from pain, at least it collaborates in the arduous form of resistance which is everyday life" (Lupo). The coincidental reference to de Certeau's crucial interests—everyday life and its "delinquent" practices—is quite uncanny, and ultimately confirms the fruitfulness of this hermeneutic path for the reading of *Dio non ama i bambini*.

More specifically, it is the choice of the detective genre that allows Pariani to thoroughly inspect this scarcely known society of immigrants in "delinquent" ways, without the scientific claim of the traditional anthropologist or the rational investigator. She instead adopts a caring eye that preserves throughout the book the distance necessary to draw her gallery of portraits while rethinking both the meaning of seeing and the map. Not surprisingly, her novel functions within a visual economy privileging the sense of sight and its related representations with a particular sensitivity toward the technology of seeing. Besides the fact that the novel works as a picture album and relies on cartographic descriptions of residential places and neighborhoods, there are powerful passages about photography (the shots that Spreafico takes of the newly arrived immigrants at the port docks with the fake background of a beach and some palm trees, 141), and paracinematic and cinematic devices, the "*biógrafo*" (a box with moving images 250) and silent films (249), respectively offering the ability to "see" life shots in motion and life in a different color. In other words, the optic on life is presented as a movable process, comparable to the process of moving experienced by immigrants. Indeed, the novel is intent on showing the ability of certain characters to "open their eyes" (100) in the new spaces of emigration and to reoccupy their daily preoccupations with new visions. Immigrants are not just the "the first victims" (de Certeau, "Idéologie" 231–32) of a culturally mixed society but also, like Pariani's children, the pioneers of a society constantly attempting to eliminate forms of preoccupation thanks to imperceptible and concrete acts of resistance.

"Unsquared" Narratives in Lakhous's Immigrant Palazzo, Piazza, and Elevator

> Since he or she moves with the marks of an idiom, a tradition, usages, tastes, and behavior that are not familiar and in which we fail to see ourselves, the immigrant teaches us how to circulate in our language and our customs (de Certeau).

Lakhous's *Clash of Civilizations Over an Elevator in Piazza Vittorio* foregrounds space in ways similar to Pariani's *Dio non ama i bambini* by focusing on those *loci* that function as points of encounter between immigrants and nonimmigrants. As we will see, he moves from the neighborhood piazza to the palazzo and inside it the elevator to show the stratification of histories and stories of movement and the contrasts they generate. Like Pariani, he adopts the detective genre to intensify these contrasts as well as to identify points of closeness. In the process, he redraws the genre's code with the aim of making migrant stories central. First, he relegates the murder story to a more marginal role compared to Pariani, and resorts to humor rather than graphic violence in order to represent the various forms of distance and resistance experienced by the immigrant characters. Through a mobile technique that fragments the story into eleven parts and offers the perspective of different characters on the crime, Lakhous operates a constant "displacement" of the truth and identity, and in particular national identity. The resulting fragmentation is brilliantly spatialized in the novel by exploding the central space of the story, which is a quintessential Italian space, the piazza (square) of the title. He thus creates what in Italian is termed as "*spiazzamento*." The subtracting suffix "*s*" indicates the lack of location and consequently of center, and points to the worrisome disorientation that this state can generate. At the same time, this "dis/placement" can produce new forms of seeing and doing, as Lakhous signals with his prismatic narrative method. Unlike Pariani who privileges the chorus to create cohesion, Lakhous adopts a strong individual voice of a semiautobiographical nature (Ahmed/Amedeo/Amara) to stitch together the multiple voices of the numerous characters as well as the echoes of other novels and films that constitute the metaliterary matter of *Clash*. As the last part of this chapter will show, the voice of the protagonist emphasizes the nonlinear development of a novel essentially built around narrative, filmic, and concrete spaces pre-occupied by and preoccupied with internal and international migrations as well as (post)colonialism.

By way of a double condensation mechanism within the spatial economy of the novel, the author brings the palette of his characters into very close contact by focusing on the palazzo or condominium they are all residents of, and in even closer contact by zooming in onto the elevator that they share. The palazzo is never depicted in the novel in terms of architectural style or physical layout; it is instead described in the different emotional and social meanings it carries for the various inhabitants or users of it. As such, it becomes a theater of actions that at the micro level represents larger mechanisms of interaction in the neighborhood, the city, and even the country. Besides functioning as the place of residence for old-time immigrants from the North and South of Italy, the palazzo hosts immigrants and a foreign student. The former group reflects the traditional fabric of the neighborhood: Benedetta Esposito, "*la portinaia*" (the doorwoman) from Naples; Sandro Dandini, the barman of Sicilian ancestry; and Antonio Marini, the Milanese university professor. The latter group represents the new international texture of the area: Maria Cristina Gonzales, the Peruvian caretaker of old Signora Rosa; Parviz Mansoor Samadi, the Iranian dishwasher trying to secure a job and political asylum for himself; and Johan Van Marten, the Dutch student intent on making a neorealist film in Piazza Vittorio.[20] The palazzo is at once a temporary shelter for struggling immigrants like Parviz counting on the generosity of friends; a workplace for cleaners like Benedetta; the delivery destination for local store owners like Bangladeshi Iqbal Amir Allah; a prison for domestic workers like Maria Cristina; and the improbable set for Johan's movie project, entitled like the novel *Clash of Civilizations Over an Elevator in Piazza Vittorio*. The palazzo presents some characteristics of the immigrants' patterns of housing in a large Italian city like Rome. In the absence of housing policies specifically designed for them, immigrants mingle with old-time residents, especially in the historical centers, in ways somehow comparable to the *case di ringhiera* (tenements with running balconies), which also hosted immigrants from the Italian South starting from the early 1900s (Fig. 12). In today's Italy there is a similar mixing among locals and immigrants: The novelty rests on the fact that there are also immigrants

FIGURE 12. Immigrants standing outside the two small apartments they rent in a *casa di ringhiera*, Milan, 1990. Photo by Rosy Schirer.

coming from various parts of the world. Ironically, some *case di ringhiera* are now inhabited by these foreign immigrants: They are residential spaces pre-occupied by prior stories of immigration. In general, these contemporary immigrants more rarely create the areas of "ethnic specialization" found in the United States and the European capitals, for instance (Natale 166–68).[21] Ultimately, as Lakhous suggests, the palazzo is an experiment in coexistence, which yields mixed results since while some residents and users are prone to exercise empathy across cultural differences, others foster the thesis of the inevitability of the clash of civilizations due to irreconcilable distinctions.

This tension becomes even more evident in the use of the elevator, the metonymy for the building. As Graziella Parati has cogently put it in her "geocritical analysis" (*Annali* 443) of the novel, the elevator is "the door to the city," alternatingly "allowing and disallowing movement and access" to the migrants (436). The use of the kinetic space of the elevator, which will be addressed also in connection to Mazzucco's *Vita* in Chapter 4, is at the center of a controversy dividing the residents over the ways in which it is utilized (frequency, decor, etc.). On the one hand, the elevator is considered a crucial instrument of control: Benedetta monitors it constantly by preventing those misuses that may jeopardize her job in the eyes of the building owner (disproportionate use, overweight charge, littering) and Professor Marini is intent on creating a decalogue of what to do and not to do with the elevator, on which he philosophizes to the point of believing that "the elevator is a question of civility" (78).[22] The victims of these discipline-and-punishment attitude are Maria Cristina, who cannot take the elevator due to her excessive weight, caused by her hypersedentary life and depression (68); and Iqbal who would benefit from using it to deliver the groceries from his store, but is denied access (46). Yet, for Parviz, the elevator is "an instrument of meditation:" Taking it to simply go up and down is comparable to a yoga session for him (16–17). The centralizing force of the elevator is even more effectively rendered in Isotta Toso's 2010 film adaptation whose shortcomings reinforce Lakhous's achievements in the novel.[23] In her *Scontro di civiltà per un ascensore a Piazza Vittorio*, the camera moves smoothly up and down the stairs of the palazzo, which wind around the elevator. Dating back to the late 1800s, the palazzo has an old-style wrought iron elevator, which melds the outside and the inside: As a see-through object in an open-view well, the elevator is a space of mutual monitoring by default. In the novel, Lakhous treats this bickering over the elevator with his distinctive humor and lightness, yet he never fails to reveal uncomfortable truths, since these arguments function as a barometer of the pettiness of the building's residents and resonate with further territorial claims identifiable in Italy at large. As Johan comments in his usual indignant mode, the debates over the elevator are a sign of Italy's backwardness and underdevelopment. According to him, Italians are prey to the "lock syndrome" ("*catenaccio*" 84), a metaphor borrowed from soccer that he uses to point out Italians' tendency to play defense rather than advancing in attack (85). As a simultaneously anchored and moving space, the elevator is an ideal locus for the author to explore people's attitude toward life, ideas, and space itself. Not surprisingly, Lakhous elects it to be the space of conflict.

These open clashes reach their zenith when the elevator turns into a crime zone after one of the residents, a young man named Lorenzo Manfredini, is found dead in it. Lorenzo was known by the nickname of The Gladiator for his bellicose attitude. His death is the antecedent to the novel, and the search for the murderer is the reason for its form. The book is effectively made up of testimonies supposedly collected by an investigator, and as such it becomes an anthology of reactions to the crime presented as first-person narratives.[24] Yet, it soon becomes obvious that the murder is an occasion for self-representation and for the description of one's opinion about who belongs where. In the same vein of Andrea Camilleri's 1995 *Il birraio di Preston* or Calvino's 1979 *If on a Winter's Night a Traveler*, Lakhous's book is a mosaic of autonomous units that could theoretically be read in any order, except for the last unit that, albeit open-ended, works as a conclusion of sorts. As the different points of view unfold in the novel, the truth becomes more diffuse in the same way that the novel's characters reveal so much about the alleged murderer, Ahmed (or Amedeo), that in some sense he becomes indefinable. A sensitive man who works as a translator, Algerian Ahmed, known in Italy as Amedeo, is married to Stefania, a long-time resident of Rome, and interacts constantly with all the tenants as he tries to understand their personalities and help them when in need. He is a profound connoisseur of Rome, a learned person with a love for literature and cinema, but also a tortured soul who carries a secret, haunted as he is by a past that he tries to keep at bay by attending to the present and the possible betterment of society. In his capacity as a diarist, and thus the alter ego of Lakhous, he plays a "seamster" role in the novel; his regular entries are direct responses to the comments of various characters, and they function at once as insights into his ideas, fears, and desires and as connectors between the autonomous sections of the book.

While consciously creating a general sense of *spiazzamento* or displacement, the fragmentary structure of the book hardly affects its cohesion thanks to the binding function of Ahmed/Amedeo's diary entries, which he calls "wailings" since they express his internal sadness. In echoing some of the information gleaned from the self-portraits, the entries recontextualize it in a thick web of literary and cinematic references gathered from the rich patrimony of the so-called Western canon as well as the Muslim tradition, which Ahmed/Amedeo places in a dialogue between civilizations in lieu of the clash buttressed by the novel's characters.[25] Yet, the more this plurivocal text lets viewpoints and personal stories emerge, the more the idea of truth, identity, and belonging collapses in a house-of-mirrors effect. This becomes particularly apparent in the characters' perception of Ahmed/Amedeo, whose identity is up for grabs as people know very little about him and his origin, but are certain that somebody with such a precise knowledge of Rome cannot be an immigrant. As the Roman taxi driver puts it with an unmistakable Roman accent: "Wow, Amede', you really know Rome! Did the wolf suckle you?" (95). The local exclamation ("Wow" is *"Ammazza"* in the original version) is followed by the appreciation of Amedeo's knowledge of the city and the question-statement about his purported adoption by the she-wolf, symbol of Rome par excellence.[26] Additionally, Ahmed/Amedeo's perfect knowledge of Italian helps in his "passing," a process that has to be read not as a negation of one's roots out of shame, but as a double operation working both at the personal level for the character and at the metaliterary level for the novel and its fundamental message. Ahmed/Amedeo's past is linked to the violence of the postindependence fundamentalist regime in Algeria: Like the protagonist of Mohsen Melliti's novel, which is analyzed in Chapter 4, Ahmed has fled his country after losing his lover in violent circumstances for political reasons (111 and 114). His desire to forget his origin is tantamount to his desire to live, and his profession as a translator allows him to migrate to another language and culture with ease. In other words, passing is not an act of hiding but a necessity for survival. At the same time, his passing is instrumental to Lakhous's central theme in the novel: The context-based and metamorphosis-prone nature of identity serves the purpose of invalidating the deeply rooted biases of the novel's characters. While they cling to their own supposedly fixed identities out of self-defense and fear, Ahmed/Amedeo develops a porous way of being in the world out of a "delinquent" performance. By showing how Amedeo can be many people at once depending on the point of view, Lakhous implicitly suggests that unbiased inquiries can be, potentially at least, a first step in better understanding a person, a culture, and an environment. An immigrant like Ahmed/Amedeo can teach locals how to circulate in their language and customs, to paraphrase de Certeau's epigraph (*The Capture of Speech* 133), and to counteract the widespread negative view of immigrants.

The reference to the ignorance surrounding the experience of immigrants in Italy is evident in the hilarious monologue of Benedetta when she takes her narrow-mindedness to a pinnacle of hypocritical racism:

> All you have to do is take a walk in the afternoon in the gardens of Piazza Vittorio to see that the overwhelming majority of the people are foreigners: some come from Morocco, some from Romania, China, India, Poland, Senegal, Albania. Living with them is impossible. They have religions, habits, and traditions different from ours. In their countries they live outside or in tents, they eat with their hands, they travel on donkeys and camels and treat women like slaves. I'm not a racist but that's the truth. Even Bruno Vespa, on TV, says so. (38)

Benedetta's simplistic statements, corroborated by the power of popular anchormen such as Bruno Vespa, are made particularly absurd since they obliterate the legacy of Italian emigration. In echoing the fears of many Italians today, she unconsciously ventriloquizes the preoccupations of so many native populations of the countries of destination for Italian emigrants who in turn used to be discriminated against for being criminals, backward, and uncouth.[27] Similarly biased positions abound in the novel, as Lakhous is interested in registering paroxysms of tension and division in order to reveal their preposterous nature. While the characters' obsession with proving the existence of incommensurable differences produces what some critics of the novel have considered monodimensional personalities, if not rigid types, Lakhous uses this fixation within a comedic genre that consciously privileges caricatures and is therefore "reductive." Intent as he is in modulating the characters' views through the dialogic form of the novel, which always offers a double take on every situation, the author recontextualizes prejudices into a larger network of cultural exchanges and borrowings that undo these very claims. Through the monologues of the characters, he draws an emigration/immigration and (post)colonial map of people's constant movements from and to Italy that paradoxically speaks of similarities much more than differences among these people and effectively deconstructs any purported concept of a homogeneous Italian identity via a process of constant *spiazzamento*.

When he shares his point of view on Ahmed/Amedeo, Parviz, a frail character who tries to reconcile his hatred for pizza and pasta with his lack of aversion toward Italians, clearly points to an internal contradiction:

> It's pointless to persist with this question: is Amedeo Italian? Whatever the answer is, it won't solve the problem. But then who is Italian? Only someone who was born in Italy, has an Italian passport and identity card, knows the language, and lives in Italy? As you see, the question is very complicated. . . . It's enough for you to know that Amedeo knows Italian better than millions of Italians scattered like locusts to the four corners of the world. . . . I don't despise the locusts; in fact; I respect them, because they procure their food with dignity—they don't count on anyone. And then it's not certainly my fault if the Italians like to travel and emigrate. (14–15)

The preoccupation over an essentialist Italian identity today proves to be problematic in the face of the massive historical diaspora of Italians around the world. This exodus remains a subtext to the main story, but the author deftly reworks it into the narrative by later mentioning the stereotyping suffered by Italians in the United States (54) and by referencing the lives of Italians in Australia as depicted in Zampa's 1971 film with Alberto Sordi and Claudia Cardinale, *Bello Onesto Emigrato Australia Sposerebbe Compaesana Illibata* . . . (72–73). As Parviz discloses the transnational emigration-based pre-occupations of Italian culture and identity, the internal interregional migrations are voiced by many other residents through references to Gianni Amelio's film *Cosí ridevano* (1998),[28] personal and family stories of relocation from Naples and Sicily to Rome, and the depiction of Roman restaurants as businesses run through the efforts of Sardinian and Calabrese waiters and dishwashers speaking Italian with a level of competence surprisingly comparable to that of foreign immigrants. In the words of Mario, the cook at a restaurant located in the Stazione Termini, the quintessentially immigrant gathering space in Rome, "we're all foreigners in this city!" (16).

The stratified migratory map of Rome also includes the figure of the Milanese professor, a sort of reincarnation of the Piedmontese bureaucrats that moved to the capital after 1871. His hatred of a city that he considers the epitome of the dirty, ignorant, and corrupt South interestingly crisscrosses other legacies of Italian demographic movements, which surface like symptoms of an unexplored malaise. In commenting on the malfunctioning quality of public transportation and the ensuing chaos that it produces in the city, Professor Marini, a historian with a not merely coincidental expertise in Roman imperialism, explodes in a bias-ridden invective cutting transversally through time and space: "Madonna! Where in the world are we? In Mogadishu or Addis Ababa? In Rome or Bombay?" (74). The use of the Northern dialect (unfortunately lost in translation) in the passage emphasizes the regionalist residue found even among educated people self-identifying as "proper" Italians, and ironically places Marini among the Sardinian or Calabrese waiters as well as the Neapolitan doorwoman. At the same time, his anathema is directed against a city that for its systemic chaos is equated with cities in Africa, which are notably capitals of former Italian colonies, Somalia and Ethiopia. The resurgence of a colonial racist sentiment in a capital of modern migrations like Rome signals to the "displaced" quality of colonial memories, to use Jaqueline Andall's and Derek Duncan's apt concept (21). A new scenario of power relations triggers a familiar one and appropriates a situation through a well-known grammar of racism, which in this case is interestingly interlaced with a new form of racism in its reference to a place like Bombay, embodying disorder in the contemporary collective imaginary.

To this complex landscape of pre-occupations in Rome, Lakhous adds another declension of foreign presence in the city with Johan, who exemplifies a very common phenomenon in Rome: the temporary residence of foreign students.[29] This presence inserts Rome (and Italy) into a more traditional set of routes by which the capital continues to be a major destination for short- and long-term visitors as well as religious immigrants, due to what Casacchia and Crisci have respectively called the "Rome effect" (the city's artistic magnetism) and the "Vatican effect" (its Catholic faith-based centrality) (64). The "fear" of foreigners in Rome thus becomes particularly misplaced. For film students like Johan (and Northern tourists at large) Rome remains an exotic South that offers a source of artistic inspiration and simultaneously creates and/or reinforces the superiority of the "North."[30] For Johan, the South, criticized as it is, needs to remain unchanged as if Rome were the same as when Rossellini or De Sica knew it; this freezing in time is aesthetically indispensable although the politically conservative implication is the stagnancy of the South.

By contrast, this South stands for the developed North in the expectations of foreign immigrants who move there from developing countries around the world. Lakhous's novel interweaves their stories of migration in its monologues: the reason why they left (political or economic); their degree of integration (linked to economic stability, language competence, valid documents); their plans for the future (return, stay, family reunion); their degree of nostalgia; their coping mechanisms (cooking out of homesickness, hanging out with compatriots out of loneliness, practicing religious rituals out of fear for cultural loss); their views of Italy, positive or negative as they are. The immigrants themselves resort to simplified perceptions of Italy and Italians, mythicize their country of origins, and often behave according to cultural norms they consider as axioms—this is quite evidently the case of Algerian Abdallah Ben Kadour who is obsessed with immutable traditions (112–13). While Lakhous subtly shows that immigrants can be biased toward Italians as well, the biased view toward immigrants on the part of natives carries more weight within the inherent hierarchies of the society due to the rhetorical and concrete powers that locals can exercise in excluding "others." Like Benedetta (39), Elisabetta Fabiani, an old-fashioned lady living in the building, considers the Chinese as a dog-eating people and is infuriated at them after the disappearance of her beloved dog Valentino, ironically named after one of the best-known early Italian émigrés. Albeit humorously, the arrival of immigrants from the Souths of the world (Asia, Latin America, Africa) is perceived in the novel as an invasion, a problem, and a form of decline for the society of destination.

Lakhous never fails to show the ludicrousness of such generalizations in order to condemn the widespread dichotomy us/them on two main grounds. The first is that of the porosity of identity, which the very advocates of monolithic cultures are sensitive or inadvertently subject to: Benedetta considers the Iranian Parviz an Albanian and the Bengali Iqbal a Pakistani, and she fears that one day people might look at her as a Filipino, while Professor Marini thinks that Amedeo is not only Italian but a Northern Italian because of his kind manners. In the entire novel, origins are important only insofar as they can be questioned: The new epistemologies that they trigger as the meaning of life and of the world is explored produce new forms of comprehension, mutual understanding, and ultimately ethics. The second ground is historical and political: Lakhous is relentless in suggesting the coimplications of past and present, and the here and there. Immigrants are not extraneous to a society, despite what Benedetta insinuates when she claims that immigrants have nothing to find in a messy unemployment-plagued country like Italy (38). They are instead the manifestation of a texture of occurrences—mostly geographically displaced—that invest the very space of destination within a framework of European colonial and emigration legacies on the one hand, and postcolonial and neoimperial entanglements, on the other.[31]

In response to self-referential and closed views of identity, Lakhous designs a character whose place in both the intradiegetic space and the linguistic-narrative production of the text is scarcely intelligible and highly "delinquent." In this intradiegetic space Ahmed/Amedeo is a chameleonlike character, coming from what he generically refers to as "the South." His ability to "walk the city" like Pariani's children allows him to try alternative routes, thus shunning impositions (he is not excluded like other immigrants). This delinquency becomes evident in his refusal to use the elevator, which reminds him of tombs (42). By opting for the stairs, a decision that Marini finds politically extremist (stairs are for him "an offense to modernity, to development, and to enlightenment!" 78), Ahmed/Amedeo distances himself from the central preoccupation of the palazzo, but he remains available to act as a mediator for those who inhabit or traverse this residential environment (he hosts Parviz, supports Maria Cristina, and entertains conversations with Johan, Marini, and Benedetta) as well as the neighborhood (with his wife Stefania, he is involved in pro-immigration activities). His role as a *flâneur* (Parati, "Where" 439) possesses a specific migrational quality: His apparent nonbelonging is actually the multiple belonging of the immigrant, since Amedeo is constantly occupied and pre-occupied by Ahmed. The linearity generally traceable in all the characters, to the point that their actions and words tend to render them into types, is nullified in the case of Ahmed/Amedeo. At the level of the linguistic and narrative production of the text, Ahmed/Amedeo is equally elusive; as a translator, and an avid reader who speaks in quotations, Ahmed is coimplicated in the writing of the text from the perspective of the philosopher injecting doubt: He asks questions, looks for multiple answers, plunges into dreamy realities, leaves sentences unfinished. Most of all, he howls. His wailings are nocturnal wanderings through the pains of the past, the enigmas of the present, and the uncertainties of the future. More specifically, they are ramblings in the form of a free-associated tale, which for de Certeau is "a spatial practice" (115). The same way Ahmed/Amedeo bridges cultures through his diary entries, he connects languages through his work as translator, which he depicts as an experience in space: "translation is a sea voyage for me from one coast to another" (109) or

"Is the Italian language my new dwelling?" (110). More specifically, he reveals the strongly "delinquent" operation entailed in this profession when he confesses: "Sometime I consider myself a smuggler across the borders of languages with a loot of words, ideas, images, and metaphors" (109). This last term is particularly relevant since the carrying-through effected by a metaphor represents the migration experience itself; the delinquency inherent in disregarding or playing with borders via language and narration is therefore even more intense from the point of view of a migrant. It is quite natural that Ahmed wonders about the habitability of the Italian language, as the epigraph suggests, and then melts into his typical howl: "*Auuuuuu.*"

The question of language is central to Ahmed as much as it is to the novel and in the extraliterary realm to Lakhous himself, who has claimed to have found a home in the Italian language. From the perspective of an Algerian in Italy since 1995, Lakhous maintains that Italian is devoid of the cultural tensions inherent to French and is a terrain to experiment with Arabic and Italian dialect influences (he rewrites his novels in Italian rather than translating them from the Arabic). Albeit devoid of the intricateness displayed by Pariani's heteroglossia, Lakhous's linguistic play is quite rich as it happens at an interlinguistic and metalinguistic level. Rather than mimetically reproducing the patois spoken by domestic and international migrants in Rome, he adopts a fairly sophisticated standard Italian for all of them and intersperses it with dialect words ("*guagliò,*" 17), unexplained foreign terms ("*qalb alluz,*" 119) and orthographically adapted loanwords ("*sibice*" for ceviche, 91). But, most of all, each character interrogates language and articulates his/her relationship with it: Ahmed/Amedeo uses the dictionary like a baby uses a milk bottle; Parviz stitches his lips out of protest since his words remain unheard; Abdallah compares Italian and Arab proverbs; Stefania teaches Italian to the migrants; and Maria Cristina speaks to the TV; Johan fixates on the pun gentile/Gentile (the adjective "kind" and the name of the Italian soccer player who introduced the self-defensive technique called the "lock").

Lakhous's fascination with acts of mis/communication is supported by his strength in reproducing the spoken voice, which provides the writing with a sonic signature, a truly unique gift for a foreign writer.[32] His dexterity with dialects compounded with his knowledge of Arabic and French, in addition to Italian, renders language pliable in his hands. In some ways, he is comparable to Carlo Emilio Gadda, who with his masterpiece *Quer pasticciaccio brutto de via Merulana* almost fifty years before *Clash* had mapped "the geography of the languages that resound in the capital" (Erbani 284).[33] Like Gadda, Lakhous is interested in Rome as a basin of languages, which now includes the Italian spoken by immigrants. Lakhous proposes a new form of "delinquent" writing via the incorporation of a foreign element that is not introduced by advertising or high culture and high-tech, as in the case of the omnipresent English language in Italy, but finds its way in through migratory routes. Similar to Laura Pariani, Lakhous adopts a linguistic hybridity from below, which within the landscape of Italy's capital only adds to the composite nature of the local language rather than, as one would superficially conclude, challenging a monolithic model. This linguistic operation is taken by Lakhous to a more sophisticated level in the book following *Clash*, *Divorce Islamic-Style on Marconi Avenue* (*Divorzio all'islamica a viale Marconi*), a novel in which, as he once again explores "clashes of civilizations" via migration stories, the "truth" is less important than the human stories it discloses.[34]

Indeed, like Gadda's and Sciascia's detective novels, which inspired Lakhous, *Clash* resists full narrative closure. Besides presenting the "truth" in two final versions (the murder case is solved in two only apparently separate and incompatible ways by Inspector Bettarini), the novel ends with Ahmed/Amedeo's diary entry melting into his idiosyncratic ancestral sound, this time even more amplified on the space of the page: "*Aauuuuuuuuuuuuuuuuuu*" (131). By obsessively questioning the meaning of the truth, he has realized how impossible it is to find it, and how risky it is to embark on its search when burdened by memories, and in particular by the unpleasant memories of a political refugee, with a legacy as threatening as Shahrayar's sword in *One Thousand and One Nights*. Seemingly, the piazza hosting this multiethnic human comedy and tragedy turns, by way of a vowel switch, into "*pazzia*" for him: His own *spiazzamento* is madness in the Pirandellian sense of the word, a keener sight defying social norms. Yet, this isolating "madness" needs to be counterbalanced in order to avoid complete loss of touch with the world. Writing is what anchors Ahmed: both writing his nightmares, and writing about writing gives him a "place." In invoking Orpheus and Shahrazad right before his visceral howl, Ahmed/Amedeo pays homage to mythopoiesis beyond territorial boundaries. Through this metaliterary device, Lakhous thus gestures toward both his numerous national literary traditions, which he rereads in a transnational frame, and the power of the word and storytelling, which he reimagines across differences.

In this sense, Lakhous offers an innovative postcolonial detective novel that travels to a displaced metropole like Italy and puts forward the possibility of an experimental nation[35] by depicting the crisis of the nation as a model. Lakhous interestingly revisits the traditional former colony–metropole relationship by choosing Italy and its history of transnational dispersion and internal fragmentation to reflect on identity. Like Pariani, he displaces the point of origin and hybridizes the point of arrival. Through multiperspectival narratives focused on mobility in space and cultural shuttling, Pariani and Lakhous use the detective story as a pretext for a subtle social and cultural investigation. For Pariani, the genre is an opportunity to recast history and tell a story of emigration from the unusual perspective of those left out by history (children, women, immigrants), while for Lakhous it is a tool to rewrite the present through the very stereotypes it rehashes from the past in a vicious circle of stale self-confirmation. The centrality of the practices of everyday life in their tales of delinquency and the experimental quality of their literary languages and narrative structures signals their radical rethinking of writing and "seeing." It is an epistemological shift that in a typical de Certeau style "seek[s] out more hospitable circumstances for heterogeneity" (Highmore 151) and allows both writers to reoccupy spaces of preoccupation with antiviolent and antiracist practices.

FOUR

Writing the Pasta Factory and the Boardinghouse as Transnational Homes: Public and Private Acts in Melliti's *Pantanella* and Mazzucco's *Vita*

> There is no thought without u-topia, without an exploration of the possible, of the elsewhere . . . without reference to practice.
>
> —HENRI LEFEBVRE

Homes are by definition intimate spaces devoted to single families and, less frequently today than in the past, to extended families. Because of their intrinsically dynamic quality, migration phenomena have reformulated and continue to reformulate this definition. Issues of precariousness, either economic or social, prompt migrants to look for residential solutions that barely fit existing conventions. Migrants are often forced into living conditions that are at once a sacrifice and an opportunity, and ultimately a social experiment for immigrants and nonimmigrants alike and also, in the case of writers, an occasion to identify vibrant cultural milieus. Whereas Chapter 3 focused on public spaces like city squares and neighborhoods and private ones like condominiums where immigrants mingle with locals, this chapter looks at residential spaces that are exclusively inhabited by immigrants.

Once again, the approach adopted offers a parallel view of such spaces through the double lens of immigration to Italy and emigration from Italy, as separate and yet connected experiences. More specifically, the two spaces chosen for this sociocultural exploration are an abandoned factory in Rome, occupied by immigrants from outside Europe, and a boardinghouse in a New York tenement shared by immigrants of different national origins. Depicted by prominent immigrant author Mohsen Mellitti in *Pantanella: Canto lungo la strada* (1992) and best-selling writer Melania Mazzucco in *Vita* (2003) respectively, these two spaces are ideal opportunities to investigate the layers of migration history present in one place or text, as well as the echoes of stories of mobility resounding across spaces and texts.[1] While Mellitti's book constitutes fictionalized reportage of the actual 1990 occupation of the former Pantanella pasta factory in Rome, Mazzucco's work is a family epos stemming from some *objets trouvés* and documents dating back to the first half of the 1900s, enriched by on-site research in New York as well as pure invention. The pasta factory and the boardinghouse in the tenement are crucial spaces for my analysis, although they do not hold the same weight in the overall orchestration of the two books. For Melliti, the occupied factory is the main engine and stage of the story, whereas for Mazzucco the boardinghouse in the tenement is central only in the first third of the novel, and is enriched by the analysis of many other spaces in the city of immigrants embodied by New York (neighborhoods, elevators, streets, workplaces). Despite the different roles these two spaces play in the respective narratives, they lend themselves to a proxemic interpretation combining housing and economic factors in new political directions. As seen in Chapter 3, the square and palazzo of Ferrente's and Lakhous's works are inevitably embedded in economic networks embracing the jobs available to and the services offered by immigrants—Maria Cristina Gonzales in *Clash of Civilizations* works as a caretaker in the palazzo, for example. But, as living spaces, they are not intrinsically sites of exchange of goods, performances, and ideas that trigger new sociopolitical and individual alliances. This is instead the case for Melliti's former pasta factory, turned into a hotel-bazaar by its international inhabitants with a utopian project in mind, and for Mazzucco's apartment in which room and board is sold from immigrant to immigrant. In defining relationships among immigrants themselves as well between immigrants and so-called locals, these spaces, a hybrid between the private and the public, design new urban spheres of signification.

Both authors are interested in showing how need prompts invention, and they explore the different levels of preoccupations engendered in and around these spaces. Borrowing from Henri Lefebvre's reading of control and resistance in space in his *Urban Revolution* (1970), I engage these spaces as both spaces of economic production and imagination, the former being "the practice of habiting and use" and the latter "an exploration of the possible, of the elsewhere" (182). Melliti's and Mazzucco's spaces are not defined simply by economic demand and supply (lodging, food circulation and consumption, etc.); in the intra- and extradiegetic realm of the narration, they clearly point to the sphere of artistic creation, specifically writing, as a political response to challenging housing conditions. In a situation of deprivation, words and writing emerge as a coping mechanism, and more; whether public as in the case of *Pantanella* or private as in the case of *Vita*, the act of writing is a liberating tool even in the most trying circumstances. The very titles and subtitles of the two works point in this direction: A song along the road signals poetic forwardness, and "life" (*vita*) is unquestionably pregnant with optimism.

Complicating the National Space in the Occupied Pasta Factory

"So, what's going on with you?"
"I am just preoccupied" (Melliti 36).

Published less than two years after the seven-month occupation of the Pantanella by roughly 2,500 immigrants, Melliti's book, part documentary and part invention, is a powerful rendition of the facts and effects of that complex event, which eventually resulted in a forced evacuation ordered by the local police.[2] Focusing on the character of Ahmad, the novel is nonetheless a choral one, constantly reflecting the experience of many within a space that is clearly represented as a container of multiple lives, or as the narrator puts it from the very outset, "the city" (11). The metaphor of the city is quite telling as it signals not just the condensation of a large amount of different people in a defined space and the layered nature of their relationships, at once economic and emotional, but also the political thrust of this experiment which challenged, albeit temporarily, preconceived ideas about urban living, national culture, and the power of the institutions vis-à-vis the freedom of the individual. To use Lefebvre's words, the Pantanella experiment restored "a heart, a face, a 'soul'" (183) to the concept and experience of a city otherwise functioning merely as urban society, that is, a repressive space (185).

The reading of Melliti's *Pantanella* has often been focused on the fabulation of this occupation experience, and its related emancipatory thrust for a migrant author.[3] Written in Italy in the first language of the author, Arabic, the novel was translated by Monica Ruocco, professor of Arab Literature at the University of Palermo, and published only in Italian translation.[4] The fact that the book leaves such a meaningful trace of this story for Italian-speaking readers reinforces both its political purport and its distancing from the more usual postcolonial framework; instead of embracing French, the author opts for the Italian language. At the same time, the preface by Algerian writer Rachid Boudjedra, one of the most important voices of Maghrebi literature, inscribes the novel in a tradition of postcolonial dissent writing. Edited by Isabella Camera D'Afflitto, professor at the University of Naples and one of the most recognized Arabists in Italy, the book belongs to the first wave of Italophone literature, the series of texts born out of the collaboration between an immigrant writer and an Italian journalist or scholar, according to Lombardi-Diop's categorization ("Italophone" 295). As in the case of *Libera*, the story of Feven Abrehe Tekle told to Raffaele Masto, analyzed in Chapter 2, the nature and degree of collaboration between Melliti and Camera d'Afflitto is not unpacked in any way. Through Boujedra's comment pointing to Melliti's use of different Arab dialects as well as a variety of languages (8–9), found, for instance, in the opening dialogues (12) and in the quotations of Aragon's verses in French (145 and 159), the reader becomes aware that the author's original denationalizing intent is unfortunately lost in translation. Ironically, the novel is further nationalized as the protagonist Ahmad, like all the other characters, speaks a plain Italian, erasing the novel language that immigrants usually forge through their use of local dialects (also, his "mistakes" are mentioned by a character, but not visible to us as readers, 128). *Pantanella*'s polyglossia, which certainly made the novel more experimental than it looks like in its printed version, is thus left to the reader's imagination.

The attack on the nation that Melliti originally articulated at the verbal level remains visible at the narrative/spatial level, mostly in his authorial choice to write about a hybrid space inside not only Italy but the nation's capital in particular. The actual unraveling of the Pantanella events can in fact be read as a denationalizing and simultaneously transnationalizing act of strong symbolic value. The erosion of the concept of the nation as a homogeneous cultural space hinges, on the one hand, on the presence of a highly international group of people in the heart of Rome and, on the other hand, on the reappropriation, albeit coincidental, of "an international symbol of Italianness" like a pasta factory (Parati, "Legal" 301). A brief analysis of the history of this connoted space will show the revolutionary purport of the immigrants' spatial intervention not only at the concrete level of what Lefebvre would have called "urban self-management" (156) but also at the metaphorical level of remapping the relationship between the center and the margin.

Born in 1882 from a previous smaller family activity, the Pantanella industry is represented in today's brochures as the epitome of "the noble Italian tradition" and its pasta as a "100% Italian product." Despite its new location in the region of Molise (Isernia), the legacy of the Pantanella is presented as profoundly linked with Rome to the point that the red oval logo continues to state "Rome since 1882" and is set below an image of the Colosseum.[5] Black and white images of the old factory adorn the brochure in order to add historical weight to the business. These images portray the inside of the original site, a building in via dei Cerchi, in the Circo Massimo area, right behind the church hosting the well-known Mouth of Truth. The building eventually proved inadequate and was left unused until it was sold to the city of Rome in 1928 and adapted, quite significantly, into the now-defunct Museum of Rome, which "celebrated the myth of the Roman spirit" by linking the ancient history of Rome with its recent colonial status in order to project an Italian capital's identity able to embrace local roots and transnational connections in the past as well as the present.[6] Meanwhile, starting in the very late 1800s, to respond to the expansion needs of a modern factory, a new Pantanella complex had been developed at 5 via Casilina. In part, it took over some existing buildings owned by the milling company Ducco e Valle and, in part, it entailed the construction of new ones in the early 1910s (the church-shaped silos) and the 1920s and '30s. This operation climaxed in the monumental additions designed by the rationalist architect Pietro Aschieri, reflecting the regime's intention to "experiment with a revitalized image of the myth of Rome" (Scatafassi 29) and effectively assigning to the Pantanella a national(ist) role. Among these additions, the most striking was the central body inspired by the nearby first-century CE Roman tomb of the state baker Eurisace, whose decorative elements incorporated the shapes of breadmaking tools. In particular, the top frieze of the tomb is characterized by circular elements representing the top of flour barrels, interestingly looking like the portholes of a ship. It is consequently of little surprise that Federico Fellini, whose father had worked at the original Pantanella plant in Rome in 1918, used the new building as "an exterior to paint" for his set of *And the Ship Sails On* (Chandler 221–22) due to its massive shiplike shape and windows. By mere coincidence, a quintessentially Italian space like a pasta factory takes the shape of a ship, thus inadvertently evoking the fate of a nation like Italy, whose very existence from its birth has been so profoundly linked to migratory dispersion through voyages, as seen in Chapter 1.

The Pantanella multiplex on via Casilina eventually covered a vast area comprising this large building (functioning as the actual pasta-making space), a mill, a grain storage, offices and access to the railway tracks.[7] It became the site of the most productive pasta factory in Europe before and right after World War II. Heavily bombed by the Americans during the war, a sign of its central role in the economy of the city and the nation, the Pantanella complex was rebuilt, in part by architect Vittorio Morpurgo, and refurbished with modern machinery in the 1950s. Around the peak of its success in 1954, the Pantanella company was at the center of a legal case whose central issues point once again to the symbolic meaning of the factory in the conceptual space of the nation. Maria Meneghini Callas, already an admired opera singer, who despite her Greek origin was held up to be the apogee of Italianness, was depicted as the testimonial in a Pantanella ad claiming that she had lost weight after eating Pantanella pasta regularly. Callas's immediate demand that the ad be declared as false and that the company pay her damages and issue a public apology bumped up against a Pantanella defender no less influential than the Pope, who intervened to protect the company owner—his own nephew. Callas had to wait until Pius XII died in 1958 to see the case come to a close according to her demands (Scott 126–27). In the late 1970s, a series of financial struggles prompted the closing of the factory; the industrial area on via Casilina was then left in a state of abandonment until the "requalification" project of what can be considered the largest example of industrial archeology in Rome was approved in the late 1990s.[8] The occupation of the derelict Pantanella factory by immigrants in 1990, thus inserted itself in a profoundly national and conservative institutional history that was challenged at its roots, unbeknownst to the occupiers.

The occupation was initially carried out by immigrant men, nine out of ten of them between the ages of eighteen and thirty-nine,[9] coming from Pakistan, Bangladesh, and India but eventually embraced a good number of immigrants from the Maghreb, Sub-Saharan Africa, and the Middle East as well. Pushed out of the historical center at a time in which the Roman government was focused on "cleaning" the area in view of a tourist influx related to the summer 1990 World Soccer Cup, these immigrants not only found a shelter in the abandoned factory but, despite its dilapidated conditions, also slowly developed a wide array of activities and facilities, ranging from a market to restaurants, a mosque, a language school, and even a "cinema."[10] To this day, the only full reportage of the Pantanella events spanning from June 1990 to January 1991 is Renato Curcio's *Shish Mahal*, published in 1991 by his own press, Sensibili alle Foglie. Once the philosophical leader of the Red Brigades and an active militant within it, Curcio has been involved in cultural activities against oppression and discrimination in the role of the writer, and *Shish Mahal* marked one of the first of these projects. The title of the book quotes the name that the Pantanella occupants gave to their "city." Shish Mahal means Palace of Mirrors or Crystal Palace in Hindi and refers to Mughal palaces characterized by elegant pavilions inlaid with intricate mirror work, examples of which can be found in Agra and Jaipur, with the most important, a UNESCO site since 1981, located in Lahore, Pakistan. The use of this nickname for the Pantanella on the part of the immigrants was a doubly ironic take on a non-regal building almost completely devoid of windowpanes. Additionally, as Curcio explains in the book's introduction, "Shish, in Hindi-Urdu language, means 'you are.' Mahal instead refers to 'a meeting point'" (7). His own choice of the term then focuses on the centrality of space in this social experiment that the Pantanella came to represent in those months. Immigrants thought a decent living space could be created out of this cradle of tension generated by job and shelter-related precariousness, lack of papers, *ghurba* (nostalgia), and rage. The plan was to install new windows and heating and water systems by employing the many Pantanella dwellers that had training in the construction sector

(Curcio 20–21), thus producing job opportunities and a living space acceptable to the residents and the neighborhood. In closely chronicling the facts in what looks like a journal with dated entries complemented by data, lists of names, and images, Curcio denounces the response of the local government, fraught as it was with delays, incompetence, but primarily prejudicial positions. Regardless of the support from many social groups, student organizations, and some media, the occupation was seen for the most part as a plague by public institutions and residents of the neighborhood, whose long depoliticized identity ironically found a renewed form of unity "in the act of rejecting the intruder," as sociologist Gallini explains in her afterword to *Shish Mahal* (155).[11] Attempts at gaining the protection of key politicians in power failed over time, while overcrowding and low standards of hygiene made the occupied Pantanella less and less livable. The ex–factory dwellers were labeled as criminals, virus carriers, dangerous loiterers, and interestingly "aliens," even though a large number of them held visas.[12] By extension, their unique house became a maxi-signifier in public discourse:

> Bewitched shelter. Lager. Dilapidated structure. Old ugly barrack. Extra-territorial fringe. Trashy hotel for street sellers. Dangerous hell. Kasbah. A monument to decay. Pigsty. Powder keg. Human maze. Hospice. Third-world corner. Immigrant purgatory. Melting pot. Duty free zone. Sewage. Ticking bomb. Non-E.U. factory. Ethnic bomb. Hotel of the desperate and outcast. Mega-camp. Kampo. Black maxi-ghetto. Mohammed's house. Dunghill. Terrorist lair. Apocalyptical den. Risky spot. Shameful hotel. (Curcio 8)

This series of epithets used against such a complex space signals the centrality of space but also the denial of the possibilities it contained as a "spontaneous city" (Lefebvre 160).[13] The widespread public resistance against the occupation coupled with the support of an alarmist media industry that "played a crucial role in the reproduction of ethnic prejudice" (ter Wal 62), eventually prompted the authorities to order the confiscation of many personal belongings, and the evacuation of the area in a forceful way on January 31, 1991 (Fig. 13), while fire was set to a section of the factory.[14] Immigrants were dispersed with various promises of support but actually providing help to such a large number of people proved to be a daunting project, especially in light of political tensions and infrastructural weaknesses. This clear display of "practices of evacuation and demolition [that] decentralize and disperse immigrant communities . . . and determine clear boundaries of settlement . . . [and] categories of exclusion" (Lombardi-Diop, "Roma" 405) killed a visionary project.[15] A city-in-progress, which with the proper resources could have become an occasion for addressing immigrant issues in a constructive way, was instead turned into a sorrowful ruin.

While the Pantanella was given increasing visibility in the media, its inhabitants were often erased as individual human beings and political subjects. Even Curcio's book, whose merit is to provide a sensitive document of that experience mostly unraveling as a reflection on the discriminatory power of language, falls short of providing systematic and full portrayals of the involved individuals or of their direct perspectives. *Shish Mahal* distinctively fails to sketch complex figures and ambiguous situations mostly due to its uncompromisingly pro-immigrant, or rather antiestablishment, stance. On the other hand, besides

FIGURE 13. The former Pantanella Pasta Factory, occupied by hundreds of Asian immigrants from Pakistan and Bangladesh, is evacuated by the police, Rome, January 31, 1991. Photo by Stefano Montesi.

bringing back to life the voices muted by official history, Melliti's novel *Pantanella* paints nuances, speaks with silence, and abounds in half-truths, undecided people, and unclear circumstances. Ultimately, it shows the irreducible character of singularities without bypassing the inevitable impact of communality. Narrated in the third person through the lens of one of the main characters, the Maghrebi Ahmad, a member of a minority community at the Pantanella,[16] Melliti's polyphonic novel is a document of the endless forms of interracial tension and collaboration generated in a space marked by multiple histories of migration and threatened by the hostility of exclusionary languages and policies. Through realistic descriptions and dialogues, interspersed with oneiric passages, Melliti captures the conflicts of the dwellers in the definition of their identities as migrant subjects caught between nostalgic emotions, utopian projects, daily fears, and selfish attitudes.

Those sections of the novel where the pre-occupation of and the preoccupation about spaces are central reveal how an experience like the Pantanella affair engaged in unique ways with national history, transnational movements related to migration and colonialism, and visions of change. Mostly, the novel is intent on showing how stories large and small constantly overlap, and despite cultural distances, mobility creates connections, and such connections leave indelible marks. The novel's focus is on stories of immigration in the present, although it interestingly avoids labeling people in terms of national origin thus sketching a global migratory space. All the main characters are defined by experiences of travel and relocation in a web of departures, arrivals, and desires for further movement. The protagonist, Ahmad, is an introverted man who functions as the Pantanella scribe— always jotting down "weird annotations" in his "notebook" (34). Invested with this specific public and historical role, that of the preservation of memory, in a way Ahmad represents the rootless and idealistic intellectual. In the first part of the novel, he is seen painfully reminiscing about his political activity as a young university student, when the "new history" (35), a revolutionary tool to make history from below, was supposed to do away with the codes of repression and silencing managed by the police and government. Indeed, from the very outset, the novel frames itself as a postcolonial text in which the violent legacy of colonialism both numbs and inspires the protagonist as he tries to formulate a working project for the "city." The failure of those past actions at home, which killed his dreams for a better future as well as his beloved girlfriend and political companion, combines with the present difficulties in identifying a successful political course in the Pantanella, given the multiple forces at work within the occupied space.[17] Ahmad's role is therefore that of registering not only the words of reality but also silence, the ineffable, and the incomprehensible, thus defining "spaces of communication that defy the norm" (Burns 374), as in his final cry so reminiscent of Ahmed/Amedeo's howl in Lakhous's *Clash of Civilizations over an Elevator in Piazza Vittorio*.

All the other characters, referred to by name only, are Muslim like Ahmad, although their compliance with religious rules is quite flexible, inserted as they are into a new cultural environment. Aziz is the cynical apolitical atheist with a weakness for alcohol and dancing; Khaled is a young immigrant forced to leave his country, and disappointed by the gloominess of his prospects in the Western world; Mustafa is an "amateurish communist" (41) whose desire to cross the Italian border with no papers, and thus see his wife in Russia, will cost him his life; and Shirkhan, originally from Pakistan, is a deserter from the war against the Soviets in Afghanistan, drafted to fight with the U.S.- and Saudi-supported forces. All of them come from areas that at some point were under the control of European powers, which is why the "city" is also compared to "an old colony" (84) or "medieval colony" (136). While highlighting the colonial matrix of contemporary immigration, *Pantanella* also shows the shifted nature of the postcolonial condition in Italy, which does not constitute the metropole to the former colonies that the immigrants are coming from, but a hybrid colonizer/colonized country, as we will see in their reaction to Italy's simultaneous affinity to their lands and inclusion in the EU. In sharing stories of transnational and local migrations, these men alternate moments of desperation and hope, and they try wholeheartedly to make their dream of a better life come true. Their challenges range from bureaucratic complications—Mustafa has lost his passport and is denied an Italian visa—to lack of economic means, which often result in the decision to resort to illegal or morally questionable means to survive. In both cases, their stories prove how the "other" is profoundly linked to the local milieu. The Pantanella dwellers are not outside elements in a national space, but new presences whose lives are intertwined with local people and places.

Ironically marked by an Italian flag at its entrance (129), the Pantanella is thus a laboratory in which the difficulties and weaknesses of the immigrants are presented in parallel with those of Italians. The easy dichotomies of good versus bad and Italian vs. non-Italian dissolve when systems of exchanges, spaces of "habiting and use" (Lefebvre 182), are looked at closely. Habiting is here linked to the "lived experience" shaped by the *habitus*, the practice of doing and being, not necessarily in permanent ways in terms of dwelling as Heidegger would suggest (Lefebvre 82), but also as a temporary adaptation inserted in a preexisting context and prompted by necessity as the Pantanella was. Interestingly, in this case the occupied factory's activities are not alien to the experience of habiting the city/nation, but are connected to it. In fact, the systems of exchange internal to the Pantanella reveal the porosity of the national system toward incorporating immigrants as cheap labor or as collaborators in underground activities. The Catch-22 situation created by the lack of a job due to the lack of a stay permit that in turn causes the lack of housing is one of the focuses of the novel, which openly illustrates the tenuous condition of these immigrants as well as the traps created by socioeconomic mechanisms. Even more troubling is the widely accepted use of immigrants outside legal norms, so that the (post)capitalist system can preserve its profit margins by exploiting this "excess" labor force, while erasing forms of protection and security for them (Mezzadra 188). For instance, Aziz has experienced harsh forms of exploitation in the tomato fields of the South (87), and Sami, the restaurant owner at the Pantanella, is co-opted by a crooked Italian merchandiser, Mario, who needs an informer to monopolize most of the food market of the "city" at the expense of the previous seller Franco. Khaled's story is even more representative: His work in the cigarette black market leaves his stock vulnerable to informal appropriation by the police, instead of official confiscation and fines. Yet this punishment against destitute immigrants only reduces their ability to improve their condition: Covering the fine and repaying the cigarette provider requires entering into the more lucrative but also infinitely more dangerous drug business, which eventually takes him to prison, a common "home" to immigrants given the absence of a systematic politics of integration.[18] In other words, immigrants in Italy land in a space pre-occupied by informal work practices that by hinging on favorable demand-and-supply mechanisms benefit from this cheap and unprotected labor force. The underground nature of work and residence coupled with the byzantine bureaucracy of the national system and the connivance of the police often keeps the immigrants away from formal recognition with papers, thus producing a domino effect in their increasing social invisibility. As Ahmad bluntly puts it in the novel, the official system reminds them that they "will always be foreigners" (130); while the eternal city, *caput mundi*, welcomes tourists with a warm sense of hospitality, it carefully separates them from immigrants, even when immigrants are visa holders (102).[19]

Pantanella hardly hides the sense of disappointment produced by the shortcomings of this so-called First World: As Khaled confesses in a melancholy moment, "I dreamt of job, money, a better life, but . . ." (21). The myth of Italy as a developed country is contradicted by its "Third World" quality. If, on the one hand, immigrants from the Maghreb feel at home when they arrive in the South, because of the climate and the physical features of the locals, they soon realize that certain Italian towns are less taken care of than their towns of origin: "This city is poorer than my town. I have to leave right away," Khaled comments about Naples (63), oddly echoing Professor Marini in Lakhous's *Clash*, albeit from an inverted perspective. The colonial condition of the Italian South strikes the immigrants as a surprise rather than as a historically explainable status. This condition generates preoccupation among the immigrants as it betrays their "American Dream" in the face of a profound North-South division in Italy that compromises the country's "European" rank in their eyes.

Equally disappointing for the immigrants is the fact that Italy itself has been a point of departure for emigrants or has experienced large flows of northbound migrations within the country itself, a condition that makes the immigrants' prospects even slimmer. As Khaled bluntly puts it, "What am I doing here? Even Italians emigrate to other countries" (62). To unpack these entanglements, Melliti focuses his attention on the neighborhood bar just outside the factory plant, a place where preoccupation is voiced between rounds of beer, and the pre-occupation of stories of Italian internal and international migration soon emerge. The waiter of this hangout, Rosario, is an erstwhile emigrant who came back from Germany after saving some money. His closeness to the immigrants bothers the bar owner, who eventually fires him; her racist stance is made even more preposterous by her questionable business ethics (she overcharges her customers and sells them illegal cigarettes, like Khaled). Yet, Rosario's support is not isolated. In the course of a flashback, Khaled remembers his initial arrival in Italy as a moment full of doubts and anguish, as well as the warm generosity of Teresa, a Sicilian woman managing another local bar. An internal migrant from Catania, Teresa was always willing to help the immigrants: "I am a foreigner myself here" (65), she used to explain upon recalling the years in which she was uselessly waiting for her husband. He had migrated to the United States with the initial intent of sending for her but never did, and she eventually decided to build a life for herself despite countless difficulties.

The recollection of her empathy, along with the experience of Rosario's friendliness and a policeman's support ("maybe a Sicilian," 86) are articulations of possible forms of alliances along diasporic lines that break the trite dichotomies of national versus foreigner or Italian versus non-Italian. Such alliances are for the most part predicated on common forms of geographical displacement, making the Pantanella experience a space pre-occupied with internal and international migrations in and out of Italy preceding the current immigration flows to Italy and yet indistinguishable from them in the social space that the Pantanella and its environs produced. In light of this stratification, the novel represents an even more direct challenge of national tenets than already seen in the initial analysis of the meaning of the Pantanella pasta factory as an Italian symbol. In this sense, as Binetti suggests, the novel is not "other" nor the space it depicts is "other," but both text and space become part of an operation of demystification of the nation's purported homogeneity from within (91 and 100).[20]

Of particular relevance in this denationalizing operation is the new space of production of meaning that, despite the hostility against them, the Pantanella inhabitants define not only for themselves but also in a dialogue with several Italian activists. Even though the police increasingly monitor the building, and there is a known informant constantly spying on the inhabitants, the narrator introduces a variety of characters sincerely involved in helping the immigrants. Among them the most present and beloved are the revolutionary Christian (a priest always available to provide suggestions and services), a sensitive doctor, and Dino, a young volunteer who organizes strikes and street protests (111), in contact with Shirkhan, leader of a large portion of the inhabitants.[21] Through these characters the Pantanella turns into a political arena while simultaneously functioning as a place of economic exchange: The "city" becomes "a true market" (82), and soon restaurants pop up (94) offering both Italian and "ethnic" products (Fig. 14). Other activities that the inhabitants organize more or less officially at the Pantanella include services like a barbershop and a mosque. Such informal businesses are the result of outside pressure as well as need and imagination, and become political because they concern unprotected subjects in an unwelcoming society. In this sense, the immigrants preoccupy the system as their agency challenges its tenets or control measures. In some cases, the "city" provides even better services than the normative institutions: There was no need to go to the immigration office to get information; at the Pantanella one could get it in one's own language or even dialect" (75). Ironically, the Pantanella had to a degree superseded Rome.

The proxemic representation of the inhabitants' experiences in *Pantanella* is not coincidental, as their revolution, while it lasted, was intrinsically linked to space, and in particular a living space. The issue of housing, "one of the black holes" (Brazzoduro 292) of the immigration question in a metropolis like Rome, could only be addressed as an urban issue. Melliti adopts many intriguing images to describe the "city," mingling the sense of possibility it offered along with the anguish it produced. To respond to the deplorable conditions of this "seedy, remote, isolated place outside of the lit area of town" (49)—"the only city in the world without any architectural style and aesthetic sense" (17)—the dwellers sweep the vast space, and later discover water underground (51), all operations that mark improvements. Such efforts are the result of internal organization inspired by the

FIGURE 14. Shop inside a freight elevator, former Pantanella Pasta Factory, Rome, June 1990. Photo by Stefano Montesi.

possibility of creating together, what Lefebvre would have termed "the u-topia" of the thought that comes from the practice in space, as quoted in the incipit of this chapter. Ahmad is the mouthpiece of this conviction: "Let's talk about internal problems. Let's try to solve them in order to eradicate the virus of internal death. Unity is not a fantasy or a catchy phrase, it is an action founded on solid bases and constructive confrontations" (105). Yet, the euphoria of the beginning gives way to the awareness of the deterioration of the building, for the logistical challenges are infinite. No wonder that the city at some point is depicted as "a traveling community, weak and tired, that doesn't even know whether to leave again for a new faraway country" (49), an interesting ship-inspired metaphor for the somewhat ship-shaped Pantanella. The sense of disorientation is so intense that the similitude is also with a "space ship" ready for solar orbit (18): The unanchored nature of immigrant communities affects the perception of this space through images of excessive or risky movement, as that of immigrants in today's world.

Ahmad's rhetoric of unity finds many supporters, but not enough. The inhabitants are split not only by cultural and religious differences (107–8), but also by political agendas: Some of them argue that they should ask for housing, others for visas, still others for jobs (32). It is a vicious circle in which all three things are essential and related to one another, although institutions usually separate them, thus creating these dilemmas even among the most energetic activists. This internal separation, worsened by the presence of many Italian activists of different ideologies ("rightist," "leftist," extremist," "communist," "atheist," 114–15), is detrimental to political action because it undermines the possibility of a strong agenda presented by a cohesive group. The scene gradually becomes bleaker as tensions erupt in open fights and chaotic growth produces constant venues for clashes between protesters, counterprotesters, and rioters (148): "in that sad 'city' there was no form of control to enforce laws" (82). Alliances fail not only among immigrants but especially with the institutions. The Pantanella case becomes an occasion to gather votes or support (as in the mayor's sensationalized visit to the "city," 153), yet no concrete action is taken. Eventually, the "city" becomes the theater of a civil war, a quintessentially preoccupied space, fraught with concerns inside and outside of it.

The final chapter is the stage for the invasion of the city by the police (167): Filled with references to anguish, fear, disorientation, and terror it climaxes in moments of random violence, which mark the explosion of the city. This is when, as Ahmad puts it, "the city sobs" (169). In a passage evocative of biblical destruction with fire and smoke in the background and the enumeration of names of people all shouting "E . . . N . . . O . . . U . . . G . . . H . . ." (172), the Pantanella's experience reaches its apocalyptic end. As the eternal city enclosing it keeps on living, the Pantanella's death sentence is pronounced. Thrown out by the police, the now former dwellers of the former Pantanella factory line up to leave their "home city"; they are suggestively compared to both colonial troops returning to the metropole, in an obviously inverted image of colonialism, and as emigrants with their suitcases and boxes on their heads (169). Both images visually encapsulate the core of the transhistorical and transgeographic perspective proposed by *Pre-Occupied Spaces*, in their embracement of immigration, emigration, and colonialism in the postcolonial era. Interestingly, sociologist Clara Gallini has seen in this shutdown an anti-Muslim operation dictated by Gulf War–related fears. Operation Desert Storm, launched in January 1991, created an enemy outside as well as inside and identified the face of such an enemy as that of a dangerous Muslim terrorist, as part of social mechanisms that have only become more widespread in the following decades leading up to the terrorist attacks in Europe. Gallini further recognizes in the Pantanella's "*sgombero*" (evacuation), the act of cleansing and separation enacted by the power system through coercive means, an event reminiscent of the anti-enemy, and thus anti-immigrant or descendants of immigrants resolution adopted by the U.S. government after Pearl Harbor (Curcio 154). Although Gallini refers only to the internment of the Japanese starting in 1942, omitting a reference to the "secret hi/story" of the internment of Italians, to use Lawrence DiStasi's notable phrase, her parallel identifies spaces and actions in the present that are pre-occupied by past stories of anti-immigrant sentiments and restrictions.[22]

In the end, a space originally marked by production (a factory) was once again turned into a vacuum, marked by the failure of this new vision for habitation: The kingdom of the quintessentially Italian icon, pasta, ended up producing exclusion, thus reversing the usual convivial quality of the image of pasta, so effectively embodied by Calvino's character, Mrs. Phink$_o$ (47), as we have seen in the Introduction of this book. *Pantanella* takes this sense of destruction to an even stronger level by offering the snapshot of Ahmad jumping off a bridge, usually a point of connection over fluid separations, to commit suicide. Anticipated by the reference to the Christlike fate of the protagonist of Nikos Kazantzakis's *Christ Recrucified*, Ahmad's act is literary to a high degree. The very last words of the novel refer not only to Ahmad's inarticulate cry or song ("ENOUGH") but also to a message "for himself or perhaps a friend yet to arrive" (172), which could be identified with the novel *Pantanella* itself. This metatextual moment returns the story to the power of fabulation and preservation of experiences that "are ignored in news discourse, or represented as a threat" (ter Wal 63). The failure of a revolutionary action like occupying the onetime factory in reality makes the writing of it into a political gesture. Ahmad labels his tale/report as a thus far unknown literature (Melliti 136) that only a city like the occupied Pantanella can produce. In this space marked by a geography of mobility Lefebvre's intuition comes through: The human being inhabits not just in pragmatic terms but by maintaining "his relation to the imaginary" (82), which is also the literary output. Burn's conclusions about the novel are particularly cogent as she indeed identifies the novel as a place: "the desire to migrate itself, the concomitant desire to return home, and the desire to tell stories are linked by the common impulse to create a coherent and fully formed other, or alternative, place" (383). Inspired by the history from below, Ahmad's diary/Melliti's novel is an intense and visionary document of diasporic spaces and identities, which despite its unhappy conclusion, offers the space for a dialogue among Italian institutions, immigrants, the media, and groups of volunteers advocating immigrant rights.[23] Unlike the Orchestra of Piazza Vittorio where immigrants interacted as part of a project designed by Italian *engagé* artists, the Pantanella was a project managed by immigrants who collaborated with locals in an attempt to turn hostility into hospitality. Ultimately, the Pantanella occupation suggested "a new epistemology: new words and new glances for new actions and new relations" (Curcio 90) in a transnational space that looked at preoccupation and pre-occupation as an opportunity rather than as a threat.

Spaces of Transnational Production and Reproduction in the Boardinghouse of Mazzucco's Vita

>I want a kiss for every word (Mazzucco).

In ways similar to the occupied factory, the equally dirty, crowded, sexually promiscuous environment of the boardinghouse for immigrants in a tenement of Prince Street in New York's Little Italy at the very turn of the twentieth century exists as a space of production (as well as reproduction) and invention. Mazzucco's *Vita* identifies in the boardinghouse and the tenement and neighborhood around it not only the crossing point of stories of human dislocation/relocation and economic activities related to it, but also of creative fabulation. More specifically, the novel assigns special meaning to the production of words, as we will see. Given the immigrant condition of the characters involved in this production, the process is bilingual and bicultural, like the very experience of relocating overseas. Precisely because this production is a linguistic transition between Italian and English, it functions as a reproduction with a powerful aesthetic value interweaving space and desire within the context of the tenement. In this sense, Lefebvre's observations about inhabiting as a multilayered experience—physical, symbolic, and lyrical at once—will provide a useful interpretive lens. In a manner comparable to Melliti, Mazzucco portrays life in this migrant space by gathering words and stories, and ultimately delivers a document of migration history that with its personal as well as collective relevance questions the nation.

The plot of *Vita* stems from the Mazzucco family's story, but it is not designed as a linear documentary-style reconstruction of facts, since memory, and in particular oral memory, is blurred by time and interpretation. As the narrator/author tells us in the chapter entitled "James Earl Jones's Twin," Mazzucco found some old objects and documents in shoeboxes and then remembered a series of loosely connected tales that her father had in turn heard from his father Diamante who had emigrated to the United States with Vita, a young girl from his own village. During a trip to New York, Mazzucco decided to dig deeper into these tales because she realized that she "didn't have any idea" (44) about her grandfather's adventure in America, which ended when he decided to return to Italy due to an illness and a profound sense of disappointment, thus giving up on both America and Vita at once. Through archival research conducted in New York (Ellis Island and other archives) as well as in Italy (especially Tufo di Minturno in Campania, where her family is from), Mazzucco found a few scattered references to the specific people she was investigating and a plethora of information about the larger context of migration-related struggles around her family's story. Indeed, *Vita* has a much broader significance than a simple genealogical inquiry. As the author stated in an interview, "Behind that daily epos of work, frustration, poverty and dreams, there weren't only my grandfather and Vita, but millions of Italians. This has been a way of providing dignity to those nameless anti-heroes, and truthfulness to literature" (Mazzucco "Intervista").

The novel is recounted along three main narrative timelines: the turn of the century, when Diamante and Vita leave Italy behind to build their new lives in the United States, which stretches for many decades and includes Vita's visit to Italy in the 1950s, after Diamante has come back for good; the wartime phase, when Vita's son is stationed in Italy as a GI and looks for traces of her family's origin; and the phase of the novel's genesis, which makes the writer into one of the novel's characters to a degree. As Mazzucco adds in the same interview, the nonlinear structure of the story reflects the ways in which she herself as the author often encountered names, places, and facts and, consequently, decided to share the story in the same roundabout way. In fact, the transatlantic voyage, which chronologically precedes the arrival, is included in the last chapter of the novel. The first part instead opens with the landing at Ellis Island, after a brief flashforward to World War II. Vita and Diamante travel on the same ship with no family or friends, at the very young ages of nine and twelve respectively (8). Diamante is sent away to relieve his dreadfully poor family, and Vita is sent by her mother Dionisia to join her husband, Agnello, Vita's father. In a novel heavily populated with characters and extras, it is no coincidence that Vita and Diamante arrive at Ellis Island on April 12, 1903, the day of the highest peak of inbound flow (over twelve thousand people arrived from all over the world on that day): The protagonists' story is not an isolated one, Mazzucco suggests; it becomes symbolic of an experience that she closely follows especially in the urban spaces of their destination.

In *Vita*, spatialization grounds and propels the storytelling. This process involves the city at large, the neighborhood, and the residential space. From the very outset, through a strongly sensorial descriptive mode that renders space through images, smells, tastes, touches and sounds, Mazzucco is able to offer a powerful gallery of crucial places in early 1900s New York through the eyes of two recently disembarked foreign children. These include a series of overcrowded halls at Ellis Island (19), skyscrapers that "tickle the clouds" (29), busy streets that are dangerous to cross (23), scintillating stores full of elegant merchandise (33), an elevator that Diamante calls the "box room" that flies into the sky (33), and a construction site (34) turned into a home where a squatting organ grinder offers a shelter to these newly arrived children in exchange, unbeknownst to them, for all their belongings, which he steals while they sleep. Yet, the space that strikes the reader from the start for its intense condensation of stories is the boardinghouse in the tenement at 18 Prince Street, in the heart of Little Italy. It was meant to be Vita's and Diamante's immediate destination after they landed, but since Vita's father, Agnello, is nowhere to be seen at Battery Park when they arrive, they wander the city and are exposed to all the aforementioned spaces before reaching the "tenement ghetto" where they will live.

Despite the noble name of the street where it is located, the neighborhood reflects a social situation that is far from princely: "the street is clogged with carts of all sizes"; "there are beggars . . . naked children wandering amid heaps of garbage . . . and the rather disturbing exotic fauna" (23). Mazzucco's rendition of this urban environment is interestingly denunciatory as the famous shots by Jacob Riis and his contemporary photographers had meant to be. Yet, Mazzucco remains sensitive to the complexity of the environment and its people; even though the immigrants' separation from the rich part of town is clearly demarcated, with Houston Street being the northern border of the ghetto that immigrants do not trespass (33), they are not depicted as "the other half," and their lives are much more nuanced and interesting than a static picture of social malaise would convey.[24] Undoubtedly, in *Vita* the Italian Lower East Side comes across as a place replete with dirt, illness, poverty, and abuse; yet, Mazzucco never fails to reveal the lyrical fragility of the characters, their ability to dream and to be moved, their remarkable resilience, and their idiosyncratic ways of bonding and providing mutual assistance even after hurting or damaging each other. In part, these networks of support were dictated by places of origin. The immigrant population tended to gravitate toward people of the same area, so that aggregations based on village, city, and region were recognizable, as the studies by Baily and Gabaccia show.[25] While a certain mingling across national borders takes place in the neighborhood of *Vita*, Mazzucco's tenement shows a strong prevalence of Italian presence.[26] Unlike Melliti's occupied factory in Rome and Pariani's *conventillo* in Buenos Aires, which are truly mixed immigrant spaces in terms of nationality, the diversity of Mazzucco's immigrant space is driven by regional variety. The tenement turns into an Italian microcosm, filled with tensions due to linguistic and cultural differences—tenants speak "different dialects and at times incomprehensibly" (13)—as well as budding relationships based on commonalities. In other words, the tenement functions as a dislocated national environment in the transnational space of the country's diaspora to the United States.

The tenement was the typical housing solution for poor immigrants in New York. As Dolkart explains in his *Biography of a Tenement House in New York City*, while the term was officially introduced in 1867, the first housing of this sort was introduced in the 1840s when single-family houses were adapted to dwellings for several families or were built for them following a model that did not favor amenities (16). The great influx of immigrants starting from the 1840s and continuing for decades prompted owners to rent less space for less money to more tenants. This claustrophobic space was soon identified as the root cause of the terrible living conditions in the tenements. Reports from the 1840s refer to poor ventilation and lighting, lack of proper heating and water supply, an inadequate toilet and sewage system, and the by now infamous overcrowding. In the early twentieth century, as Dolkart remarks, reports were denouncing the same issues (15). While the section of the novel *Vita* under discussion here technically takes place after the 1901 Tenement House Act, which included several provisions for betterment of the structure and management of tenements, it shows how such provisions "did not radically improve conditions" due to the owners' resistance (Dolkart 80) and the tenants' persistent ability to endure difficult circumstances. Apartments were often 300–350 square feet, and tenants stuffed them to the brim with their possessions. A tenement dwelling was usually made up of a kitchen/entrance room, a tiny bedroom, and a parlor/living room, often referred to as the front room, since it was the only one with a window; tenants filled them up with people, since "every room could be used as a bedroom" (52). The apartment *Vita* depicts, in the "blackened, run-down and decrepit" (13) Prince Street building, follows this model, and its adaptation to a boardinghouse makes it particularly messy:

> The house on Prince Street is crammed full of pans, bowls, tubs, sacks of flour, barrels, and trunks . . . wooden cages with plump clucking chickens and a pot of half-dead basil . . . damp undershirts, sheets, and socks dangling precariously from wires that slice up the room . . . a double bed behind a screen in what seems to be a kitchen . . . there are cots everywhere, in front of the stove, behind every curtain, bend, and trunk. (15–16)

When Diamante reaches the apartment, he counts fourteen men and one woman. Eventually both Vita and he himself will live there, seventeen people in three jam-packed rooms.

In a typical Lefebvrian mode, the boardinghouse represents "the practice of habiting and use" in the sense of economic use (Lefebvre 182). It was a common housing solution in the era of mass emigration, when a large number of young male workers were in need of housing (Fig. 15) but could afford only a sleeping spot in a family apartment where food, cleaning, and washing were included in the rent. As Baily reminds us: "About a fifth of the Italian immigrant households in New York City had boarders and lodgers" up to World War I (107). The boardinghouse was the opening up of a family apartment to family members, acquaintances, or co-workers. The resulting living conditions were appalling not only to the parochial views of the American reformers who found these places to be "primitive" like its inhabitants (Mazzucco, *Vita* 106–108), but also to the boarders themselves, who are aware of the discomfort of their lives as much as they are of the lack of alternatives, especially right after their arrival. In the novel the boardinghouse is ironically presented as owned by a "rich" immigrant (16, 50): Agnello seems to have achieved a solid financial position in working for railway construction as a labor contractor and supervisor, which has allowed him to buy a food store. The boardinghouse is another source

FIGURE 15. *Lodgers in Bayard Street Tenement, Five Cents a Spot, 1889.* Photo by Jacob A. Riis.

of income for Agnello; the living conditions of the place hardly speak of a solid economic position even by immigrant standards, yet they show the Italian families' willingness to "accept crowded living accommodations . . . to make ends meet and to save" (Baily 100). What is relevant to this analysis is the shift of a residential space to a space of production with the adaptation of domestic chores into paid services, which nonpaying tenants such as the young men in the family also enjoy. In reality, this economic production remains unpaid for the actual laborers, who are practically reduced to a condition of serfdom. Unsurprisingly, the uncompensated domestic work is performed by women, who in this way "remain at home and still contribute to the family budget" (Baily 107), yet only for the benefit of the male owner/manager who collects the rent. While the Pantanella brought together in an overcrowded space only male inhabitants who volunteer their labor to clean and arrange the abandoned factory and also offer paid services as food sellers and the like, the boardinghouse presents a mixture of men and women, with the former representing a clear majority. The gallery of male figures includes a wide palette: Geremia is Diamante's cousin and works as a laborer; Rocco, a heavyset man who uses his hands more than his brain, is involved in illegal activities; Nicola Coca-Cola is Vita's brother, although he joined his father in the United States when she was young, and she barely knows him. The only two women in the apartment are Lena, Agnello's undeclared partner, and Vita. Even though she is so small that she cannot reach the pot to cook the pasta (26), Vita is sent to New York from Minturno with the clear function of helping a weakening Lena.

The boardinghouse is a further hybrid between the domestic space and the space of production since it regularly turns into a factory, as was common in that era. In an anthropomorphic twist, Mazzucco describes the entire tenement as a "factory of sweat," a word that in Italian is a metaphor and not a technical term as in the English translation, "sweatshop" (107). Clothing, cigars, artificial flowers, mattresses, and other products were produced in the tenements' apartments (Dolkart 54). Lena and Vita work as artificial rose makers for many hours a day and a miserable pay: 720 flowers had to be completed to make one dollar, which is why Mazzucco calls them fake roses "devoid of scent, devoid of beauty" even though they "bloomed" fast thanks to the women's manual dexterity (108). The combination of the two sets of chores (domestic for boarders and manufacturing for factories) turns the women's lives into perpetual work commitments. When the men return from the factory, the construction site, or the street, the women serve them dinner; then the women return to making flowers after the meal (Fig. 16). For Lena there is a third shift: As Agnello's partner—even though he is supposedly still married to Vita's mother Dionisia, who never joined him from Minturno—she has sexual obligations to fulfill as well. In the course of the story, the reader learns that Lena was a prostitute Agnello met in Chicago and took with him despite her desperate status, in part because there was something irresistibly exotic about her, and in part because he needed a partner for his family and business projects in America. Yet, Lena actually provides enjoyment to several men; in the promiscuous environment of the boardinghouse, Rocco as well as Diamante become Lena's lovers, except that this "service" of hers, like the domestic one, remains unpaid.

The intersection of domestic (unpaid) labor, sexual (unpaid) labor, and industrial (poorly paid) labor at home makes the boardinghouse into a space of production hyperoccupied by work, while the secretive sexual activity at night makes it into a space of potential reproduction. Lena's unexpected pregnancy and later (self-induced) abortion is an intense narrative thread of the novel that produces some of the most powerful scenes in it: On the one hand, the collective moment of female support in the tenement for a moribund Lena whose bleeding could be fatal, and on the other, the theatrical funeral that Vita, Diamante, Rocco, Geremia, and Coca-Cola decide to give to the fetus. "The American brother," as they call him, is the protagonist of a sacred ritual in which the young generation of the household takes the fetus to the top of the still-under-construction *New York Times* building in order to burn the "brother" and let the ashes ascend to the stars, since no cemetery would take it. The illicit nature of the act coupled with the high danger associated with it makes this suspenseful scene particularly effective; its subtheme further adds to its symbolic meaning. As the seat of the English-language newspaper par excellence, a paper that often published critical articles against Italian immigrants, seeing them as criminals, this in-progress tower embodies a non-Italian space that these young Italian immigrants appropriate as an act of "delinquency" against the social norm that excludes them. Reaching the top of the *New York Times* building and performing such a daring act on the border

Figure 16. "Mortaria family, 8 Downing Street, New York, making flower wreaths, 1912." Photo by Lewis W. Hine.

between life and death makes its protagonists into creative agents that, albeit only ritualistically, conquer the city: "The American brother will look out over the city and spit on it" (77) is their own interpretation of the act.

The entire novel is characterized by moments in which the immigrants reinterpret space using the scanty resources available to them to fight the exclusion imposed on them by the system. As Lefebvre suggests, inhabiting has the quality of turning into "an exploration of the possible" in relation to the imaginary. In the very tenement that has witnessed the denial of reproduction due to lack of means—Lena cannot afford a child physically or economically, especially if Agnello is not the undisputed father—Mazzucco places other modes of reproduction that hinge on words. In the economy of the novel, words acquire different roles: They are an occasion for formal entertainment, vehicles of information, instruments for opportunities, and secretive objects of desire and loyalty. As for formal entertainment, words really constitute lyrics, and in particular the lyrics of operas that immigrants listened to thanks to the introduction of a device that marked a technological revolution in the reproduction of culture.

In a lyrical section of the first part of the novel, Mazzucco deftly inserts this device as if it were another character, so to speak: a gramophone reproducing the words sung by popular artists such as Enrico Caruso. Upon hearing Enrico Caruso's voice traveling throughout the tenement, Vita thinks that the singer is actually visiting in order to look for her, "to collect his daughter" (56). Indeed, out of spite against Agnello, she prefers to believe that she is Enrico Caruso's daughter instead. Only when she reaches the source of the music and the words does she realize Caruso is not there and that he "is hidden in the trumpet . . . on a black plate where an angel etches the disc with the feather from one of his wings" (56). Vita is thus introduced to the phonograph, a mechanical device that reproduces reality and as such is wrapped in a magical aura. Albeit brief, this scene in the novel is important for two reasons at once: It points to the accessibility of "high" culture (opera in this case) at all levels of the social ladder thanks to a technological advancement that the immigrants discover in the "New World." *Vita*'s characters have to steal the gramophone, given their limited economic means, but elsewhere the gramophone added new customers from immigrant groups through installment plans offered by the companies and the informal practice of sharing records among buyers. At the same time, the phonograph created a whole new market by making immigrants into specific consumers of targeted music and plays/skits on vinyl, as Kenney has shown in his study of what were called "'ethnic' recordings" (67). Interestingly, the repertoire offered to the immigrants "ascribed a unified musical nationalism upon the village and regional musical traditions of immigrants" (Kenney 66). The unforeseen result of these recordings for foreigners is that regional immigrants become national in the international space of emigration. In the case of Italians, opera becomes a shared legacy in the quintessential immigrant space of the New York City tenement.

The gramophone scene is also relevant as it complements the mode of economic production so typical of the tenement with the mode of leisure, of "useless" reproduction of music in this case. This image of the tenement as a space where tenants enjoy moments of pleasure defies popular reports whose view often dehumanized tenants. Mazzucco is instead keen on restoring her immigrant characters to a condition that also embraces culture. Diamante's announcement—"from now on in this house there'll be music all day long" (56)—speaks of the aesthetic reappropriation of space toward the production of pleasure in an otherwise unwelcoming environment like the shabby tenement. What Lombardi-Diop has argued about the inventive use of residential space by immigrants in Rome is applicable to this passage in *Vita*: "Within the hegemonic and inhospitable host space, such operations of creative consumption of places . . . represent tactical reactions to . . . marginalization and exclusion" (409) and produce a "sense of closeness and solidarity . . . through a lived practice of space" (Lombardi-Diop, "Roma" 417).

Words are also part of the production of information, a space that in the novel is identified with the circulation of Italian papers in Little Italy. For Diamante, who sells one of these papers, the *Araldo*, in the streets, this is also a space of knowledge production. Thanks to his reading skills, which he acquired in Italy, dialect-only-speaking Diamante becomes fluent in Italian. He reads the newspaper for himself but also reads it aloud to the Italian workers in exchange for free beer (65), thus both becoming well informed about the news and expanding his vocabulary. In Mazzucco's clever narrative twist, the regional and the national meld in the transnational space of the immigrant neighborhood. Yet, Diamante perceives this newly acquired Italy-focused knowledge as limited since it is just national. He needs to learn English in order not to be excluded in the international destination of his emigration: "The *New York Times* rebuffs him with pages carpeted in unknown words" (77). Diamante is not alone in this condition. Many immigrants did not know English and were illiterate even in Italian, which made the managers of Italian papers such as the *Araldo* complain about the low circulation of the paper in the community (62). While their dialects were often sufficient in work and living spaces, the lack of English-language skills historically relegated the Italians to the lower ranks of the broader society for an extended period. Mazzucco is clearly aware of the racial debate of those years; in the novel, she quotes the words of a doctor at the Bellevue Hospital she herself met during her visit in New York. As "the most pitiful ethnic minority in the city . . . [Italians] 'were like blacks who couldn't even speak English'" (41), she says in a statement that vividly renders the degree of exclusion and suffering of Italians in the United States.

Precisely because the knowledge of Italian words is insufficient to make it in the United States and the acquisition of the local language is difficult for young boys who are forced to work to live and support the family in Italy, Diamante is jealous of Vita's opportunity to go to school, which she is compelled to attend by the social workers despite her open reluctance. She will end up in having "something no other woman in the neighborhood had: words." Eager to acquire words in the new language, Diamante begs Vita to teach him these words, "the first step to give a name to things" (117). Yet, the dispensation of words does not come as a one-directional sharing, but is inserted in an interesting mechanism of exchange in which words are the secretive object of desire and loyalty. Vita and Diamante seal a pact by which she teaches him an English word in exchange for a kiss:

> "If you learn American, will you teach me?" Diamante said all of a sudden. "What will you give me?" Vita answered back, disappointed he wasn't more sympathetic. "I'll tell you about the knights" he proposed. "I already know about them." . . . He did not know what would convince a stubborn little girl . . . Money? He didn't have enough. Presents? He had already given her plenty. Attention? Between his new job and new friends he didn't have much time for her. . . . "A kiss." Vita burst out all of a sudden. "What's gotten into you?" Diamante was flabbergasted . . . "I want a kiss for every word." (116–17)

This word-kiss exchange operation, which gives a poetic spin to an only apparently commercial interaction, reflects an intercultural and incipient sexual discovery and ultimately identifies fabulative reproduction as the infrastructure of the novel. In the space of pseudo-innocent exchanges between the two young protagonists of the novel, the words are disarmingly simple and essential to describe their world: "job, train, bed, fire, water, earth, hearth, hurt, hope . . . butchery . . . elevated . . . help, work, cry . . . kill, live, pray" (117). Their secret affair coalesces the double function of lips—speaking and kissing—in a dance between Logos and Eros that interestingly happens on the roof of the tenement. Comparable to the famous attic space that phenomenologist Gaston Bachelard in his 1958 book

The Poetics of Space associates to a dreamscape of rationality (17), the tenement's roof is the space that the young protagonists enter in order to acquire the tools that over time may potentially help them exit their current condition of subjugation. Bachelard's poetic view of the vertical house as a receptacle of dreams, memories, and desires has been repeatedly challenged by critics who underscore how the house is often an environment for abuse and repression: Diamante's and Vita's tenement house, despite its verticality, is indeed this latter type of environment.

In the diegetic space of the novel, the exchange of words and kisses happening on the roof is violently interrupted as a matter of fact: Agnello suspects that Vita is hiding something from him and asks a miserable street urchin, Cicchitto, to spy on them. Found on the roof terrace at night exactly at that point when two kisses are exchanged for the words "boy" and "girl" (125), Vita is brutally beaten by Agnello. Locked in a rabbit's crate for hours in the scorching sun on that very roof that was supposed to provide some initial form of liberation to her, Vita will be separated from Diamante, and her dream of escape will temporarily come to a halt. Eventually, she will be able to leave the boardinghouse and the tenement behind, thanks also to the level of education she has achieved, and build a rich personal and professional life marked by a high degree of autonomy. While the novel is not intent in weaving a tale of success for this immigrant woman, her story stands out as unusual, since women's immigrant tales are even less known.

It is precisely this process of unearthing and sharing the story in the extradiegetic space of the novel that further emphasizes the value of words for Mazzucco. Inevitably prompted and/or enhanced by images, traces, and documents, the story's reconstruction turns into an investigation, as Mazzucco has called her research and writing process (Melania, "Intervista"). Like any investigation, it entails extratextual elements that Mazzucco decides to include in the novel. In the same vein of Sebald's 1992 *The Emigrants*, she includes unlabeled visuals without an explicit illustrative purpose, simply as a complement to memories: a postcard of Minturno, the shot of a ship, the drawing of a black hand, reproductions of fingerprints and identity cards, and so forth. Through this delicately interwoven archive of images, the reader is exposed to the nonlinear workings of recollection. Yet, despite these visual interpolations, *Vita* does not embrace any daring experimental mode, even if it resorts to complex flashbacks and flashforwards, the frequent use of dialect or "Italglish" words, and its inclusion of quotations from supposedly real documents. It is instead its intrepid challenge to the national archive that turns the book into an experiment: The story is almost uninterruptedly told from the point of view of emigrants, and in particular emigrant children (in this sense close to Pariani's narrative choice) and emigrant women, for whom she claims a different space.[27] As one of her characters states in *Vita*, "only what gets told is true" (7). This urge to fabulate is not just a personal urge, but it becomes almost a moral imperative. The more Mazzucco archeologically unearths the story of her family, the more she realizes that she is writing a collective story, built on tiny fleeting elements in the absence of large archives, bulky literary texts, or famous monuments. As she stated in an interview published in *La Repubblica*, "for us the only legacy of that American Dream was made up of words. We had nothing else, but they are a rich trove. For me it was like closing the circle" (Mazzucco "Melania e il mondo"). The process of recollection entailed in the book is thus a gesture that counterbalances the Italians' "congenital diffidence about remembering, eternity, and the universal, or maybe to ward off bad luck" (Mazzucco, *Vita* 91).

In opening these lesser-known archives, Mazzucco complicates this understanding through a hybrid technique that rewrites the center through the margins. Her mixing of history and fiction marks a new approach toward the past that is meant to remember the forgotten, that is, the legacy of emigration in Italy. The fact that the ancestors who left Italy were often very poor made Italian families identify in amnesia the only way to eliminate the stigma; this way, "the memory of departures sunk into oblivion" (Nicotra 369). *Vita* is thus a plea for memory against amnesia, as the epigraph to this section highlights. Ironically, in the novel, the person who forgets, or rather remembers selectively, is Diamante, who eventually leaves the United States and brings with him not his beloved Vita, who has in the meantime chosen to stay, but "words—they will be his only baggage, the only wealth he takes with him from America" (410), since his dreams have not come true in the new land. Those words will get eroded over time, and the holes left in the net will prompt Melania the writer to rebuild the story, in particular from the perspective of the person she finds hardly any information about, Vita. If in "Seval," Mazzucco's first acclaimed piece, a short story about a Turkish woman who moves to Italy, the female migrant is portrayed as silent—"she would never say anything" (76)—and eventually condemned by the normative system to eternal silence because she is an outsider, in *Vita* the female voice leads the story. In this sense, not only is Mazzucco bearing witness to the story of Italian demographic dispersion, but she is also doing so through the specific lens of an anonymous woman who starts her American adventure in a poor boardinghouse and to whom she assigns the task of embodying the national and transnational experience of Italians abroad.

Vita is much more than a novel set in a boardinghouse catering to Italian immigrants abroad. Yet, for the purpose of this book, the boardinghouse is a particularly cogent space of social preoccupation whose echoes will be found in the contemporary Italian domestic space, as we will see in Chapter 6. Today's kitchens are thus pre-occupied by these tenement stories. The boardinghouse and by extension the tenement that condensed modes of economic production and aesthetic reproduction for Italian immigrants at the turn of the twentieth century represent yet another occasion to reflect on the preoccupation generated by the immigrant condition as well as the opportunities it granted in the residential space. By bringing together "home" and "language," and thus joining urban realities and discourse, *Vita* confirms Lefebvre's profound intuition that "the human being cannot do anything but inhabit as poet" (82). In the same passage, he adds that if the human being is not given "the possibility of inhabiting poetically or inventing a poetry, he will create it as best he can." The boardinghouse of *Vita* certainly reflects this need and the related reproduction of words in both the intradiegetic and the extradiegetic dimension of the story. It is the simple location of this production—the boardinghouse and the tenement—that enhances its spatial quality; "even the most derisive everyday existence retains a trace of grandeur and spontaneity," Lefebvre adds (82). What Lefebvre is not contemplating is that home and language in the case of immigrants are inescapably double. The new home is pre-occupied by the old, just as the new language is pre-occupied by the old one. It is in this tension that a new poetry and a new space are created to defy preoccupation and design possibility via transnational exchanges.

PART THREE

Workplaces: A Creative Re-Occupation of Labor Spaces against Exploitation

APERTURE III

Labor on the Move: Rodari's Construction Workers and Kuruvilla's Babysitter

This Aperture and Part III at large address yet another area in which Italian emigration stories furnish tools to decrease and possibly reverse preoccupation about current immigration in Italy, as a reality pre-occupied by emigration. After looking at the experiences of traveling to and residing in new environments, the attention will now be turned to working in those new environments. Occupation, which is coincidentally contained in the term pre-occupation, is the key word of Part III. While the term has already appeared in another meaning, squatting and taking over a space (Chapter 4), here it refers to work, and specifically construction and domestic work. Emigrants and immigrants have historically entered a number of different job sectors, yet some occupations have been particularly accessible to them based on the low level of skills they apparently require. Among these, construction work and domestic work are some of the most common jobs secured by immigrants in many parts of the world; strongly defined by gender (construction work for men and domestic work for women), these two occupations represent the dominant pathway into Italian society for many immigrants today, the same way they were for Italian emigrants abroad in the past. The representation of the two sectors and their workers in cultural texts reveals common elements across time and space as these experiences can be probed in terms of desires, fears, expectations, struggles, and so on. Each of the chapters in Part III deals with one of the two sectors by providing a socioeconomic background to both the condition of Italian emigrants abroad and foreign immigrants in Italy. In particular, Chapter 5 offers the analysis of François Cavanna's 1978 novel *Les Ritals* and Mariana Adascalitei's novella "Il giorno di San Nicola" (St. Nicholas's Day) about the plight and creativity of migrant construction workers, while Chapter 6 brings together Renata Ciaravino's script for the 2005 play *Alexandria*, directed by Franco Però, and Gabriella Ghermandi's short story "The Story of Woizero Bekelech and Signor Antonio," about the invisible struggles and achievements of migrant domestic workers. The differences between past emigrant workers and contemporary immigrant workers are superseded by a range of commonalities showing that these occupations are today occupied with similar stories of work-based relationships and projects belonging to the past. A combined reading thus reinforces the need to examine these experiences from multiple perspectives in order to avoid trite perceptions of migrant workers and to foster more layered conceptualizations of nation building as well as family expansion hinging on what I am calling here labor on the move.

This Aperture anticipates the analysis of more complex texts in the two chapters by addressing the themes under discussion through children's literature. This genre constitutes a natural space for the development and distribution of stories mostly because the presence of immigrant children in the Italian school system has only soared, and materials to address this changed cultural landscape have become necessary for both the curriculum and private reading at home. Written by both immigrants and "locals," published by a vast array of publishing houses—specialized and established at large alike—and addressing both immigrant and nonimmigrant readerships, these books have multiplied over the past decade.[1] Despite the risk of oversimplification intrinsic to the genre, publications for children distill reality into its essentials and prompt straightforward questions about our place in the world. When they are not afraid of denouncing or challenging the norm, thus avoiding simplistic good-heartedness and trite stereotypes, books in this genre succeed in denouncing or unmasking, as is the case of the texts chosen for this Aperture: two nursery rhymes by Gianni Rodari,[2] "Case e palazzi" (Houses and palaces) and "Il muratore della Valtellina" (The bricklayer from Valtellina), and an illustrated book for children, *Questa non è una baby sitter* (This is not a babysitter), by Gabriella Kuruvilla.[3] The texts chosen contain in a nutshell some of the strident contradictions inherent in these jobs and openly question issues of national belonging. The protagonists give voice to the perspective of immigrants in cultural texts that afford them a new dignity through the devices of the inversion/paradox and deception, thus challenging commonsensical views.

In the nursery rhyme "Houses and Palaces" included in the volume *Favole al telefono* (Fairytales on the telephone, 1962), Gianni Rodari addresses themes of migration history with his usual incisive candor.[4] The piece recounts a meeting between an old bricklayer and an unidentified narrator who tells the story in the first person. The nursery rhyme develops around a recurring pattern in which the bricklayer asks the narrator if he has visited a series of places ranging from Paris to the Americas, from Australia to Berlin, and from Algiers to Cairo. The latter replies "Yes," but it is not his visits that are the focus of the conversation: It is instead the memories that the bricklayer has kept of the places mentioned. His recollections are completely based on his work, and in particular on how his labor, as a helper first and a bricklayer later contributed to the growth of the places where he lived as a temporary worker: a beautiful palace on the Seine River in Paris; flag-topped houses and skyscrapers in the Americas; a private villa in Berlin; always "solid beautiful houses" (295) with straight walls and waterproof roofs.[5] The narrator interrupts the enumeration of places and projects and takes it to a conclusion by making the exchange of information more personal: "You have built quite a few houses . . . around the world . . . but what about yours?" To which inquiry the bricklayer sadly replies: "I have built houses for others and remained without one myself. I live in the old people's home. That's the way the world works." The narrator empathizes with him, but situates the bricklayer's fatalism in a frame of reclaiming justice: "Yes, that's the way the world works, but it is not fair" (296).

In "The Bricklayer from Valtellina," Rodari revisits the paradoxical condition of the emigrant construction laborer who is a victim of historical irony. This time, it is not the lack of dwelling that makes his condition absurd but his entrapment in it. The protagonist, Mario, originally from the northern valley of the title, leaves Lombardy for Germany in search of work.[6] Despite his strength and forward-looking attitude—he dreams of working and saving hard in order to return to his fiancé in Italy—he meets an ironic end, or rather an ironic beginning. In the collapse of a bridge on the construction site, he falls into the cement flow and remains pinned to the building he was helping erect.[7] The peculiarity of Mario's experience is that, ensnared inside a pillar, he can still see the activity around him; not only does he witness the completion of the construction project, but also the life of the tenants who eventually move in. He "spies" on their daily routines and shares their feelings. By an unexpected turn at the story's ending, it is the war that makes him die for real: If the first time he was embalmed at work, the second he definitively disappears due to a bomb explosion. The same way he had become an intrinsic part of the life of the building, he partakes in its demise.

For the purpose of this Aperture, what is interesting in these two nursery rhymes is the inversion of the drive lying behind edification: Rather than building, a forward action by definition, these construction workers are left empty-handed or destroyed in the process. They are occupied in the building sector or occupy its projects, albeit inadvertently in the latter case, but building is ultimately a source of preoccupation for them. Through simple narrative figures such as the paradox and the inversion, Rodari effectively points to two common conditions for laborers in this sector: struggling economic conditions that leave them "homeless" despite their hard work, and dangerous workplaces that jeopardize their safety and in some cases even their lives.

These nursery rhymes serve as anecdotal texts to address other issues that are central to Chapter 5, i.e., the complex relationship between nation building and national roots in the scenario of transnational labor. Rodari's ability to steer clear of the easy celebration of his compatriots as well as of the pathos normally embedded in the tragic experience of these unnamed bricklayers foregrounds a reflection on the flexibility of cultural affiliations and the need for protection of the subjects involved when labor is on the move. Through these two texts, Rodari is also defining alternative maps of traveling and living spaces. Unlike visitors, immigrant laborers affect the foreign countries as much as they are affected by them, even if their migration is temporary. With their disarmingly simple style, Rodari's writings aim at revealing the international contribution of laborers as a counterpoint to the more common amnesia about their existence and their work. In his footsteps,

Chapter 5 brings attention to the experience of Italian construction workers around the world. In providing an introduction of a socioeconomic nature to the presence of Italians in this sector, the chapter recontextualizes the act of building to both afford it dignity and invest it with creative power through, on the one hand, Cavanna's autobiographical novel, which recounts the toil and inventiveness of Italian construction workers in France, and, on the other, Mariana Adascalitei's unpublished novella about the invisible world of undocumented immigrant construction workers from Romania who are exploited in Italy by their own compatriots as well as by Italians.

The anonymous nature of construction labor, which often produces tangible if not outstanding and famous results in architectural terms but leaves the actual builders unrecognized, is paralleled by the invisible nature of domestic work. Carried out within the walls of apartments and houses, and traditionally by women, this labor tends to be particularly hidden because in the first place it is not fully recognized as a job. Usually associated with wives, mothers, grandmothers, daughters, and so forth whose contribution to the family was identified through unpaid domestic chores, this sector is female par excellence and often feminizes men who carry it out in lieu of women. In industrial and (post)industrial societies, laborers from other regions and countries, read outsiders, have cyclically been offered jobs as cleaners, cooks, nannies, and the like, all positions that ironically bring the "alien" into the most intimate spaces of the family. This contradiction becomes particularly strident with two figures, the wet nurse and the elderly caretaker, whose relationship with fragile family members are so body-centric that the perception of immigrants as "others" becomes questionable.

These issues will be further addressed in Chapter 6, which connects two interesting aspects of domestic labor on the move: Renata Ciaravino's play recollects the practically unknown story of women from the Friuli region who in the early 1900s emigrated to the cosmopolitan city of Alexandria in Egypt in order to work as wet nurses or maids. By a fascinating simultaneous reversal, Italian families in the colonies hired local women for domestic chores, and in some cases they decided to take them to Italy upon their return. Gabriella Ghermandi's text, which can be considered as an independent story within her 2007 novel *Queen of Flowers and Pearls*, gently explores the pre-occupation of domestic work in Italy today side by side with the history of an often repressed or misinterpreted colonialism. Read in tandem, the two texts shed light on an important chapter of Italian emigration, that is female emigration, characterized by a dynamic interplay between stigma and emancipation for these women, in ways that are reminiscent of Vita's experience in Mazzucco's novel analyzed in Chapter 4. Today's immigrant domestic work exposes similar alternations of control and agency, albeit within family environments that tend to control the workers' time, space, and ultimately individuality.

The piece chosen here to introduce the later in-depth discussion of these issues in Chapter 6 is *Questa non è una baby-sitter*, written in 2010 by Gabriella Kuruvilla and illustrated by Gabriella Giandelli. Unlike works in which immigrants are elder caretakers, nannies, and domestic workers and speak about their experience of marginalization, Kuruvilla's book focuses on a woman who is not a babysitter but is taken for one just because of the color of her skin and her attire. Based on a real incident in which Kuruvilla was asked whether she was the babysitter of her son, a fair-skinned child with light eyes, the story revolves around the concept of perceptions and misperceptions. In this specific case, the confusion is born out of the rooted idea that immigrants and especially immigrants of color are part of the society as service providers. The lack of awareness about their private lives, heightened by the lack of a visual language to understand "difference" in broad terms, prompts among the "locals" inferences about social roles that are effectively defined by external appearance: A dark-skinned woman is categorized as a babysitter before being conceptualized as a mother. The theme of people's response to physical traits, and in particular skin color, is a running thread throughout Kuruvilla's work and a theme that she often addresses in public interviews. *Questa non è una baby-sitter* allows the writer to explore the theme not in theoretical terms but through visual means and through one of the typical modes of children's narrative: deduction by comparison. Essential, yet nonetheless incisive, this mode offers the author the opportunity to work on basic shapes and elements of everyday life to prove how external looks can be deceptive, since they are often subject to existing preconceptions.

A series of images presented in the fashion of a primer opens the book. Each image is first shown for what it is *not* and then labeled for what it is (a spoon turns out to be a ladle, a ladder a bookshelf, a washing machine a camera, a circle an oval). Hinging on the negation of the first impression, the format borrows from René Magritte's famous painting *The Treachery of Images*, yet it veers its semiotic play toward explanation and comprehension rather than the separation of signifier and signified. The series invites the reader to overcome the superficial reaction fostered by deception and to look closer to gain better understanding. The last image of the series is the portrait of a dark-skinned woman with blue hair, a nose ring, and a yellow hairband—the line underneath the drawing vividly concludes: "This is not a baby-sitter: it is a mom." The rest of the book unravels the context around this final statement by backpedaling to the situation that provoked it. Interestingly, it does not just show the prejudice of Italians toward immigrants or descendants of immigrants—a young girl cannot imagine a mother called Ashima—but it also probes the mechanisms of deception and consequential exclusion perpetrated by, in this case, children of immigrant descendants. Ashima's son discriminates against a Chinese classmate of his, Ginko, as well as a Sicilian one, Salvatore, because they speak a "strange" language he cannot understand. The overall message of the book—advocated by the mother—is one of exchange and encounter. All the classmates, including Ginko and Salvatore, are invited to play at her family's house. Once there, the game they choose is that of drawing objects that look like what they are not, as in the primer-like opening. The story thus loops back to the beginning, and its core message is reinforced in the end when Ashima's son confirms she is not his babysitter, but his mom with both her virtues and shortcomings.

The space defined by *Questa non è una baby-sitter* is both pre-occupied by a notion of domestic work linked to race and infused with a preoccupation over social roles. But precisely because the book addresses and embraces children the deconstruction of the notion of race as monolithic and of roles as rigid formulas is presented as an educational moment. Yet, the book eschews didactic solutions in its playfulness about appearance and substance—at some point, the son jokingly refers to his mom as his babysitter. The fluidity of images, linguistic labels, perceptions, and appropriations is seized by the author to create a space of sharing and mixing against the more common philosophy of difference and exclusion. In so doing, it also restores the voice of descendants of immigrants in the context of Italian society while affording child rearing a dignity and social function that pertains to both mothers and babysitters, native or immigrant alike. By relying on a voice that reflects the author's experience, namely that of the Indian-Italian woman raised and residing in Italy, the story provides a view that is "foreign" and yet domestic, what Geneviève Makaping has called "the participant observation of an eccentric subject" (109): the perspective of the minority looking at the majority from within.[8] In ways similar to Kossi Komla-Ebri, who affectionately analyses the ironies produced by the discriminatory attitudes of Italians—what he calls "*imbarazzismi*," mixing racism and embarrassment—Kuruvilla opts for an inversion of common perspectives that makes immigrants into full members of Italian society. The power afforded by this move, which is narrative and political at once, exposes a whole range of questionable views embraced by Italians. Written at a time in which India developed into one of the fastest growing economies in the world, *Questa non è una babysitter* critiques the usually unopposed views of the so-called First World and offers a palette of possibilities that dispels preoccupation about diversity in reminding Italian-speaking readers that the Indian community,[9] along many other immigrant communities, is an integral part of Italian society.

For the purpose of this Aperture and later chapters, both Rodari's nursery rhymes and Kuruvilla's book prompt reflections on the invisibility of migrants, and yet paradoxically hypervisibility, namely the ultracodification of their look and role in a society that functions by dividing and separating. They also propose a rewriting of the experience of immigrants from new perspectives—an operation that literature and artistic creativity afford by definition. Finally, they force an investigation into the contributions of laborers on the move, in particular for a country like Italy that for decades benefitted from the remittances of emigrants and is now relying on the contribution of immigrants. Written in the 1960s and the late 2000s, these texts indisputably show how Italy has transitioned from the status of being a country of emigration to one of immigration in just a short time. A crucial portion of its economy can be understood only through the movement of labor force and resources that migration entails.

FIVE

Edification between Nation and Migration in Cavanna's *Les Ritals* and Adascalitei's "Il giorno di San Nicola"

> Who builds bridges? And once the bridge is built, who remembers the builders?
> —GAY TALESE

The relationship between construction and foreign immigration embraces a wide range of issues from labor conditions to social in/visibility and creativity. As a work sector with usually high margins of profit and equally high safety risks, despite the regulations in place, construction traditionally tends to emphasize profits for the building companies while offering minimal compensation and protection to individual workers, especially when the workers are foreign immigrants. These issues have been at the center of several controversies in various parts of the world where imported labor has been subject to abuse as part of modern indentured servant contracts.[1] At a time when countries search for opportunities of national growth thanks to projects of international relevance such as worldwide sporting events or educational programs, the gain from transnational capital rests on the availability of transnational labor—read immigrants—whose vulnerability intensifies in environments with lax labor laws and in a condition of utter displacement. Saskia Sassen's established identification of "two epistemic communities" (22), one that allows for the circulation of capital across borders and one that restricts the circulation of immigrants across those same borders, is quite useful to understand the coimplication of national interests, international pressure, and transnational labor and capital, especially in the construction business.

Construction comprises many areas next to the more obvious development of private residences and public buildings. It entails the introduction or expansion of infrastructural systems (water, gas, electricity) and transportation systems both on the surface (railways) and underground (subways). Technically, it also embraces quarry work for the provision of building materials. The ironic clash between the hypervisibility of these grandiose projects and the invisibility or negative visibility of the hired workers (especially when they strike, when they are arrested or deported, or, worse, when they perish at work) is another aspect of the building sector. By definition, the work of the manual laborers remains unrecognized as compared to that of architects, engineers, and building companies, notwithstanding its crucial importance in the actual development and completion of the projects. As noted journalist Gay Talese cogently reminds us in the epigraph: "Once the bridge is built, who remembers the builders?" (2007 CUNY Lecture). The invisibility of the immigrant, especially if undocumented, is heightened in this context of erasure, even though paradoxically immigrants constitute a large number of employees in the building sector, especially for unskilled tasks.

The construction site (or the quarry) is thus the preoccupied space par excellence, since the life and health of the workers are constantly jeopardized. Yet, it is a space that hosts a creative activity by definition for its intervention in space, whether natural or urban; its addition of physical volume and presence; its functional service; and its stylistic statement. It is therefore a space in which workers, and migrants in particular, encounter some of the cultural elements of the society they live in in terms of social relations, economic investment, and aesthetic choices. When they are employed in vast projects of expansion, they effectively contribute to the concrete growth of the nation at large and to the reinforcement of its image internationally.

Interestingly, all of these aspects pertaining to the relationship between building and immigration can be traced along a historical continuum all the way up to today. Italy is once again an interesting case that connects past and present insofar as it plays the role of both a country of departure for millions of emigrants active in the construction business around the world as both skilled and unskilled workers, and a country of destination for large numbers of immigrants, most of them employed under the table in the Italian construction business. The mechanism of pre-occupation at the core of this book is thus applicable also to this realm: The experience of today's migrant construction laborers is a reverberation of that of Italians abroad in the past (and, according to some accounts, the present as well, as we will see in analyzing the current outbound migratory flow of Italians). Despite this continuum, migrants on the construction site are still perceived as "aliens" and their presence fosters preoccupation, when in reality they themselves experience a constant sense of preoccupation due to their physical and social vulnerability. Once again the main focus here is the representation of this migrant experience in texts that transform this preoccupation into a possibility by visualizing the invisible and uttering the unsaid about immigrant construction workers.

A large body of cultural texts focuses on Italians active in the building sector of foreign countries. These texts include canonical novels like *Christ in Concrete*,[2] classic works by popular writers such as John Fante,[3] autobiographies,[4] documentary works,[5] and films,[6] as well as outsider art.[7] Italian writers who have been attentive to the topic of construction and immigration include prominent authors such as Andrea Camilleri and Erri De Luca.[8] Surprisingly, the theme of construction is not a common one among immigrant writers based in Italy, despite the high incidence of immigrant involvement in the building sector.⁹ Notwithstanding their differences, all these texts show that, while representing a hyperphysical realm in which sweat, risks, damage, and exploitation abound, the construction sector can easily be turned into a philosophical one that hinges on the nexus building/being, two words that share the same Indo-European etymological root, *bheu*. Existing in a space that the subject edifies and inhabits is a unique experience for immigrants: Their condition of alienness is theoretically reversed by a process of concrete edification, which prompts forms of participation in a collective process such as urban development. In other words, immigrants—generally the least recognized group in a society—are profoundly instrumental in the material expansion of that society whether vertical through buildings, horizontal through streets and railways, or underground through subways.

In this chapter, this experience of preoccupation and participation will be addressed with specific reference to France, a country rarely connected to the Italian diaspora in part because of the high level of social assimilation made possible by a system that has traditionally focused on civic rights and duties over ethnicity and soon erased the marks of the immigrants' foreign descent. *Les Ritals* by François Cavanna is the text chosen to investigate the story of Italian construction workers and their families in a linguistically inventive novel that is considered a literary jewel in France.¹⁰ The experience of foreign immigrants in Italy will be explored through the novella "Il giorno di San Nicola" (Saint Nicholas's Day), an unpublished text by a Romanian woman who lives in Italy, Mariana Adascalitei.¹¹ While in both texts the presence of immigrants in the construction business is only one of several thematic threads, it clearly plays a pivotal role in addressing the immigrant experience abroad, whether that of Italians in France in the 1930s or that of Romanians in Italy in the 2000s, and to investigate the broader socioeconomic mechanisms of the context immigrants work and live in. Through different styles and genres—the irony-imbued autobiographical novel and the meditative detective story respectively—both texts engage with issues of exclusion, exploitation, denigration, and pain on the one hand, and with mediation and exchange on the other. Ultimately—to stay within the metaphor—they offer a model for the construction of bridges across cultures by emphasizing the crucial role of words, oral and written alike, and the equally crucial role of word-builders and carriers in edifying or at least imagining to edify a different world beyond national separations.

Italian Construction Workers in France: Building (Trans)National Memory through Humor and Realism

> "My home country's wherever I can earn enough to eat."
> "Yeah, that's why you're fat." (Jean Renoir, *Toni*)

The long tradition of artisanship in Italy notably produced a large pool of transnational workers in the building sector, ranging from bricklayers to stonemasons, stonecutters, and architectural sculptors, whose work often crossed the traditional boundaries between art, artisanship, and manual labor. The high incidence of Italian workmen in the profession consequently speaks of the enormous material contribution of Italians to urban construction and nation building around the globe. Donna Gabaccia in her 2000 study *Italy's Many Diasporas* argues that "by far the most important Italian occupational niche world-wide was that of male construction worker" (74). She describes the role played by Italian workers in both public and private projects: "On five continents, Italian men were earth-movers, masons, and hod carriers—veritable human steam shovels who built the transportation and urban infrastructures of modern capitalism" (74–75). Much literature has been produced about the experience of construction workers in the United States, especially because the modernization enterprise of this rising country coincided with the arrival of a massive number of immigrants; the United States officially became a country of immigrants as the immigrants were supporting its development both horizontally with the transportation system and vertically with public and residential buildings.

Less attention has been devoted to the European continent, even though the involvement of Italian immigrants in the construction business was equally pervasive to the point that in 1900 future President of the Republic Luigi Einaudi wrote, "*Gli operai dell'arte edilizia formano il blocco più saldo della nostra emigrazione*" (The artists of the construction trade represent the largest portion of our emigration; 530), interestingly defining their construction skills as an art. Within the European context on which Einaudi commented, France played a key role as the country of destination for these Italian immigrants. Geographic proximity created the conditions for seasonal migration flows of the "transalpines," but as a result of an eight-decade migration span, Italians came to constitute one of the most substantial communities in the country.[12] Their historical role in the construction business is undeniable. As Eric Vial demonstrates in his essay "In Francia" (In France), by the turn of the twentieth century, Italy furnished 50 percent of the foreigners who worked in the construction sector (135). In this period, Italian workers—often "competent auxiliaries to real professionals" rather than expert masons, tile setters, or plasterers (Milza 33)—were seen as indefatigable workers who accepted low salaries and replaced the strikers. Criticism mounted, and some protests were staged against them as in Nancy in 1893 (Vial 136). In the post–World War I period, reconstruction needs and the presence of low-skilled workers marked an increasing presence of Italian construction workers to the point that in 1931, 60 percent of the foreigners in the sector were made up of Italian immigrants (138). Before and during World War II, Italians became the preferred immigrants over Algerians. For instance, to respond to the housing crisis, France largely employed Italians on construction sites since this sector was by now considered to be their specialty (144).[13] It is only after the war that they started being site supervisors or self-employed, and with the economic boom they received "historical legitimation" in the sector even though in the midst of several contradictions. On the one hand, Jean-Francois Roverato became the owner of the largest construction firm in the country (and in Europe), and on the other, levels of specialization among Italian construction workers had not improved that dramatically (145).

The story narrated in Cavanna's autobiographical novel, *Les Ritals*, falls in the span of time that roughly coincides with the rise to power of Fascism and Nazism and the outbreak of World War II. The decade of the very late 1920s to the late 1930s, with its complex web of international relations and social tensions at the national level, is seen through the lens of the young protagonist, François Cavanna himself, the teenaged son of an Italian immigrant construction worker and a French woman who becomes a naturalized Italian by marriage and works as a maid.[14] It is this double perspective that allows the author/narrator to offer a perceptive insider's view of the Italian immigrant community in France while maintaining a genuine distance that shields him from both resentful deprecation or sentimental eulogy. The compass used by Cavanna to experience and relate this world is humor, a natural resource for a man who eventually became one of the most renowned French satirists. This entryway into the community does not erase the documentation of the challenges and tragedies of the lives of Italians in France, but it grants them a dignity that humor succeeds in reinforcing. The author does not laugh at Italians but with them. Even more so, he learns to laugh thanks to them, and in particular thanks to his amusing father.

As Cavanna himself confesses at the end of the novel: "I started out with the idea of talking about Italians and I believe that in the end I talked mostly about my dad" (280). This is hardly the case, but his father certainly plays a pivotal role in the book. Indeed, the very first chapter is a homage—and a memorable one at that—to his father Gigino (Vidgeon in the original French version) Cavanna, an illiterate construction worker employed by the company "D. Cavanna & D. Taravella"—the Cavanna owning the company is a distant relative, linked to the "rich Cavannas," while Gigino belongs to the "poor Cavannas" (19). The first chapter is a gem that encapsulates the entire novel and reflects many of its themes and sentiments as well as Cavanna's unmistakable comic style. The opening depicts Gigino as a hoarder of materials both useful and useless at his various jobs on construction sites, at home, and in the private gardens he tends. He collects these materials in several heavy boxes scattered around these locations; the key implement in them is the folding wooden measuring tape that his father creates out of discarded sticks from old tapes by carefully assembling the pieces and the springs. That the sticks do not follow the usual order of numbers—in Gigino's idiosyncratic assemblage 60 comes first, followed by 25, for instance—does not seem to bother him:

> Why would you need numbers? You look at the sticks and that's it, it's fine. Four sticks makes eighty. That's it. And for those little centimeters on top, just measure it with your finger, more or less, what the heck, one should not waste time with these trivialities 'cause the plaster, you know that one, the plaster, it's not gonna wait, that one. (12)

In this magnificent short speech—the first of many in this flamboyant and yet intimate novel—Gigino reveals his characteristic qualities: inventiveness, pragmatic attitude, an *ante-litteram* recycling philosophy, and an incurably positive take on life which is simultaneously a source of admiration and laughter for young François. This is why his father is a second-tier worker at the construction company, a step above the assistant. He could be a specialized worker for his technical skills, except for the fact that he cannot read. This apparently small yet crucial element frames the entire novel in two ways. First, it makes Gigino into an endless well of working-class wisdom and entertainment (both of them expressed in unvaryingly Piacentine dialect) that contains a precious yet limited value in the new environment of emigration. Gigino is a "Rital," an Italian in France who ingeniously pieces his old parts together, as in his unique measuring tapes, to make something new that is not yet French. The root of the disparaging word "Rital" is not clear, but is most likely the abbreviation of the French word for Italian (*italien*) with the addition of the quintessential French sound in front ("*r*"), and is possibly also an echo of the word "*ricain*," short for "*americain*" (American).[15] In the novel, Gigino's illiteracy also marks the inherent distance between him and François, so typical of the relationship between first- and second-generation immigrants. The son's very question about the odd structure of his dad's makeshift measuring tapes reveals that he is already "leaning towards the bureaucrat" (12). The distance determined by education within immigrant families, to which I will go back later, is interestingly a source of inquiry and empathy for François and not one of deepening contrast and open conflict as in many Italian American novels, especially those about construction workers, notably di Donato's *Christ in Concrete* and Fante's *Brotherhood of the Grape*.[16]

The first chapter thus establishes the "Ur-figure" of this Ritalian—so I render *Ritals* in English—story, the father, and sets it against the other point of origin of this bildungsroman, the mother. Yet, her traits, which are explored with a similar attentiveness and compassion on the part of François but not as systematically, are not as inspiring as those of his father.[17] A strong, hardworking woman from the central mountains of France, she is depicted as bitter, whining, driven by norms and routines, and ultimately dissatisfied with her marriage to an Italian, whom she often disparages along with "his people." The transition from the private space of the Cavanna household to the public one of the neighborhood is seamless as the reader moves from the first to the second chapter: The neighborhood is effectively a mosaic of households, almost all Italian. The novel is craftily prefaced by a map that simultaneously discloses Cavanna's drawing abilities and his overall vision for the novel, which can be considered "a story in place." The place is rue Sainte-Anne, in a town called Nogent-sur-Marne, in the Parisian outskirts, only six kilometers from Place de la Nation. This is a street that unexpectedly continues after an apparent dead end by designing two sharp turns that make it self-enclosed and unappealing to visitors both for its narrow shape and its unequivocal Italian smells and noises: "The French have abandoned to the Ritalians the winding roads, the rows of yards and gangways, and the basements full of sewage rats" (18). Cavanna provides a seal of pedigree to the neighborhood in his usual humorous style; he lists all the Ritalian resident families (thirty-seven last names) in the book's dedication. Indeed, with the exception of a few remaining French who still run businesses, the neighborhood is profoundly Ritalian. The author renders this attribute in vivid ways through a multisensorial snapshot of the Sunday afternoons at the Piccolo Cavanna, a tavern where Italian men fight, loudly play card games and *morra*, and sing a cappella, to the shame of their wives. The scenario corresponds to a narrative version of an Ashcan School canvas swarming with people, odors, and sounds; or a Rabelaisian bacchanal that the author abruptly juxtaposes with the story of an inadvertent fatal accident in which a truck ran over a small child, the son of the truck driver himself by tragic coincidence (17). The culprit is the same narrow rue Sainte-

Anne where the Ritalians have fun on Sundays. The sudden alternation between comedy and tragedy that Cavanna masters in the very first pages of the novel remains a constant in the rest of the text, a reflection of the stark contrasts that characterized the lives of these immigrants especially from the perspective of François who looks at them as an Italian and a French person at the same time (and for this reason, he is a *Rital* himself, according to the French).

The physical space that the community occupies is the cultural ghetto so widespread in the many other countries to which Italians moved. It is a space in which Ritalians transplant their place of origin thus establishing an axis between not two countries but effectively between a village in Italy and a neighborhood in France, as Donna Gabaccia demonstrated for the case of Sicilians in New York in her classic study *From Sicily to Elizabeth Street*. The Cavannas and their neighbors are from the area of Piacenza in the Emilia region, and more specifically Bettola, Ferriere, and Farini in the Apennine valleys called Val Nure, Val d'Arda, and Val Trebbia (Cavanna 51–52). Their concentration in Nogent-sur-Marne was so high that the place is rebaptized "Nogent des Italiens," although it may have also been called "Nogent des Piacentines."[18] Unlike other Italian immigrants who mingled with co-nationals from different regions, the people from Emilia created homogeneous settlements (Vial 137). Their pervasive use of dialect is then attributable to this demographic uniformity. Yet, in a typical Cavanna comic twist, this dialect paradoxically makes the immigrants closer to the locals, since it is quite similar to French; the province of Piacenza is adjacent to Lombardy, whose dialect belongs to the Gallic language family and has been strongly influenced by French. The unique language that Cavanna has created for his novel, an untranslatable mix of "*piacentino*" and French, is then a blending of two elements that were already close to each other.

When the narrator offers an early portrayal of his father—invariably full of gusto and tenderness at once—he remarks that his Italian friends call him either "Vidgeon Grosso" or "Gros Luis (to be pronounced as Louvi)" (21). Oscillating between the Italian dialect expression and the French one that is adapted to the Italian pronunciation (Italians are not prone to pronounce too many vowels in a row and add a consonant as a bridge, as François explains), "they do not really know whether they speak *dialetto* or French anymore, they sit on top of both" (21). An even more obvious passage in the book that signals this space of linguistic overlay comes when François's father meets some locals originally from the area of Limousin in the Massif Central. Historically employed in the construction business, these French people were substituted by Italians as workers in the sector in what seems to be a striking coincidence with the experience of Southern Italian workers active on the construction sites of Northern Italy substituted today by foreign immigrants, as Adascalitei's story shows. In the passage from *Les Ritals* this form of pre-occupation is heightened by another unexpected parallelism: In talking to the people from Limousin, Gigino discovers that these "hillbillies that spoke their coarse French dialect understood his dialect and he could understand their *limousine*" (52). This coincidental similarity creates a form of pre-occupation that so far this book has not analyzed, a linguistic one. The language spoken in the country of destination is pre-occupied by the language spoken by the immigrants or actually vice versa, in a delicate equilibrium of distinction and resemblance that constitutes a solid reason not to foster preoccupation over the presence of immigrants.

In reality, despite these points of cultural convergence, Italians were the targets of discrimination. Often depicted as violent or drunkards, they were easily associated with murders; the infamous lynching of Aigues-Mortes in 1893 was the result of this perception. Italians were attacked most often for being invaders who negatively affected the job market (Vial 136). This aspect is amply registered in Cavanna's novel, where Italians are seen as "bread stealers" (33) or "bloodsuckers" (37), an image that François promptly dismisses by retorting that they actually buy the bread they eat and humbly pick the jobs the French refuse due to their petit-bourgeois desire to climb the social ladder. The worker goes where the bread is, as the iconic phrase reproduced in the epigraph reminds us; with its good-hearted comic twist (the immigrant can also get fat from too much eating abroad), the phrase acquires a hyperbolic meaning in the hands of Jean Renoir in his classic proto-neorealist 1935 film *Toni*, about an Italian immigrant (Antonio Canova) working in the quarries of Southern France.[19] Abundance is not a matter the Cavanna family can contemplate, as *Les Ritals* meticulously portrays; the work of the father in the construction business is clearly one of toil, risk (even lethal), and limited gain. Nonetheless, the novel succeeds in celebrating it without falling into the trap of the bombastic panegyric and in granting it dignity without resorting to a populist rhetoric.

Construction in the novel is at once a source of income, a religious creed, a reason for trouble and a lifestyle. The job is like a second skin that the narrator vibrantly renders in a number of occasions: In describing his father's work-roughened hands "full of plaster spots and pieces of insulating tape" that Gigino prizes over band aids for their solidity (46), or his cement-coated wallet (70), or his body and clothes whitened by stucco or grayed by concrete (19), François suggests that his father (and his co-workers) wear their jobs. A process of identification between life (both family and neighborhood life) and the Cavanna & Taravella Company accompanies this anthropomorphizing of the job. Representative elements of the construction site are referred to by the definite article as if there existed no other essence outside of it: "The" owner, "the" house, "the" construction site, "the" truck are the accepted and recognizable coordinates used in the neighborhood to indicate the geography of work. Additionally, all actions are related to the construction job: Gigino thickens his soup with bread chunks that turn his food into "cement" (245) and holds the flag pole at the biannual street parade as it were a scaffold pipe (92). It is thanks to humor that such comparisons run smoothly in Cavanna's narration, which eschews denigration for this identification between man and job, while also skirting easy redemption. With their "fingers hardened by cement encrusted in the skin folds and the nails reduced to naught by the red bricks—one blur of nails and skin, even exposed flesh," Gigino and his co-workers play the trumpet in the street band; the keys are too small for their callused fingers and must be played two at a time, but when it comes to blowing into them, they can count on their strong breath—"darn, what lungs!" (91). Cavanna redeems the crushed worker through humor by constantly inserting contrapuntal elements that liberate the subaltern through Apollonian and Dionysian routes.

It is not a coincidence that Gigino, a potential underdog, is restored to a creator in several forms despite his wife's criticism, widespread social discrimination, and the challenges of the market. Portrayed as an artist leaning toward Apollonian elegance when active on the construction site, he is the emanation of a whole community that has made a reputation for itself in the sector. Like many Italians, he has the attributes in place for this job—"too refined, too delicate of a thing. One needs the right eye for it. It requires thinking with your head," Gigino explains to François (35). And when a construction job is not well done, he scientifically concludes that the French are responsible for it (46). The sanctuary of the business is "the" construction site, not just a construction site where a project is demolished or built, but also the "barn" hosting all the paraphernalia for work. It is a sacred spot made even more sacred by Gigino's idea to add a fruit and vegetable garden to it that he volunteers to tend; to do so, he relies only on his solid construction tools, since for him gardening tools are instruments for embroiderers (182). This commingling of art, nature, and technology characterizes several passages in the novel, but it reaches its peak in the chapter "The Peach Tree" where Gigino is so intent on making sure that the tree yields its first fruit that he protects the first peach against all outside attacks. He finds a large umbrella to tie to the tree trunk in a hailstorm, thus shielding the olive-sized peach. His co-workers humorously comment that he might want to wrap a little scarf around the peach to make sure it does not catch a cold! (*"Eh, Gigetto, bisognia metterci anche una siarpina, se no si prende un fredür"* 100). It is a moment of perfectly pitched teasing that is conveyed in dialect to add incisiveness as well as warmth. In passages such as this, Gigino is gently consecrated to eternity as a Ritalian Charlie Chaplin, full of not only inventiveness but also poetry and delicacy, two characteristics rarely adopted to depict a construction worker. At the same time, his Dionysian qualities are equally highlighted as unique. In particular, he is represented as a tireless storyteller of moral tales in dialect or the unique Ritalian language (see, for instance, the tale in "The Donkey" chapter). Fully rooted in the folk tradition of his Italian region, these tales are made special by his unmistakable delivery style, which encompasses his own wild laughter, an element that François can grasp more easily than his father's actual stories:

> He always laughs, my father. He stops abruptly in the middle of the street to laugh at his own silly stories; he lands on his knees; arms stiff, he shoves his fists in the pockets of his jacket; throws his head backward and hurls his side-splitting laughter towards the sky. People stop and laugh as well, it's impossible to hold it; look, it's a force of nature. (21)

Cavanna's talent rests on his ability to occupy with imagination and visceral emotions an occupation like construction often flattened to the provision of mindless labor and anonymity for the worker crushed by a grimy job (44).

Cavanna's book documents this close relationship between his father's community and this business sector. Since construction is defined as the barometer of the economy—"when the construction business works everything works. Corollary: when everything is a mess, the construction business has been bad for a while" (109)—and Italian immigrants are so heavily represented in it, they are subject to unexpected trends and perceptions. Despite their numbers in the business, Italians do not enjoy financial security—junkmen seem to be better paid than masons, quite mysteriously according to François (237). Even though they all entertain the dream of buying a plot of land and building a house whether in France or in Emilia (see the chapter "Il Villino," meaning the single family home), they are unable to build for themselves the houses they build for others, in an ironic twist that echoes Rodari's nursery rhymes in the Aperture.[20]

When the 1930s crisis hits, Ritalians suffer from increasing unemployment, a word they had never heard of (183). The post–World War I reconstruction in France had created manifold job opportunities for laborers and the memory of those migratory flows is still vivid in Gigino's mind (88). Cavanna illustrates the nexus between unemployment and social discrimination with his usual wit, showing how foreign workers become the target of collective anger along with Jews, Communists, blacks, and Germans (189). Yet, with equal skill, he shows the illogical nature of this preoccupation and discrimination, which compounds elements and oscillates between one extreme and another. For instance, during the Fascist regime, Italians are also labeled as politically problematic for their closeness to the Right at a time in which the Popular Front is growing in France; yet, for those very reasons, they are particularly liked by the upper-class French clients as well as by the Church. The nuns whose gardens Gigino tends explicitly prefer Italian workers (29) and some French upper bourgeois clients even praise Mussolini for his strong statesmanship. These French are struck by Mussolini's politics in urban architecture, characterized by solid materials and colossal dimensions; they see Il Duce as an enviable leader and Italy, quite ironically, as a "construction site" full of vitality in this historical period (87). Cavanna's robust humor inexorably surfaces at the end of this image of national power with the following observation: "Simultaneously, who knows how, never before have so many Italians arrived at the Lyon train station with their cardboard suitcases fastened by a rope" (87). In a matter of a few sentences, Cavanna captures the dissonance between the international image of Italy that Mussolini boosted and the reality of life for Italian people during the Fascist era.

Despite outside perceptions, Italian immigrants in the book do not seem to be very involved politically. They are aware of the risks entailed in joining the strikes (86), including forced expulsion after following a convoluted route of special permits to stay or to work limited by expiration dates (191–92). When Gigino realizes that his days are being counted, he opts for naturalization, pressed by a wife who is shocked at the idea of having to leave her own country to go to Italy "like gypsies" (193–94). His compatriots think that *"turaliser,"* their term for the act of naturalization, is a form of betrayal, but then they all bend their heads to it not only because, as Gigino states in echoing Renoir's film *Toni*, "Homeland is where work is, that's it" (194), but also because France offers opportunities to their children and mostly access to the great equalizer of all, the school system. Through these vehicles of integration the Italians start moving from difference to transparency in French society over time (Vial 142).

The role of the school system is central in a novel about edification like *Les Ritals*. Young François is introduced to a multifaceted world of books, which molds his views in unique ways from the age of four; he literally feels that his schoolteachers have "brought him to this world" (39) and that the public library was his nursery school (147). In exposing him to the classics of French literature, reading allows him to both acquire knowledge and hone critical views. Very early on, his favorite authors are the ones whose works show robust humor and bold naturalism (Molière, Rabelais), two characteristics that he absorbs in his own writing. Reading for him is mostly pleasure—of all pleasures "this was the stronger of all" (149)—but also a vice that possesses his body and soul—"the vice of the printed page" (41)—if not even a condition that he inventively calls "bulimia of the printed page" (188). In his usual fashion, Cavanna provides a hilarious example of his reading compulsion, when he describes his urge to read everything, from the Camembert cheese boxes on the dinner table showing the ingredients, seals, and production details to street posters including the small print about legal regulations (144–45). This hyperconsciousness about his relationship with the written word defines a metaliterary space in and outside the novel that works at different levels: the intradiegetic reference to books (especially an informative *excursus* through the history of comics that prefigures François's real calling and eventual profession); the overall goal of the book in "edifying" outside the construction site and on the printed page; and the love for language, grammar and genres that affects the content and form of *Les Ritals*. The love for language is demonstrated in the very idiom that Cavanna created for the book by carefully listening to and analyzing the environment of his youth: Dialect and French overlap and intermingle to create a unique lingo that, instead of excluding, attracts the reader and makes the novel effective in crossing boundaries. Young François sees words before understanding things and concepts in a debonair Wittgensteinian style and describes the words as if they were things based on their letter composition and sound (145–46).

The result is a buoyant fiction whose quick pace reflects the thirst for life of a young boy first and teenager later in whose environment he is not just a documentarian but also a direct protagonist. He experiences sex, delinquency, nature, politics, religion, sickness, betrayal, and much more in ways that are in some cases oddly reminiscent of John Fante's vibrant novels. In Cavanna's episodic text, each chapter is almost a story in its own right: Cavanna is comfortable in adopting repetitions, flashbacks, and ellipses—not only does he make use of these literary devices with ease, he also signals their presence to the reader. For instance, the memoir-like style of the text always presupposes the presence of a reader/listener that the narrator addresses repeatedly in pointing to the act of narrating: "Let me breathe" (13) or the jocular "this one I have already told some other place" (237) or "I don't know if I have said this already" (247), with the most entertaining being: "I am not going to waste time describing the scene again, just go back to the chapter in which I tell the way in which dad laughs" (101). The footnotes are particularly straightforward: "Do not go to Nogent-sur-Marne!" (13) or, "Thank you for your attention" (271). Cavanna plays with the readers by making them responsible for engaging with the novel: They are expected to get the meaning of Piacentine words since if he can get it as a small child they can too and should not expect a translation (46). The narrator is not a puppeteer of the plot but a discussant involved in a process of recollection comparable to a building process. His storytelling agilely moves from an unmarked multiperspectival dialogue (55–56) to a fable ("The Donkey") and an adventure-filled comic tale about his own escape from home, which constitutes a masterpiece in and of itself ("The World Tour").

Theatrical and cinematic at the same time—at some point the narrator inserts the word "Cut" (254) as if he were stopping the shooting of a scene and not just the narrating of a story—this coming-of-age novel is a clever experiment in building (trans)national memory through humor and realism.

Whereas Italian American novels about construction workers often relay grandiose desires of success and end up dealing with losses or tragedies, Cavanna starts from a position of observation, modest acceptance, and warm humanism that yet remains shielded from a didactic espousal of good values. François ultimately loves his father with all his shortcomings and mostly loves both his humble job as a construction worker and his unique storytelling talent. In *Les Ritals* he melds these two characteristics of his father and turns oral tales into written stories in a book conscious of its architecture but never burdened by it. Understatement and witty relativism expressed in "Cavannese" are the special ingredients of this unique literary gem, which gently deals with the thorny issues of deprivation and exclusion. François is accepting of his condition as "Ritalian" and confortable with the deprivation that poverty entails; by resorting to the present conditional of the verb "to have," he can pretend to own toys and play games he cannot afford (243). Next to this poetic irony, Cavanna resorts to relativism, a device that allows him to maintain a critical view of things and people without judging them negatively altogether. A telling example of this approach is an astute illustration of the dynamic of stereotyping by which groups find cohesion in downplaying another group while in turn they are downplayed by yet another. As the men from the Piacenza province denigrate the Italian Southerners for being lazy violent liars and womanizers, and thus a source of social preoccupation, François remarks on their limited perception of things: These men are not aware that the French characterize all Italians in the same way, short, curly-haired, and dark, with no distinction between the North and the South.[21] However, François has also noticed that the French are represented in American films in the same manner: short, curly-haired, dark men who end up defeated by the cowboys! His morale is incontrovertible: "Each one needs some shit below them. When a French thinks of an Italian, he feels like a darn hunk with gold teeth like an American" (51). Exclusionary formulas are inescapably pre-occupied by existing racist epithets and occupied by new ones.

This mechanism of self-recognition by exclusion, if not outright racism, is recounted in other passages of the novel especially with reference to Jews (36). Africans who, unlike Jews, are not dangerous plotters against the West are depicted as ignorant and backward, and as such laughable. François often talks about them as characters in the comics he reads (196). By a mechanism of recycling and adaptation of the grammar of racism, "Blacks" are identified by François's father as *"marochèn"* (Moroccan), a category universally applicable to Indians, Chinese, and Turkish in his view (196). The term "Moroccan" to refer to "foreigners" grew in usage in the 1990s in Italy when it became an overall derogatory definition for "immigrants" at large. Interestingly, in the region of Emilia Romagna and the surrounding areas, the term "Moroccan" had also been previously used to denigrate Southern Italians by resorting to a generic geographical concept such as Morocco aimed at defining difference. This application of the term by an Italian in France takes on a specific local meaning given the geography of colonialism that the country is still presiding over at the time of the novel's story. More generically referred to as "Arabs," in this era immigrants from North African colonies in France became the target of racism in lieu of Italians, who by comparison became "good" (read Catholic and European) (Vial 133) and over time were more accepted. Cavanna inserts a brief reference to an Arab character at the outset: an Algerian rug seller who in reality sells a constellation of objects from the most mundane to the most useless, none of which are typical of his place of origin. The Algerian is clearly represented as an outsider that people avoid and is labeled as a "lazy butt," a typical trait of his conationals that adults around young François attribute to the hot climate (35).

As a counterpoint to these preoccupation-filled comments, Cavanna spins a powerful tale of solidarity toward the very end of the book, in the chapter "The Arab," which recounts the story of a struggling man looking for work at Gigino's construction company. His incessant request for work, which does not subside despite the direct explanations he receives about the lack of available jobs, is a reflection of his desperation. Cavanna distills the plight of the poor immigrant into a single straightforward line: "Job." The unexpected twist in the story does not just lie in the eventual offer of a small job to him—a sign of the power of stubborn determination and work opportunities in the system—but can be found in the hidden actions of Gigino. As François learns after a while, his father had provided the Arab with money to eat during the three weeks he was begging for a job, standing like a statue at the construction site in the cold weather. The reason why the construction owners find out about Gigino's generosity is that the Arab in turn asks the payroll office to deduct some money from his paycheck and pay Gigino back. Even more admirable is Gigino's refusal of the Arab worker's offer, as the money Gigino used to help him was the small extra pay he was getting from the nuns for tending their garden. In his inimitable style, Cavanna stays clear from moralistic conclusions, and yet he recognizes the humanism of the gesture. He ingeniously adds a footnote in which, while acknowledging his "melodramatic" reaction to this news, he laughs at himself crying. The awareness of this "edifying" "thing" (271)—note the use of the adjective in a novel about construction work!—provides further material for humor. Through a brilliant metaliterary/metacritic device, the author anticipates that the critics in love with allegories and figurations would consider this passage a missed opportunity on the part of the writer for a disquisition on the high social and philosophical meaning associated with the Italian immigrant who passes a shovel to an Arab immigrant. He lightly concludes: "Oh, well, they will be so much better at this than I am!" That I now find myself attributing this meaning to the story is an example of Cavanna's sharp prescience as well as of his knowledge of human nature, the mechanism of cultural formations, and the dynamics of writing. That I am doing it better than Cavanna is quite doubtful . . .

Besides its wit, this chapter is important for the interethnic solidarity it reveals across experiences such as emigration and colonialism: Working as an antidote against social preoccupation, this alliance seems to incarnate at the human level Gramsci's intuition about the cohesion among the subalterns. Far from being an act of revolutionary politics, the silent alliance between the two men, symbols of historical experiences with global dimensions beyond their individual spheres, corroborates the imbrications of international phenomena that are pre-occupied by each other. In a telling game of mirrors, the Arab colonized subject is an immigrant in the metropole the same way the Italian immigrant is treated as a colonized subject in the land of arrival. Yet, a hierarchy can be discerned in this passage, where the Italian possesses a slightly more stable base of social and financial capital, a sign of the emancipation that from this period on, and especially after the war and the economic boom, will turn him into a transparent subject, that is, an unmarked citizen that does not foster preoccupation anymore. The eventual transition "from transparency to success story" (Vial 145) coinciding with the hypervisibility of celebrities of Italian descent in different sectors of French society (Ungaro, Smalto, Platini, Riva, Piccoli, and so on) marks the emancipation from a legacy of exclusion and consequently a rediscovery of ethnic roots versus assimilation. Cavanna's *Les Ritals* is the result of this rediscovery and functions as a vindication against humiliation that starting with the transformation of an insult like "Ritals" into an endearing if not glorious term marks a new relationship with Italian immigrants and descendants in France.[22] According to Italo-French historian Milza, Cavanna is a great French writer who has actually contributed in making "Ritalian-ness" concrete and likeable (407–408). Despite its weak ending—perhaps justified by a sequel (*Les Russkoffs*)—and its diffused machismo flair, *Les Ritals* remains a masterpiece of French literature as well as Italian migration literature that awaits discovery in the English-speaking world through a long overdue translation as well as a reappraisal in Italy at a time in which the country's construction business is increasingly defined by the presence of foreign immigrants in a telling loop of pre-occupation/preoccupation.

Italy Builds Romania Builds Italy: The Construction of Linked Identities

Construction constitutes a sector of quick absorption of immigrant labor in Italy (Fig. 17)—especially undocumented labor—and a realm in which many social contradictions and tensions can be identified in order to understand both national socioeconomic mechanisms and international dynamics, especially at a time of crisis. According to the IX IRES-FILLEA Report (2015), the presence of foreign workers in construction has increased over the years; in 2014, the sector was ranked third for its use of foreign workers only after the tourist industry and sectors categorized as "personal and collective services" (3), which includes domestic work. In 2014, immigrants constituted 30 percent of the construction sector if one embraces both EU and non-EU workers, while the average for all economic sectors (agriculture, industry, commerce, transportation, etc.) is slightly over 10 percent (Galossi 1). Immigrants are heavily employed in all aspects of the construction industry, except for management and planning (only 2 percent): They constitute the backbone of unqualified or little qualified labor on construction sites. Data show very minimal margins of skill improvement over time, and hence rank and salary improvement (3–4). Like Italians, but more than Italians, they have been heavily affected by the crisis but with consequences that are unique to them as foreign workers such as exposure to blackmail and informal agreements (6). In the past, this labor force in the metropolitan areas and in particular in the industrialized regions of the North was represented by immigrants from Southern Italy, another example of how this occupation is preoccupied by stories of Italian migration.[23] Often recruited through a *padrone* system that disregards job regulations (minimum salary, benefits, work hours, security standards) and that is particularly prone to tax evasion, immigrants have in some cases found the courage to protest and denounce, but for the most part they remain victims of a system of exploitation that can in some cases spiral down into tragedy.[24]

Mariana Adascalitei's 2005 detective novella "Il giorno di San Nicola" reflects this harsh reality and takes it to a hyperbolic point precisely to denounce it. Still unpublished and made available by the author in a final draft form for the purpose of this book, the text represents an unripe yet overall convincing attempt at capturing some of the core issues of the construction business and immigration in Italy. It focuses in particular on the Romanian community, which has a prominent role in the sector as part of the labor force. Interestingly, the novella also addresses themes related to domestic work and caretaking that create an appropriate bridge to Chapter 6. By inserting the nexus construction/immigration in a broader context of social, institutional, and personal relations, the author dissipates any risk of oversimplification in representing the "good immigrants" versus the "bad Italians." The novella is set in 2005, when Romania was still a non-EU country, and therefore Romanian immigrants were seen as "extra-community" people

FIGURE 17. *Young Bricklayer*, Turin, 1992. Photo by Uliano Lucas.

and fell under the category of undocumented when ineligible for a work or stay permit. Romania joined the EU on January 1, 2007, and its citizens' status changed overnight on that date, although some restrictions remained in place; a number of mechanisms described by the novella are thus historically situated and point to the socially constructed nature of exclusion. The reading of the novella offered in this chapter will also provide an extratextual context related to the presence of Italians in Romania in the present and in the past with particular reference to the building sector in order to complicate the otherwise widespread notion of the Romanian invasion of Italy.

The story of the novella takes place in Milan and revolves around the murder of Michele Mascaro, a ruthless Italian boss who manages the construction work and housing assignments of undocumented workers from Romania. Well known for his exploitative methods and his boundary-pushing approach, Mascaro is found dead in his own apartment for no apparent reason. Three people show up at the police station to tell what they know about the circumstances of the murder: his partner Lenuta, an undocumented woman from Romania who both works for and lives with him; Ion, a documented worker from Romania, who accepts to work for Michele due to the crisis-related paucity of jobs; and Ursu, an undocumented Romanian who joins Michele's system in order to earn the sum necessary to cover his wife's lifesaving surgery. Conveyed in the form of a police testimony, their reports reveal the network of relations between Romania and Italy for the human traffic of workers, the life and work conditions of Romanians once in Italy (in this case the North), and the forms of exploitation exerted by Italians who remain untouched by the law as they cannot be reported by undocumented workers. The novella is as much about these three characters, besides the figure of Michele hovering in the background, as it is about three women who through their work help uncover the truth and try to support the people involved: Anna Attarian, the protagonist and narrator of the story, a Romanian woman who works as a translator and interpreter both in the import-export office of an Italian firm and for the Milan police and court; Caterina, a policewoman from Southern Italy who after six years at the immigration office counter has switched to the immigrant investigation office; and Marta, an upper-class lawyer who, despite her background, works indefatigably to defend the dispossessed, and successfully at that.

The strength of Adascalitei's narrative relies in her deft choice of these female characters: While she adopts a very popular genre in Italy, the detective story, she turns it on its head by designing an all-female group of "readers" of the immigrant situation for whom immigration is not a chore or an added problem but either a personal story with collective implications or a social issue to be sensitive to and to fight for at the ethical level. The center of this female world is Anna, who tells the story in the first person, and as an immigrant from Romania herself she allows for the story to always maintain two perspectives defined by two different geographies and cultures that meet because of the migratory trajectory. The fact that Anna is a translator and as such a carrier of words, thoughts, and emotions across two worlds adds to this double perspective which ultimately offers the possibility of constantly avoiding black-and-white solutions and monolithic judgments.

Because of the impossibility of rendering the translation that Anna is engaged with, which would have added the equivalent of one third of the story lengthwise, the narrative unfolds in Italian only. This said, Adascalitei's own knowledge of Italian as a second language lets some imperfections slip through, which make the text particularly realistic unlike the polished Italian language of many writings by immigrants.[25] It is not easy to infer whether Adascalitei included these as voluntary mistakes or if they represent natural flaws of a bilingual speaker, and in a way it is not of major relevance here since some specific incidents are becoming common "mistakes" among Italian speakers themselves.[26]

The shuttling back and forth of words, thoughts, and feelings is much more than a service that Anna offers to the immigrants and the Italian institutions. It also functions as a memory trigger and a device to assess her present. The stories of these Romanians, albeit apparently so distant from her, prompt flashbacks and comparisons that allow Anna to better understand her situation while the readers learn indirectly about her. More specifically, the testimonies at the police station turn into unexpected psychoanalytical sessions in which Anna confronts her weaknesses while the defendants confess or protect theirs. Yet, whereas the suspects' stories reveal, Anna's flashbacks and references to the present remain for the most part vague if not utterly mysterious. What they seem to suggest is that the dialogic nature of the exchange is at once a revealing and a masking process, and that the truth is as clear as it is obfuscating, as the final twist of the story hints at.

What "Il giorno di San Nicola" exposes is the functioning, or rather malfunctioning, of the construction business, if not all the time but certainly in a number of cases: The defendants' stories, albeit in different ways, all converge in depicting the *caporalato*, a criminal phenomenon of workers' exploitation that is particularly effective when applied to (undocumented) immigrants. For the purpose of this chapter, the sections of the novella that recount the recruiting in Romania through intermediaries providing for the trip, the arrangements once in Italy and the threatening and abusive practices of the bosses are the most relevant to investigate the obvious preoccupations at the heart of this occupation, construction. As Ion relates, Michele

> would pick [the immigrants] up at 10 P.M. with a van and took them to work. An ugly one this work: on the construction sites taking care of the heavier tasks, we even had to break that stuff there, that stone that looked like marble. At night, in the dust with water that was trickling down non-stop, and as a protection I would put a handkerchief . . . on my nose. Ugly job and ugly pay. The last time he paid us it was barely for the work of two months ago. For a month of work at night in those conditions: 600 euros and immediately he kept 200 for the rental of that dump, a building owned by his aunt that he managed. Ah . . . the rent money he kept right away . . . for the pay we had to wait until his clients paid him . . . (48)

This story is corroborated by Ursu as well in his later report: night-shift work—"not to be seen by indiscreet eyes"—in disgusting environments full of dust so unbearable that the sites where workers were asked to dismantle old walls, load the debris on trucks, and carry cement bags actually felt like a relief (85). Further details emerge about the place in which

Michele "hosts" the workers: an abandoned unheated building not far from the freeway, hence very noisy, "equipped" with dirty mattresses, where fifteen people sleep in the same space and share the same bathroom. Michele never fails to collect the rent for this "service" since, according to their agreement, the rent is deducted from the pay. Whenever the workers complain or protest, he makes false promises, while blaming defaulting clients. Considering that many workers also had to pay back debts for the Romania-Italy trip paid in advance (1,800 euros plus fees), the financial pressure is unbearable. In addition to saving money and sending it back home, daily survival itself is a challenge given the high cost of living in Italy. Anger against Michele mounts. His "style" is bound not to work out, as Marin Gheorghe, a "smaller" boss, points out.

The inclusion of Marin in the story is relevant for two reasons: He is from Romania himself, and he deals with immigrant women. His involvement shows the complexity of the exploitation system, which contemplates both locals and nonlocals. Yet, even in this realm, the immigrant subject has to be more careful for the risk of being reported. Marin circumvents the risk by treating his abused people better, as he puts it. His "girls" would never report him as he does not push the envelope with them and in a tough environment he is well regarded for being "fair." Marin deals with the women's aspects of the business: The "girls" provide domestic service to the construction industry by cleaning spaces—they start at 5:00 in the morning and work for ten to twelve hours. Then the lodging is once again an ice-cold storage space where twenty people sleep on old mattresses and share eating and washing spaces. Unlike Michele, Marin pays his workers; his business works despite the fact that some of the women go back to Romania as the physical toil is unbearable. The inclusion of women in the scenario of the construction business breaks the typically gendered paradigm applied to this sector while complicating the domestic one: Women are still considered the "cleaners" by definition in this scenario but are expected to clean unusual environments such as in-progress buildings. The overlapping between the two sectors becomes even more evident when Lenuta secures a job with Michele via Marin by which she will be a maid and cook at his place. Over time, she is invited to take a room, give up the afternoon shift with Marin and work for Michele's aunt as a part-time caretaker; she is even allowed to bring her daughter Marinella in from Romania to live with her and Michele. The "only" price to pay is Michele's random and harsh violence, which Lenuta handles "well" both because of a history of abuse in Romania with her first husband and thanks to some techniques she has developed with her daughter (leaving the apartment at the moment of Michele's anger outbursts and spending some hours at the mall until he calms down).

Lenuta's ability to cope is at once a form of resilience stemming from a past condition of submission due to a traditional gender configuration and a subtle compromise that she frames within her migratory project. Independence comes at the price of risk and exploitation, she seems to suggest. Additionally, by articulating her experience in a narrative that responds to her own logic, she can be understanding toward Michele and accept his violent outbursts. She plays down his aggressiveness and highlights the benefits of her situation, even though the lack of documents makes her vulnerable, and indeed she is eventually affected in an indirect way (she is given an expulsion injunction). Adascalitei subtly interweaves the forms of interdependence between Italians and Romanians rather than presenting a dry distinction between abusers and abused, and actually blames the legal and economic systems for this perverse relation. The exploitation is paradoxically fostered or at least not contained by the abused because of the lack of protection for undocumented workers and the limited number of economic opportunities. Ironically, the socioeconomic situation creates ideal conditions for exploitation, and the legal system in place allows abusers to count on a way out thanks to the help of skilled lawyers (61). Besides recognizing the participation of Romanians in the exploitative system and the complicity of the Italians, Adascalitei creates a series of parallels that further contribute to the dismantling of the typical distinction between good and bad and even more so of the assignment of that distinction to national categories, so common in the media and as a result in the public opinion. It is Anna, with her in-between experience and her memories, who constantly bridges and questions both worlds.

Manual construction and architecture play a crucial role in the exploration of the character Ursu, whose experience turns from edification to destruction due to a sadly failed migratory project. Clinics, stairs, doors, and so on, especially as loci recuperated by memory, design a map of disorientation for both Ursu and Anna walking on a tightrope stretched between two cultures. In an interesting game of mirrors, Anna relives traumas of the past and shudders when her present vulnerability is made tangible by the weaknesses of the people whose words she is translating. The moment Lenuta remembers the university clinic of Via where her mother had to be hospitalized, Anna has a flashback into a brief moment in which the grandeur of the past is shattered by the corruption of the present. The clinic is a pink villa with baroque staircases and lean statues that a lawyer had built for his sick wife, an excellent pianist who died of tuberculosis; as a public institution, Anna recalls, it turned into a bastion of bribery where patients had to pay nurses on the side to be granted even basic services like some physical support to go down the stairs (32).

This narrative thread, which is merely touched upon, resurfaces during the story of Ursu, whose wife Anita at that very clinic is diagnosed with cancer and informed that only an immediate operation can save her. The high price of the procedure ($2,000) prompts Ursu to go to Italy illegally and work for Michele in order to gather the necessary money in what he thought would be a quick enterprise. The gain proves to be a chimera in the web of exploitation that Ursu is trapped in once in Italy. In desperation, the good-hearted man finds himself begging a drunk and furious Michele for a loan. Michele refuses while threateningly laying a knife blade on his neck. Blinded by anger and humiliation, Ursu kills Michele as if he were the pig sacrificed on Saint Nicholas's Day, according to the tradition of his region of origin in Romania, Maramures. The quick and bloody fix with a knife cut that goes straight to Michele's heart is at once a concentrated gesture of universal vengeance against abuse and a respectful act on the part of this delicate man (the technique reduces pain to a minimum). The cogency of the moment and its metaphorization into the religious calendar explain the choice of the title, up to this point left quite obscure. The irony is not too subtle as Saint Nicholas's Day is the equivalent of Christmas Day, the designated day to receive the gift one deserves. In the process, Ursu experiences a double erasure: Not only does he turn into a killer despite his mild and generous personality, but he is also forced to turn his work skills into a destructive force when in reality he is a truly creative man. Back in Romania, Ursu worked as an expert wooden builder in a region famous for its picturesque wooden churches, carved portals, and decorated tomb blocks.[27] His migratory path provides him with a job in which he is asked to build, but his skills could not be more negated. At the same time as his art of building dies in the transition to a new country and job, his work paradoxically produces death with the killing of Michele.

The novella explicitly unveils forms of corruption both in the country of arrival and in that of origin pointing to the countless forms of preoccupation experienced by migrants on both sides of the border, so to speak. The consequences for Ursu will be heavy, since even the partially legitimate self-defense cannot take him out of prison. But the real irony of his story is that, as the policewoman Caterina and the lawyer Marta, discover and later relate to Anna, Ursu's wife was not operable since her cancer's metastasis was too widespread. For Caterina and Marta, the misdiagnosis is a mistake that if anything reflects poorly on the Romanian health system, but in the final line of the story Anna finds the courage to challenge that reading and legitimately insinuates that the misdiagnosis was an act of vicious manipulation designed for self-interested profit: "Caterina, why do you say that they made a mistake?" (126), she bluntly concludes. She thus condemns Romania's widespread corruption system of pitiless doctors and nurses who gave Ursu and his wife hope and set in motion Ursu's migration project, which eventually became a prison sentence for him while his wife's life sentence was definitively declared by the illness. The preoccupation over life prospects in the country of migration is pre-occupied by the one in the country of origin. Adascalitei rescues this vortex of desperation from the risk of melodramatic rendition in the text by adopting the rational and empathetic perspective of the women involved in the case.

This revelation for Anna is the first of several occasions in which she becomes vulnerable to the pain of others as well as sensitive to their resilience—in this case the strength of Lenuta and the determination of Ursu despite their trials as well as Anita's self-dignity even after she discovers the truth. In another quick flashback, we learn that Anna was sick herself, and through her stories we are privy to her resistance against her oppressive husband, who teases and offends her for being a foreigner coming from an "ugly country" (91). She also finds the courage to officially claim the money that the court owes her, four hundred euros that should have been disbursed months earlier and that the very police Inspector Riva, who calls her at any time of the day and night in desperate need for a Romanian translator, never helped her claim. That money, we learn, at some point was crucial to make her father's operation possible in Romania in circumstances uncannily similar to those of Ursu and Anita. It is precisely in the tension between her as abused employee and her employer that the mechanism of exploitation denounced by the testimonies who were abused by Michele echo in the middle-class environment of educated, institutional Italy (107). By pointing out the inappropriateness of overstepping institutional boundaries, Riva finds a self-justification and endorses the malfunctioning of the system. In other words, Anna realizes that she is a victim like the other Romanians whom her translation may help, since apparently respectable functionaries of a democratic advanced society such as Riva can be eerily close to the Italian and Romanian abusers of immigrants on the construction site as well as to the corrupt doctors and nurses in Romania. Interestingly, the victims' apparent weakness turns into Anna's strength, and while the construction work she learns about clearly reeks of destruction, she engages in building new forms of alliances. Adascalitei's story subtly plays with this inversion of the function and mechanisms of building.

Anna's incipient form of liberation happens thanks to a shared solidarity with women also fighting against prejudice: Caterina as a woman from the South with an institutional role and Marta as an upper-class woman active in defense of working class people. This network is not flatly presented as a strong alternative to the system: What makes these women strong is their vulnerability—and the resilience they have developed to contain it—against outside attacks. It is their connectivity that allows them to be mutually supportive but as a result supportive to others with their skills, contacts, and resources.[28] As the author herself stated, "under the pretext of the detective story I wanted to reveal the humanity of the women protagonists: the policewoman, the lawyer, the interpreter, Lenuta. Women with very different jobs, cultures, personal stories, brought together by that fate that has women struggle more just because of their gender status."[29] The web of support is not a guarantee of security but rather a shared weakness that creates forms of understanding and sensitivity among subalterns and equips them with humor: "They did not have other people to face this difficult situation [the murder case] and have put us out there on the front line. Oh well, didn't we want equality? Was it perhaps better to stay at home and embroider?" Caterina remarks (64).

A similar network of understanding is established along cultural lines: Not too surprisingly, Southern people—whether Caterina or the vice inspector—share with immigrants a sense of exclusion in a town like Milan. Despite the same national belonging and the number of years spent in the North, there is a remaining residue of difference that does from time to time create humorous moments. In other words, the running thread of the story is cultural mediation, the ability to understand beyond differences and to build bridges in part thanks to a dislocation that by being geographical is also mental and emotional. It is not surprising that Anna quotes from Pirandello as well as Ionesco—respectively an Italian and a Romanian playwright whose work on the meaning of human existence she invokes as a reminder of the inevitability of human miscommunication. Yet, Anna's awareness of the emptiness of human life—certainly reinforced by a degree in literature that she ridicules for its economic uselessness while valuing it for the power of insight it provides—does not result in desperation or nihilism. Her ability to cling to life is depicted through her love for multiple places: a wanderer at heart she reveals her simultaneous liking for her town of origin, for her grandmother's village, for Padua where she studied, and for Milan where she works, as well as Bonn where she escaped after a fight with her husband. Multiplicity is represented by Adascalitei as a source of richness against the conventional myth of belonging, as Marta confirms in her spontaneous remark:

"What's wrong about that? . . . Some love more than one man and some more than one city" (100). The porosity of this approach produces an attitude toward listening in Anna that ultimately allows for a real construction, that of human relationships, in a text about the destructive nature of the construction business. Even though in the conclusion the women feel disappointed by the outcome—they would have liked for Ursu to be acquitted, for Anita to be effectively operated on and cured of her cancer, and for Lenuta to stay in Italy—their edifying efforts speak of a mentality of cooperation that dispels preoccupation. Ultimately, the novella is an invitation to exercise a reversal of perspectives. In identifying well-meant and good-hearted Romanians (Ursu, Lenuta) as well as selfish and exploitative Italians (see Riva and Michele), the text offers a counterpoint to the prevalent negative image of Romanians as invaders (given the size of their community) and as criminals.

Due to a substantial incidence of crime and the easy parallelism drawn between Romanians and Roms—the latter considered as intrinsically unassimilable—the community has been negatively labeled despite its size and widespread presence in many aspects of Italian life. The largest immigrant group in Italy—according to the latest data, it amounts to almost a million people (Dossier 2014, 2)—Romanians are mainly occupied in two sectors: construction and domestic work. While they have become citizens of the EU, their level of official integration was in any case limited (the Schengen Treaty did not apply immediately, and only as of 2014 has free circulation been approved). Italy has had an open-door position from the inception of EU membership, allowing Romanians to find jobs in Italy once on site rather than before moving. In reality, this flexibility is also the result of an increasing presence of Italian companies in Romania, especially in the Timisoara region, where the labor and production costs have made delocalization very attractive (the most famous case is that of the Italian company par excellence, Bialetti, maker of the stovetop espresso machine). At the same time, major Italian companies are present in Romania as part of further developing the country's infrastructure: see for example, Astaldi/Italstrade and Todini Costruzioni Generali in the construction business.[30] In other words, while a flat-out preoccupation is expressed toward the Romanian invasion, especially at the time of elections in Italy, the relocation of Italian production in Romania, with visible consequences for the Italian economy, is not always factored in as part of what is effectively a bidirectional movement and consequently a web of mutual interests and forms of dependence (Italian production thrives thanks to foreign infrastructure and Romania grows thanks to new job opportunities provided by Italy at the local level).

This web of correlations can also be identified in other historical moments, thus corroborating my interpretive filter: pre-occupation. Since the time of the Austro-Hungarian Empire, but with a particular increase right after Italy's unification and around the very end of the nineteenth and beginning of the twentieth centuries, Italian construction workers were employed in Romania for the development of public projects ranging from transportation infrastructure to buildings.[31] The presence of Italian construction companies as well as architects and engineers was particularly prevalent in the provinces of

Moldova and Dobrogea. Workers were originally from Veneto and the whole northeastern region of Italy, but migrants from the Adriatic South were also employed by both Italian and Romanian companies. The contribution of Italian immigrants was particularly relevant in terms of technique and style: masons, bricklayers, stonecutters, plasterers, and tile setters were sought after for their expertise and precision, received prizes and recognition for it (Tomasella 237), and were able to secure decent pay and send remittances home. The immigrant group also comprised engineers and architects whose contribution has left "a decisive and tangible sign of their stay on the Romanian soil and participated in nonmarginal ways to the construction of the new kingdom's identity" (236).[32] With World War I, the flow of Italian migration from Italy stopped but Romania continued to benefit from Italian investment on infrastructure (and labor supply) in the interwar period and later during the regime of Ceausescu and even after it. This unknown history of pre–World War I migrant flows from Friuli and Veneto surfaces in a short section of the novel *Dispute Over a Very Italian Piglet* (2013) by Amara Lakhous, author of *Clash of Civilizations* analyzed in Chapter 3. As pointed out by the novel's protagonist, detective Laganà, "Italian history is full of surprises. There are always new things to discover. I think that there does not exist a people stranger than ours. We Italians have not neglected any place in the world. We've gone everywhere, including to Romania to work as bricklayers. Today it's the Romanians who come to our country to do the same work. Irony of history" (89–90).

Indeed, today, not only do Romanian immigrants represent the largest group in the building sector, but they also have a respectable track record of opening their own building companies. "Italy builds Romania builds Italy" is a circulatory pattern that acquires special meaning within the context of this book since it confirms the transnational quality of national building projects.[33] It is precisely this strong link between the two countries—further heightened by the Latin root of the language and the adoption of the Latin alphabet in the mid-1800s and some Italian grammar rules, given the proximity of the two languages—that should dissipate forms of preoccupation in the name of these instances of pre-occupation. These instances function as strong reminders of the connections between the two countries, peoples, and cultures and the empathy that Italy can exercise toward Romania as a result.

Empathy is the *fil rouge* of the two texts analyzed in this chapter; whether across generations in the case of François Cavanna toward his father or across ethnic groups and geographies in the case of Adascalitei, the texts design a relational space built through experience. If the fate of construction labor is by definition one of anonymity, according to Gay Talese's insightful comment, it is labor's transformation into dignified work, and more specifically into works of art via its representation in literature, that marks its transition into the realm of visibility and, as such, history. In particular, in Cavanna's book, the invisible immigrant worker on the construction site becomes one of "the workers of the construction art," to use Einaudi's expression again. The same way construction came to constitute "the ideal type" of Italian emigration (Corti 228), it represents a typical professional sector for immigrants in Italy today. The trajectory of cultural conflict and connection that these narratives by Cavanna and Adascalitei unravel furnishes another valuable starting point for a remapping of the Italian national project and its discontents. The textual and sociopolitical architectures of both works identify the participation of Italians in the building projects of foreign nations and of foreigners to Italy's expansion.

SIX

The Circular Routes of Colonial and Postcolonial Domestic Work: Però's and Ciaravino's *Alexandria* and Ghermandi's "The Story of Woizero Bekelech and Signor Antonio"

> Someone should explain to me, for example, why the majority of Italians consider immigrants the primary cause of their lack of security when, at the same time, they entrust the persons dearest to them, children and old people, and the key, to their houses, to immigrant caretakers and housekeepers.
>
> —AMARA LAKHOUS

The condition of invisibility that the construction site forces upon immigrants is made more acute in the domestic space. Largely hidden from the public eye and regulated by idiosyncratic norms, caretaking—whether of people or the house—is one of the most unnoticed contributions that immigrants provide to a society. Yet, by inversion, it is also one the most central for the economy not only of families but also of entire countries in some cases, despite its widespread under-the-table nature. Domestic work generally entails housekeeping, but at very particular historical junctures it has also embraced care of the elderly and nursing, dry or wet, but especially wet nursing (in Italian, *baliatico*), an ancient practice common in the Western world until the mid-1900s, when artificial milk became a viable alternative to breastfeeding. (Luigi Pirandello, for instance, addressed the topic in a 1903 short story entitled "La balia," adapted to film by Marco Bellocchio in 1999.) Domestic work has been pivotal in maintaining a socially proper role for upper-class women in the past and granting new forms of autonomy to middle-class women in the postindustrial era.

Immigrant work in the house has in other words been a catalyst for the re/definition of gender roles in the family and the workforce over time. Yet, the experience and identity of domestic workers are inevitably obliterated or highly stereotyped in the process.[1] Along Italy's outbound and inbound migratory routes, domestic work has played and continues to play a key role thus defining an unlikely connection between the experience of Italian women working abroad from the late 1800s through the mid-1900s and foreign women (and men, as we will see) working in Italy today. The overall framework of the book acquires a specific declension: Not only is domestic work in Italy pre-occupied by a history of Italian domestic work abroad, as we have seen for other categories in the rest of the book, but the preoccupations that both phenomena express are over key notions for any society primarily based on reproductivity and economic productivity: the well-being of babies, women, and old people. Domestic workers lift this preoccupation from women otherwise in full charge of parenting and elder caretaking, yet their "foreignness" preoccupies the system insofar as it poses questions about these workers' actual belonging to the society and in particular to the private space of the home they work in.

The history of Italian literature and film is marked by several tales of domestic workers "on the move" over the arc of a long century: Italians emigrating abroad on the one hand,[2] and foreigners in Italy on the other. The latter category of foreign domestic workers in Italy is the subject of an increasing number of films[3] and literary texts,[4] a sign that the domestic economy is largely run by immigrants, including highly educated immigrants.[5] This chapter focuses on the two contrasting and complementary experiences of Italian domestic work in foreign countries and foreign immigrant labor in Italy through respectively the play *Alexandria*, written by Renata Ciaravino and directed by Franco Però in 2008 (a previous version of it entitled *Quando la sera ad Alexandria* was presented in 2005), and Gabriella Ghermandi's "The Story of Woizero Bekelech and Signor Antonio," a short story woven into her 2007 novel *Queen of Flowers and Pearls*. Despite their differences in terms of genre and approach to the topic, they both shed light on the mechanisms of national formation in connection with migrations and colonialism. From a purely spatial perspective, the two texts prompt an inversion of perceptions: While domestic work is usually associated with indoor spaces, these texts exceed the "home," so to speak. *Alexandria* leaves the space of labor in the background and gives priority to the semicolonial city under direct and indirect European control—it was under British control from 1882 to 1953—thus counteracting the usually claustrophobic nature of domestic work. Ghermandi's tale is set in an apartment that allows for the simultaneous denunciation of the closeness of domestic work and the critical recuperation of the vast space of transnational migrant labor along colonial routes. The geography that both texts combined describe is a map that spans from the northern region of Friuli to Egypt, and from Ethiopia to Emilia-Romagna: Different historical moments and different life experiences echoing each other occasion a rewriting of the country from a "home" that also lies abroad.

From the Province to the Cosmopolis: Italian Domestic Workers in Egypt

In the course of the first wave of emigration after Italy's unification, women normally traveled on their own to join their family members or husbands: Their emigration was only rarely an independent project. Yet, from the late second half of the century, it is possible to identify seasonal, temporary, and long-term flows in various sectors, including domestic labor and in particular wet nursing. No comprehensive study on the topic has yet been produced, and the literature tends to focus on highly regional phenomena: Still, essays on specific areas of Friuli and Toscana have proven to be very useful in defining the broader scenario as they trace the transnational nature of these economic and cultural movements.[6] Departure points were mainly Friuli/Veneto, Tuscany, and Calabria followed by Abruzzi, Piedmont and Apulia, as Ada Lonni's and Bruna Bianchi's essays explain, with France and Egypt, and later Australia, as the main foreign destinations.[7] This occupation was uniquely female and profoundly linked to sexual and family life and as such regulated by specific norms, especially in societies that considered women as subordinate to men. The work they accepted, or were forced to accept by family members, spoke of the dire conditions they came from. A woman's sacrifice in giving up her own children to make money away from the village by relying on her breast milk was the ultimate tragedy for her. While a *baliatico* in the same village for a local well-off family or for a charitable institution supporting orphaned children was compatible with one's birth children, wet nursing abroad implied separation from one's newborn, which was a heavy price to pay. France was an exception in this respect as women were encouraged to give birth across the border with the guarantee of citizenship to the child as part of the country's campaign for demographic increase; yet, in some cases, women abandoned their children in France itself as they could not find a shelter for them while they worked full time.

In Italy, newborns were either left with an institution (*esposti*, meaning exposed, was the term used for them) or given to other women who in exchange for compensation would raise them along with their own children. This decision could be handled financially by migrant wet nurses since abroad they would earn wages five to ten times higher than in Italy, but it was somewhat of a gamble as these caretakers would occasionally neglect the children under their care while pocketing the money. In some cases, wet nurses returned home to their men to plan other pregnancies and capitalize on their precious milk for longer (one pregnancy could yield up to two years, during which work was then secured). Such decisions resulted in some of the harshest forms of social stigma and affected these women's families and social relations over time in terms of trust and acceptability (Lonni, "Protagoniste" 441).[8] Yet, the opportunities they embraced were in reality the effect of a "natural" job offered to women whose professional alternatives were very limited. Theirs was not a form of abandonment of their families, but actually a separation that through remittances provided vital support. Despite the image of fragility (unfit) or brutality (cold-hearted) that often accompanied these women to the point that upon their return they consigned the experience abroad to oblivion, what becomes apparent through a closer analysis is that the female occupation par excellence that they chose or were forced to choose actually revealed these women's ability to control their resources, make decisions, regulate their bodies, and plan for the future, in ways that were otherwise unavailable to them in that era.[9]

In other words, while "women's corruption, emigration, and wet nursing are all intersecting elements in a way" (Lonni, "Protagoniste" 441) in the understanding of this historical phenomenon, it is also important to interrogate the unexpected possibilities for emancipation, not only financially but also culturally, that wet nursing (and domestic work at large) opened up along the migratory routes. This was the case for a particularly stimulating and liberating environment like Alexandria. The flow of women's emigration to Egypt had started in the 1880s when parts of Northeastern Italy were under the Austrian Empire: Women from Trieste, Gorizia, Istria, Dalmatia, and Slovenia moved to Alexandria in large numbers to the point of marking a veritable socioeconomic phenomenon, that of the "aleksandrinke" (Boz 259), as these women were called. In the 1920s, Egypt now independent but still under the indirect control of British forces, experienced an economic, political, and cultural resurgence. The booming cotton economy, archeological findings and a renewed national spirit resulted in a financial resurgence that made the country open to receiving foreign laborers on a large scale: Greeks, Italians, Slavs, Armenians, Syrians, Lebanese, and so on. Within this semicolonial context, work was available and at a high pay relative to Italian standards for women interested in working as wet nurses, ironing maids, wardrobe maids, seamstresses, and in some cases housecleaners. Italian workers of the first wave were particularly attractive since, as citizens of the Austrian Empire, they were literate and employers perceived them to be above the level of purely menial workers, such as cleaners. Regulated through binational agreements that secured legal visas for emigrants (Boz 253), this domestic work offered the advantage of providing food and board, yet also implied volatility (families tried to pay the nurses less after babies were weaned, for instance) and even physical pain (nipple bleeding was not infrequent). At the same time, the experience was an opportunity for these women to be on their own for the first time, to reside in comfortable houses and to live in large cities. What is of relevance for this study is their double form of autonomy, as work allowed them to send money back to Italy to help their families, while offering them the chance to explore new cultures and new forms of freedom, both personal and sexual.

Renata Ciaravino's play *Quando la sera ad Alexandria*, also simply known as *Alexandria*, is based on the research work of Franco Però.[10] It focuses on this unexpected process of emancipation in the febrile climate of Alexandria in the 1920s. As a Mediterranean port, Alexandria was a particularly cosmopolitan city: Hosting since time immemorial Christians, Muslims and Jews, it was known as a haven of ethnic coexistence where French, Greek, English, Maltese, Italian, and Slovenian were regularly spoken alongside Arabic. Often compared to the New York or New Orleans of the 1920s, Alexandria was exceptionally vivacious at that time and attracted many established families from Italy (and other parts of the world), which settled in this British semicolonized area as expatriates,[11] as well as migrant laborers in many sectors.[12] Ciaravino decides to focus on the experience of a group of women from what today is the Friuli region who moved to Alexandria to serve in the domestic sector: Milena, Olga, and Irene are joined by Alexandra, the daughter of Milena's aunt Albina. By placing these women at the center of the story, the playwright reverses the usual paradigm that sees women as appendixes or companions in the history of emigration. As women on their own, even though married in some cases, Ciaravino's protagonists acquire an especially meaningful role inasmuch as they question their gender roles and their national belonging. Work in a domestic environment ironically opens an entire world to them in a cosmopolitan city like Alexandria where living abroad for these Italian women meant much more than discovering just one country. In particular, it also meant exploring a broad range of foreign worlds, cultural and otherwise

(Petricioli 470). In a telling scene in which the women reminisce about a party, a simple act such as cooking for a social gathering turns into an amusing conflict in which the Jewish women have to be mindful of the separation of milk-based from meat-based dishes; like the Jews, the Arab women have to avoid pork, and even beef does not work if it is not kosher or halal. The Jewish women object to the Italian Catholic protagonists' idea to serve clams, and in the end they decide that each will bring what they individually prefer, since only vegetables would have worked otherwise.

The play rebuilds the 1920s immigration experiences of these women through flashbacks that take place in 1960s Alexandria; whether through tales recounted informally among them or through monologues, their stories emerge at once as trajectories of desperation and liberation. The performance starts with the blast of a ship horn in the dark, a sound that is reminiscent of Crialese's choice in *Golden Door*, where this aural sign condenses an entire experience of familial and national severance. *Alexandria*'s main setting is the dock of a port. In the background, a moored ship waits to depart the next morning. What was supposed to be a brief good-bye turns into a long session of memories and revelations for the four protagonists and ultimately as the stage for migration-related sentiments across the Mediterranean.

Milena is the fulcrum of the story. She is both an immigrant of yesterday (born in 1920, she arrived in 1935) and an emigrant of the present in the play (she is about to return to Friuli). She carries the vivid memory of leaving Italy with her mother and grandmother to visit and then stay in Egypt: Prompted by the death of her father and the ensuing poverty of an all-female household, the trip to Alexandria was back then encouraged and paid for by her aunt Albina. A defiant and courageous woman, Albina had already left years earlier to escape the strictures of her village life and to look for work in a place where her free, anti-Catholic spirit would find a home. The visit of Albina's female relatives further fractures the family as Milena decides to stay with Albina and to send half of her pay back home to her mother and grandmother. While less fiery than Albina, Milena is a strong woman in her own way: She will remain single and work until the new developments in Egyptian politics convince her that the cosmopolitan and rich environment of the past is fast disappearing.

Olga and Irene have complementary yet equally rich roles. Their stories are conduits to understanding both the harsh conditions of life in the Friulian towns of origin and work life in Egypt. Coming from a village between Udine and Gorizia, Olga has left behind an indebted family. In ways similar to Marco's mother in De Amicis's "From the Apennines to the Andes," Olga becomes responsible for the destiny of the entire family nucleus. Under the pressure of an impending property foreclosure, Olga's mother-in-law suggests the migration plan to the young woman who has just given birth to a child. This pattern was not unusual as the literature suggests: Both in her essay and in the exhibition catalogue she curated with Mara Tognetti,[13] Lonni reminds us that in joining the husband's household, women were under the additional control of their mother-in-laws who often saw in the *baliatico* a way out for the entire family, and forced their daughters-in-law in this direction despite the pain involved in this decision.[14] Olga is torn between her role as mother and her duties toward the family. The prospect is that of leaving her child with another woman who will breastfeed and take care of him. Yet, the recent story of the death of a child of a wet nurse working abroad, who was neglected by the woman in charge of him, and the caretaker's ensuing tragic death at the hands of the child's father leaves Olga terrified. She is nonetheless forced to leave. Her child will live, but she will not see him for five years until his visit to Alexandria with her husband. As she bluntly puts it, leaving her son was an emotional death: "He was not dead, but he could not recognize me and did not want to be with me."

Irene's experience is comparably desperate. Originally from Prvačina, a village once belonging to Gorizia and eventually absorbed into Slovenia, she has an unemployed and alcoholic husband who is physically abusive toward her. Irene's decision to leave is again due to economic necessity but also a flight from violence and oppression, a theme addressed in folksongs from that time (Barbič 168). Olga's work as a wet nurse and caretaker will support the family back home through regular remittances. In the course of her tales, she also reveals that her grandmother had made the same choice: She lived and worked in Alexandria and went back to Prvačina only in order to give birth to a new child whom she would leave behind before taking off again with a renewed "richness" of milk. Indeed, the generation of nurses that Ciaravino decided to focus on is the second or third one. Considering that the initial flow started in the very late 1800s, these women arrived between the 1910s and 1920s relying on the experience of other women before them as part of a "migratory chain" (Boz 253) and the stories about these experiences that circulated through the informal channels. This genealogical element is important in *Alexandria*'s plot as well as in the history of Italian domestic work "on the move." Irene's grandmother is portrayed as a champion of wet nurses; her expertise as a midwife saves a newborn's life, and she receives a prize in Alexandria in recognition of that deed. The definition of putative mothers in the experience of domestic workers abroad is a typical feminist operation of legitimization and empowerment that is working quietly and yet incisively in what could be defined as the protofeminist environment of the play's story.

Alexandria also constitutes an important repository of information about the lives of these Italian female workers in Egypt. What emerges clearly is that the promises of compensation turned out to be true: Entrepreneurship, determination, and physical strength all helped in securing jobs in a market that offered substantial compensation compared to the prevailing salaries available in Italy. The jobs also gave these women the possibility of living in pleasant environments, having access to healthy and rich diets, and wearing nice clothes and even jewelry, effectively transitioning to an upper class lifestyle overnight.[15] The play *Alexandria* does not address this aspect openly in the script, but the attires of the women as well as their attractive bodies on the stage speak of a general physical wellbeing that contradicts the more common images of domestic workers as modest, if not invisible women.[16] As Bianchi notes, "wet nursing allowed them to unshackle themselves from coarseness and ignorance" (263): The archival photo of wet nurse Gemma De Marchiò reproduced in Boz's essay shows how caretaking often went hand in hand with personal care (Fig. 18).

Additionally, the experience in Egypt offers an occasion for cultural discovery and social experimentation. In the play, the women repeatedly refer to the French and En-

FIGURE 18. Gemma De Marchiò, wet nurse, with children under her care. Alexandria, Egypt, 1930s.

glish theaters, dance nights at the tango hall, large parties, informal occasions for socialization among themselves, and encounters and relationships with men coming from diverse parts of the world. The tales are injected with sensuousness and pleasure and speak of a Belle Époque, long past by 1960, that opened possibilities for personal exploration. Aunt Albina is remembered as the one who not only absorbed the cosmopolitan air of Alexandria but pushed her limits even further when she met "the Maltese," a prosperous onion merchant (he is represented as perpetually smelling of onions) who combined the characteristics of the farmer with those of the successful immigrant who has built a comfortable life for himself. In addition to being a passionate lover, he also becomes a doting father for Albina's daughter, Alexandra, born out of wedlock from a man who soon vanished. One of the most telling lines of the play captures the cosmopolitan and bohemian flair of the city with a lyrical twist: Albina "already knew Arabic, Greek, English and French, but to talk about love she learned Maltese too." The line is also a powerful reminder of how multilingual these women had the opportunity to become in this environment, despite their relatively low level of education. *Alexandria* dedicates much space not only to the emotional but also to the sexual satisfaction of these women; undoubtedly, emigration is a route away from oppressive models and toward forms of physical attraction and affinities that were not available in the village of origin. References to *One Thousand and One Nights* furnish the women with a code to talk about sexual appeal and curiosity, and the friendship with Marcel, a gay man, allows them to experience difference in accepting ways. These are all modes of expression and relation that only emigration (in ways more diffuse than urbanization, that is, internal migration) and only emigration to a particularly diverse place like Alexandria can open up.

Nevertheless, the flexibility of behavioral codes was not necessarily always a freeing opportunity. Women could easily fall prey to the prostitution business or similar forms of exploitation in illicit circles. *Alexandria* does not ignore this other side of the bohemian life and acknowledges the traps of the environment. Yet, instead of treating it in moralistic terms, it turns it into an arena of personal assessment for women and eventually of independent decision making. The general view of Egypt was that of a place of perdition, and of the wet and dry nurses as not only easy preys to racketeers but as women particularly prone to the "wrong" way because of their "unnatural" choices as mothers. It is no surprise that in 1899 the government of the Austrian Empire announced the introduction of a "hostel" for its female citizens who had moved to Alexandria for work and needed to be "assisted and protected" from the local criminality that could entrap them. In *Alexandria* there is a quick reference to this "asylum" (12) as it was also called, and the document that circulated to declare its opening. Yet, the characters see it as a patronizing gesture toward women: In a powerful scene Milena mocks the voice of the Austrian reporter reading the document in front of local officers in Alexandria. The full document was included in the play's version entitled *Quando la sera ad Alexandria*; even in its shorter form in *Alexandria*, it functions as an extension of the prudish view of the destination and the work of these immigrants on the part of the people back in the homeland (see also Barbič 168).[17] In opposition to this dichotomy between acceptable and questionable work, Ciaravino's play actually addresses the illicit places of pleasure as regular workplaces as well, quite unexpectedly. The mythic harem of Arab culture remains a forbidden attraction for the protagonists but it is also demystified by one of them, because "it's normal to be curious about what's in the dark" (13). As Milena recalls she learned about the harem through Albina who once worked there as a seamstress making beautiful dresses for the women. Some of the fascination of the harem is "domesticated" by taking the fabric remnants home to make other dresses for the nights at the dancehall with her friends.

The scenario described by Ciaravino is far from rosy, and it would be incorrect to gather from her play an easy trajectory from suffering to happiness, and from oppression to liberation. Each woman is clearly invested on denouncing the challenges and the losses entailed in her courageous decision. Olga deplores the sense of displacement experienced when her husband joined her and was unable to fully comprehend the autonomy that she had reached: "it was not easy at the beginning to explain to him what I had become, that I would go out by myself, that I liked going to the theatre . . ." (22). Other struggles are registered in terms of labor: As women and foreigners, these immigrants were subject to a volatile market redefined by the established families with newborn children. Yet, interestingly, women learned to defend themselves by negotiating. Their newly found independence as workers opened up the possibility of defining and not just accepting work conditions. Next to this newly gained strength in the labor market that grants them a more secure financial position, these women show an equally strong capacity to create a nonviolent environment around them by staying away from abusive men. Reading from old letters and reminiscing about her family, Irene reveals for the first time that once in Egypt she asked the Consulate to deny her husband entry into Egypt. In what was effectively a reversed repudiation for the codes of that time, Irene finds a form of relief from violence in this self-designed divorce that only the expanded geography of migration can afford her.

The financial security reached by the women and their sense of independence was not always complemented by emotional gratification: Milena, the most accomplished of these women, is still single, a condition that further prompts her to go back to Italy. In the course of the conversation in front of the ship, she confesses that she had a man, but he was a POW in British hands during World War II, and since then she has been alone—"I have always been unlucky in love" (15), she bluntly concludes. The theme of loneliness runs through these stories, while simultaneously the value of friendship is celebrated throughout, and especially reinforced in the farewell scene where the women share experiences and confess secrets. Ultimately, these characters are at once foreigners and locals: Decades of stay in Alexandria have made them alien to their place of origin, and oddly at home in the cosmopolitan world of Alexandria. Given that in the 1960s the country is driven by a nationalist sentiment, immigrants are more "foreign" than before, and some feel the need to return to Italy—in this sense Milena's departure is vaguely reminiscent of that of thousands of Italians leaving Libya at the time of the establishment of Gaddafi's dictatorship in 1969.[18]

Dissolved by cultural exchanges, national affiliations easily resurface under pressures from above; once the homogenization of the country prevails, Alexandria loses its unique charm. The city that had functioned as a home for these migrant denizens now sends them home. Milena, Olga, and Irene on the one hand and Albina's daughter Alexandra on the other share a similarly idealized perception of the immigrant city but from different time perspectives. The Egyptian port of the past emerges as a welcoming city to immigrants, to single women, to people from all religious backgrounds—a Tower of Babel where it was possible "to find a job without being exploited" (26). As the senior women look at the city nostalgically, Alexandra embraces it in its still active potential for being the ideal city: "What do you mean Egypt is theirs? Isn't it of those who live in it?" (26). In other words, the notion of foreignness that Milena embodies is counteracted with the one of belonging expressed by Alexandra. Born in Egypt and now left with no family, she is supposed to follow Milena back to Gorizia, but right when they are about to board the ship, she opts to stay in what is effectively her country. She is bilingual and a native, and she claims a sense of belonging that Milena instead discards: "You are not Egyptian enough" (28). In an intense exchange toward the end of the play that takes place on the liminal topos par excellence, the edge between land and sea, Alexandra, whose name assumes iconic power in the conclusion, reveals that as much as people see her as Italian, she has not even seen Italy once. The sentence powerfully gestures to the condition of today's new Italians, the children of immigrants born in Italy, where they are forced to feel foreign.[19] The future of Milena is as uncertain as Alexandra's but they both need to continue to assert the call toward independence and exploration of new mixed worlds. While Alexandra remains in what she sees as the utopian city, Milena considers other migratory destinations such as Canada, confirming once again how the Italian national identity was also defined in its diasporic dimension. Alexandra's decision to stay is nothing but a mirror of Milena's many years before and, as a result, Milena's return is her voyage reversed.

This inversion and refraction is rendered in the text with the iteration of some lines that in mapping the trip by ship functions as a circular refrain linking past and present in space. Part prayer, part travel diary, this long section in the script is the voice of the old generation, the one that experiences the voyage from Friuli to Egypt by ship to accompany the new generation. The old generation sees in the voyage a funerary walk demanding the protection of the saints—"Thanks Saint Ilario . . . . and Saint Taziano for this flat sea that does not flip the boat over and for this sun that does not let musk grow on our feet" (30)—and the new one as an exciting adventure pregnant with possibilities. The unexpected twist of the verses lies in the fact that they become an accurate description of the actual trajectory of the trip even though they are surprisingly described by a woman whose eyes are closed during the voyage and has never traveled: "My grandmother that geography she knew it well, she had people tell her and knew everything" (31), Milena first and Alexandra later remind the spectator/reader. The grandmother describes the archipelago of islands along the Croatian coast, the enchanted city of Dubrovnik/Ragusa "where people make love to seduce fortune" (31), the ghost- and bandit-ridden beaches of Albania where illicit traffic takes place, the fine coast of Greece full of short mustachioed men who use their refined minds, and then Turkey with its mysterious god "Allahdino." This simultaneously provincial and magical view of the Mediterranean's Adriatic coast incarnates ancient wisdom, tradition, as well as modernity since the voice is carried by a modern ship for that time and will take the new generation to a space of innovative experiences, Egypt (for Milena first and eventually for Alexandra).

The litany/travel report has a double function. On the one hand, it draws a geography of movement that once again explodes the constraints of the domestic and reveals the transnational nature of identity formation for people active along the sea routes (sailors, merchants, traffickers, as well as migrants). The Mediterranean, including the lesser known upper eastern section, the Adriatic, serves as the stage of these movements and interestingly enough it is traversed in a direction opposite to today's voyages. While the play does not make any direct reference to the contemporary northbound flows, the spectators/readers can hardly ignore those reverberations. On the other hand, the story told by the grandmother poignantly shows that knowledge of the migratory routes was also acquired through shared tales: She had learned that geography in the same way people learned about migrations, through first and secondhand stories that effectively produce as well as forge memory in the absence of official records.[20] This process becomes important in understanding the history-writing operation underlying *Alexandria*, which revolves around picking up echoes, traces, documents, and even personal reports of returned migrants who were still alive. The memory loop of the litany that gets repeated sheds light on one of the most profound truths about emigration and its cyclical nature—Italy clearly embodies a place of repeated departures in the script, a condition that in this book of mine has been frequently emphasized. The novelty in the case of *Alexandria* and the stories it recounts lies in the fact that the destination is unusual, especially from the contemporary perspective, which inscribes Egypt as a non–First World country. Interestingly, Egypt has been a place of departure for Egyptian migrants heading to Italy for decades now.[21] This return to the past also functions as a metaphor for the actual archeological research operation that this play and the larger initiative around it with the conference and its proceedings have entailed.[22] Its goal has been that of rescuing the story of the "aleksandrinke" from the silences of the returned migrants that are still alive and their family members, who did not see any pride in that "Levantine" experience of their women characterized in their views by split couples, child separation, and "libertine" lifestyles: in a word, by shame. The play functions as an experiment in reversing this sentiment.

An example of research work interweaving oral interviews and archival findings conducted by the play's director, Franco Però, that was then handed over by him to a female playwright (Renata Ciaravino) in order to provide the story with a distinctive gender perspective, *Alexandria* is the result of a collaboration that apparently held much more potential than the production allowed for. If on the one hand the material generated interest and fascination mostly because it relied on true stories, such as that of Milena herself, on the other it translated into the artistic project in relatively contained forms. As Però has himself stated in an interview with Sarah Gerbitz, "This is vast material, with which one could have done much more and many more shows could still be developed." The production at the Rossetti Theatre of Trieste gained strength from the presence of a solid actress, Elisabetta Pozzi, interpreting Milena, and the chemistry among the women worked out well; yet the use of some pseudo-footage from the Roaring Twenties in Alexandria introduced a dissonant note that hardly captured the magical atmosphere described by the women. Their words and memories prove to be much more powerful in evoking that magical era and what it meant to them. Additionally, some of the literary references are so subliminal that the cultural richness of this Mediterranean human tapestry is lost: Albina is vaguely inspired by an aunt of Fausta Cialente portrayed in one of her novels, and the aunt's love story with a Greek man seems to be modeled after a novel by Enrico Pea.[23] Despite these marginal shortcomings, the play and the work behind it are of great relevance in historical terms for their sociopolitical quality, and as an indirect window into contemporary Italy.

Interestingly, the play talks about domestic work but precisely because the experience of these Italian immigrants in Egypt was for the most part one of discovery and emancipation it frees them from the closed space of the houses where they worked and places them outdoors (the street, the port) or in the dance hall rather than the "safer" space of gardens and churches mentioned by more conservative reports. The foreign urban space allows these women to reduce or at least compensate for the preoccupation born out of their family situations in Italy while they enjoy a city pre-occupied by several migration experiences. The dynamic quality of this metropolitan space at least temporarily dissolves the sense of foreignness that immigrants usually feel and actually designs the ideal city of coexistence, in which difference is not erased but valued. While in Italy the city of Alexandria was seen as a place of damnation, for these women it was their place of origin that damned them to a sad fate, which the migration project to Alexandria instead in part transformed. The very domestic work experience abroad effectively broke the "purity" of the family by intrinsically embracing a "foreign" element (even in physical terms via the wet nursing process): By extension the exclusionary national parameter so embedded in the construct of the Western family was equally challenged. The result is a transnational map of movements and form of belonging that can also be traced in today's foreign immigration in Italy. The story of the domestic workers of Alexandria pre-occupies the experience of many women working in the same sector in Italy in environments that unfortunately are not always as cosmopolitan and embracing.

Colonial and Postcolonial Intimacies along the Italy/Ethiopia Trajectory

> At least some of the guests of today were the hosts of yesterday . . . (Curti)

The immigration phenomenon in Egypt was often independent from nation-based encapsulations. The wet or dry nurses as well as the maids from Italy did not always work for Italian families settled in the area, given the demographic diversity of Alexandria.[24] Yet, in the official Italian colonies, the *baliatico* was governed by a colonizer-colonized structure in which local women fed Italian babies. Known as *letté* in Eritrea,[25] these women were incorporated—I am using this "physical" verb on purpose—into the life of the baby and by extension the family in profoundly intimate ways despite the fact that they were racially "other." This close relationship with local people on the part of Italians was analogous to the practice of *madamismo*, by which Italian men entertained relationships with African women as part of temporary *more uxorio* contracts. Both these practices were suspended by the racism-imbued laws introduced by the Fascist regime in the 1930s: The recourse to indigenous wet nurses was deemed dangerous by "modern" medicine as a potential carrier of disease and mothers' breastfeeding was promoted instead. As Lombardi-Diop writes, "the role of the *letté* . . . was no longer central to the domestic economy of the colony [and had to be erased] in order to offer white women a frontier space and a 'proper' space as they settled in it to create modern Italian homes" ("Postracial" 181–82). Local women continued to serve as domestic workers in the homes of Italian settlers who stayed well after the post–World War II dismantling of the colonial empire, effectively creating a continuum of hierarchies between the colonial and postcolonial eras in the very colonized/decolonized space.

Today's scenario of domestic work in Italy is hardly postcolonial in the sense that immigrants active in this labor sector are not originally from the African Horn or other territories of the former Italian Empire in the Mediterranean, with a small number of exceptions (Bonizzoni 137). For the most part, domestic workers in Italian homes share a condition that in other parts of the book I have already referred to as "indirect postcolonialism" by which they come from places that were under a colonial rule different from the Italian one or were under Communist regimes. Indeed, they are from Romania, Ukraine, the Philippines, Moldavia, Peru, Poland, Ecuador, Sri Lanka, Morocco, and Albania in order of magnitude (Fondazione 13): As of 2011, roughly 710,000 immigrants worked as domestic workers in Italy, and they represented 81.5 percent of the entire sector, within which their presence has tripled in the past ten years (Fondazione 11).[26] Women represent 80 percent of the sector (Agostini 5). After a flow in the 1960s from Eritrea ("Indagine" 2), domestic workers came from the Philippines as part of one of the first steady flows, which starting in the mid-1970s was regulated by a binational agreement contemplating visas, contracts, and even paid flights.[27] In the 1970s, the practice of hiring a person from the Philippines was so widespread that the expression "*il filippino/la filippina*" came to refer to maids and housecleaners, and in some cases caretakers or babysitters, whatever their ethnic or national origin. This blend of nationality and labor, whose racist nuance was completely lost on upper- and middle-class families, was prompted by a social hierarchy that effectively reproduced a colonial discourse in the Western world and in a condition of indirect colonialism, since the Philippines were under Spanish and American imperial control.

The perception of immigrant domestic workers—largely women—is that of precious helpers in the sustenance of both the productive and reproductive economy of the family (and the nation by extension) at a time in which the aging population is growing steadily in Italy[28] and the birth rate is one of the lowest in the world.[29] Elderly caretaking has become the most common form of employment in the domestic sector for immigrant women under a category known as *badante*, that has transcended the widespread discrimination applied to both employed and unemployed immigrants and has come to represent a cherished presence instead, as Patrizia Pulga's photo suggests in its warm depiction of the relationship between caretaker and senior person (Fig. 19). In replacing the role that family members would play in the extended family structure of the past, the *badanti* become ideal young daughters or "paid *traditional housewives*" whose presence allows for the norm to be still in place, as Degiuli shows ("Laboring" 348). As she further remarks, "the presence of migrant women workers therefore allows the perpetuation of a fictional reality both at a private and at an institutional level" (349) insofar as neither the family nor the state need to rethink their basic structures in terms of elderly care. The "special care" exercised toward the caretakers, as I refer to it, has consequently created a separate paradigm for these immigrants who in the eyes of both employers and policymakers constitute an integral part of Italian society while immigration continues to represent a sore spot.[30]

Whereas the combination of duties, hours to perform them, and compensation vary, the literature shows how the utilitarian view of immigrant women easily becomes exploitative: Caretakers/housekeepers are much needed but not necessarily protected. The convoluted bureaucratic process needed to provide a legal contract to domestic workers and the assumption that compensation can be minimal because the job often comes with food and board—monthly salaries ranged from $500 to $1,000 in 2010 (Fondazione 14)—has relegated these women to a condition of semi-servitude or, in Pojmann's definition, to that of "servants in a hostile culture" (182). The totalizing nature of this employment which reduces/eliminates free time, vacation, and private space/time, as pointed out by Degiuli ("A Job" 196) reifies these subjects while at the same time the family and national

FIGURE 19. *Bologna. Hassanatu e Serena*, 2002. Photo by Patrizia Pulga.

discourse makes them feel precious because they are "different" from other immigrants who are seen instead as undesirable. The tendency to tolerate migrants for their utility instead of accepting them as complete individuals, with relationships, families or needs of their own is at the core of Gabriella Ghermandi's story "The Story of Woizero Bekelech and Signor Antonio." Ghermandi's text delves into the intimacies of this relationship by adopting a colonial and postcolonial historical lens with the goal of questioning the hierarchies introduced by that history.

"The Story" is included in Ghermandi's novel *Queen of Flowers and Pearls*, which is considered to be one of the most cogent responses to a reductive if not positive representation of Italian colonialism[31] with particular reference to Ethiopia, a country whose fierce resistance to colonization kept Italy from subjugating it completely.[32] The Ethiopian-Eritrean origin of Ghermandi's family and her own work as a writer, performer and cultural activist contesting race and gender discrimination are essential to understand the genesis and message of the overall book.[33] In adopting the traditional structure of storytelling common among the elderly in her place of provenance, Ghermandi has built a circular novel that ranges from the Italo-Ethiopian conflict and the dictatorship of Mengistu Haile Malram to contemporary Italy. In following the vicissitudes of a young Ethiopian woman, Mahlet, who moves to Italy and then recollects memories of the past in order to make sense of her role and destiny as a *trait d'union* between tradition and the present, the author forges a semiautobiographical text that is both a rewriting of Italian colonial history and a powerful reflection on the postcolonial condition in Italy. The first part of the book, called "Promise," is devoted to the life of Yacob and the detailed life of Mahlet, while the second, "Return," hosts a series of five tales ranging from Aesop-style fables to stories of colonial abuse and anticolonial resistance including that of women fighters. The protagonist Mahlet is the listener of these tales conveyed to her by the local sage Abba Yacob and will eventually learn how to share the stories herself after the repeated invitation not to forget the ancestors who like "a star [will] guide [her] pride" (262). An alter ego of Ghermandi herself, in what proves to be an artful metaliterary device, Mahlet is the "*cantora*," a female singer/storyteller entrusted with maintaining the patrimony of Ethiopian tales alive for future generations, a gendered choice of relevant weight. The overall message of the book is that of identifying in memory a process of recognition and awareness that fastens together the microhistory of individuals to the macrohistory of civilizations along the diachronic line. As the book's narrator, a hardly disguised Ghermandi herself, reveals at the very end referring to Yacob: "And so, that is why today I am telling you his story. Which is also my story. But now yours as well" (270). It is with this specific mechanism of temporally shifting from back then to now that Ghermandi "pre-occupies" the Italian present with a colonial history that is not other but rather intrinsic to the country.

This time-shifting device is the central engine of "The Story," the last of the five tales that Abba Yacob shares with Mahlet. This story provides an ideal bridge from the colonial to the postcolonial period and condition as it focuses on an indigenous domestic worker, Bekelech, who is employed half time by an Italian family, the Mandriolis, about to return to Italy from Ethiopia. While it is not clear what year the action is set in—the only temporal reference at the very beginning is "20 years ago" (216)—the story presumably refers to the mid-1970s when the Derg Communist dictatorship took over and foreign settlers fled the country and tried to take their maids along (Amato 22). In this sense, "The Story" barely carries any trace of official history since it privileges the intimate space over the public and institutional one. When the Mandriolis decide to return to join Franca Mandrioli's aging mother, they ask Bekelech to consider following them at a later time. After a period of full-time work for the Barbieris, Bekelech receives an official invitation and contract from the Mandriolis. Despite the fact that her social condition is not desperate, Bekelech decides to emigrate out of loyalty, given the strong bond she has developed with Franca.

As we learn later in the story (235), her choice to emigrate is also a self-imposed test that would prove her ability to handle life in a country that many consider preferable to Ethiopia. In reality, life in Italy is far from glitzy, even though people abroad think of the country as a "paradise" (221). Italy soon appears to be a place where, ironically enough, people privilege the private over the public sphere when compared to Ethiopia: a country with "wealth, road that lit up at night with rows and rows of streetlights, . . . hospitals that heals you, trains, buses," yet one full of solitude where people do not share and are often in a rush even though it is not clear where they are going (231). Bekelech finds herself in a place "full of older people" (218) unused to novelty, and is wrapped in a silence that she finds uncomfortable when compared with the liveliness of her neighborhood in Addis Ababa. Like many immigrant women today who come to Italy in search of better opportunities, Bekelech is trapped in a job that is fully absorbing and highly isolating, as many studies and cultural texts confirm.[34] In charge of Franca Mandrioli's old mother, Anna, Bekelech is relegated to a hyperdomestic and maddeningly quiet, disorienting life in the provincial environment of a small mountain village not far from Bologna.[35] The lack of personal relationships and social life is compounded with the racist abuse she is subjected to by the old woman, who sees her as an exotic creature. Bekelech's skin—more than her origin, as the narrator seems to suggest—prompts all kinds of questions about the presence of cannibals among her people, the use of huts instead of houses, and so on, which point to the exoticization of as much as ignorance about the "other." Bekelech's patience wears thin over the months, in particular after she discovers that she is underpaid, in the course of a conversation with the Barbieris who are visiting from Addis Ababa for the summer. Instead of quietly leaving or passively accepting the situation, Bekelech confronts the Mandriolis and asks for a raise, but is brutally dismissed as ungrateful and invited to consider the unique opportunity they offered her in taking her out of her "African hole" (223). While this negotiation about labor reveals Bekelech's agency and sense of self-dignity, her decision to stay speaks of her sense of allegiance. Ghermandi's choice to leave her with the Mandriolis signals the entrapments produced by colonial language and practices, as Bekelech is not a subject of the system but is instead subject to the control of the employer's family. The domestic space is clearly pre-occupied by the colonial experience (or postcolonial experience in Africa itself, since it is not clear in the story when the Mandriolis moved to Ethiopia). The colonial hierarchies are reproduced in the postcolonial condition: The relationship is effectively neocolonial given the economic exploitation and racial discrimination Bekelech faces in Italy.

After battling with her sense of nostalgia and loneliness for another season and her frustration over Anna's relentlessly racist comments, Bekelech finally quits and does so in a dramatic form reminiscent of the anticolonial fighters that Ghermandi depicts in other stories of *Queen*. When Anna insensitively inquires about Bekelech's genitalia, she challenges the old woman by flashing her (224) and promptly leaves the house to join the Barbieris who in the meantime have offered her a position as a domestic worker with a respectable family in the city of Bologna. This move confirms Bekelech's growing self-awareness and defiance of the system of oppression, as well as her ability to identify networks of support: The repressive nature of the domestic work for the Mandriolis family and environment does not thwart her, and her decision to move to Bologna proves to be rewarding. With an interesting narrative twist, Ghermandi assigns her a domestic work position that, while maintaining housekeeping tasks, turns her into a babysitter for an adorable child, thus providing her with the rewards of childrearing (playfulness, affection, a sense of gratification) that can be less frequent in eldercare assistance. Yet, Bekelech continues to be an alien presence, a condition most likely produced by her clear lack of belonging in the eyes of the locals. Assuming the story is set in the 1980s, Bekelech would have likely been a fairly unusual presence in the Bologna area and, by extension, Italy. As Bekelech states when commenting on the surprise of the old residents at seeing her: "I think that, around here, no one had ever seen a black person except on television" (218). Ghermandi masterfully interpolates a stream-of-consciousness section in which Bekelech expresses her frustration at being considered either "African" by people at large or a generic product of the Italian Empire (225) by better informed Italians, two visions that are equally reductive and inherently colonial in nature and that ultimately make her feel "other."

The only person that interrupts her isolation and provides Bekelech with a sense of warmth is a senior neighbor of hers, Signor Antonio, who speaks Amharic, having spent time in Ethiopia in the 1930s both as a military and a civil officer. Their initial encounters are characterized by, on the one hand, a growing excitement on the part of Signor Antonio who can finally interact with a close manifestation of Ethiopia, a land that he fell in love with, and on the other hand, by a mix of pleasant discovery and hesitation on the part of Bekelech. The previous experiences in Italy have taught her to be cautious and she decides to exercise her discretion, thus showing her agency once again. The relationship between Signor Antonio and Bekelech pivots around language and writing; he functions as her scribe in charge of writing letters to her family. A typical subject of many stories of migration,[36] letter writing becomes an ideal turf for performance of affect and intellect. By inserting this mechanism in a colonial/postcolonial context, Ghermandi inflects it in novel ways: Antonio, a foreigner to Ethiopia, is helping Bekelech write in her own language in a doubly displaced fashion. While she is illiterate, he speaks the language of the formerly colonized and activates his knowledge away from the former colony in their service. The vertical structure of the relationship (the colonizer

በስመአብ በወልድ በመንፈስ ቅዱስ በጌታችን በመድህኒታችን በኢየሱስ ክርስቶስ ስም ለምወዳችሁ ወድ እናቴ ወድ አባቴ ወንድሞቼ እንዲሁም አሁቶቼ ለጤናችሁ እንደምን አላችሁልኝ? እኔ ከቡር አምላክ ይመስገነዉ ለጤናዬ በጣም ደህና ነኝ። ...

FIGURE 20. Excerpt from a letter written by Signor Antonio in Amharic and included in the short story.

knows the colonized language and owns power over knowledge) cannot be escaped, and Bekelech legitimately doubts his intentions. Through a clever solution, Ghermandi makes the letter unintelligible to both the diegetic reader (Bekelech) and the extradiegetic reader (ourselves) by reproducing it in its original form on the printed page of the short story (230) (Fig. 20). Only when the letter arrives in Addis Ababa and she has her family read it to her over the phone, which means for us readers seeing it as a transcription of the call on the page, does Bekelech realize for sure that Signor Antonio has faithfully transcribed her words (she tests him twice through this same mechanism). He means well and is not the *talian sollato* ("Italian soldier," read conqueror, 218) that colonial history had led her to think.

The regained trust constitutes the basis for a friendship that understandably shows its unevenness: Signor Antonio knows Amharic better than Bekelech does; he is referred to as Signor, while Bekelech does not have a title;[37] he uses the informal "tu" in addressing her and she uses the formal "voi". But the relationship develops along the lines of mutual respect. Bekelech thus finds herself spending time with an elderly person outside the usual restrictive obligations and expectations produced by the domestic service industry. Their conversations in his kitchen or in the course of walks around the neighborhood are independent from imposed entertainment and effectively become an occasion to reverse many hierarchies and ultimately historical records and perceptions in the name of an unexpected friendship. The exchanges between Bekelech and Signor Antonio reveal a man who was so profoundly touched by the beauty of Ethiopia, its people and its culture, that already during his stay in Africa, first as a soldier and later as a civic officer, he defended the locals from the abuses of the colonizing Italians and the lies they circulated about the effectiveness of Ethiopian resistance. As a result, he has developed a unique *mal d'Afrique*: Ethiopia has left such a deep mark on his soul that he cannot return even for a visit. While initially the reader is led to believe that there is some personal secret behind that decision or that he is nostalgic about colonial times, the very last line of the short story reveals that he is ashamed to go back because of what Italy has done to Ethiopia (270). The domestic environment with its letter writing, translations, and revelations therefore turns from an intimate to a public space in which transnational relationships are discussed and revisited.

Through the encounter with Signor Antonio, Bekelech loses the position of the inferior domestic worker—imposed by her gender, race, and national difference—and surprisingly becomes the object of an apology that she is asked to face in the name of her country.

While she herself does not feel equipped to incarnate what Signor Antonio attributes to Ethiopia as a whole (an ancient tradition, a fierce spirit of resistance, and a refined language), the short story repositions her on the map of international relations and grants her a position of respect. Signor Antonio's shame works as a form of recognition that sets in motion a form of cognition on the part of the reader, that is, a different assessment of history that is ultimately an attempt at decolonizing the mind and the spirit, and at focusing on exchanges rather than exclusions. His offer to translate from the oral to the written and thus allow for a transaction of words across continents is a form of service toward the one-time colonial subject and, to a degree, a catharsis for himself. His choices and sense of shame offer a factual response to Lidia Curti's incisive invitation to consider that "at least some of the guests of today were the hosts of yesterday" (60); indeed, some of the immigrant workers in Italy today come from places that hosted Italians in the past and in some cases were abused by their presence. Adopted as the epigraph of this chapter section, Curti's words function as a call to adopt a new vision in reading immigration that is inclusive of the legacy of Italian colonialism, a vision attentive to "pre-occupation." Ghermandi herself adopts this reversed lens to bring visibility to this complex history informing the personal and cultural world of immigrants from the former colonies. In the space of a kitchen, the least official space by definition, Ghermandi stages the offer of a national amendment to the usually most "invisible" transnational migrant, the domestic worker.

From Domestic Preoccupation to the Pre-Occupation of Transnational Intimate Spaces

A number of aspects related to both "The Story" and *Alexandria* are better addressed in tandem, since they create an implicit dialogue thanks to a conjoined examination: a general consideration of the connection between subaltern stories such as those of domestic workers and hegemonic history; the question of language in the text; the role of space; and gender dynamics. Unlike the vast space of the ocean/sea and the layered space of residential/living places, the domestic space is rarely addressed to probe broad issues such as immigration and colonialism. Yet, it yields fascinating vistas over human relationships, historical linkages and cultural formations, and holds both preoccupation and possibilities within it. In a revealing article on the role of servants' narratives about the Dutch colonization of Java, Ann Laura Stoler and Karen Strassler perceptively remind us that "in contrast to nation-centered narratives, the domestic occupies a space that is neither heroic, nor particularly eventful, nor marked by the brash violences in which colonial relationships are more often thought to be located" (9). When the colonial intersects with migrations and thus the postcolonial, the emotional economy of the everyday becomes transnational; additionally, in the case of Italy, the national is questioned by the fact that contemporary immigration is pre-occupied by emigration abroad. *Alexandria* occupies "The Story" indirectly in the sense that the two texts show a circulatory movement of women leaving Italy and going to Italy along colonial and postcolonial routes exposing similarities as well as differences. Together, they point to the pre-occupation of Italy's present with a past that is full of stories and suggestions. These stories are subaltern narratives meant to substitute hegemonic history; they certainly work against it but are also profoundly intertwined with it, and they reveal the formation of the nation in the kinetic space of the transnation defined by colonialism and immigration. By relying on the only apparent uneventfulness of these women's lives, the two texts portray women who are resistant to subservience both at home and in the new country in different degrees. Their decisions to leave, stay, and return are dictated by complex family, personal, and contextual mechanisms that vary over time, showing the fluidity of choices and the shifting nature of situations. Their paths are not linear but ultimately transcend exclusion thanks to the women's adaptability in what is effectively a process of negotiation of modernity mediated by migration. This depiction is not as common. Female domestic workers are often consigned to literal or metaphorical silence. The work of contemporary Eritrean writer Hamid Barole Abdu, for instance, showcases this effacement via death-imbued stories about the lack of communication across cultures.[38] By the same token, Amara Lakhous's character Maria Cristina Gonzales in *Clash of Civilizations*, discussed in Chapter 3, and Cristiana de Caldas Brito's "Ana de Jesus," addressed in this chapter, generally convey a sense of claustrophobia and regimentation. *Alexandria* and "The Story" instead privilege life and possibilities, while remaining sensitive to the forms of suffering that the relocation entails (nostalgia, loneliness, challenges, and losses).

From a stylistic point of view, the two texts present two forms of verbalization of this experience: *Alexandria* hinges on a choral model in which different voices enrich each other without blending uniformly while "The Story" opts for a first-person narration. Linguistically, they are both uninterested in registering the richness they articulate: The "aleksandrinke" speak Italian rather than dialect and the Tower of Babel environment they live in is rendered in just a few foreign words that pepper the text. Similarly, Ghermandi chooses a canonical Italian for Bekelech, an improbable choice for a woman who cannot even write in her own language; far from the daring experiment by Cetta Petrollo in *Senza permesso*, where the Italian reader is as displaced as a foreigner in Italy in trying to follow the story, Ghermandi opts for an impeccable literary language relying on the simple-past-based standard literary narration which is interrupted only by transliterated words from and expressions written in Amharic. The power of the word in both stories rests in a more subtle space then: the articulation of the protagonists' stories takes place not just at the level of the narration via the story and script, but also at that of the alphabet on the page and the transcription of the phone calls in "The Story," and the reading of letters in *Alexandria*. This verbalization recasts domestic workers as people and not just invisible presences.

Spatially, the two texts unfold in quite different directions: *Alexandria* is about the topic of domestic space rather than being set inside it, and substitutes the home with the city in order to emphasize the unique opportunities open to the Italian women it references. The Egyptian capital offers an intimate canvas of life stories infused with the port's breeze of Alexandria, which Paolo Rumiz defined as "the New York of the Mediterranean" in his review of the play in 2005. By contrast, Italy embodies a place with little opportunity and no vibrancy as the experience of Bekelech in "The Story" reminds us. The levels of integration and enjoyment of the new country's social fabric are vastly different even though all these women come from similar family backgrounds (if anything, Bekelech seems to be more privileged in her choices rather than being compelled to leave). The migratory project for each woman may assume a different meaning, but what their stories as a whole reveal is that their acceptance or exclusion is the result of ideological conditioning, and one fraught with contradictions at that. The "aleksandrinke" enjoy acceptance insofar as the cultural climate created by the government does not represent them as alien to the system (at least until Arab nationalism takes over), while Bekelech is clearly the victim of a doubly exclusionary system: The color of her skin and her immigrant status both constitute grounds for discrimination. Signor Antonio's openness toward her is the result of an ideological revisitation. He realizes that Italian colonialism was an iniquitous occupation and is now preoccupied with identifying ways of giving back to Ethiopian people in order to compensate for injustices. In today's Italy, targeted pragmatism takes the place of ideology: A country often paralyzed by the fear of immigrant invasion actually opens the doors of its most private spaces to entrust these very immigrants with the most fragile family members, as Lakhous remarks in the epigraph, taken from his novel *Clash of Civilizations* (72). This oscillation between rejection and acceptance exposes the inner tension of a relationship between locals and immigrants that is always mediated by history and through public discourse via the media, but also by personal discoveries. By occupying the private space, immigrants preoccupy Italians, yet at the same time they define unlikely connections.

From a broader spatial perspective, *Alexandria* and "The Story" design a more nuanced international geography attentive to the place of origin and destination alike. At a time in which Italian society legally "imports" foreigners for the domestic sector—effectively declaring the failure of the welfare state and the health system in providing solutions for elderly care (Parati, *Migration* 156)—the risk of reducing these workers to mere labor force is high. The tendency to see domestic workers as people "without a past, with nothing interesting to say, and coming from places without a history" (Bekelech's words in Ghermandi, 238) is a way for Italians to manage the sense of preoccupation about the "other" within their own spatial coordinates. Narratives such as the ones offered by *Alexandria* and "The Story" reverse this approach and consider the cultures of origin and destination and, even more so, the enrichment that their contact produces. Otherwise obliterated by an economic prison that expects only service from them to the point of extracting a heavy physical toll,[39] immigrant domestic workers instead find a much fairer representation in projects that, in paying attention to their "homes" in Italy as well as their "homes" at home, show the sacrifices they face in effectively supporting two families across countries.[40]

As a result, when viewed together, *Alexandria* and "The Story" indicate a remapping of the nation defined by the affective production and reproduction linked to these "global women," according to the expression used by Barbara Ehrenreich and Arlie Hochschild to refer to domestic workers in their book. By designing a geography of intimacy in the public sphere and bringing the globe to the domestic sphere, the two texts and by extension the experience of these global women point out how the nation always exceeds its physical borders and redraws the cultural ones on new territories. Current immigration to Italy is thus pre-occupied by past emigration abroad, despite the systemic amnesia or lack of knowledge about the past. This circularity is made even more complex by the recent exodus of Italians abroad and the type of official rhetoric used to represent it. The economic and political crisis of the last decades has forced many to relocate both within Europe and to the United States The literature on this phenomenon abundantly embraces portraits of Italians who have reinvented themselves somewhere else in all possible professional roles and with different levels of success, interestingly mirroring the experience of Italian migrants of the past or immigrants in contemporary Italy.[41] Stories about their jobs have even come to include domestic employment, yet it is worth noting how Italians involved in this sector abroad are represented in bombastic ways by the media. A case in point is the story of "the Italian housekeeper" par excellence which I am embracing here anecdotally to point to the inner ideological contradictions related to the representation of migrant work in Italy's cultural sphere. Originally from Tuscany, and employed by the Queen of England for thirteen years, forty-four-year-old Antonella Fresolone was chosen as the housekeeper for Kate and William in preparation for the arrival of their son. Italian newspaper articles hailed the news as a point of pride for Italy, not only for Fresolone's qualities (ethical rigor, abnegation) but mostly for her ability to function as a typical made-in-Italy product thanks to her unique cooking skills (see "Una 'tuttofare'"). In an unexpected inversion of rhetoric, an Italian housekeeper at the British royal family's residences makes the news, while thousands of *badanti* in Italy remain invisible except when writers, filmmakers, and photographers are preoccupied by their only apparently uneventful lives, which instead tell so much about the transnational life of the country past and present.

CONCLUSION

Italy as a Laboratory for Imagi-Nation: The Citizenship Law between Inbound and Outbound Flows

This book has attempted to create a space or rather a map of interconnected spaces to address the layered history of movement that has made Italy into a nation whose unifying process has been incessantly sustained and yet defied by dispersion. Homi Bhabha used the term "dissemiNation" to highlight this phenomenon. His aim was to address the margins of the nation in order to discover its "alterity" in the colonial space, and thus the limitations (impossibility?) of national projects and of modernity at large (148). My view embraces this intriguing concept, inflects it in terms of emigration in addition to colonialism, and at the same time swivels it 180 degrees to investigate how the nation has become the receptacle of the reversed dissemination (postcolonial immigration). In linking such apparently disconnected events as emigration/immigration and post/colonialism, the book has thus reconsidered in systematic ways their nexuses in the understanding of Italy and its culture. The result is a transnational vision in which dislocation allows us to make sense of a place and in which diffusion carries a unique potential for fusion across boundaries.

The concepts of pre-occupation and preoccupation have guided a voyage through three centuries (nineteenth, twentieth, and twenty-first) and five continents (Africa, South America, North America, Europe, Asia), bringing together various levels of meaning: occupation as "invasion" of space (colonialism) or reversed "repossession" (postcolonialism); occupation as occupancy of space in terms of living (migrants residing abroad); occupation as work production in and of space; and occupation as "attention" and "concern," indeed preoccupation, and its embedded term pre-occupation. The suffix "pre" separated by the hyphen has defined a temporal axis in this book about space in order to highlight the centrality of the past in the comprehension of the present due to its obvious reverberations. This investigation in the book has been undertaken through cultural texts from a very broad range of genres embracing written, spoken, and sung words as well as (moving) images as part of a remapping of Italy's cultural history, which is also a remapping of its canon.

These various approaches were designed with three objectives in mind. First, connectivity allows for a comprehensive view of topics usually addressed as separate or as competing (colonialism being a more established field than emigration in U.S. academia) with the aim of questioning and making sense of the nation in motion at large.[1] Second, the thematic thread (pre-occupation/preoccupation) offers a reading of these inbound and outbound movements that is diachronic and synchronic at once, and triggers the political thrust of the book's argument. Recognition (acknowledgement) toward cognition (understanding) means facing what has been experienced before as the precondition for empathizing in the present, and thus for dispelling preoccupation against those widespread forms of exclusion and racism that are increasingly more normative. Third, the use of cultural texts along with data about migration (rather than privileging one over the other) provides a humanistic reading of migrations, in itself a political choice if political is seen as an act for the polis. The stories narrated in these texts tell us about and address a community that is invariably implicated with motion and yet is constantly pulled toward a definition: The nation knocks at the door of the diaspora. Yet, precisely because of the tension created by the push-and-pull movement of the national narrative (fictional by definition) and the national dispersion, this process of definition, which entails some essentialism even if only strategically, opens up the possibility of what I call an imagi-nation, expanding on Cassano's insistence on the regenerative role of "imagination" (44) in a diverse national space like that of Italy where purity is limited and transits abound (4). In a space of this nature, creative possibilities become infinite. In this book, such possibilities have been traced in travel, living, and work spaces or rather in the cultural texts that represent and express these spaces, and ultimately make them even more meaningful than they are in real life via transposition. In the process, the book has developed into a brief survey of the works on the specific subjects being treated with many chapters offering short annotated bibliographies of related texts. Ultimately, the book has turned into a layered space in which cultural texts are always somewhat pre-occupied by other texts, often despite the geographical distance; as a result, the space of the national canon has been disseminated.

The juridical space, in addressing the polis by definition, designs potential forms of transcendence from the nation while measuring up to it. The occasion for this reflection is Italy's citizenship law, which brings to the surface the forms of historical and contemporary overlapping discussed in this book. While in its current form the law breaks the strictly national mold and opens up to demographic dispersion, it still clings to an exclusionary paradigm thus defeating its "elastic" vision. To unpack some of these contradictions, the conclusion analyzes two audiovisual texts (Maria Rosa Jijon's *Forte e Chiaro* and Fred Kuwornu's *18 Ius Soli*) along with an educational project ("Cultural-Shock") and then concludes with a reference to a project that bears much potential for new forms of citizenship on this planet for which Italy is proving to be a "laboratory," to borrow a term from Michael Hardt's fruitful concept.

A Citizenship Law for Immigrants Pre-Occupied by and with Emigration

> A people of poets, artists, heroes, saints, thinkers, scientists, explorers, and transmigrators. (Palace of Italian Civilization, EUR, Rome)

This inscription appears in large characters on the façade of what is also known as the Palace of Italian Civilization—informally known as the Square Colosseum—in Rome. Built between 1938 and 1943 at Mussolini's initiation, it is one of the most canonical examples of Novecento architecture and of the monumentality of the Fascist Era at its peak. The most striking aspect of the inscription is its choice in extending the famous saying "Italy: a people of saints, poets and explorers" to the category of the *trasmigratori*, that is, emigrants. The inclusion of the term prompts two considerations, of a linguistic and political nature respectively. For the former, "to transmigrate" is mainly used with reference to the passage of souls from one body to another in metempsychosis and only infrequently to indicate mass migration. Additionally, the term *trasmigratori* is a derivative that almost makes the subjects of this action into machines. As for the latter consideration, the term was used by Mussolini in a 1934 speech aimed at justifying Italy's colonial aims: It reflected his drive to identify the national ethos with its geographical dispersion and to recuperate its diaspora into the "fatherland" as a point of pride. As part of his colonial and imperial vision, this attitude simultaneously erased Italy's responsibility for the massive emigration up to the 1920s in terms of economic weakness, and couched its aggressive intervention into foreign territories in a rhetoric of "natural" demographic expansion.[2] Mussolini's transnational remapping interestingly rethought the nation outside its borders, but only as part of a self-interested rhetoric. My view is that Italy ought to reform in the opposite direction the most nationalist of all laws—the citizenship law—which, at the moment, privileges Italian descendants abroad over the children of foreign immigrants in Italy, also referred to as "new Italians."

In illustrating the most salient moments of the formulation of Italian citizenship since the country's unification and their effects in and outside the country, my analysis reveals some of the contradictions of the current Italian approach, namely the prioritization of the past (Italian emigrants' descendants) over the present (immigrants in Italy). My reading calls instead for a view that, despite the procedural challenges involved, shows a deeper awareness of the country's unique experience of migrations since the unification and dynamically connects pre-occupation and preoccupation. This is the "imagi-nation" mentioned before—a nation able to remain actively linked to the Italian diaspora out of the nation's territorial boundaries while engaging the immigrant population living in

Italy with a more attuned understanding of the colonial and postcolonial implications of its presence in Italy. This complex triangulation, even more necessary in this second decade of the twenty-first century, in which Italians are emigrating again in large numbers,[3] is in many ways embedded in the history of Italian citizenship; a triangulation that has been resistant to allowing positive energies to flow across its nodes, thus short-circuiting the generation of sensible opportunities.

Introduced in 1992, Law 91, the governing citizenship law, fundamentally confirms the right of Italian descendants to acquire an Italian passport and the benefits attached to it, but in addition to previous laws, it also extends the category of blood-based eligibility into previous generations while definitively endorsing dual citizenship. Quite surprisingly for a country like Italy, which had at that point clearly become a point of destination for contemporary immigrants, or perhaps precisely due to this new role in the Mediterranean, the Parliament passed a law that in the uncompromising words of historian and economist Luca Einaudi was designed "for the Italians abroad and against foreigners in Italy" (186). Indeed, compared with the previous law dating back to 1912, the children of foreigners would not be able to acquire the citizenship automatically by showing proof of birthplace and residence as part of an administrative procedure to be initiated within one year from their twenty-first birthday. Instead, the current law requires uninterrupted legal residence in Italy from birth to the age of eighteen or at the time of submission of paperwork, which has to be before turning nineteen (the window for submission is thus less than a year).[4] By introducing the assessment of the request in lieu of the automatic administrative process, the granting of citizenship has now been turned into a discretionary operation that opens up the possibility of a denial.

Despite the increasing number of immigrants in Italy, at least up until 2011, the number of naturalizations has not grown proportionally, and Italy remains the country with the lowest citizenship-granting index within the EU.[5] Additionally, the prerequisite for naturalization for residents born in other countries was taken to ten years compared to the previous five-year threshold of the 1912 law, thus reversing the general trend in so-called developed countries that experience growing immigration flows. It comes as no surprise then that naturalization by marriage is the most common route for immigrants in Italy today.

The consequences of this law on the second generation, referred to as G2, are quite serious: The lack of citizenship until the age of eighteen, which often extends for a few years given the bureaucratic complications and the possibility of denial, may place these young people in a condition of limbo for longer than two decades after their birth. Unlike the children of immigrants in the United States who in some cases are fully undocumented and as such invisible or at risk of deportation,[6] many in Italy hold a renewable stay permit, which expires as often as every two years (some fortunately hold a residence card for "extra"-EU citizens, which is comparable to a U.S. green card). The lack of citizenship limits their ability to leave the country for trips with their schoolmates or for family visits abroad, and over time their access rights to scholarships, jobs, sport competitions, and benefits entailing a citizenship requirement. A particularly challenging requirement for eligibility to citizenship is the proof of a regular annual income of over 8,000 euros for a period of three years. This constitutes a particularly substantial obstacle for the second generation, in light of the structural instability of the Italian economy.

While people such as the second generation who are born and raised on Italian soil, schooled in the local system, fluent in Italian (often with a regional dialect inflection), and very much attuned to local habits cannot benefit from the rights granted by citizenship due to the prevailing regulations, Italian descendants abroad are readily able to become citizens due to the privileging of *ius sanguinis* at the exclusion of *ius soli*.[7] Some restrictions apply to them as well (for example, the interruption of Italian citizenship holding in the family tree at some point due to the acquisition of citizenship in the country of immigration), and the bureaucratic process can be quite time-consuming. But there is not a discretionary decision-making process, and obtaining citizenship can be quite straightforward for, say, a twenty-year-old residing in New Jersey, while it can potentially turn into a nightmare for the son of a Brazilian immigrant in Rome. In other words, it is not just the level of difficulty imposed by the citizenship law that is so aggravating for the second generation of immigrants in Italy, but the generous attitude that the country has institutionalized for the emigrant community regardless of the level of knowledge of the Italian language and culture on the part of the applicants and despite their lack of or often limited active participation in the economic, social, and cultural life of the country. Other consequences of Law 91 affect national resources and international relations. Italian descendants' citizenship applications have produced unmanageable amounts of administrative work at consulates abroad.[8] The dual citizenship recognized by Law 91—coupled with the 2001 electoral law, which grants Italian citizens abroad the right to vote and elect their own members of Parliament, that is, candidates running for jurisdictions in foreign countries—has created citizens with double civic loyalties. This ability to have active rights in national elections in more than one country at the same time has been a controversial point in international debates. Additionally, the granting of Italian citizenship, and thus the ability to travel freely in the EU or with no visa to such countries like the United States, has been considered a unilateral decision on the part of Italy that affects other countries that had no say in the matter. For example, studies show that a number of irregular immigrants from Italy in the United States have Argentinian citizenship, thus indicating that Law 91 as the source of what Tintori calls "a Carsic river" between the Americas (85), in which Italianness resurfaces from the underground like the rivers of the Italian Northeast.[9] In the meantime, roughly a million people born in Italy of immigrant parents or brought to the country at a very young age cannot benefit from the rights granted by citizenship and as a result live a shadow existence in what is effectively their primary if not only country—in most cases they are not familiar with the country of origin of their parents, since they cannot visit due to the lack of papers (Fig. 21).[10]

FIGURE 21. L'Italia all'Italiani (Italy to "Eyetalians"), 2006. Photo by Roberto Cavallini.

Immigration, Emigration, and Postcolonialism in the G2 Cultural Production

"I asked to become Italian despite feeling Italian." (*18 Ius Soli*)
"I'm Roman: Do I look like a tourist to you?" (*Forte e chiaro*)

Along with the very vocal 2012 campaign called "I am Italy too,"[11] responses to the peculiar structure of the law have come primarily from the Rete G2 (second-generation network) over the years, an association run by and for the children of immigrants born in Italy or taken to Italy by their immigrant parents. Besides concrete political actions pushed forward by a branch called G2 Parlamenta with a focus on reform of the citizenship law, Rete has also developed a variety of materials to educate a broader audience about the specific situation of the G2 and their claim to fuller recognition in Italian (and thus European) society. Among its several tools—including short stories, novels, memoirs, a musical album, and even more unusual formats such as a *fotoromanzo* and a game[12]—the 2006 video *Forte e chiaro* by Maria Rosa Jijon addressed for the first time the urgent need to revisit the law in order to make the lives of the immigrant descendants manageable.[13] The short video emphatically denounces the impact of the current law on these young people in terms of job opportunities, access to civic rights, and mobility, but mostly for its power to deny them the peace of mind that comes with official papers. Simply put, one of the most unbearable elements of these young people's existence is repeatedly being in line to renew a stay permit that makes them legal and acceptable in the country where they were born and/or raised. Another aspect that they underscore is the fact that consequently they are anomalies and outsiders.

The uniqueness of *Forte e chiaro* lies in the perspective it offers. In representing this body of youth as protagonists and articulate voices, it emphasizes the preoccupation constantly experienced by them instead of giving space to the preoccupation of the political system that ought to make them citizens (generally speaking, politicians fear that an inclusive law will encourage an increase in immigration flows). Interestingly, the video's tone is not one of concern or fear; on the contrary, it is infused with indignation, provocation, and irony in order to turn these "innocent victims" of the system from marginal subjects into reformers. Jijon's aesthetic choices are clearly molded by youth culture: Hip-hop is not just the musical genre of the soundtrack but a language itself in the script of the video. Interweaving the sharing of casual comments, the singing of lyrics, and the recitation of official texts and data about immigration and integration, the video clearly relies on utterance as a political act. The straightforward verbalization of problems and equally direct requests for change oppose the indistinct and unfocused reactions of the media, the politicians and the public at large, all unable to address the situation by taking action through a reform of the existing law. In one powerful scene of the video, all the protagonists join in to repeat "blablablabla," thus mimicking the inane discussion that so far has characterized the debate around reform. As excerpts from the last pages of Albert Camus's *The Stranger* (1942) form the visual backdrop of the video, the protagonists express their frustration not as a dead end but as the starting point of the fight: Their cry "*basta*" (enough) is a reminder that will is power in a fight that has gathered increasing attention.[14]

As part of the campaign for reform of the citizenship law, the filmmaker Fred Kuwornu has produced *18 Ius Soli*, a 2011 documentary that adopts the perspective of the second generation and invites the reader to face in unequivocal ways the absurd situation that the children of immigrants are experiencing in Italy.[15] As former President of the Republic Giorgio Napolitano, who appears in the film, states, the conundrum of being born and/or raised in a country of which they are not citizens is "an aberration." Supported by Anolf Giovani, the Second-Generation Youth branch of the National Association Beyond Borders, as well as many other organizations and institutions in Italy (G2 network not included), Kuwornu's documentary assembles a range of interviews with "new Italians." At the same time, almost as an echo of *Inside Buffalo*, a previous work about African American GIs in World War II Italy, the director splices into the main narrative of contemporary Italy references to the colonial past and the emigration experience that are crucial in the understanding of the country today. This solution makes *18 Ius Soli*'s framework richer than *Forte e chiaro*'s; yet, as we will see, it also detracts from its arguments.

The gallery of characters chosen by Kuwornu is quite mixed—students, activists, artists, medical interns—and reflects the diversity of the roles of the "new Italians" in Italian society. Besides sharing biographical information along with their views about Italy and Italians, his protagonists illustrate the challenges imposed by the current law and the perception of themselves that it fosters, as well as their dreams. Kuwornu has selected a group of particularly determined and sensitive young people who as part of their studies (biotechnology, law, business), jobs (banking, cultural mediation), and personal activities (volunteering for the Red Cross, the blood bank, or the immigration office) show a serious attitude toward their futures, which they identify with the future of their country—Italy. Their fluency in Italian, often inflected by local pronunciation, their fondness for the cities they live in and the Italians they date or have married, are all characteristics that the director emphasizes in order to indicate their Italianness. As a result, what looks like a heterogeneous group on the surface turns into a homogenous voice; the lives of Kuwornu's interviewees are paragons of commitment to strong personal passions as well as declarations of love for Italy as their country of belonging to the point that their family origins are secondary to their "national traits." Whether they are originally from Morocco, Nigeria, the Philippines, or Sri Lanka, these young men and women are not seen as bridges between two cultures. References to their parents' cultures are practically absent. Rather, they are incarnations of an Italianness that ironically no young Italian would feel forced to prove in these terms, given the proverbial fragility, disunity, and vagueness of Italian identity.[16]

In the process of embracing his legitimate support of a law reform, Kuwornu presents G2 youth that paradoxically offer a monolithic idea of Italianness. Interestingly, Jijon's *Forte e chiaro* adopts exactly the opposite approach. Her protagonists do not gently plead to be included, but rather forthrightly claim their right of inclusion. With their straightforward style, their informal look, and ironic if not defiant attitude that does not shy away from insults, her protagonists indirectly express their desire to be taken for who they are. They define themselves as "normal" people and are comfortable in being overweight, in smoking, or in wearing casual attire that diametrically opposes the image of Italy as the capital of fashion. They are young people who are tired of being seeing as tourists when they are at home: "*Io so' romano: che te paro un turista?*" ("I am Roman. Do I look like a tourist to you?") asks a young man of African origins speaking with a clear dialect inflection. The resulting humorous friction conveyed by sound and image is in turn heightened by the fact that the Roman accent is often synonymous with jokes in film and TV productions. Elsewhere in the video, as one of the protagonists puts it in a disarming way, "Are you saying that the second generation is *the* problem?" thus unmasking the hypocritical narrative that finds in immigration issues the scapegoat for broader social tensions as well as for the economic and political crisis. Ultimately the G2 youth is tired of being seen as second-class people instead of just second generation.

The strength of Kuwornu's vision lies instead in his injection of a diachronic reading that interprets immigration in terms of colonialism and postcolonialism, while also comparing it to emigration. In telling the story of boxer Leone Iacovacci and Resistance fighter Giorgio Marincola, both of them dating back to the Fascist period, the director brings attention to forms of institutional exclusion that are at the core of his argument. Iacovacci, the son of an Italian man and a Congolese princess, was brought up in Italy but was not allowed to represent Italy in sports competitions as a black person, while Marincola, originally from Somalia and educated in Italy, fought in the Resistance, although his contribution is not part of any official history. In both cases, the director resorts to Italian stories that clearly bring attention to the pre-occupation of the country's history with a colonial past that by definition complicates issues of belonging and adds "color" to Italianness. Kuwornu is unequivocally approaching the question of citizenship from the viewpoint of race. Xenophobic slogans against the soccer player Ballottelli open the film, and Martin Luther King's speeches and statements provide the grammar of hope and resilience in the fight that this reform seems to require in the view of Kuwornu and his interviewees. Besides the pre-occupation of colonialism in the debate about Italian identity in this post-postcolonial era, Kuwornu interestingly interpolates another relevant reference to Italian transnational history. In a brief slide followed by some archival footage of transatlantic ships and passengers, he reminds the viewer that in the twentieth century, four million Italians moved to the New World. The inaccuracy of the statement is somewhat secondary. Effectively, many more emigrated to the Americas; indeed, even this underreported data gives a sense of the size of the Italian diaspora to the audience and reminds it of the irony of granting Italians abroad access to citizenship.[17] Unfortunately, relevant as they are, these postcolonial and emigrant detours remain largely decontextualized in the documentary, and their function is effective only to a limited degree inasmuch as they do not fully erode the "natural" conceptualization of citizenship that the documentary perhaps unconsciously offers. Assuming that acceptance and integration come automatically with citizenship, *18 Ius Soli* reessentializes Italianness and opts for a patriotic discourse that serves the political purpose of supporting a reform law on the principle of nationalism instead of righteous inclusion.[18]

In this sense, the third project analyzed here is a dynamic initiative that moves away from this desire of Italianness at all costs among the youth and posits Italianness and by extension national identity as "an approximation" rather than a goal. Launched by Zenit Arti Audiovisive in collaboration with the Italian public TV RAI and the Italian Ministry of Internal Affairs, *Cultural-Shock* is a cross-media project with both entertainment and educational goals.[19] It addresses the experience of the G2 by pairing up a young immigrant or descendant of immigrants and an Italian young person in the course of a journey through the country of origin of the former. Essentially, the project is developed around the question "What does it mean to be a foreigner?" and instead of erasing or generically representing the story of the origin, it makes it dynamic and attractive. Through a national call, the project's designers invited people to submit their casting applications online as a pair via a short video with a travel plan and objective. Four thousand people voted online to choose one of the forty submitted videos. The winning one featured a boy of Roma origin from Bosnia and a girl from Turin. They traveled for twelve days under the program's special restrictions (no taxis, no fast food, no hotels, no souvenirs, no flights), and along their journey they reported on their experience on Facebook, Twitter, Instagram, and the web site of *Cultural-Shock*. The project was covered via TV and radio and became the starting point for the development of educational materials about the history of the Balkans, Islam, Roma culture, and mixed marriage on RAI Scuola, the education branch of the RAI network. Overall, *Cultural-Shock* has reached two million people.

The project revolves around a dialogic structure by which an experience lived by two people of different origins—yet brought up in similar environments—was shared via social media. In the process the project emphasizes the discovery of roots and the representation of them in a narrative, thus breaking the more common trajectory of movement from "ethnic" identity to assimilated subject or its reverse, which likewise pointedly emphasizes differences in unchallenged ways. In engaging young people in research as protagonists and broadcasters via an adventure, *Cultural-Shock* bypasses the limitations of other denunciations and opts for a dynamic model that inverts the traditional national categories presumed as normative. As the subtitle of the project reads, *Cultural-Shock* is the radio, TV, and web program in which "you are the foreigner," a sentence that makes the viewer into an outsider in order to change his/her perspective. The protagonists' discovery and analysis of culture is particularly insightful because they access it from the vantage point of a sensitivity that is simultaneously Italian and international in ways similar to much G2 cultural production, as Clarissa Clò has pointed out ("Hip" 275).[20] In this sense, these children of immigration (technically they are not a second generation of immigrants, since they did not immigrate themselves) are the new form of the "children of World War II" that poet Amelia Rosselli identified in her generation, a group born out of a fracture and forced to bear the consequences of situations that reflected a specific historical moment outside of their control (25–26). The condition of the second generation of immigration, and I would add their activism and creativity, make them into the "most symptomatic group in contemporary politics" to adapt Hannah Arendt's definition of stateless people (277); they embody global dynamics and the potential for innovative change due to the redefinition of categories that they prompt, as shown in this graffiti (Fig. 22).

FIGURE 22. "Immigrants, please, do not leave us alone with Italians" (graffiti on a public wall).

Understanding Pre-Occupation, Dispelling Preoccupation

The view subtending to projects such as *Cultural-Shock* as well as, by extension, the combined embrace of emigrants and immigrants in the reformed law analyzed here may sound utopian. Yet, to quote from Hardt, "continually proposing the impossible as if it were the only reasonable option" (7) seems to be a sound option to fully face the complex imbrications of Italy's past and present, and to soundly remap the country in cultural and political terms, as the subtitle of my book suggests. In this sense, Italy's itinerant paradigm with its outbound and inbound migrations offers a unique national/transnational model, and makes it into "a laboratory." According to Hardt, "Laboratory Italy refers no longer to a geographic location but to a virtual space of hope and potential that may be actualized anywhere . . . it refers to a modality now available to all of us" (8), experimenting "in new forms of political thinking" (1). At a time in which Italy's uniqueness is most often predicated on its fashion, food, and design goods, turning the entire country into a high-end consumer good (Italy is eaten, drunk, driven, sported, and otherwise enjoyed at large), its history of demographic and cultural movement should provide much broader and deeper food for thought. This is especially relevant in the third millennium, an era so profoundly characterized by global migrations, human relocations, and the displacement of peoples. To stay within the language of my book, the invitation is thus to reoccupy Italy's history of emigration and colonialism through critical eyes and a fundamental ethical empathy while also occupying anew the present country with ideas, strategies, and organizations that can challenge the overly homogenizing process of globalization on the one hand and retrieval into national myths on the other. In the face of social and political destabilization prompted by violent attacks, the risk of nationalistic drifting is high, yet a balanced understanding of historical events (Italians were considered to be anarchist and socially dangerous in the United States at the turn of the twentieth century in ways similar to contemporary terrorists, for instance) and an attuned ear toward the constructive position taken by immigrants who are active in our society (see the G2 work) can provide an alternative route. But, I would add in particular, a plain recognition of the continuous overlapping of inbound and outbound flows will by itself prompt a transnational vision and thus, one hopes, less preoccupation about migrants and more understanding of if not identification with them, as shown in *Sola andata*, a recent song and video by the Tarantella revival group from Apulia Canzoniere Grecanico Salentino.

In putting to music Erri De Luca's incisive poems about immigration from *Sola andata: Righe che vanno troppo spesso a capo* (One-way only: Lines too often moving to a new paragraph), this music video, directed by Alessandro Gassman, clearly plays off of the concept of pre-occupation. As immigrants emerge from the Mediterranean waters in front of a fisherman sitting along the shore, one of them turns into an emigrant of the past, a perfect figure out of an Ellis Island picture—a melancholy look, heavy clothes, and a veiled head. As the concluding thoughts of the poem/song remind the listener, the migrants may die in trying to cross the Mediterranean, but there is a biblical quality to their journey that makes them immortal, as they will continue to arrive: "Sure, I may die, but in three days I resurrect and come back." Ultimately the video suggests that this coming back is also in the form of memory: The newly arrived bring back the past. Letting the immigrants drown is equal to an act of denial, as the pun *annegare* (drown)/*negare* (deny) underscores, a practice of ignoring made even more contradictory by the ever-present images of dead immigrants along the Mediterranean shores, with that of a Syrian toddler having acquired iconic status in 2015. Yet, by extension, I would argue that letting the memories drown, painful as the memories of Italian emigration can be, is an equally dangerous act of denial as it may trump empathy in the present.

As I write, boats loaded with migrants continue to reach the Italian South from North Africa. They are still traversing the Mediterranean looking for new opportunities. They are just more numerous and more desperate and courageous now. While they attempt (sometimes even for the second or third time) to enter Europe despite the mortality risks which dissolve in front of the somehow more tangible risk of wasting their lives in poverty, exploitation, and violence, Italians leave the country to reach other parts of Europe, Asia, and the Americas, seeing their own lives as wasted in Italy. *Mutatis mutandis*, albeit with clearly different levels of pressure and hazard, they are engaged in a very similar adventure, looking for better opportunities, fleeing a situation that denies their ability to be what they desire to be. What occurs, in ways that are still subterranean or marginal, yet still worth highlighting, is a form of empathy that is effectively a reversal of the preoccupation via a mechanism of pre-occupation. Immigrants to Italy are pre-occupied by past emigrants from Italy, and current emigrants from Italy are pre-occupied by immigrants to Italy in a complex web of echoes and coincidences. Gianni Amelio's recent film *A Lonely Hero* reminds us of this by inverting the trajectory proposed in his *Lamerica* twenty years ago: Poor Italians look for jobs in Albania in the third millennium.[21]

The dialectical tension created by the recollection of the past (distant or close) turns the preoccupation in the sense of worry into new worldviews and different accounts of the past and the present. The cognitive path designed by the active connection of emigration and immigration and, as such, migrations in general, opens spaces of recognition of the cyclic nature of demographic movements, and in some cases of solidarity and civic responsibility. It is what Gayatri Spivak has termed as "planetarity," a sense of global belonging that far from pretending to own the present and the future through technology and reason, proposes to learn from below (100), add sympathy to reason, and combines institutional agency with dreaming (75). I thus argue that it is not just in its "excellences" (high-end made-in-Italy goods, scientific discoveries, industrial products) that Italy can find its place in the current international scene to overcome its stasis. It is primarily through its own remapping in the diaspora and the reconsideration of the multiple maps designed by immigrants within its borders that it can propose a new way of being (Italian) on the planet. This remapping may even affect the other old cliché about Italy, that of the land of the perfect holiday tour, whether for the enjoyment of culture, art, history, nature, craftsmanship, or food.

In the course of a conversation with a student of mine, Italy became the destination of a journey of an unusual nature. The student explained that she was studying Italian to get ready to visit her family in Italy. Knowing her Peruvian nationality, I was initially perplexed, since it was not clear what kind of family reunion this trip to Italy actually meant:

"Are they returned Italian emigrants who had originally moved to Peru and moved back recently?" was my question. The student soon made me realize that a family reunion in Italy can also be linked to recent immigration to Italy from abroad! A branch of her Peruvian family moved to Milan, and she is thinking about visiting them, the same way my Italian American students often visit their relatives in Italy or my friends in Italy visit relatives who emigrated to New York. Interestingly, this Peruvian student is taking advanced classes in Italian along with young Italians who, fatigued by an alarming unemployment rate, left Italy just a couple of years ago to find an opportunity as teachers of Italian in the New Jersey school system. They are here with a spirit not too dissimilar from their Peruvian classmate's relatives in Milan, that of searching for new life opportunities. Italy's transnational map becomes only more occupied by new migratory routes and stories.

NOTES

INTRODUCTION. ALL AT ONE POINT: THE UNLIKELY CONNECTIONS BETWEEN ITALY'S EMIGRATION, IMMIGRATION, AND (POST)COLONIALISM

1. Specialists agree that the total number of Italians living abroad is in actuality twice as much, if not higher (see Tirabassi, Cucchiarato, and Nava's blog "La fuga").

2. See http://demo.istat.it/strasa2014/index.html (click on "Tavola"). The number is actually higher, since the statistics do not include undocumented/irregular immigrants.

3. If all the Italians abroad registered in the AIRE list were to go (back) to Italy, they would be able to count on medical coverage, emergency subsidies, access to job opportunities, voting rights, and mobility within the European Union. All these opportunities are not always available and certainly not automatically offered to foreign immigrants living in Italy.

4. Statistics concerning return flows were produced only after 1905 for overseas countries and 1921 for European countries: They indicate that between 1905 and 1976, 8,500,000 people returned to Italy (Favero 12). Assuming that the annual rate of return for the period 1876–1904 was the same as for 1905–1976 (118,000 per year), we can conclude that 3.4 million migrants returned to Italy between 1876 and 1904, leading to a total of approximately 12 million returnees over the period 1876–1976. When applied to all 27 million émigrés, the return rate equals almost 50 percent over the entire period.

5. For a detailed account of this multifarious history of relocations and the effects it had on both Italy and the destination countries, see Vecoli, the two volumes edited by Bevilacqua et al., Audenino and Tirabassi's book, Gabaccia's 2000 classic, and Franzina's works.

6. As Baily notes, "by the beginning of WWI, the Italian colonies of New York and Buenos Aires were by far the single largest concentrations of Italians anywhere in the world outside of Italy," with São Paulo ranking third (47). The highest levels (on a relative basis) of Italian presence were reached in Argentina in 1895 and 1914, when Italians represented 12.5 percent of the total population (Devoto 26) with peaks of 50+ percent of incidence within the overall international immigrant community (vis-à-vis the 14 percent in the United States; Baily 54).

7. The very first Italian colonial presence in Africa is recorded in Asseb (1869): today's Eritrea, eventually created under Crispi's regime in 1890 and maintained as a colony until World War II. Today's Libya was acquired in a series of phases from 1911 to 1934, when it was effectively assembled into one country by Italians, who controlled it until World War II. In 1936, the Empire of Oriental Africa was officially formed to be on par with other European powers that Mussolini competed with in the "Scramble for Africa." Somalia was an Italian colony first and protectorate later for a total of fifty-two years (1908–60) and Albania was invaded in 1939 and remained in Italian hands until 1944. A small area of Tianjin, China, belonged to Italy from 1900 to 1945, while the islands of the Dodecanese were an Italian possession between 1923 and 1948. In the post–World War II period, a certain level of control was exercised by Italy, as the fate of countries such as Eritrea, Ethiopia, and Libya were being decided by the European powers.

For an overview of Italian colonialism, see Ben-Ghiat's "Italy and Its Colonies." For more in-depth readings, see Labanca's canonical *Oltremare* and Del Boca's seminal volumes *Italiani, brava gente*, *Gli italiani in Africa orientale*, and *Gli italiani in Libia*.

8. On Liberal and Fascist Italy's demographic colonialism (human labor intensive rather than financial capital intensive) in the Italian colonies, as well as French and English colonies in Africa (Egypt and Tunisia), see Labanca's essay "Nelle colonie."

9. The actual number according to the ISTAT data is 60,782,668 (see http://demo.istat.it/pop2014/index.html, and click on "Tavola").

10. This growth is not just a function of new arrivals or births, but also of a very low naturalization rate among immigrants due to a highly restrictive citizenship law (see Conclusion) that ensures that virtually "none of them ever becomes Italian" (Giustiniani 38).

11. While immigrant communities from different parts of the world are present throughout the country and in particular the large metropolitan areas of Rome and Milan, special concentrations are quite discernible even in smaller towns: The Chinese community is often associated with Prato in Tuscany, the Ecuadorian with Genoa, the Tunisian with Mazara del Vallo and Vittoria in Sicily, and the Albanian with several towns in Apulia ("La popolazione" 2–4).

12. See Fiore's "Migration Italian Style" and "Immigration from Italy since the 1990s." Tirabassi also points out that foreigners leave Italy as well due to the country's economic instability, as their cancellations as residents from the city records indicate (25).

13. Calderoli compared the Minister to an orangutan in the course of a public speech on July 14, 2013. Asked to resign, he simply apologized publicly (see Gandolfi).

14. In 2013, the average was of almost 1.4 children per woman (see http://www.istat.it/it/archivio/140132), which placed Italy as 212 in a list of 224 countries in the world, according to the CIA World Factbook (https://www.cia.gov/library/publications/the-world-factbook/rankorder/2054rank.html).

15. Among the scholars who have addressed issues of Italian emigration to single countries from various disciplinary perspectives, but primarily through a cultural lens see (in alphabetical order): Giorgio Bertellini, Mary Jo Bona, Nancy Carnevale, Simone Cinotto, Francesco Durante, Thomas J. Ferraro, Fred Gardaphé, Edvige Giunta, Stefano Luconi, Martino Marazzi, Joseph Sciorra, Anthony J. Tamburri, and Robert Viscusi for the United States; Pierre Milza for France; and Vanni Blengino for Argentina. Various articles on the culture produced by Italian emigration are included in the fourth part of the two volumes *Storia dell'emigrazione italiana: Partenze* and *Arrivi*, edited by Bevilacqua et al. For some of the main scholarly works on immigration culture in Italy, see the publications of Daniele Comberati, Jacqueline Andall and Derek Duncan, Armando Gnisci, Àine O'Healy, Cristina Lombardi-Diop, Graziella Parati, Sandra Ponzanesi, Tiziana Quaquarelli, Caterina Romeo, and Sante Matteo, among others.

16. Scholars and journalists have connected emigration and immigration as a premise of their projects (Stella's 2003 *L'orda*), a subtext (Portelli's 1999 article "Mediterranean Passage"), or adopted it as a partial focus: Ruberto's 2007 *Gramsci, Migration, and the Representation of Women's Work in Italy and the U.S.*, which connects internal migration, U.S.-bound emigration, and immigration to Italy from a gender and labor perspective, while Schrader and Winkler's 2013 *The Cinemas of Italian Migration: European and Transatlantic Narratives* focuses exclusively on film. A recent edited volume embraces a similar approach to mine (connecting emigration, immigration, colonialism) and opens up to tourism and *irredentismo* as aspects of national formation in motion: Ben-Ghiat and Hom's *Italian Mobilities* offers mostly a history- and sociology-based framework, while in the cultural sphere it opens up almost exclusively to cinema.

17. See Parati's *Migration Italy* for a reading of national identity through immigration (2005); Gabaccia's *Italy's Many Diasporas* (2002) through transnational diaspora; and Fuller's *Moderns Abroad: Italian Colonial Architecture and Urbanism* (2006) and Ben Ghiat's articles in *Interventions*, *Modern Italy*, and so forth through colonialism. Other works have adopted a combined lens to

read processes of national formation: emigration/colonialism (Choate's 2008 *Emigrant Nation: The Making of Italy Abroad*), and colonialism/postcolonialism (Lombardi-Diop's various articles in *Interventions* as well as the volume *Postcolonial Italy* coedited with Romeo in 2012; and the 2005 volume coedited by Andall and Duncan, *Italian Colonialism*). "Italy's Margins," a poignant photographic exhibit presented for the first time at the British School of Rome in 2010 probed issues of national identity formation through the concept of the margin. While colonialism and immigration featured in it (along with physical disability or poverty as paradigms of marginality and exclusion from the main discourse), emigration was not included (see http://www.iitaly.org/20538/italys-margins-social-exclusion-photography-and-film-1860-2010 for an interview with curator David Forgacs).

18. Interestingly, an older meaning of the word "*preoccupazione*" in Italian is that of "prejudice" (see Garzantilinguistica.it).

19. For an overview of the numerous books, essays, and newspaper and magazine articles, as well as websites and blogs on the subject, see Fiore's essays "Migration" and "Immigration from Italy since the 1990s." Curiously, the majority of these studies tend not to read contemporary emigration in connection with the current phenomenon of immigration in Italy. Despite their progressive perspective on mobility, they remark on the "loss" of new Italian emigrants as if they had left a vacuum in a static country of origin, whereas, in reality, many new people have arrived in the past forty years, albeit with lower levels of education than those who left, generally speaking.

20. See the works of Andall and Duncan, Ponzanesi, Lombardi-Diop, Matteo, Ottaviano for a special issue of *Zapruder* (n. 23) and mostly Lombardi-Diop and Romeo.

21. Even though Foucault never refers openly to the issue of migration, he poses the space question as one linked to demography: "In a still more concrete manner, the problem of siting or placement arises for mankind in terms of demography. This problem of the human site or living space is not simply that of knowing whether there will be enough space for men in the world—a problem that is certainly quite important—but also that of knowing what relations of propinquity, what type of storage, circulation, marking, and classification of human elements should be adopted in a given situation in order to achieve a given end. Our epoch is one in which space takes for us the form of relations among sites" (23).

22. See, for instance, the works of Balbo and Manconi; Dal Lago; Macioti and Pugliese; and Martinetti, De Lourde Jesus, and Genovese. More attention has been paid to the cultural production since the mid-2000s: see the journal *Scritture migranti*, directed by Fulvio Pezzarossa; the web sites "El ghibli" (www.el-ghibli.provincia.bologna.it) and "Letterranza" (http://letterranza.org), and the special issues of *Narrativa* (curated by Lucia Quaquarelli and Silvia Contarini, 2006) and *Quaderni del '900* (edited by Tiziana Morosetti, 2004), all focusing on literary issues (language, genre, etc.). Very recent publications bring together socioeconomic and literary issues, but in separate essays (see *Italian Culture*, September 2010).

23. This ambiguity is inevitably reflected in the very language of any study of this subject. The term "migrant" allows for circumventing the ambiguity, but erases some of the specificities of the experience of leaving and arriving by emphasizing a more general mobile condition. The term has also been embraced by scholars such as Mezzadra for the stronger agency it affords to migrating subjects who are thus not defined by the countries of destination and arrival but by their decision to relocate in a defiant act against border regulations.

24. Given this international quality, a number of texts were not available in English translation. Unless otherwise noted, all translations are my own.

25. See Fiore's essay "Post-'Colonia.'"

26. Written in the aftermath of 9/11, this bestselling book was an open invective by a journalist, traditionally well known for her progressive political stance, against immigrants (and in particular Muslim immigrants), responsible in her view for damaging both materially and

metaphorically Italian high civilization (and the world). Her reductive and mythicized reading of Italian emigration as a path to success and as a model for successful integration as well as her support of the deportation of undocumented immigrants acted as an amnesiac device necessary to propose European/Western superiority again.

27. A similar interest in both migrations can be found among independent film producers. After two films on immigrants in Italy (Carlo Luglio's 2006 *Sotto la stessa luna* and Guido Lombardi's 2010 *Là-bas*), the Neapolitan company Figli del Bronx will finance a film on emigration, Abel Ferrara's *Grandfather*, a family story set between Campania and California. The company's main producer Gaetano di Vaio openly admitted his interest in "comparing old and new migrations" when he embraced Ferrara's project (Del Pozzo).

28. The conferences were part of a Leverhulme Trust–supported multiyear project called "Destination Italy" that, while focusing primarily on Italian immigration, systematically embraced contributions in the areas of colonialism and emigration (http://www.italianstudies.ox.ac.uk/di-outline). The Dartmouth College conference in 2007 entitled "The Cultures of Migration" (http://www.dartmouth.edu/~news/releases/2007/06/20.html) set up a systematic linkage between the three phenomena of emigration, immigration, and colonialism within a global framework through a program of presentations (www.dartmouth.edu/~complit/docs/cultures-schedule.pdf) later included in a volume (edited by Parati and Tamburri).

Many of the "similar initiatives" center on photographic exhibits juxtaposing images of Italian emigrants and foreign immigrants, thus entrusting the still image with the role of creating empathic associations. In 2010, the symposium "Altrove" (somewhere else) complemented by the exhibit "Gli Altri" (the others) focused on the representation and self-representation of emigrants and immigrants over the decades with a regional emphasis on the city and province of Bergamo (http://www.comune.bergamo.it/servizi/notizie/notizie_fase02.aspx?ID=7394). The photographic exhibit "MigrAzioni" (a neologism effectively highlighting the dynamic component *azioni*, actions, in the word *migrazioni*, migrations in Italian) was presented in 2007 in Lamezia Terme: it was a part of a larger EU-funded project "Pane e Denti" (Bread and Teeth) led by communication firms, unions, immigrant centers, coops, etc., to create a heightened awareness of prejudices against immigrants (http://tinyurl.com/PaneDenti). Similarly, a photographic exhibit called "Balie italiane & Colf straniere" (Italian wet nurses and foreign domestic helpers) adopted a mirror effect to represent the different and yet parallel conditions of Italian caretakers working abroad in the past (black-and-white pictures) and contemporary foreign caretakers working in Italy (color pictures) (http://www.cestim.it/sezioni/mostre_musei_teatro/balie-e-colf/donne.htm).

29. See, for instance, Pugliese's *L'Italia tra migrazioni internazionali e migrazioni interne* (2002) focusing on the post–World War II scenario; *Quelli di fuori: Dall'emigrazione all'immigrazione, il caso italiano*, edited by Di Comite and Paterno (2002); Mauro's 2005 ethnographic work *La mia casa è dove sono felice (Storie di emigrati e immigrati)* collecting stories of outbound and inbound migration; the volume *Emigranti e immigrati nelle rappresentazioni di fotografi e fotogiornalisti* by Corti (2010) opting for argumentation via visual parallelisms; and Ledgeway and Lepschy's collection of essays on language and linguistics *In and out of Italy: Lingua e cultura della migrazione italiana* (2010).

30. Interestingly, all the authors of these books are immigrant scholars in the United States and United Kingdom, or descendants of immigrants.

31. Three meaningful works that offer ideal opportunities to read migrations and colonialism in connected ways to produce empathy are Carmine Abate's 2010 short story "Prima la vita" from *Vivere per addizione e altri viaggi*, Melania Mazzucco's 2003 short story "Loro" from *Patrie impure*, and the 2011 play *Italianesi* by Saverio La Ruina.

32. In his essay on museums devoted to Italian emigration, Sanfilippo argues that a look at past emigration as prompted by current immigration has clearly defined two opposing fronts: on the one hand, support of the importance of making connections between the emigration and immigration, and on the other, a radical dismissal of this take (131).

33. For instance, Rinauro, in *Il Cammino della speranza*, clearly separates the subject of his research—Italian undocumented emigrants to France—from the current scenario of undocumented immigrants in Italy. Because he analyzes the different restrictions implemented over time by the countries of origin and arrival, he claims that he does not subscribe to the "we were the Albanians" argument—the reference to Stella, albeit implicit, is clear here (xiv).

34. As Corti continues, it is important "to reflect jointly on the two migratory experiences that have our country as a protagonist, with the goal of underplaying the impact of recent immigration vis-à-vis the dynamics of long established phenomena, strengthening with the example of our national experience . . . the long duration of the migratory flows, their complexity, their multi-faceted motivations and their diverse social composition" (126).

35. Pellicani in *Quelli di fuori: Dall'emigrazione all'immigrazione—il caso italiano* claims that acceptance of the immigrants as the response to an aging population is not sustainable as their presence is not substantial enough, and an increase in numbers due to higher quotas would create social instability in terms of cultural tensions. Internal problems such as care of the elderly or a young labor force should find internal solutions rather than resorting to immigrants, according to her (237–38).

APERTURE I. AN O*SEA*N OF PRE-OCCUPATION AND POSSIBILITIES: *L'ORDA*

1. *L'orda* is available in a package called *Il viaggio più lungo: L'Odissea dei migranti italiani* (see Stella), which includes a booklet and DVD.

2. Many other texts could have been the focus of these first two chapters, but the ones chosen allowed for a more cogent consideration of the diachronic and synchronic connections the book establishes. Among these alternate possibilities are Marco Tullio Giordana's film *Quando sei nato non puoi più nasconderti* (2005), Andrea Camilleri's detective novel *Rounding the Mark* (2003), Mohsen Melliti's film *Io, l'altro* (2006), Ron Kubati's novel *Il buio del mare* (2007), and Natasha Shehu's fictionalized reportage *L'ultima nave* (2001). A particularly powerful creative work on the Mediterranean's transformation into a cemetery as a result of harsh regulatory policies at the European level is *Rumore di Acque* by Marco Martinelli, a 2010 monologue that has been brought to the stage by his company Teatro delle Albe and is available in English at http://www.escholarship.org/uc/item/95d7c407. When applicable, these texts will be referenced in the course of the analysis or in the footnotes.

3. The former is accompanied by a thoroughly illustrated web site with instructive charts, multimedia materials, and interactive spaces: http://www.orda.it/rizzoli/stella/home.htm. Bertelli's website contains information on the show: http://www.gualtierobertelli.it/inscena-orda-main.htm and http://www.gualtierobertelli.it/inscena-odisee-main.htm.

4. For the most complete study of stereotypes in the Italian American context, see Lagumina; for a more geographically encompassing text, see Stella and Franzina; for a listing of derogatory terms worldwide, see Stella's *L'orda* (Appendix 2) and web site: http://rcslibri.corriere.it/rizzoli/stella/nomignoli/nomignoli.spm. For an analysis of the formation of stereotypes within the context of immigration in Italy today, see Dal Lago. Both Lagumina and Dal Lago devote space to the transformational nature of the grammar of racism with reference to black slavery and colonialism, respectively.

5. On the complex representation of the Brazilian Dream, see Fiore's "Post-'Colonia.'"

6. See the case of the ship *Carlo R*, which left with cholera cases on board and ended up with 211 deaths due to different illnesses (79). Moored out at sea for days waiting for provisions or quarantine approval for its passengers from the destination port, the ship eventually returned to its departure point in what was a two-month voyage. For a chilling list of the systematic deaths of passengers due to illnesses and malnutrition, see Stella's *Odissee* (74).

7. For the show, Stella includes a story from his book *Odissee* about the ship *Utopia*, which collided with a docked ship on a stormy night of March 1891. The ship sank with 576 people

aboard. No compensation for the families of the victims was ever offered, since crewmembers were not considered responsible for the accident (87).

8. Here, Stella selects the story of the ship *Principessa Mafalda*, which, despite well-known engine problems, was allowed to leave the port of Genoa in 1927. It experienced additional complications along the voyage and sank eighty miles off the Brazilian coast, with 314 of its more than 1,250 passengers dying (foreign sources indicate twice the number of losses), many of them in badly organized rescue operations. The Fascist press quickly transformed the tragedy into "a terrible deed of fate" (*Odissee* 97).

9. For a study of the ship sector and its "maximization of profit with a minimization of investments" in Italy, see Molinari (241).

10. The lyrics of the songs can be found on the *Odissee*'s web site: http://www.orda.it/rizzoli/stella/canti/canti-emigrazione.spm.

11. The song was composed and written by Bertelli (see Bertelli *Quando emigranti* . . . 2).

12. See also Franzina's *Traversate*.

13. See Del Grande 49, 53, 81, 137.

14. For an analysis of this tragicomic short story on a circular migrant voyage cunningly crafted by a swindler in the post–World War II period, see Fiore's "Lunghi viaggi." Interestingly, Del Grande contains a similar story of voyages ending practically where they started (109).

15. For images of the ex-voto, see the rich CD-ROM accompanying the second volume of *Storie dell'emigrazione italiana*, edited by Bevilacqua et al. See also Briscese for a catalogue of a special collection of ex-votos.

16. References to the involvement of Italians in human smuggling in the late 1800s are included in a series of sections of *Macaronì: Romanzo di santi e delinquenti* (Macaronì: A Novel of Saints and Criminals) by Francesco Guccini and Loriano Macchiavelli (1997). Through brief tales of secret voyages and arrivals along the Italian and French coasts, Macchiavelli and Guccini signal the continuous involvement of Italians in the smuggling business as both victims and perpetrators (including smugglers of children), in that same Mediterranean basin where today the public opinion cries out against the "illegal" arrival of foreign immigrants.

17. The show addresses in detail the workings of this business, comprising migrant recruiting, ticket sales, the signing of job contracts, and service provisions during the various segments of the trip and at the port, and so forth: More often than not it involved well-planned scams at the expense of illiterate people. For a study of this business, see Martellini.

18. What is clearly new in the current scenario is the level of militarization of the spaces crossed by the migrants: They are turned into "soldiers" fighting at every border, and many perish in the process of crossing or even waiting to cross. For a detailed account of the deadly nature of contemporary immigration, see Del Grande's book, as well as the portal Fortress Europe he himself launched: http://fortresseurope.blogspot.com.

19. For a study of these illegal routes, see Rinauro.

20. See Marazzi for a report by Edward Corsi, Ellis Island Immigration Commissioner between 1931 and 1933, in which the arrival of these "gate crashers," as Corsi calls them (276), is presented as a frequent occurrence of large proportions at Ellis Island.

21. Composed by Isabella Zoppi, a songwriter from Turin, with lyrics by Bertelli, "Noi" is included in the CD *Quando emigranti* . . . (see Bertelli).

22. On the oxymoronic concept of the amnesia of the present, see Del Grande's analysis of the use of the past tense to talk about deadly crossings in the Mediterranean today. He instead proposes counterinformation (155–56) to prompt action.

23. Information on this show is available at http://www.gualtierobertelli.it/inscena-bilal-main.htm. It is available in its entirety at http://espresso.repubblica.it/dettaglio/gatti-bilal-in-scena/2125823.

24. See Bertelli *Quando emigranti* . . . 2.

25. An integral part of the iconography of the migrant voyage, ships started being slowly replaced by airplanes in the 1950s and early 1960s. They were eventually retired from this function in the mid-1970s, when cruise ships took their place for leisure purposes, and emigrants turned to planes to reach new destinations.

26. For De Amicis, who himself traveled with the emigrants to Argentina, the ocean is not a source of "preoccupation." Despite the dangers it holds, it appears "immense" and "good-hearted" (27). For a close analysis of the migrant ship and voyage in De Amicis's complex work, see Fiore's "The Ship" (31–35).

1. CROSSING THE ATLANTIC TO MEET THE NATION: THE EMIGRATION SHIP IN MIGNONETTE'S SONGS AND CRIALESE'S *NUOVOMONDO*

1. For a study of both letters and autobiographies written by immigrants, see Serra's *The Imagined Immigrant* and *The Value of Worthless Lives* (Chapters 3 and 4).

2. As Brunetta notes, the presence of Italian emigration to the United States on the American screen is by far larger and qualitatively more complex than that on the Italian screen. No Italian film has been able to capture "the dimensions and the power of the phenomenon" ("Emigranti" 496–97). See also Cicognetti on the topic.

3. Although set on the mountains instead of the ocean, the film that more closely resembles Crialese's trajectory is Pietro Germi's 1950 *Cammino della speranza* (Path of Hope), which describes the condition of the Italian emigrants waiting to leave and their "illegal" trip across the snow-covered Alps to reach France through treacherous paths. The film documents a flight that is uncannily similar to today's Mediterranean crossings from North Africa.

4. The verses are taken from Viscusi's project *Ellis Island*. It consists of 624 sonnets and is available in both printed and digital form; online, a poem generator randomly recomposes the individual verses of the original sonnets into new ones. For more information on this project, which Viscusi aptly calls a "book of changes," see http://ellisislandpoem.com/viscusi.php.

5. Mignonette's songs are now available on CD as part of a series still published by Phonotype in Italy. Included in these CDs are just a few classics of her broad emigrant repertoire, notably "Mandulinata 'e l'emigrante" and "'A cartulina 'e Napule."

6. Antonio Sciotti, author of the only full biography available on Mignonette, refers to 1886 as Mignonette's year of birth, unlike practically all other sources, both Italian and American, including the recent book by Marc Rotella, *Amore: The Story of the Italian American Song*, which quote 1890 instead. Sciotti does not provide a reason for this different date.

7. For a discussion of the term "colony" in the realm of Italian emigration, see Choate as well as Fiore's essay "Post-'Colonia.'"

8. See Haenni for a study of the amusement industry between the nineteenth and twentieth centuries focusing on the participation and agency of, as well as influence upon, foreign immigrants.

9. The translations of the titles are literal and mine. In the United States, some of these songs were recorded and catalogued with both an Italian and an English title, which I am not reporting here.

10. See Musco.

11. A list of the U.S. recordings with Geniale, Columbia, Victor, and Brunswick, among others, is contained in Spottswood (463–71), while Sciotti provides a more comprehensive list of both the Italian and the U.S. recordings (177–98). Both are truly impressive catalogues of hundreds of titles, a sign of the successful career of Mignonette on both sides of the Atlantic.

12. Another famous song (or rather song cycle) of these years was dedicated to the intercontinental flights of Francesco de Pinedo, a hero of the early years of the Fascist regime. At the same time, songs with an emigration theme continued to be proposed: "Me so 'mbarcato" (I got on

board the ship), "Stornelli all'emigrante" (Stornellos of the emigrant), "America," "L'emigrante chiagne" (The emigrant cries), "Terra straniera" (Foreign land), and "La gita della morte" (The death tour), depicting such diverse themes as the sadness of the emigrant for the loss of family relatives back in Italy, the happy return home, and the transatlantic voyage.

13. Bertellini looks at a similar process in early cinema: In characterizing it as the expansion of the "picturesque" already developed in painting and drawing, he also shows the effects of this aestheticization of the Italian South on U.S. racial formation, as well as immigrants' social integration and artistic (self-)representations.

14. The Phonotype/Phonoelectro catalogue codes for the songs are in order: 7315, 7316, 7317, and 7318.

15. The song was composed by E. A. Mario and performed with the Orchestra Ernesto Tagliaferri.

16. Mignonette's songs contained rare references to specific aspects of the emigration experience: Women's forced prostitution was addressed in "Mala fine" (1925), inspired by Mignonette's real-life experience of meeting and providing help to an abused woman (Sciotti 51).

17. Composed by E. A. Mario and performed with the Orchestra Ernesto Tagliaferri, the song is mentioned in the composer's biography by Catalano, who reports that it was originally published in 1928 with the title of *Cantano ll'emigrante* (75). Mignonette's version incorporates parts of another song ("Santa Lucia luntana") already present in "Partenza degli emigranti per l'America," and it includes some recitation.

18. As the recited part in the song explains, "Bella 'mbriana for Neapolitans is the name of a fairy bringing good luck."

19. This is an excerpt from another song made famous by Gilda Mignonette, "Santa Lucia luntana". Written by the same composer, E. A. Mario, the song was first published in 1916. Excerpts from it appear in "Partenza degli emigrati per l'America" as well.

20. Her ability to function in both worlds hinged on various forms of protection and support. She had a permanent helper and secretary, Esterina, who in the United States was also her interpreter, since Mignonette did not speak English fluently. In New York, she counted on the protection of some Mafia heads—Sciotti mentions Vito Genovese among her close friends (80)—in order to avoid the pressures and violent threats of the Black Hand. Although this aspect begs more investigation, it speaks of Mignonette's ability to move in the local environment by negotiating through forms of power and cultural mechanisms active across the Atlantic.

21. Other titles include "Tarantella imperiale" (Imperial tarantella), "Passione tricolore" (Tricolor passion), "Abissinia napulitana" (Neapolitan Abissinia), "Marcetta nera" (Black march), "Macallè," "Stornelli bianco neri" (Black and white stornellis), "Africa tricolore" (Tricolor Africa), "Marcetta Africana" (African march), and "L'Italia addà vince" (Italy must win). For a discussion of these titles, see Sciotti 129–34.

22. For a reading of the African American reaction to Italy's 1935 Ethiopian invasion, see Bekerie.

23. For an introduction to the various topics, political stance, and musical genres of this musical heritage, see the selection of songs on Stella's web site *L'orda*: http://rcslibri.corriere.it/rizzoli/stella/canti/canti-emigrazione.spm.

24. For a brief analysis of Crialese's first feature film, see Fiore's essay "Migrations."

25. Crialese's 2011 film *Terraferma*, chosen as Italy's entry for the 2012 Oscar Award competition, interestingly centers on immigration to Italy, and in particular on the arrival of an Eritrean woman and her small child on the island of Linosa, located between North Africa and Italy. With a cast of Italian and immigrant actors, the film probes the challenges posed by the encounter of different cultures in a remote place cautiously transitioning from tradition to modernity, while still attempting to retain its enchanted quality. While the film confirms Crialese's talent for narrating liquid spaces (there are a couple of memorable boat scenes) and his genuine interest in

migration and the South, the density of the plot threads, certain inaccuracies, and the icon-like representation of the African woman lend an overall stiffness to the work.

26. Initially formulated within a framework of circular dispersion by Gabaccia in *Italy's Many Diasporas*, this notion is central to Choate's book about emigrant colonialism, *Emigrant Nation*.

27. See the chapter "L'occupazione militare alleata (10 luglio 1943–10 febbraio 1944)" in Renda.

28. The total number of emigrants from the island is calculated at about 2,600,000 between 1876 and 1976. For more information, see Rosoli 362–64 (Table 4). During the years 1876–1930, 90 percent of Sicilian emigrants choose the Americas, and in particular the United States, over Europe as their preferred destination. See Martellone 379–423 (Table 4).

29. The credits make specific reference to Sergio Pelliccioni, director of the Cultural Association "Archivio della memoria," devoted to the recuperation and documentation of oral history, and Dr. Paul A. Lombardo, Professor of Law at Georgia State University, an expert in genetics and legal regulations, who consulted on the Ellis Island section of the film.

30. For a close reading of the representation of emigration in Sicilian literature, see Fiore's essays "Andata e Ritorni" and "La Sicilia."

31. For a study of the iconography of this imaginary world and its cultural impact, see Del Giudice.

32. The interview, not available in print, was collected by Gabriella Bellorio on February 13, 2009.

33. To Chaplin's 1917 bittersweet and darkly ironic short *The Immigrant*, Crialese adds an organic and structured historical documentation; while to Kazan's 1963 epic and picaresque *America America*—the most obvious narrative model for *Nuovomondo* (see de Marco)—he adds a more unassuming register, next to a sense of grandiosity borrowed from Amelio's 1996 idiosyncratic neorealist *Lamerica*, *Nuovomondo*'s more direct predecessor. Crialese's film also shares a certain fantastic impalpability found in Fellini's 1983 carnivalesque *And the Ship Sails On*, a film that explodes the national norm with references to issues of fleeing citizens and negotiations over belonging.

34. The former tendency in De Amicis's book is exemplified in the initial representation of the ship moored in the port as "an enormous cetacean . . . sucking . . . Italian blood" (6) during the passengers' embarking. The second is evident in the closing figuration of the ship as "a floating limb of my country" (257) with an Italian flag fluttering toward the disembarking emigrants, defined as the "wandering children" of Mother Italy. By keeping the nation as the fundamental axiom of his view, De Amicis reads emigration as a loss for or an extension of the nation rather than a formation process for or a fundamental challenge to it.

35. See Bonsaver about the lack of contextualization of her presence in the film, and de Marco about the credible mystery surrounding her, like the mystery of many emigration-related myths.

36. Augé defines it as "a space which cannot be defined as relational, or historical, or concerned with identity" (77–78). His concept is applied to realities that are connected to "transport, transit, and . . . commerce" (94): In this sense the concept could be related to the ship here under discussion. Yet, his inscription of the "non-place" in the sphere of "supermodernity" is characterized by "new experiences and ordeals of solitude" (93). The ship in *Nuovomondo* predates supermodernity and deals instead with the formation of modernity and the contact/overlapping of premodernity with modernity.

37. It is worth quoting the entire section about the boat from Foucault's essay on heterotopias: "The boat is a floating piece of space, a place without a place, that exists by itself, that is closed in on itself and at the same time is given over to the infinity of the sea and that, from port to port, from tack to tack, from brothel to brothel, it goes as far as the colonies in search of the most precious treasures they conceal in their gardens. . . . The ship is the heterotopia par excellence. In civilizations without boats, dreams dry up, espionage takes the place of adventure, and the police

take the place of pirates" (27). While this quote needs careful problematization, especially for its hasty reading of colonialism and omission of the slave trade related to it in the transoceanic economies he refers to, it also sheds light on the mythopoeic power of the boat, that is, its transformational power, which is at the core of Crialese's film.

38. A literary work that relies heavily on the magical quality of Sicilian life and stories is Tony Ardizzone's *In the Garden of Papa Santuzzu* (1999), which includes a section on the transatlantic voyage and the Ellis Island passage.

39. This vision of unity is contradicted by a recent Swiss ad promoting anti-immigration measures: Two pictures in sequence show two different scenes at a local lake. The first picture depicts four naked women in great physical shape who are walking into the lake's waters in an orderly fashion. The second one is a shot of a jumbled group of older and overweight women wearing traditional dresses and scarves, smoking and bathing with their clothes on. It is this second image that with its discriminatory take contradicts the encounters and cross-pollinations suggested by Crialese's closing shots in the milk river. See the pictures at http://www.repubblica.it/esteri/2010/11/18/foto/no_agli_immigrati_campagna_shock_in_svizzeta-9238368/1/#.

40. Within the country, the institutional memory of Italian emigration has been characterized by fragmentation; several museums with a regional breadth and/or local accessibility are scattered over the country. For the first project designed to create a unified space, see the web site of the MEI (Italian Emigration Museum), opened in Rome in 2009, at http://www.museonazionaleemigrazione.it (the site contains the list of all the other museums).

2. OVERLAPPING MEDITERRANEAN ROUTES IN MARRA'S *SAILING HOME*, RAGUSA'S *THE SKIN BETWEEN US*, AND TEKLE'S *LIBERA*

1. The song "Ritals," which provides the epigraph for this chapter, is contained in a concept album released by Gian Maria Testa in 2006: *Da questa parte del mare* (On this side of the sea). The late Testa, who found his success in France initially, devoted the entire CD to songs on migrations, relying on his usual sonic repertoire rather than "ethnicizing" his work. By mixing ballads à la De André, delicate elegies to the water, musical poems on the invisibility of arriving, and a rearranged original emigration song, Testa blends images of emigration and immigration without ever slipping into sentimental registers or politico-ideological assertions. "Ritals" (the nickname given to Italians in France) opens with this straightforward and yet poetic call against oblivion, which links current immigration and historical emigration: "after all we ourselves knew/ the smell of the ship holds/ the bitterness of departures/ we knew it ourselves."

2. For Giordana, the out-at-sea accident is a prologue to a broader narrative about encounters and clashes between migrants and nonmigrants, while Melliti's focus on a fishing boat to explore shifting perceptions of immigrants in the contemporary culture of terror paradoxically turns an open-air environment into a claustrophobic stage of violence and death.

3. For a close reading of the documentary, see Fiore's "From Exclusion."

4. The song "Il passo e l'incanto" (The step and the enchantment) delicately weaves images of physical movement (the step as metonymy of the migrant's travel) and of its related emotions, from awe to fear. These lines capture the sense of lightness of the arriving immigrant: "better not to be noisy when you get there/ a stranger at the mercy of another shore."

5. For instance, over the period 2000–2010, Sicily alone has experienced a massive emigration: 40,281 young people between the age of twenty and forty (Nava, "Dalla fuga" 74).

6. This "looking-like-them" condition is a theme effectively exploited in both Giordana's and Melliti's film as a temporary and permanent condition, respectively. For a reading of these two films, see Benelli's and Pastorino's essays, as well as Pell's, in Bullaro's edited collection on contemporary Italian film.

7. In it, through interviews with undocumented emigrants from Tunisia who either made it to Italy or were deported back home, as well as with various NGO activists in Tunisia, Northern Europe, and Italy, directors Annika Lems and Christine Moderbacher recognize in the migrants a high level of awareness about the risks involved in the voyage and the challenges awaiting them once in Europe. Thirsty for alternatives these young "economic migrants" are willing to "harg," that is, do something illegal (as the verb is used in Tunisia) in response to the oppression they suffered. Ultimately, *Harraga* calls for a reconsideration of the distinction between categories of migrants (economic vs. political) by indirectly foregrounding Mezzadra's "right to flee."

8. See Introduction with references to Nava, Cucchiarato, and Tirabassi, as well as Fiore's "Migration Italian Style" and "Immigration from Italy since the 1990s."

9. In the first chapter of his *Bound by Distance*, Verdicchio offers this reading of the postunification colonized South, borrowing from Gramsci's theory and embedding into it an analysis of how the racialization of the South was a sign of the "failure to integrate the South" (29).

10. See Vincenzo Consolo's essay "The Bridge over the Channel of Sicily" for a short summary and insightful commentary, as well as the more extensive study (albeit introductory in nature) by Marinette Pendola.

11. Roughly the seventh or eighth, according to the Caritas Dossiers of the last decade.

12. Ironically, the Tunisian Samir is the most comprehensible to a non-Neapolitan audience, since he speaks Italian, albeit with some inflections of dialect and foreign interferences.

13. For a close reading of Amelio's film in relationship to Marra's, see Fiore's "Lunghi viaggi."

14. *Lamerica* has also been read as a fundamentally Italian film in which Albania is instrumental in reflecting on the country's history and current situation, and in which agency is detracted from the immigrants (Diaconescu).

15. "I have already been here/maybe in another enchantment/I have already been here/I recognize in me the trace." The last word (*passo*) in Italian means step, pace, and mountain pass at once. The word "trace" conveys a similar complexity as evidence of presence, reference to movement, and trajectory.

16. For a consideration of the gender dynamics in *Lamerica*, see Ruberto's "Neorealism."

17. This approach is enriched by the inclusion of some glimpses into the life of Kym's father—a man who linked his life to women of color (after Kym's mother, he lived with Carmen from Puerto Rico), loved music, and made a living as a chef, but never recovered from his military experience in Vietnam and fell victim to addiction.

18. For an embryonic version of the memoir, see Ragusa's "Sangu du sangu meu."

19. For a reading attentive to the redefinition of the South, see Evelyn Ferraro (Chapter 3). On the recuperation and reconstruction of story and history from nontraditional points of view, see Romeo's "Una capacità."

20. The Italian presence in Harlem (specifically East Harlem) grew exponentially between the 1880s and the 1930s, turning the area into the largest Italian neighborhood in the country with a strong presence of Southern Italians who lived in clusters defined by regional or city origin. On Italian Harlem's politics, see Chapter 6 in Meyer. See also Chapter 2 in Orsi about the role of devotional rituals in the neighborhood, what he calls "theology in the street" (219). About the Italian section of the Bronx, see Ultan and Unger.

21. In his essay "Mediterranean Passages," Portelli completes the cycle by offering an equally daring but substantiated parallel between slavery and contemporary immigration. While he shows that the Mediterranean passage is "less bloody and dramatic" (284) and that the proletarian condition of the immigrant is not as marginal as that of the slave, he sets up a comparison in terms of cultural uprooting and expression (in writing) of the experience of relocation.

22. For a subtle treatment of the encounter between blacks and Italians in the rural American South of the second half of the nineteenth century, see, for instance, Mary Bucci Bush's short story "Drowning" and her novel *Sweet Hope*.

23. For the connection between slavery and colonialism in the reading of contemporary race relations and identity, see Gilroy, Oboe, and Scacchi for their transnational approaches.

24. See Antonucci's "Fermo" for a Barthes- and Ricoeur-based reading that focuses on "the border between image and imagination" (4).

25. Ragusa is also a documentary filmmaker: Her early *Demarcations* (1991) and her award-winning shorts *Passing* (1996) and *Fuori/Outside* (1997) are explorations of racial divides and encounters developed around the elusive and equally palpable skin color that she so painstakingly focuses on in *The Skin Between Us*. Since both documentaries can be seen as visual prologues to the memoir, the memoir itself can be read as the work of a filmmaker, according to Ragusa (Antonucci, "Fare" 5). For the analysis of her documentary work as a "visual meditation" on the boundaries between family memories and official history, in which "the personal is political," see Giunta's "Figuring" (225), which also refers to Ragusa's never-released first documentary *Blood of My Blood* as a specific exploration of the legacy of emigration and slavery in her family (313).

26. The word is important in the text, as suggested by its inclusion in the title. Ragusa explains how for these women beauty was "a means of transcending mere survival . . . [and] to seek out their own dreams, to live those dreams, however partially and temporarily" (77–78).

27. See Orsi for a close reading of this religious *festa*'s history and sociocultural impact.

28. Testa's song "Rock," included in the same album *Dalla parte del mare*, captures the painful experience of the sea crossing for undocumented immigrants. The shame associated with this underground escape, which turns people looking for a better opportunity or for a chance to survive into criminals, is central to the refrain of this song: "But it was not like this/that I thought I would go/no it was not like this/like thieves, at night/in the hands of a sea thief."

29. Radio Popolare (http://www.radiopopolare.it) is a counterinformation broadcast, independent from large news conglomerates and close to the leftist politics of the unions. It works as a cooperative, and its coverage includes Europe and parts of Africa and the Middle East. In 1980, it introduced a program in Arabic for immigrants ("Shabi") and has offered pro-immigration specials over the years.

30. The *testimonio*, a Spanish word meaning "witness account," is a first-person narrative offered by a disenfranchised or subaltern individual and made available through the mediation of a person (journalist, writer) who not only transcribes, translates, polishes, and edits the text, but fundamentally makes its publication possible thanks to his or her contacts in the publishing world.

Among Masto's publications, see *La nuova colonizzazione* (1998), *No Global* (2001), and *L'informazione deviata* (2002). Masto embarked on two other as-told-to narratives in 2003 and 2008 respectively: *Io, Safiya* (I, Safiya) is the personal story of a Nigerian Muslim woman who was almost lapidated due to an out-of-wedlock pregnancy, while *La scelta di Said. Storia di un kamikaze* (Said's choice. A kamikaze story) is the story of a man that reflects the broader infiltration of terrorism and fundamentalist Islam among impoverished youth.

31. Military service also includes construction work supervised by soldiers, and since 2003 has extended into the last high-school year. The brutal treatment and abuse reigning in the barracks, the high degree of isolation from family and society, the constant threat of being sent to fight on the border with Ethiopia, and the interruption of studies that the conscription entails have led many Eritreans to flee the country, despite the harsh punishment for desertion or evasion (including the death penalty). For details on the violations of human rights in Eritrea due to the conscription, see "Immigration and Refugee Board of Canada."

32. For a succinct but comprehensive history in English of all the Italian colonies, see Fuller (23–38) and for a brief overview of the Eritrean colony, see the entries by Negash, Labanca, and Iyob in Ben-Ghiat's "Italy."

33. This random *refoulement*, which moves migrants around, on the other side of chosen borders that are not related to the countries of origin of the individual migrants, was for a while

quite common (and is still practiced), even though it is considered illegal on the basis of international agreements. (Italy was officially condemned for it by the European Court in 2012 with reference to a 2009 case—see "Italy"). While on the one hand this is a "blessing" for asylum seekers (being repatriated to their own countries would very strongly reduce their ability to escape), in reality returning migrants to generic points of departure has created a worrisome situation for their vulnerability to forms of abuse in countries they are not citizens of and for the complications arising from either lack of money or papers while in transit.

34. For a critical reading of the *testimonio* at large in the context of Latin America, see Gugelberger. For the Italian case, see Parati in her "Introduction" to *Mediterranean Crossroads* (19–20), Portelli in "Mediterranean Passages," Boelhower, Meneghelli, and Curti (68–69) among others.

35. Alternative approaches to the use of Italian language—broken Italian, influenced by the languages of origin of the immigrants—can be found in Cristiana Caldas de Brito's short story/monologue "Ana de Jesus," for writings by immigrant themselves, or in Carmine Abate's short story "Prima la vita," for writings by native speakers. In the case of Amara Lakhous's novels, Italian is used with a sophisticated level of experimentation, and includes formal Italian, slang expressions, dialect, and, in a particularly original turn, an attempt at "Arabicizing" the Italian language (see Chapter 3 of this book).

36. Besides Liberti (149) and Del Grande (146–56) on this topic, see Andrijasevic and d'Apollonia. An element that emerges in practically all these studies is that the aggressive nature of the EU response to the flows is bound to be endless—"more security creates more insecurity" in Europe (d'Apollonia 204)—if it is not substituted by a politics of effective foreign aid, the management of regular access routes, and integration programs within the Union. All other attempts based on technological, political, and financial resources as well as on a culture of fear are bound to be constantly defeated by migratory projects driven by the more impalpable, yet no less powerful, structures of need, courage, and dreaming. It is a resistance that does not simply speak of the often unrecognized migrants' agency, but also of "the constituent force [of migration] in the production of the European polity and citizenship" (Andrijasevic), whose sovereignty is constantly questioned at its heart by these migratory flows.

APERTURE II. A MULTICULTURAL PROJECT IN A NATIONAL SQUARE:
THE ORCHESTRA OF PIAZZA VITTORIO

1. On the formation of village- or city-based clusters in the Little Italy of Mulberry Street and that of East Harlem, as well as their contact zones see Baily (133 and 135). People from Italy often became Italians abroad through the mixing that the ethnic enclaves engendered (122), as seen in Chapter 1 through the analysis of the ship scene in Crialese's *Nuovomondo*. See also the Tenement Museum's website at http://www.tenement.org.

2. Incidentally, in the case of large metropolitan centers of the North, immigrants have also settled in the neighborhoods that were once the residential areas of immigrant workers from Southern Italy (Amato 89). See Figure 12 in this book.

3. Among his early documentaries are *Poco più della metà di zero* (A bit over half of a zero, 1993) and *Opinioni di un pirla* (The opinions of a moron, 1994), while more recent works include *Intervista a mia madre* (Interview with my mother, 1999) e *Il film di Mario* (Mario's film, 1999–2001), both made with Giovanni Piperno. Before fully concentrating on cinema as a producer, director, and artistic director, he worked as an editorial coordinator for radio and TV programs addressing Italian communities abroad, an experience that prepared him to a degree for a documentary on immigration in Italy.

4. In January 2014, the city had roughly 2,872,021 residents. See http://demo.istat.it/pop2015/index.html (select in order Central Italy, Province of Rome, and City of Rome).

5. See Golini on the postunification migratory flows (125).

6. Golini defines the exodus from the central neighborhoods as a "hemorrhage-like" (133) expulsion due to politics of high-end real estate development and control in the downtown areas (135). He clearly shows how the analysis of migratory flows is important not just for the definition of population changes but also for the social and cultural transformation of the city (137).

7. See ISTAT table at http://demo.istat.it/strasa2015/index.html (select in order Central Italy, Province of Rome, and City of Rome).

8. For a detailed analysis of the urban development of the Third Rome since 1871, see Agnew 33–39 and 42–47.

9. For an interesting reading of the effects of the 1997 relocation, which has decreased the Romanness of the market and transformed it primarily into an ethnic market with a "ghetto" quality, yet kept it very vibrant, see Elkadi and Forsyth.

10. On the complex relationship between documenting and "redocumenting" outside the traditional paradigm of "truth-recording," see De Lazzaris.

11. The making of the orchestra was linked to the rescuing of the local Apollo Theater, hence the name of the association, Apollo 11, involving activists, residents, intellectuals, and artists in Rome. See the group's Facebook page.

12. See Keating for a critical reading of the documentary which "paradoxically and consistently tend[s] to thematically evoke" "the local/global, national/postnational, Self/Other binaries," even though as a whole it invites us to consider a transnational view (207).

13. Ironically, multiethnic Piazza Vittorio hosts not only Apollo 11 but also the headquarters of the Rightist organization Casa Pound, literally on the opposite side of the square (Elkadi 9).

14. After two CDs (*L'orchestra di Piazza Vittorio* and *Sona*) and hundreds of concerts at the national and international levels, the Orchestra has presented its own multicultural version of *The Magic Flute* in 2009 and a tenth-anniversary show called *Around the World in 80 Days*, which Tronco refers to as "the autobiography" of the orchestra in an interview (http://vimeo.com/65649956). For more information, see their official site: http://www.orchestrapiazzavittorio.it.

15. While it is true that the formation of the orchestra remains in the hands of Italians and is not truly a collaborative project (see Keating), as Ferrente has remarked, the immigrants could not identify funds, political support, and the like, which even Italians can hardly secure (Clò "Orchestrating," 216). Yet, the film rarely shows moments in which Tronco, who maintains a disciplining role as orchestra director, openly admits that he is learning from the immigrant musicians and that the project is changing because of their creative input.

3. DISPLACED ITALIES AND IMMIGRANT "DELINQUENT" SPACES IN PARIANI'S
ARGENTINIAN *CONVENTILLOS* AND LAKHOUS'S ROMAN *PALAZZO*

1. The term *conventillo* comes from *convento*, "convent," since the tenement was made up of single rooms along common corridors. It was also used to refer to a brothel or a prison, with reference to the term *conventículo*, meaning a group of people involved in illicit activities.

2. The word *palazzo* in Italian refers to a generic tall building (roughly three floors or more) made up of either owned or rented individual apartments. While the term in English correctly but exclusively evokes an aura of prestige and stylistic refinement, in Italian palazzo can also indicate a dilapidated structure or a modern skyscraper.

3. Translated into Spanish (2008) and French (2009), Pariani's novel is not available in English. Page numbers refer to the Italian edition. Pariani's interest in stories of migration is central to another choral novel of hers set in Argentina, *Quando dio ballava il tango* (When God used to dance tango, 2002), and to her collaboration on the script of Amelio's 1998 film, *Così ridevano*, focusing on Southerners in Turin in the post–World War II period. For a full list of her

publications, prizes, and collaborations on play productions and illustrations for comic books, see http://www.omegna.net/pariani.

4. Both located in the heart of Buenos Aires and often collapsed into one, these two neighborhoods are still considered working-class, despite an ongoing process of change. An attractive spot for artists since the 1920s (tango was very popular here), this area still hosts the building of a former bank and pawnshop that served immigrants starting in the late 1870s.

5. Baily's study indicates that Italians settled primarily in urban areas: Buenos Aires was by far the largest "Italian" city in the country, and the most "Italian" city in the world outside of Italy up until 1910, when New York took over that role. Other destinations in Argentina included Santa Fe, Entre Rios, and Cordoba (47), as well as Rosario and La Plata (Devoto 41). In the period covered by *Dio non ama i bambini*, there were roughly 300,000 Italians in the city, representing slightly over 20 percent of the entire population (down from the peak of 32 percent in 1887), which was made up of 48 percent foreign-born residents (this made Italians roughly half of the immigrant population). Return rates from Argentina remained quite high over the decades and were as great as 43 percent in the period under consideration (Baily 59). See also Introduction note 6.

6. Baily underlines the fact that "Italians in Buenos Aires were evenly dispersed" (143) throughout the city, although very high concentrations remained in the areas of La Boca and San Nicolas (123).

7. See Devoto on Argentina's fears of Italian immigrants for sociopolitical reasons (36), the widespread anti-Southern biases (38–39), and the presence of anti-Italian sentiments even among Italians (39).

8. An abbreviation of *napoletano* and *papolitano* (a local mutation of the adjective *napolitano*), which may have originated from the high incidence of Neapolitans among the army sutlers as early as 1870, *tano* was applied to practically all Italians, but especially the Southerners (Stella, *L'orda* 267–68).

9. These brief comments, prompted by the lived experience of people, eloquently speak to two historical aspects of Italian immigration, and immigration in general, to Argentina. In response to what was conceived as a threat, the central government aimed at assimilating immigrants through the 1901 law on mandatory conscription and the 1912 law on voting; in addition, a "patriotic" curriculum was designed for immigrant schools (Devoto 39). The level of assimilation for the second generations was quite high, since they considered themselves Argentinian (48).

10. Franzina reports that at the end of the nineteenth century there were 2,000 *conventillos* in Buenos Aires renting out to 100,000 renters, mostly Italians and Spaniards (*Italiani* 345).

11. See De La Torre for a comprehensive study of the *conventillo*: Chapters 2 and 4 analyze the tenement houses in Buenos Aires from an urban and social point of view, and also for the cultural production they yielded, from tango songs to popular comic plays.

12. In reality, Italian residential patterns were quite diverse. Devoto indicates that 47 percent of the *conventillo* owners were Italian and rented out to tenants, of which Italians themselves made up 45 percent (37). The Italians' long-term presence in Buenos Aires as well as their advanced level of economic integration allowed them to move out of poor lodgings and rent in better buildings, or eventually buy property. As Baily notes, "Italians, who in 1904 represented 24 percent of the city's population, were 45 percent of all home owners.... By 1914, the percentage ... increased even more" (141).

13. As Devoto cogently puts it, "Almost anything in Argentina can be related to Italians, but we do not know exactly what is specifically Italian" (25).

14. See Choate 177 and 187–88.

15. For the origin and use of *cocoliche* and its commonalities with *lunfardo*, see Franzina's bibliographic references in *Italiani* (589 n. 64).

16. See Chapter III "'Making Do:' Uses and Tactics" in *Practice* for the analysis of tactics of use as "an art of the weak" acting against/despite the system of rational power (37).

17. Terrorist activities in Argentina were less common. This relative absence is ironically attributed to the ideological role of an Italian, the anarcho-communist Errico Malatesta, who offered a viable alternative to both individual terror and reformist unionism (Moya 194).

18. See Franzina's *Italiani* (351–55).

19. Pariani's is an in-depth picture of just a portion of the Italian community in Argentina and specifically Buenos Aires, otherwise characterized by rather high levels of economic success and social integration (see Franzina's *Italiani*, especially the section on the industrialists, 356–61).

20. It is not just a coincidence that Piazza Vittorio is where Antonio and Bruno of De Sica's neorealist masterpiece *The Bicycle Thief* (1948) look for the famous stolen bike.

21. Italy has traditionally been only relatively segregated when it comes to class divisions in urban environments (Natale 182), and high- and low-cost property markets can coexist in the same neighborhood. While this pattern has continued with the arrival of immigrants, more concrete forms of ghettoization cannot be fully excluded in the future (190).

22. In Italian, *civiltà* means both civility and civilization, a double connotation which Lakhous plays with throughout the novel; what is a question of manners (civility) is easily taken as one of civilization by the novel's characters who describe and perceive manners by way of cultural/ethnic affiliations.

23. The film uses Lakhous's plot quite freely, and loses its ironic quality. As the focus shifts onto the family of the Gladiator, who does not even appear directly in the novel, the film pays much more attention to a local story (tensions between two Roman brothers and a dwindling love relationship) than to the intricate network of migratory stories of the novel. Another film addressing issues of immigration in Rome is Claudio Noce's *Good Morning, Aman* (2009), set in the Esquilino neighborhood.

24. Somehow reminiscent from a structural point of view of Bernardo Bertolucci's first film, *The Grim Reaper* (1962), which in turn was inspired by Kurosawa's 1950 *Rashomon*, composed of different people's perceptions/explanations of the same murder, Lakhous's first novel can also be read in conjunction with Andrea Camilleri's 1996 *The Snack Thief*, a detective novel focusing on immigration.

25. The list is incredibly rich and transcultural. Lakhous discusses Sciascia and Carlo Levi, quotes from Djaout, Cioran, Maalouf, Yacine, Freud, René Char, etc., and mentions Valentino's *The Sheik* (1921), Kubrick's *Spartacus* (1960), Germi's *Divorce Italian-Style* (1961), Bianchi's *Il conte Max* with Alberto Sordi (1957) and Fassbinder's *Ali: Fear Eats the Soul* (1974), among others.

26. Lakhous published the novel *Clash* in Arabic first in 2003, under the title of *Come farti allattare dalla lupa senza che ti morda* (printed by Al-ikhtilaf in Algeria, and three years later by Dar Al-arabiya lil-ulum in Lebanon). The original title, meaning "How to be suckled by the she-wolf without being bitten by it" pointed more clearly to Ahmed/Amedeo's desire to be painlessly integrated into Roman society, iconically symbolized by the legendary she-wolf that fed the founders of Rome, the abandoned twins Romulus and Remus. Yet, Ahmed/Amedeo's wailings seem to indicate that, as a result of this suckling, he has instead turned into a lycanthrope, a condition that signals his hybrid location rather than his integration.

27. For an analysis of the forms of exclusion of Italians in the United States, see Connell and Gardaphé; Lagumina; Stella; and Stella and Franzina.

28. Incidentally, Pariani collaborated on the script of the film.

29. The United States alone has a plethora of programs in Rome (see Association of American Colleges and University in Italy at http://www.aacupi.org/members/frames/members-frameset.htm), as Italy at large continues to be one of the most popular study abroad destinations (see http://www.iie.org/Research-and-Publications/Open-Doors).

30. For an analysis of the creative and ideological function of the representation of the South as opposed to the North, see Moe.

31. On the topic of the receiving countries as nonpassive participants in international migrations, see Sassen 26.

32. Even though, as Lakhous humorously claims, he is a "minor" in the Italian language (he is not an adult in it yet), the Italian Ministry of Foreign Affairs chose him to represent Italian literature in New York in 2008 as part of the Week of the Italian Language, devoted to the theme of the Italian piazza. For a country still trying to grapple with a fast-forming multicultural society, the choice of Lakhous signaled a step toward diversification in an institutional environment.

33. Originally published in journals between 1946–47, Gadda's detective novel, set in the Fascist period came out in 1954. Lakhous's work has been often compared to Gadda's, mostly because of *Quer pasticciaccio*'s location in the same Esquilino neighborhood of *Clash* and for its systematic dissolution of the truth. Lakhous himself has recognized its debt to Gadda but has humbly pointed out the more contained scope of his literary enterprise. From a linguistic point of view, *Clash* is indeed by far more intelligible and less experimental than Gadda's novel.

34. Lakhous's declared intention of "Arabicizing the Italian language" is not really traceable in *Clash*, while *Divorce* presents a dynamic mixture of Italian, Arabic, and Sicilian (a dialect heavily influenced by Arabic). Nevertheless, in *Divorzio* the migratory palette described by the author is thinner than in *Clash*, mostly because Lakhous is focusing on the internal complexity of the specific community of Muslims in Italy, and the ways in which it intersects with the migratory movements of Italians over time from Sicily to Tunisia.

35. See Bensmaïa on the role of North African writers of the former French colonies in recasting their nations through literature and film, in conjunction with and not just against the canon.

4. WRITING THE PASTA FACTORY AND THE BOARDINGHOUSE AS TRANSNATIONAL HOMES: PUBLIC AND PRIVATE ACTS IN MELLITI'S *PANTANELLA* AND MAZZUCCO'S *LIFE*

1. Mohsen Melliti (Tunis, 1967) is himself a diasporic subject who moved from Africa to the Middle East and Europe. Since 1989 he has lived in Rome. In 1995, he published a book of fiction on immigrant children in Italy (*I bambini delle rose*, The Rose Children). Two years later, he codirected the TV documentary on immigrant journeys titled *Verso casa* (Homebound). He is also the director of what is arguably the first film by an immigrant in Italy, *Io, l'altro* (2007).

A well-respected and prolific author of the contemporary Italian literary scene, Melania Mazzucco (Rome, 1966) started out with a powerful short story, "Seval," on the theme of the invisibility of immigration and the silent cruelty of the so-called developed world. Her first two novels—*Il bacio della Medusa* (1996) and *La camera di Baltus* (1998)—were Strega Award finalists, while *Vita* actually won this prestigious prize in 2003, and it is available in English translation as *Vita: A Novel* (New York: Farrar, Straus and Giroux, 2005). Other works include: *Lei così amata* (2000), *La lunga attesa dell'angelo* (2009), *Jacomo Tintoretto & i suoi figli. Storia di una famiglia veneziana* (2009), and *Limbo* (2011). Her 2005 novel, *Un giorno perfetto*, was adapted to the big screen in 2008. She has also written for cinema and theater and contributed to collective literary projects.

2. Numbers ranging from two thousand to more than three thousand are interchangeably mentioned in the related literature. According to the only systematic set of data gathered about the Pantanella occupation, the Caritas study included in Curcio's *Shish Mahal*, the Pantanella was inhabited by a total of 3,532 people over the whole period, but not necessarily by all of them at the same time (100). The initial total of 2,332 for the August–September period seems to have been adopted as the average total.

3. See Binetti as well as Burns.

4. English translations of passages of the novel are available in Parati's *Mediterranean Crossroads* (106–20).

5. See both the Pantanella pasta website (http://www.pastapantanella.com/english) and that of the U.S. importer, Ronson (http://www.ronsonfoods.com/pasta).

6. For more details see http://en.museodiroma.it/il_museo/storia_del_museo.

7. For a gallery of images of the original blueprints of the plant, the Pantanella changing over the decades, and the Roman baker's tomb, see http://pasqualeaiello.weebly.com/area-ex-pantanella.html. .

8. Acquired by a real estate group (Acqua Pia Antica Marcia-Caltagirone), the area was eventually turned into a residential and commercial complex bearing very few traces of the original history of the factory (for a description, see http://www.appartamentiportamaggiore.com/it/component/content/article/34-demo-content/50-aino-sony-ericsson). In the aftermath of the migrants' occupation, the Pantanella redevelopment had two objectives: "to liberate the area from this marginal population and to integrate the abandoned brown field area into the rest of the city" (Atkinson and Bridge 251).

9. According to the Caritas data (Curcio 102).

10. For a series of illuminating shots of the Pantanella and its inhabitants, see the reportage of Stefano Montesi available at http://tinyurl.com/MontesiPantanella, and in part in both the volume *Album italiano* edited by Castronovo (57–65) and Curcio's book enriched by photographs by Tano D'Amico and Patrizia Copponi as well. Montesi's pictures have been at the core of two interesting projects: They have been paired with images from the Fondazione Cresci on the occasion of a photographic exhibit called "Pane e denti" (Bread and teeth) linking Italian emigration and contemporary immigration in Italy (http://tinyurl.com/PaneDenti). Additionally, in 2003, they were presented at the Piccolo Apollo theatre with the musical accompaniment of the Orchestra of Piazza Vittorio during an evening called "Shish Mahal" (http://www.apolloundici.it/PiccoloApollo/ProveAperte/Locandine/ShishMahal.html).

11. Gallini adds that these protests are particularly disturbing not only as openly racist manifestations, even when they purport not be as such, but also because they are not part of a sustained effort at requesting better conditions for the residents' urban spaces. Eroded by years of little faith in democratic institutions, struggling neighborhoods paradoxically adopt the tools of the 1970s protests to identify the problem in the arrival of the immigrants rather than in the indifference of public institutions to their plight; their cohesion is "symbolic and false at the same time" (155).

12. The Caritas data indicates that at least 60 percent had a stay permit (Curcio claims that in August 1990 up to 90 percent did, but the table for this statistic is not included, 107).

13. Amateur footage of the Pantanella's living, religious, and economic spaces is contained in *Via Casilina n. 0—Storia della Pantanella, nel 1990* (see http://www.youtube.com/watch?v=aR62UXhhyRU). The title of this "film" (*sic*) by Roberto Angelis and Carmelo Albanese echoes Vinicius de Moraes's song—made famous in Italy by Sergio Endrigo as *La casa* (1970)—about an odd house located on Mad Street no. 0, which despite its lack of a roof, floor, bathroom, and kitchen, is "beautiful, very beautiful" anyway.

14. Ter Wal's article highlights the prejudiced position of even supposedly progressive newspapers such as *La Repubblica*: Their use of numbers in place of human stories; of a language full of binary oppositions (foreign/Italian; white/black; etc.); and of "exoticizing" images or vague descriptions of the immigrants all "failed to challenge the model of the official discourse" (62) and contributed to the formation of a culture of fear around what was perceived as a crisis.

15. Lombardi-Diop's study addresses a story similar to that of the Pantanella: the functioning and eventual evacuation of the Roma Residence, where various immigrant communities lived between 2001 and 2006. In focusing on the Senegalese community's commercial, consumption-related and political exchanges within the complex, Lombardi-Diop points out that "similar to other 'ghettos,' Roma Residence's dilapidated conditions soon became a self-fulfilling prophecy";

yet the residence remained "a transnational place that fulfilled the function of combining reality and the imagined" (410).

16. According to the Caritas study, the share of Pantanella dwellers from Maghreb was approximately 15 percent, versus 76 percent from the Indian subcontinent (Curcio 100). The international community had a common denominator in Islam, although some dwellers were not Muslim.

17. Ahmad's view of gender relations is quite progressive as companionship is for him both emotional and intellectual. He is also open to relationships with European women; his encounters with Sandra, the Belgian tourist, and with Mary, a Venetian student of anthropology in Rome, are a mix of daring actions of discovery across difference and unhappy retreats into cultural essentialism or isolation. For an analysis of female characters in the novel, see Binetti (97–99).

18. For an overview of public policies and programs for immigrants in Rome, see Brazzoduro.

19. Many of the Pantanella dwellers had received a stay permit through the amnesty provided by the Martelli Law, a decision that the conservative forces considered to be responsible for the challenging housing issues that the local government had to face in the aftermath of the amnesty. As Melliti writes, the problem was seen as belonging to those who were pro-immigration; the rest could wash their hands of it ("We do not want them! Take them to your place!" 152).

20. In relying on such concepts as Virilio's "panic city," Deleuze's and Guattari's "minor literature," Said's exile as an ontological condition, and Agamben's "coming community," Binetti suggests that Pantanella as a place and *Pantanella* as a text have drawn the possibility for a different way of being in the world that weakens traditional forms of affiliation and instead places emphasis on "one's being and singular exteriority" and on forms of familiarity and proximity in specific social spaces (95).

21. These two Italian characters were inspired by Father Di Liegro of Caritas, to whom the novel is dedicated, and Dino Frisullo of Senzaconfine and Rete Anti-razzista, all networks active in combating violence, racism, and war. Long gone by now, they both continue to be symbols of social struggles in the defense of immigrant rights: It is not a surprise that Ferrente closes his documentary *L'orchestra di Piazza Vittorio* with images of a protest at which Frisullo spoke in favor of the local immigrants. The immigrant leader is sketched after Sher Khan (the tiger), aka Mohammad Muzaffar Alì, a Pakistani political refugee, activist, and founder of the United Asian Workers Association (UAWA), who indefatigably defended the Pantanella occupation in many official contexts. After years of battles to guarantee better living standards for immigrants, Sher Khan eventually died homeless in 2009. See "Trovato morto" for details.

22. For a reading of the colonial concentration camps as archetypes of contemporary measures against immigrants, see Fiore's essay "From Exclusion."

23. The events of the Pantanella have inspired a 1995 role-playing research/game called *Pantanella Shish Mahal: Una simulazione giocata sul conflitto inter-etnico* (a simulation based on interethnic conflicts). As author and sociology professor Luca Giuliano notes, the game is an occasion to fight prejudice and engage in unbiased negotiation (http://www.gdr2.org/archivio/studio/pantanella.htm).

24. A picture from the muckraker's collection of images—*Mullen's Alley, Cherry Hill* by Richard How Lawrence, an amateur photographer who worked with Riis—was used for the first printing of the novel in Italy. The U.S. book versions feature images conveying the dynamism of the neighborhood's commercial activities, or as in the case of the Picador's publication, a telling shot of a fruit store owned by a certain Caruso, perhaps not a coincidence since Vita's father, Agnello, in the novel owns a fruit store while in Vita's dreams, her father is singer Enrico Caruso (114).

25. See Chapter 5 in Baily's and Gabaccia's "Tenement."

26. A similar alternation can be found in di Donato's *Christ in Concrete*, which also includes references to the contact between young Italian and Jewish characters, for instance, in scenes that point to the role of incipient intellectuals played by the Jewish boys (see di Donato, 121–27, and Mazzucco, 147–54).

27. The other section of the archive that Mazzucco opens is colonial history. Even though the references to Italy in Africa are quite sparse in the novel, she seamlessly weaves in issues of race perceptions that for Italians in the early 1900s are mediated by the colonial experience. Diamante's encounter with an African American elevator boy in a department store is filtered through his memory of a play performed when he was in school, called *The Capture of Africa in 1896*, and representations of African people as "savages" in popular magazines (33). The colonial experience indirectly furnishes the Italian emigrants with a racist syntax that they use out of an attempt at self-preservation as they try to carve out a space for themselves in a U.S. society that openly discriminates against them.

APERTURE III. LABOR ON THE MOVE: RODARI'S CONSTRUCTION WORKERS AND KURUVILLA'S BABYSITTER

1. See Lorenzo Luatti's *L'immigrazione raccontata ai ragazzi: Vent'anni di proposte dell'editoria per l'infanzia—catalogo della mostra bibliografica* (2011) and an annotated list at http://www.vanninieditrice.it/fileup/Inserti/Libri%20che%20parlano%20di%20immigrazione%20marzo%202011.pdf.

2. Winner of the prestigious Andersen Prize, Gianni Rodari (1920–80) was one of the most popular Italian writers of children's literature, who also devoted his pen to leftist journalism. Rodari published extensively: His *Filastrocche in cielo e in terra* (Nursery rhymes in the sky and on earth, 1960), *Favole al telefono* (Fairy tales on the telephone, 1962)—both illustrated by another key figure in children's literature, the writer-designer Bruno Munari—*Il libro degli errori* (The book of mistakes, 1964) and *Il libro dei perché* (The book of the whys, 1984, illustrated by Emanuele Luzzati) are all masterpieces in the genre.

3. Born in 1969 in India and raised in Italy since the age of one, Kuruvilla is the daughter of an Indian father and an Italian mother, which makes her into what is humorously termed a "knock-off G2," that is, a second-generation person whose parents are not both immigrants. Kuruvilla is the author of several short stories collected in various anthologies ("India" and "Ruben" in *Pecore nere*, 2005; "Documenti," 2007; as well as "Piazza Vittorio" and "Nera a metà" both adapted for the stage), of a collection of short stories (*È la vita, dolcezza*, 2014) and two novels (*Media chiara e noccioline*, 2001, published under the pseudonym of Viola Chandra, and *Milano, fin qui tutto bene*, 2012). She is an active voice in the G2 movement, which seeks fuller recognition of the rights of immigrants' children (see Conclusion). A graduate of the School of Architecture, she is also a visual artist (see www.piazzadellearti.it/artista/gabriella-kuruvilla.aspx).

4. Other texts by Rodari about emigration include "Essere e avere" (To be and to have) and "Italia piccola" (Small Italy) in *Il libro degli errori*, and "Il treno degli emigranti" (The emigrants' train) in *Un treno pieno di filastrocche* (A train full of nursery rhymes, 1952).

5. All the quotations from Rodari's texts are from the comprehensive anthology *I cinque libri*.

6. Many Northern Italians actually moved to Germany to work in the construction sector: They were part of a larger flow that was particularly prominent in the period before World War I (Pugliese, "In Germania" 127). Emigration to Germany has been active since the Middle Ages and with the exception of the period from World War I to World War II, it has remained steady up to the 1990s and beyond. Even in the 1990s, when Italy was already a country of immigration, Italians were the third largest immigrant group in Germany.

7. The passage is strikingly reminiscent of Pietro Di Donato's 1939 Italian American novel *Christ in Concrete*, a vivid portrait of Italian immigrants from Abruzzo struggling to survive in New York during the Depression Era. At the beginning of the novel, the protagonist Geremio, a

construction worker, is overcome by a flow of cement and symbolically dies in the position of a crucified Christ (13–18).

8. Makaping's work reverses the tenets of traditional anthropology insofar as it places the "eccentric" subject, that is, the marginal immigrant, at the center and makes her/him into the observer. Cognizant of the fraught relationship between viewer and viewed, she also adds the observation of herself observing Italian society. The result is a new perspective on the relationship between local and "other" that questions traditional tenets reinforcing separation.

9. The Indian community is the sixth largest community in Italy and represents 4 percent of the entire immigrant population in the country. Women count for one-third of a community that remains mainly male and active in the agricultural/dairy, domestic, and construction sectors, in order. Primarily coming from the states of Punjab and Kerala, the community has been growing extensively in the past decade and is strongly concentrated in Lombardy, Veneto, and Lazio. The presence of Indian children in the school system has been increasing as well, especially in the nursery school and kindergarten levels. See "La collettività indiana in Italia."

5. EDIFICATION BETWEEN NATION AND MIGRATION IN CAVANNA'S *LES RITALS* AND ADASCALITEI'S "IL GIORNO DI SAN NICOLA"

1. See Ariel Kaminer and Sean O'Driscoll, "Workers at N.Y.U.'s Abu Dhabi Site Faced Harsh Conditions" (*New York Times*, 18 May 2014); Aleksandar Vasovic and Maja Zuvela, "For Migrant Workers, Olympic Dream Turns to Nightmare in Sochi" (Reuters, February 5, 2014).

2. Pietro di Donato's *Christ in Concrete* (1939) offers a dramatic depiction of the construction site articulated in an innovative language at once sensitive to the "Italglish" of the Italian immigrants in New York and the avant-garde experimentations of the first half of the 1900s. See also Pietro Corsi's *Winter in Montreal* (1982), an Italian-Canadian classic.

3. See *Wait Until Spring, Bandini* (1938), *The Brotherhood of the Grape* (1977), *Full of Life* (1952), *1933 Was a Bad Year* (posthumous 1985), "The Bricklayer's Snow" (in the 1940 collection *Dago Red*), and "The Orgy" (in the posthumous 1986 collection *West of Rome*), which offer biting and humorous portrayals of the life of Italian construction workers and their families in Colorado and California. For an in-depth reading of Fante's as well as Di Donato's works focusing on construction, see Fiore's "Architextualizing."

4. A representative text in this genre is Pascal D'Angelo's 1924 pick-and-shovel autobiography, *Son of Italy*.

5. The works by Mari Tomasi—*Like Lesser Gods* (1949) and *Men Against Granite*, a collection of interviews conducted in 1938–40 with Roaldus Richmond and published in 2004—record the life of the quarry workers in Vermont in a documentary style.

6. For instance, Paolo and Vittorio Taviani's 1987 film *Good Morning, Babylon* is an homage to the concrete contribution of Italian builders and carpenters to the early Hollywood industry, in itself a project of U.S. national formation relying on foreign hands. John Turturro's 1992 *Mac* is a realist-style comedy-drama about a family-based construction business in Queens inspired by Turturro's father's actual work in the sector. An interesting reversal of roles in which Italian Americans the managers of construction job assignments to undocumented Latin American migrants can be found in one of the episodes of *La Ciudad* ("Bricks"), David Riker's 2005 lyrical neo-neo-realist film about immigration in New York.

7. See migrant builder *par excellence* Sabato Rodia's Watts Towers in South Los Angeles, and two visionaries such as Achilles Rizzoli and Marino Auriti, designers of grandiose architectural projects that were never built.

8. Camilleri's novella *Maruzza Musumeci* (2007) traces the bizarre architectural project of a returned migrant from Sicily (see Fiore's "Builders"), while De Luca's 1994 short story "Una specie di trincea" (A sort of trench) from the volume *In alto a sinistra* captures the mortal risks entailed in

the harsh work of a Neapolitan laborer hired on a French construction site. For a satirical text about construction and internal migration from the South, see Stefano Benni's monologue "Il sogno del muratore" (*Teatro 2* 2003) about the safety of death versus the dangers of life as a bricklayer.

9. Hamid Barole Abdu's proselike poem "Il volo di Mohammed" (Mohammed's flight), published in the newspaper *Il Manifesto* (December 27, 2007), functions as a prayer for the loss of an Eritrean construction worker who dies "flying" off the scaffolding for lack of safety measures.

10. A French writer of Italian origin, Cavanna made a name for himself as the cofounder of two satirical newspapers; *Hari Kiri* became *Charlie Hebdo* in 1970. He was active in various genres ranging from prose to essay, reportage, and humorous vignettes. Born in 1923 in the Italian enclave of Nogent-sur-Marne, on the outskirts of Paris, he paid homage to his immigrant upbringing in two novels *Les Ritals* (1978) and *L'oeil du lapin* (1987). Other autobiographical works followed: *Les Russkoffs* (1979) about his experience as a soldier in World War II Russia; *Bête et méchant* (1981) and *Les yeux plus grands que le ventre* (1983), about his adventures as director of censorship-challenging satirical newspapers; and *Lune de miel* (2010) about his way of coping with Parkinson's disease. His working-class origin and biting political commentary replete with humor made him into an unconventional yet much respected and loved voice among French intellectuals. He died in 2014, leaving behind a large body of untranslated work, much of it characterized by inventive twists of language. In 1991, *Les Ritals* was adapted into a two-part TV production featuring Gastone Moschin and Christine Fersen and directed by Marcel Bluwal.

11. Adascalitei is originally from Romania herself. She earned a degree in foreign languages and literatures in Iasi, Romania, in 2000, and spent long periods at the Universities of Padua and Venice as a student. In 2010, she earned a second degree in communications from the University of Bergamo with a thesis on the relationship between TV language, news, and immigration. In Italy, she has worked as an interpreter and teacher, besides collaborating with the Media Observatory of Pavia. She has completed other short stories and another detective novel (along with an Italian friend). A lover of poetry, she finds in the realism of Tolstoy an ideal model; yet, the more immediate sources for her writings are the works of Andrea Camilleri and the socially engaged Italian detective novels of Marco Malvaldi and Gianrico Carofiglio, as well as the gender-inflected ones by Spanish writer Alicia Gimenez Bartlett. The books of Tahar Ben Jelloun have a special place on her bookshelves.

12. Italians furnished between one-quarter and one-third of the foreigners to France in the period 1880–1965. Within three to four generations, roughly five million French people had at least one Italian ancestor (Vial 133). According to Milza in his *Voyage en Ritalie*, in the early 1990s there were 3.5 to 4 million Italo-French, French citizens with at least one ancestor born in Italy (94).

13. See also Corti's "L'emigrazione" for a discussion on the "professionalism" of emigration across the Alps (230).

14. During this decade, the number of Italians in France was estimated at one million (Vegliante 26).

15. Another derogatory term used against Italians in France before "Rital" was "macaroni," hinging on the common image of Italian food. The term is now obsolete, but in order to document its existence and its related stories of racism (including the notorious Aigues-Mortes lynching in 1893), noted detective story writer Loriano Machiavelli and famous singer songwriter Francesco Guccini cowrote a novel by the title of *Macaronì. Romanzo di santi e delinquenti* (Novel of saints and criminals).

16. For a reading of the clash between bricklaying fathers and educated sons, see Fiore's "Architextualizing."

17. As Sylvie Schweitzer notes, women have suffered from invisibility in the history of emigration and labor under the incorrect assumption that they were not active workers. Schweitzer uses the Italian naturalized mother of Cavanna as the symbol of this invisibility in French historical accounts, given that she is mentioned several times as the home caretaker. It is only one-third of the way into the novel, though, that there is a more concrete sense of her job as a

domestic worker outside the house (31). In 1931, the statistics show, Italian women constituted the largest number of salaried domestic workers (37).

18. The expression "Nogent des Italiens" is the title of a book (Paris: Autrement, 1995) by two historians, Pierre Milza and Marie-Claude Blanc-Chaléard, whose goal was to document the story of the Italians in this section of the Parisian outskirts, and in particular their substantial contribution to the construction projects of the area.

19. In the film, the reference to immigration remains quite marginal, yet immigration is the not-too-invisible engine of this film, a mechanism that becomes obvious in the beginning and ending scenes. The arrival of a train carrying Italians and Spaniards at the outset—with its beautiful fusion of intradiegetic songs in dialects and images of passport and cardboard suitcase carriers—is iterated in the final scene to hint at the endless cycles of migration. In between there is a story of abuse, betrayal, care, desire, and in the end tragedy, which does not seem to stop immigration despite the killing of an immigrant, the Toni of the title.

20. This same topic is the narrative engine of a little known 2000 TV film entitled *Les Ritaliens*, directed by Philomène Esposito, with a cast made up of Ennio Fantastichini, Veronica Pivetti, and Margarita Lozano. Focusing on the last wave of immigration to France around the 1950s and '60s, *Les Ritaliens* tells a fairly conventional story of the immigrant's sense of displacement, rage, and dreams through the lesser-known lenses of the construction business in France.

21. In turn, Italians see the French as dirty, perverted, lazy, and Communist, married to whores with syphilis, while they perceive themselves as law-abiding, hardworking, pious people who enjoy the community and take care of their families (Cavanna 18–19).

22. Along the same lines, singer songwriter Gian Maria Testa's track "Ritals" in the 2006 album *Da questa parte del mare* (On this side of the sea) vindicates the term with a poetic spirit. See Chapter 2 for a discussion of Testa's music and lyrics.

23. A classic example of the involvement of Southern workers in the construction sector of the North can be found in a 1972 comedy by Lina Wertmüller, *Mimí Metallurgico ferito nell'onore* (*The Seduction of Mimi*), which follows the vicissitudes of a Sicilian immigrant in Turin, hired by exploitative bosses who disregard basic safety rules on the construction site.

24. A study completed by Pierpaolo Mudu, "L'immigrazione straniera a Roma: tra divisioni del lavoro e produzione degli spazi sociali" (Foreign immigration in Rome: between labor division and production of social spaces) shows that in 2006, foreign immigrants represented about 50 percent of the entire labor force in Rome. His study reports on forms of protest (128) prompted also by the high incidence of foreign workers in the sector.

25. With regard to the use of standard Italian language in immigrant writing, see Chapter 2 about Tekle's *testimonio*, Chapter 4 about Melliti's novel, and Chapter 6 about Ghermandi's short story.

26. See, for example, her use of the article *un'* with the apostrophe even in front of masculine nouns starting with a vowel, which, albeit considered a mistake, is not rare on the Internet or newspaper articles or documents in Italian by now.

27. Maramures's architecture is considered to be like wooden embroidery, and as such a precious patrimony. A number of its wooden churches are UNESCO's World Heritage Sites.

28. The narrative contains many instances: Caterina hosts Anna when she is reluctant to go back home (105); Marta provides for Anita to be visited by Italian doctors and to be furnished with medicines for five months before her return to Romania (125); Marta helps Anna claim a late-arriving four hundred euros for her translation service, and in turn Anna offers it to her Romanian friend, Cristina, for the service (111).

29. The statement comes from an email exchange I had with the author in the summer of 2013.

30. See Focacci.

31. For a study of this migration, which produced both seasonal flows and permanent colonies, see Rudolf Dinu's article "Appunti per una storia dell'emigrazione italiana in Romania nel periodo 1878–1914."

32. Among the architects it is worth mentioning Domenico Ruopolo, active in the health sector in the 1930s. See Fontana's "Domenico Ruopolo architetto alla corte di Mogoşoaia (1913–1930 e segg.)," in Popescu 230–35.

33. By another historical irony, Italians who have recently decided to leave the country find new opportunities abroad, including small jobs in the building sector, as reported by journalist Giovanni Russo in his *I cugini di New York* (30–31).

6. THE CIRCULAR ROUTES OF COLONIAL AND POSTCOLONIAL DOMESTIC WORK: PERÒ AND CIARAVINO'S *ALEXANDRIA* AND GHERMANDI'S "THE STORY OF WOIZERO BEKELECH AND SIGNOR ANTONIO"

1. For an in-depth analysis of domestic work at the global level, see Lutz; Ehrenreich and Hochschild; and Henshall Momsen. For the specific case of Italy, see Andall's *Gender, Migration and Domestic Service*.

2. The most notable example of a domestic worker of the early period is Marco's mother in De Amicis' "From the Apennines to the Andes" (1886), a woman who emigrates to Argentina to help her indebted family and reunites with her son after his tenacious search for her. Her story stands out because she acquires a substantial amount of autonomy as a wage earner, in what may be termed a gender revolution that only immigration could make possible to the working class at that time. As seen in Chapter 4, a more recent work that devotes special attention to the Italian migrant domestic labor is Mazzucco's *Vita*, whose chapters set in a boarding house of Little Italy articulate with crudeness and lyricism an otherwise untold story of female exploitation and quest for freedom in the early 1900s.

3. Tornatore's film noir *cum* thriller and horror *The Unknown Woman* (2006) subtly portrays the relationship between an Italian upper-class family and their Eastern European babysitter/home caretaker who is in charge of their adoptive daughter. A disturbing tale of abuse and doubt, the film is an exploration of how the most personal experiences are carriers of transnational collective stories and reflect societal issues—in this case, a low birth rate, professional women's reliance on nannies to raise their children, and fears about the reliability of foreign domestic helpers often seen as potential thieves or child abusers. For an in-depth reading of the film, see O'Healy, "Border Traffic." A more recent film, *Mar nero*, directed by Federico Bondi (2008), turns the topic on its head to occasion the unexpected rethinking of the Italian senior person's life in her caretaker's Eastern European country, despite age and cultural differences.

4. "Un giorno d'aprile a Pescara" (An April Day in Pescara), a short story written by the Albanian journalist Diana Ciuli (1998), shows how invisible the stratified experience of immigrant domestic workers remains by focusing on an educated Albanian woman who courageously challenges the patriarchal system with her choice to migrate to Italy. In "Ana de Jesus" (1999), Cristiana De Caldas Brito's monologue-dialogue written in an Italian-Brazilian *patois*, the experience of the protagonist, an exploited Brazilian maid, is a dramatic combination of discomfort and nostalgia for her country, eerily echoing some of the disappointing experiences of Italian emigrants in Brazil. Equally attentive to content and form, Cetta Petrollo's 2007 *Senza Permesso: Avventure di una badante rumena* (Undocumented: Adventures of a Romanian caretaker) is a highly experimental text in prose that relates the story of a Romanian domestic worker in her own immigration-forged Italian *patois*, which represents the new condition of a mixed Italy looking for novel forms of communication across cultures.

5. See Degiuli's "Laboring" (348).

6. See Boz for the village of Fontanafredda in Friuli and Dadà for Buggiano in Tuscany. See also Barbič for the Slovenian region—back then part of the Austro-Hungarian Empire, which also embraced Italian areas—and the essays in Però's coedited volume.

7. The phenomenon can be traced within national boundaries as well: As Nadia Boz remarks, even up until the period between World War I and World War II, women from Friuli migrated to Venice or Milan as seasonal wet nurses (252).

8. During the Fascist era, this stigma became particularly strong: The Church was openly critical of these women who, instead of incarnating the angel of the hearth, "abandoned" their families (Boz 256).

9. This trajectory is particularly evident in two stories by the expatriate Anna Messina, included in her short story collection *Cronache del Nilo* (Chronicles from the Nile, 1940): "Il basilico" and "'Caro sposo, ti faccio assapere,'" an interesting source for the portrayal of Alexandria in the twenty years corresponding to the Fascist regime in Italy, in which Italian cooks, wet nurses, and housecleaners saved enough money abroad to be able to buy a house or support their children's education and weddings. The stories reveal a fascination for this lively city that is on the one hand mitigated by nostalgia for Italy and on the other rekindled upon the return home, a home that is not the same anymore after the intense Egyptian experience for many Italians (see "Ritorno in colonia," "Cronache dal Nilo: Il giornale," and in particular "Ma tu non partirai" for snapshots of the city's cosmopolitan scene). In Messina's nostalgic rendition, these domestic workers share with the upper-class families they work for the same *mal d'Afrique* suffered by dislocated Italians upon their return to the home country.

10. Born in Milan in 1973, Renata Ciaravino studied at the Drama School of her town of origin and was selected for international workshops at the Théâtre du Rond-Point in Paris and Le Centre des Arts Scéniques in Brussels, led by Laura Betti and Luca Ronconi, among others. Founder of the Compagnia Dionisi in 2000, she has been the artistic director of the Festival Mixité in Sesto San Giovanni. She writes for theater, radio, and television and has collaborated with singers. In 2007, she published her first novel, *Potevo essere io*. She is also the author of a short play about Italian migrants to the United States who returned home.

Originally from Trieste, Franco Però is a fairly established theatre director who has also worked as an actor. After working as an assistant director with Gabriele Lavia, Aldo Trionfo, and Giorgio Pressburger, he began to producer contemporary theatrical works, both Italian (Cerami, Siciliano) and foreign (Mamet, Shepard). He has also directed classic plays by Pirandello and Beckett; operas (Verdi, Schoenberg); adaptations of works by Camus and Primo Levi; and newly developed works such as *Alexandria*. He is a member of the Teatro Festival of Parma.

11. Some of the most notable Italian names include writers Filippo Tommaso Marinetti (born in Alexandria in 1876) and Enrico Pea (who lived in Alexandria between 1897 and 1918 and later published *Vita in Egitto* in 1949); poet Giuseppe Ungaretti (born in the same city in 1888); Italian cuisine expert Marcella Hazan (based there with her family as a young girl in the early 1930s); and writer and journalist Fausta Cialente (a resident between 1921 and 1947), among others.

12. According to Petricioli, between 40,000 and 70,000 Italians lived in the Levantine country in the years 1917–1937, although local data underrepresented the actual size of the community. In 1927 less than 4 percent of it was registered as active in the domestic sector (7). Interestingly, Petricioli's substantial study does not include any specific analysis of Italian migrant laborers in Egypt. Instead, while highlighting the initially prominent role of Italians in Egypt in the postal, security, legal, and health systems, Surdich briefly mentions the presence of prostitutes, beggars, and street players from Italy after 1882. He calculates that roughly 500 women were present in Alexandria that year (189), which reinforces the prevalent sentiment of shame toward the migrants. In quoting the Consul General of Italy in Egypt in 1892, he points out that low-skilled jobs were infrequent and "temporary" (190). In reality, the relocation of low-skilled workers was not a marginal phenomenon. According to Però's research, one in every three families in Trieste had a woman working in Alexandria (see http://xoomer.virgilio.it/nuovopapiro/in_egitto_file/balie_italiane.htm).

13. The exhibit Balie e Colf Straniere (Wet nurses and foreign domestic workers) was organized by CESTIM (Center for the Study of Immigration) based in Verona, Italy. An

itinerant educational project made up of thirty posters connecting archival photos of Italian female domestic workers abroad and contemporary shots of migrant domestic workers and providing information about historical, sociological, and legal issues related to this professional sector, the project was designed to dispel racist prejudices by highlighting commonalities. See http://www.cestim.it/sezioni/mostre_musei_teatro/balie-e-colf/donne.htm.

14. The decision to leave was at times linked to social unsuitability due to out-of-wedlock pregnancies, but was also often forced on legitimate mothers by their husbands and mothers-in-law (Bianchi 262).

15. The site of the eminent Migration History Foundation Paolo Cresci lists all these benefits in a section devoted to the *balie*: "a full wardrobe with a pretense of elegance; a rich set of personal and house linen; wearable ornaments called 'wet nurse jewels,' including necklaces, brooches, and earrings, often made of red coral; and the certainty for many months of a beautiful and comfortable house, as well as the care and respect of the employing family." See http://www.museoemigrazioneitaliana.org/il-lavoro/le-fragili-donne.

16. Most of the photographs of that period confirm this point: see for instance the images of well-dressed nannies whether during their leisure time or during job shifts in Boz's essay (262–64). The original notes accompanying the photographs reveal the tendency to emulate the tastes of the bourgeoisie lifestyle but are also replete with a sense of guilt or inadequacy on the part of the migrant workers writing to their families back home (257).

17. Another relevant document that addresses the same issue of "risk of perdition" but is not included in the play is a 1896 report by the baron Filippo Marincola San Floro, in which he points out in patronizing terms that women from Calabria would count on their physical attributes and add some side activity of "intimate" character to their domestic work or what he called "occasional occupations in the pleasurable system, which yielded many golden" coins. See http://www.brigantaggio.net/Brigantaggio/Storia/Altre/Lamezia.htm.

18. For a reading of the novels and memoirs of Luciana Capretti, Arthur Journo, David Gerbi, and Victor Magiar on this topic, see Derobertis's "Sperduti in mezzo alla rotta" and Comberiati's "'Province minori' di un 'impero minore'" in Derobertis, as well as Comberiati's "L'esodo dei ventimila" in Comberiati.

19. See the Conclusion of this book for a broader analysis of this topic.

20. Boz shows that some traces were also left in the language: Nilo (as in the Nile River) was the name given by returning migrants to their newborns in Friuli in order to keep the memory of Egypt alive, while "Nasser" was the epithet used to refer to these returned migrants (258–59).

21. According to the Ministry of Labor and Social Policies' 2013 Annual Report "The Egyptian Community in Italy," as of January 2013 the Egyptian community was the eighth largest in terms of size among the non-EU communities: 123,529 people, 71 percent of them men (6). While the very early migrants who left Egypt in the 1960s initially came from the educated class, in more recent decades they represent low- to middle-range-skilled workers and have primarily found jobs in the construction and restoration industries (it is more frequent to have a pizza prepared by an Egyptian than by a Neapolitan in Milan today). Rome hosts the second largest Egyptian community in Italy after Milan. It is also the set of the most important novel focusing on the Egyptian community, Amara Lakhous's *Divorce Italian Style* (2010).

22. The 2008 symposium "Le rotte di Alexandria" (The routes of Alexandria) covered the topic of migrant domestic workers as well as that of the relationships between the Italian Northeast and Egypt (migrant construction work for the Suez Canal, financial support of this engineering project coming from Trieste, etc.). For the full program, see http://www.consiglio.regione.fvg.it/pagine/comunicazione/informazionieventi.asp?infoEventoId=86286. See Però for the symposium's proceedings.

23. The pamphlet *In ricordo delle Aleksandrinke—Le Alessandrine* (In memory of the Aleksandrinke) describes a series of texts in Slovenian which functioned as sources to the play *Alexandria*:

From Marjan Tomsic's novel to the work of journalist Dorica Makuc and a TV documentary, the pamphlet briefly documents the story of the Slovenian women who joined a large community of migrants in Egypt (7,000 Slovenians, of which 4,500 just in Alexandria). See http://www.aleksandrinke.si/mma_bin.php/$fId/2008112014142627/$fName/aleksandrinke+zgib+ITL.pdf.

24. Work opportunities were amply available in the various communities of well-to-do expatriates in the cosmopolitan atmosphere of Alexandria. The comment made by the Italian Minister in Egypt, Roberto Cantalupo, that the Italian language was considered to be useful primarily in order to communicate with domestic workers speaks to this mixed labor relationship as well as to the high concentration of Italian immigrants in this sector (Petricioli 221).

25. The *letté* practice is depicted in Erminia Dell'Oro's novel *Asmara addio* (1988).

26. According to the *Dossier Statistico Immigrazione 2011* (3), there were approximately 1.5 million domestic workers in Italy in 2010, half of whom were not registered with a regular contract. The irregular nature of the job market in Italy and its tendency to rely on family-based formulas (informality, etc.) makes these workers particularly unable to claim their rights (Bonizzoni 139).

27. Supported by the Catholic missions network, this "niche" immigration involved Cape Verde, the countries of the Horn of Africa, and eventually Sri Lanka (Amato 23).

28. According to the *Dossier Statistico Immigrazione 2012*, by 2050 this population will be 33 percent (3). The ISTAT data for 2014 indicates that the ageing index has reached 154 percent. Defined as the percentage of the old age population (over 65) divided by the percentage of the young population (under 15), in 2014 the aging index for Italy was ranked second in Europe, just behind Germany. For more information, see http://noi-italia2015.istat.it/index.php?id=7&user_100ind_pi1[id_pagina]=22&P=1&L=0.

29. According to the CIA data, the total fertility rate in Italy in 2015 was estimated at 1.4 children/woman, which corresponds to 213th in the list of 224 countries in the world. A rate of 2.1 is considered necessary for the population to not decline (in industrialized countries). For more information see: https://www.cia.gov/library/publications/the-world-factbook/geos/it.html.

30. This aspect became particularly obvious in the special provisions of the Bossi-Fini Law, which granted extensions and higher quotas specifically for the *badanti*, thus recognizing them an integral part of the nation/family's economy. In responding to this apparently favorable but ultimately exclusionary measure, immigrant women activists identified a troubling equating of woman with caretaker—*"donne migranti quindi badanti"*—and called for a broader spectrum of job opportunities in order to avoid the risk of being seen only as servants (Pojmann 177).

31. For an overview of Italian colonialism, see note 7 in the Introduction of this book.

32. Ethiopia constituted one of the most difficult territories to conquer for Italy. The first attempt at subjugation notoriously failed in 1896 in the Battle of Adua, which is considered the only European defeat at the hands of local warriors. The territory was eventually taken over in 1935 and lost during World War II, although a form of interposition was in place all the way through to 1947. Among all the Italian colonies, Ethiopia is the one that has played a central role in the experience and memory of colonialism due to its prominence in African history and politics, its international stature in relation to Western countries, its ancient history and culture, and the fierce resistance of the local fighters. For comprehensive readings of this chapter of Italian colonialism, see Del Boca's *La Guerra di Etiopia* and Labanca's *Oltremare*.

33. Gabriella Ghermandi was born in 1965 in Debre Zeit, a village located a few miles away from Addis Ababa, Ethiopia, and has lived in Bologna since 1979. She comes from a racially mixed family where two generations of women had relationships with Italian men, and as such she considers herself a product of Italian colonialism. Her mother's family was originally from the border between Eritrea and Ethiopia (a border that was fictitiously fabricated by Italian colonialism). Her grandmother's affair with an Italian during the early colonial phase was interrupted by the passing of the miscegenation laws against the *madamato*. The daughter born

from this relationship, Ghermandi's mother, was brought up in an Italian boarding school where the local language was banned and in an environment where racism against mixed-raced children was rampant. She later met her own Italian partner, who was posted in Eritrea in 1935 as part of the World War II military defense operation of the colonies and stayed behind. Gabriella Ghermandi is the result of their relationship; after his death, at the age of fourteen, she moved to Bologna. She has become one of the most relevant voices in the scene of immigrant and postcolonial culture in Italy thanks to her publications—besides the novel, her writings have appeared in *Quaderni del '900* (2004), *Nuovo planetario Italiano* (2006), *L'Italiano degli altri: 16 storie di normale immigrazione* (2006) and *Tolomeo* (2007)—and her performances (*All'ombra dei rami sfacciati carichi di fiori rosso vermiglio*, *Un canto per mamma Heaven*, and the adaptation of *Queen of flowers and pearls* for the stage). She is the recipient of two Eks&Tra Prizes (1999 and 2001) and the founder of El Ghibli, an online journal of immigration literature in Italy (http://www.el-ghibli.provincia.bologna.it).

34. See in particular Bonizzoni (143). The same sentiments of isolation and claustrophobia as well as distance from the elderly person she is taking care of are expressed by Lakhous's Peruvian character Maria Gonzales in *Clash of Civilizations* and the Bolivian protagonist of the 2009 documentary *Ritratto di famiglia con badante* directed by Alessandra Speciale (as the caretaker puts it: "I did not know that there were so many old people here!"). The absorbing nature of the job erases the individuality of the women working in this sector as it equates work and life in indissoluble ways and recasts them as family members with professional duties rather than workers with rights.

35. Bekelech's experience has echoes in real life. In her essay "Laboring Lives: The Making of Home Eldercare Assistants in Italy," Degiuli shows how immigrant women are often unaware of the real nature of the job they accept (349).

36. See Pirandello's "L'altro figlio" for a refined treatment of issues of trust and betrayal in the relationship between scribes writing letters on behalf of illiterate people.

37. Woizero, the term that appears in front of her name in the title of the story, is an old title bestowed on nobles. It came to refer to a married woman over time (it is unclear why Ghermandi uses it as there is no reference to a spouse): In the story Bekelech is only addressed as such.

38. See the short story "Saviceveca la badante/Saviceveca the Caregiver" and the poem "Seppellite la mia pelle in Africa/Bury My Skin in Africa," which provides the title to the entire bilingual collection containing the two texts. The former focuses on a young Slovenian woman who tries to join the prostitution business as an alternative to the effacing experience of domestic work but ends up in a detention camp for undocumented migrants where she commits suicide. The latter is a discursive poem about an African woman who, after working as a maid/nanny for three decades, finds herself old, ailing, and with no pension, simply wanting to be buried in Africa. Written in a conventional Italian, both texts suffer from a rigid religious framework that privileges moral considerations over nuanced portrayals that instead open up to new visions and exchanges as part of transnational visions such as those offered by Ciaravino and Ghermandi.

39. Interestingly, in Ukraine, doctors have introduced the term "Syndrome of Italy" to refer to the sense of depression experienced by women who in working as *badanti* are expected to only provide to others and, as a result, feel dispossessed of their own identity. See one of the interviews included in Katia Bernardi's documentary *Sidelki* (Caregivers).

40. See the photography project "Badanti" by Roberta Valerio, who splices together images of these migrant women's work in Italy, trips back in Eastern Europe via day-long bus rides, and actual visits at home: http://www.robertavalerio.com/OLD/badanti/synops.htm.

41. See the Conclusion of this book, as well as Fiore's "Migration Italian Style" and "Immigration from Italy since the 1990s."

CONCLUSION. ITALY AS A LABORATORY FOR IMAGI-NATION: THE CITIZENSHIP LAW
BETWEEN INBOUND AND OUTBOUND FLOWS

1. Lombardi-Diop and Romeo call this connectivity "intersectionality" in their manifesto "The Italian Postcolonial" (432).

2. This is the period of time when the term "colonialism" worked effectively for both the emigrant colonies and the territorial colonies. See Fiore's essay "Post-'Colonia'" and Choate.

3. See Fiore's essay "Migration Italian Style" and "Immigration from Italy since the 1990s."

4. Children of immigrants below the age of eighteen can automatically acquire citizenship only if both parents have been naturalized, a fairly rare situation given the residence requirements for eligibility and the long administrative procedures, coupled with the fact that immigrants themselves are not always informed or proactive about the naturalization process (see G2 network website: http://www.secondegenerazioni.it/legge-cittadinanza).

5. See Fondazione Moressa's study, http://www.fondazioneleonemoressa.org/newsite/wp-content/uploads/2014/02/Comunicato-stampa_stranieri-e-cittadinanza.pdf (1).

6. See the campaign DreamAct (http://dreamact.info) in support of an amnesty for young people who have not chosen to be undocumented, and Define American (http://www.defineamerican.com), the José Antonio Vargas–led project questioning the meaning of American citizenship in favor of a more embracing concept of belonging, especially in response to Arizona and Alabama laws criminalizing undocumented immigrants. Given the long-standing opposition of Congress to the Dream Act, a presidential order—the Deferred Action for Childhood Arrivals program—has since 2012 allowed undocumented youth to apply for a residence permit that protects them against deportation and provides work authorization. Note that the program does *not* provide a pathway to citizenship.

7. See Tintori on this naturalization and institutionalization of blood ties as part of what he calls an "asymmetrical treatment" of emigrants over immigrants (123).

8. For an analysis of the requests submitted in a country with a large pool of potential citizens like Brazil, see Del Pra'.

9. Tintori's analysis shows the difficulty in extrapolating definitive data about undocumented Italians abroad from the statistics (85–90).

10. The photograph captures a racist invocation of the need to give Italy back to Italians and juxtaposes it with the presence in front of it of a mother and a child of African origin, hardly the incarnation of dangerous invaders from outside stealing Italy from Italians. Further irony is added by the fact that the Italian language in the graffiti is grammatically incorrect ("*all'italiani*" should be "*agli italiani*"), revealing an intrinsically fragile relationship with the national standard on the part of Italians, including those driven by a nationalist creed. Within the context of this Conclusion, the image acquires further meaning as it could be read, despite the actual intentions of the graffiti's author, as an invitation to embrace "new Italians" into the extended notion of Italy, i.e., a country made up of Italians abroad as well as (direct and indirect) postcolonial immigrants in Italy.

11. For information about the "L'Italia sono anch'io" campaign, see http://www.litaliasonoanchio.it.

12. Among the edited collections of short stories or memoir-like tales, see the Somali-Italian Scego for *Pecore nere* (Black sheep), Indian-Italian Kuruvilla for *Italiani per vocazione* (Italians by vocation), Palestinian-Italian Masri for *Amori bicolori* (Two-color loves), and Zairian-Egyptian-Italian Mubiay for *Quando nasci è una roulette* (When you are born it is a game of roulette).

The album *Straniero a chi?* (Foreigner to Whom?) features thirteen songs by Italians from diverse cultural heritages in a wide range of musical styles, including hip-hop, reggae, rock, punk, and electronic. The songs confront issues related to belonging and status and openly criticize Italian culture for not being more inclusive.

The playful *fotoromanzo* (photo-illustrated comics book) *Apparenze* (Appearances) denounces prejudicial assumptions about G2 youth: The often-quoted instance is the surprise that people share at hearing them speak Italian so fluently. The game *Indovina chi?* (Guess Who?) smartly challenges the readers to determine the citizenship or heritage from the picture of the G2s, in itself an impossible task. The answer key reveals each person's citizenship, cultural heritage, and time spent in Italy, but mostly it reveals how flawed ethnic profiling is.

13. Included in the Venice Biennale 2011, artist Jijon is originally from Ecuador (1968 Quito) and moved to Italy in 2000. She works primarily with audiovisual tools (documentary, video, photography) within a genre that she calls *"artivismo,"* an art that is inseparable from activism. She has collaborated with several associations to defend the rights of immigrants, women, and regional cultures in several parts of the world. Her preferred mode of artistic production is what she calls *"arte partecipata,"* through projects that involve other people, develop relationships, and advance social causes. See interview at https://www.youtube.com/watch?v=ECexNwpP33s.

14. There are more than a dozen reform proposals ranging from the request for a pure *ius soli* to either a "temperate *ius soli*" which envisions the automatic recognition of children born in Italy from parents that are legal residents, or a *ius culturae* by which the recognition is based on a certain number of school years completed in Italy. Parliament has resumed discussion of the reform in 2015, and immigrant descendants and their civic supporters highly desire a nonpartisan resolution; as they claim, through an apparent contradiction, the right to citizenship is not a political matter. An ISTAT poll of 2012 indicates that over 70 percent of the people living in Italy (immigrants and nonimmigrants alike) are in favor of the recognition of citizenship at the time of birth (see http://www.istat.it/it/archivio/66563).

15. Fred Kuwornu is an Italian-born director of Ghanaian origin. After working for TV and radio, he was chosen by Spike Lee to be an assistant on his film *Miracle at St. Anna*. Kuwornu also used that occasion to develop his own spin-off, entitled *Inside Buffalo* (2010), a video that documented the experience of U.S. African American soldiers in Tuscany during World War II. Currently splitting his time between New York and Rome, Kuwornu has also completed a new documentary called *Blaxploitation: One Hundred Years of Afro-Stories in Italian Cinema*.

16. See Dickie's "The Notion" and Baranksi's "Introducing."

17. Roughly 11 million Italians moved to the Americas between the mid-1800s and the mid-1900s (Favero 12), with 5.5 to the United States alone (16). Interestingly, the number of foreigners in Italy is equal to the same number five million (*Dossier 2014*, 1).

18. Additionally, this documentary seems to claim that papers automatically grant integration at the cultural level, whereas, in actuality, a sense of displacement if not utter exclusion is experienced even by Italian descendants who have acquired the Italian citizenship in Brazil and moved to Italy, thus corroborating the centrality of race and culture in the perception of "others." See Fiore's "Post-'Colonia.'"

19. See http://www.culturalshock.org.

20. For another essay on the G2's denunciatory and creative power, see Andall, "The G2 Network."

21. *A Lonely Hero*'s protagonist is a struggling underpaid and exploited worker in Italy who, despite his acrobatic adaptability, finally decides to emigrate to Albania and work there as a miner. Albania is the very place where the immigrants came from in Amelio's 1994 film *Lamerica* (see Chapter 2). In a telling scene toward the end of the film, the protagonist (played by Antonio Albanese) is asked by his co-workers to translate a series of Albanian words into Italian. In a masterly exercise in self-quotation, Amelio revisits the scene from *Lamerica* in which a young Albanian girl teaches other Albanians the translation into Italian of some basic words right before they board a ship heading to Italy.

WORKS CITED

Abate, Carmine. "Prima la vita." *Vivere per addizioni e altri viaggi*. Milan: Mondadori, 2010. 129–37. Print.
Adascalitei, Mariana. "Il giorno di San Nicola." 2005. TS.
Agnew, John A. *Rome*. New York: J. Wiley, 1995. Print.
Agostini, Chiara, Ernesto Longobardi, and Giuseppe Vitaletti. "Donne migranti. Quali opportunità nel nostro paese?" *L'economia dell'immigrazione* (February 2012). Web. August 1, 2016. http://tinyurl.com/leonemoressa.
Amato, Fabio, ed. *Atlante dell'immigrazione in Italia*. Rome: Società Geografica Italiana, 2008. Print.
Amelio, Gianni, dir. *Lamerica*. Mario & Vittorio Cecchi Gori, 1994. Film.
———. *A Lonely Hero*. [L'intrepido] 2013. Film.
Andall, Jaqueline. *Gender, Migration and Domestic Service: The Politics of Black Women in Italy*. Burlington, VT: Ashgate, 2000.
———. "The G2 Network and Other Second-Generation Voices: Claiming Rights and Transforming Identities." *National Belongings: Hybridity in Italian Colonial and Postcolonial Cultures*. Ed. Jacqueline Andall and Derek Duncan. Oxford: Peter Lang, 2010. 171–93. Print.
Andall, Jaqueline, and Derek Duncan. "Memories and Legacies of Italian Colonialism." *Italian Colonialism: Legacy and Memory*. Ed. Jaqueline Andall and Derek Duncan. New York: Peter Lang, 2005. 9–27. Print.
Andrijasevic, Rutvica. "From Exception to Excess: Detention and Deportations across the Mediterranean Space." *The Deportation Regime: Sovereignty, Space, and the Freedom of Movement*. Ed. Nicholas de Genova and Nathalie Peutz. Durham, NC: Duke University Press, 2010. 147–65. Print.
Angelone, Anita, and Clarissa Clò, eds. *Other Visions: Contemporary Italian Documentary Cinema as Counter-discourse*. Special Issue of *Studies in Documentary Film* 5.2/5.3 (2011). Print.
Antonucci, Clara. "Fare memoria delle storie perdute." *Leggendaria* 80 (March 2010, Speciale Memoir): 5–7. Print.
———. "Fermo immagine." ibid.: 2–4. Print.
Ardizzone, Tony. *In the Garden of Papa Santuzzu*. New York: Picador, 1999. Print.
Arendt, Hannah. *The Origins of Totalitarianism*. New York: Houghton Mifflin Harcourt, 1973. Print.
Atkinson, Rowland, and Gary Bridge. *Gentrification in a Global Context: The New Urban Colonialism*. New York: Routledge, 2005. Print.
Audenino Patrizia, and Maddalena Tirabassi. *Migrazioni italiane: Storia e storie dall'Ancien régime a oggi*. Milan: Mondadori, 2008. Print.
Augé, Marc. *Non-Places: Introduction to an Anthropology of Supermodernity*. 1995. New York: Verso, 2008. Print.
Bachelard, Gaston. *The Poetics of Space*. 1958. Boston: Beacon Press, 1994. Print.
Baily, Samuel L. *Immigrants in the Lands of Promise: Italians in Buenos Aires and New York City, 1870 to 1914*. Ithaca, NY: Cornell University Press, 1999. Print.
Baranski, Zygmunt G. "Introducing Modern Italian Culture." Baranski 1–15.

Baranski, Zygmunt G., and Rebecca J. West, eds. *The Cambridge Companion to Modern Italian Culture*. New York: Cambridge University Press, 2011. Print.

Barbič, Ana, and Inga Miklavcic-Brezigar. "Domestic Work Abroad: A Necessity and an Opportunity for Rural Women from the Goriska Borderland Region of Slovenia." Henshall Momsen 164–77.

Barole Abdu, Hamid. *Seppellite la mia pelle in Africa/Bury My Skin in Africa*. Modena: Artestampa, 2006. Print.

———. "Il volo di Mohammed." *Poesie scelte*. Lucca: Libertà Edizioni, 2010. 25–26. Print.

Bekerie, Ayele. "African Americans and the Italo-Ethiopian War." *Revisioning Italy: National Identity and Global Culture*. Ed. Beverly Allen and Mary Russo. Minneapolis: University of Minnesota Press, 1997. 116–33. Print.

Bellu, Giovanni Maria. *I fantasmi di Porto Palo*. 2004. Milan: Mondadori, 2006. Print.

Benelli, Elena. 'The 'Other' from Another Shore: Identity at Sea in *Quando sei nato non puoi più nasconderti*." Bullaro 219–39.

Ben-Ghiat, Ruth. "Modernity is Just Over There: Colonialism and the Dilemmas of Italian National Identity." *Interventions: International Journal of Postcolonial Studies* 8:3 (2006): 380–93.

Ben-Ghiat, Ruth, ed. "Italy and Its Colonies." *A Historical Companion to Postcolonial Literatures: Continental Europe and Its Empires*. Ed. Lars Jensen, Prem Poddar, and Rajeev Patke. Edinburgh: Edinburgh University Press, 2008. 262–312. Print.

Ben-Ghiat, Ruth, and Stephanie Malia Hom, eds. *Italian Mobilities (Changing Mobilities)*. New York: Routledge, 2015. Print.

Bensmaïa, Réda. "Is an 'Experimental' Nation Possible?" *Experimental Nations*. Princeton, NJ: Princeton University Press, 2003. 1–9. Print.

Bernardi, Katia, dir. *Sidelki*. KR Movie/Culture Department of Trento, 2007. Film.

Bernardini, Paola. "Intervista a Emanuele Crialese." *Corriere canadese* (Toronto), October 8, 2006. Web. August 1, 2016. www.bibliosofia.net/files/Bernardini__Intervista_a_Crialese.htm.

Bertelli, Gualtiero. *Quando emigranti. . . .* Nota, 2003. CD.

———. *Quando Emigranti . . . 2. Povera gente*. Nota, 2004. CD.

Bertelli, Gualtiero, and Gian Antonio Stella, dirs. *L'orda. Storie, canti e immagini di emigranti*. 2002. DVD.

Bertellini, Giorgio. *Italy in Early American Cinema: Race, Landscape, and the Picturesque*. Bloomington: Indiana University Press, 2010. Print.

Bevilacqua, Piero, Andreina De Clementi, and Emilio Franzina, eds. *Storia dell'emigrazione italiana: Arrivi*. Rome: Donzelli, 2002. Print.

———. *Storia dell'emigrazione italiana: Partenze*. Rome: Donzelli, 2001. Print.

Bhabha, Homi. *The Location of Culture*. New York: Routledge, 1994. Print.

Bianchi, Bruna. "Lavoro ed emigrazione femminile." Bevilacqua, *Storia dell'emigrazione italiana: Partenze* 257–74.

Binetti, Vincenzo. "La città nomadica: Esodo intrasocietario e deterrotorializzazione urbana in *Pantanella. Canto lungo la strada* di Mohsen Melliti." *Città nomadi: Esodo e autonomia nella metropoli contemporanea*. Verona: Ombre corte, 2008. 91–100. Print.

Blengino, Vanni. "Nella letteratura argentina." Bevilacqua, *Storia dell'emigrazione italiana: Arrivi* 641–60.

Boelhower, William. "Immigrant Autobiographies in Italian Literature: The Birth of a New Text-type." *Forum Italicum* 35.1 (Spring 2001): 110–28. Print.

Bondi, Federico, dir. *Mar nero*. 2008. Film.

Bonifazi, Corrado. *L'immigrazione straniera in Italia*. Bologna: Il Mulino, 1998. Print.

Bonizzoni, Paola. "Undocumented Domestic Workers in Italy: Surviving and Regularizing Strategies." *Irregular Migrant Domestic Workers in Europe; Who Cares?* Ed. Anna Triandafillydou. Farnham, UK: Ashgate, 2013. 135–60. Print.

Bonsaver, Guido. "Golden Door." *Sight and Sound* 17.7 (July 2007): 54. Print.
Borroni, Chiara. "C'era una volta la terra promessa." *Cineforum* 458.8 (2006). 43–46. Print.
Boz, Nadia. "L'emigrazione femminile in Egitto da un comune del Friuli occidentale, Fontanafredda, nel Novecento: Un caso di studio." Però 249–64.
Brazzoduro, Marco. "Politiche pubbliche in favore degli stranieri immigrati." *Roma e gli immigrati: La formazione di una popolazione multiculturale.* Ed. Eugenio Sonnino. Milan: Franco Angeli, 2006. 278–320. Print.
Briscese, Angela, and Joseph Sciorra, eds. *Graces Received: Painted and Metal Ex-votos from Italy.* New York: John D. Calandra Italian-American Institute, 2012. Print.
Brito, Cristiana De Caldas. "Ana de Jesus." *Mediterranean Crossroads: Migration Literature in Italy.* Ed. Graziella Parati. Madison, NJ: Fairleigh Dickinson University Press, 1999. 162–64. Trans. of "Ana de Jesus." *Le voci dell'arcobaleno.* Ed. Roberta Sangiorgi. Santarcangelo di Romagna: Fara Editore, 1995. 59–61. Print.
Brunetta, Gian Piero. *Cent'anni di cinema italiano 2: Dal 1945 ai giorni nostri.* 1991. Bari: Laterza, 2004. Print.
———. "Emigranti nel cinema italiano e americano." Bevilacqua *Storia dell'emigrazione italiana*: *Partenze.* 489–514.
Bucci, Mary Bush. "Drowning." In *Growing up Ethnic in America.* Ed. Maria Mazziotti and Jennifer Gillan. New York: Penguin Books, 1999. 136–48. Print.
———. *Sweet Hope.* Toronto: Guernica, 2011. Print.
Bullaro, Grace Russo. *From Terrone to Extra-comunitario: New Manifestations of Racism in Contemporary Italian Cinema.* Leicester, UK: Troubadour, 2010. Print.
Burns, Jennifer. "Exile Within Italy: Interactions between Past and Present 'Homes' in Texts in Italian by Migrant Writers." *Annali d'Italianistica* 20 (2002): 369–84. Print.
Burns, Jennifer, and Loredana Polezzi, eds. *Borderlines: Migrazioni e identità nel Novecento.* Isernia, Italy: Cosmo Iannone Editore, 2003.
Calvino, Italo. "All at One Point." *Cosmicomics.* 1965. Trans. William Weaver. New York: Harcourt, 1976. 43–47. Print.
Camilleri, Andrea. *Rounding the Mark.* New York: Penguin Books, 2003. Trans. *Il giro di boa.* Palermo: Sellerio, 2003. Print.
Caniffe, Eamonn. *The Politics of the Piazza: The History and Meaning of the Italian Square.* Burlington, VT: Ashgate, 2008. Print.
Cannistraro, Philip. "The Italians of New York: An Historical Overview." *The Italians of New York: Five Centuries of Struggle and Achievement.* New York: The New-York Historical Society and the John D. Calandra Italian American Institute, 1999. 3–20. Print.
Carnevale, Nancy, C. *A New Language, a New World. Italian Immigrants in the United States, 1890–1945.* Champaign: University of Illinois Press, 2009. Print.
Carravetta, Peter. "Migration, History, and Existence." *Migrants and Refugees.* Ed. Vangelis Kyriakopoulos. Athens: Komotini, 2004. 19–50. Print.
Casacchia, Oliviero, and Massimiliano Cresci. "Roma e il suo hinterland: Dinamiche recenti della presenza straniera." Sonnino 19–66. Print.
Cassano, Franco. *Paeninsula: L'Italia da ritrovare.* Bari: La Terza, 1998. Print.
Castronovo, Valerio, ed. *Album italiano: Vivere insieme. Verso una società multietnica.* Rome: Laterza, 2006. Print.
Catalano, Bruna Gaeta. *E. A. Mario: Leggenda e storia.* Naples: Liguori, 1989. Print.
Cavanna, François. *Calce e martello.* Trans. Mariagiovanna Anzil. Milan: Bompiani, 1980. Trans. of *Les Ritals.* Paris: Belfond, 1978. Print.
Cerchiai, Claudia. "Rione XV. Esquilino." *La grande guida dei rioni di Roma. Storia, segreti, monumenti, tradizioni, leggende, curiosità.* By Giorgio Carpaneto et al. Rome: Newton and Compton, 2004. 968–1014. Print.

Chandler, Charlotte, and Federico Fellini. *I, Fellini*. New York: Cooper Square Press, 2001. Print.
Chaplin, Charlie, dir. *The Immigrant*. Mutual Film Corporation, 1917. Film.
Choate, Mark. *Emigrant Nation: The Making of Italy Abroad*. Cambridge, MA: Harvard University Press, 2008. Print.
Cicognetti, Luisa and Lorenza Servetti. *Migranti in celluloide: Storici, cinema ed emigrazione*. Foligno: Editoriale Umbra, 2003. Print.
Ciuli, Diana. "Un giorno d'aprile a Pescara." *Alì e altre storie: Letteratura e immigrazione*. Ed. Genovese, Raffaele, Paolo Giovannelli, Felice Liperi, Angiolino Lonardi, and Maria Chiara Martinetti. Rome: RAI-ERI, 1998. 37–44. Print.
Clò, Clarissa. "Hip Pop Italian Style: The Postcolonial Imagination of Second-Generation Authors in Italy." Lombardi-Diop, *Postcolonial Italy* 275–91.
———. "Orchestrating Reality through a Cinema of Relation: Interview with Agostino Ferrente." Angelone 211–21.
Comberiati, Daniele. *La quarta sponda: Scrittrici in viaggio dall'Africa coloniale all'Italia di oggi*. Rome: Caravan Edizioni, 2011. Print.
Connell, William, and Fred Gardaphé, eds. *Anti-Italianism: Essays on a Prejudice*. New York: Palgrave, 2010. Print.
Consolo, Vincenzo. "The Bridge over the Channel of Sicily." *Reading and Writing the Mediterranean: Essays by Vincenzo Consolo*. Ed. Norma Bouchard and Massimo Lollini. Toronto: University of Toronto Press, 2006. 241–45. Print.
Corti, Paola. *Emigranti e immigrati nelle rappresentazioni di fotografi e fotogiornalisti*. Foligno: Editoriale Umbra, 2010. Print.
———. "L'emigrazione temporanea in Europa, in Africa e nel Levante." Bevilacqua, *Storie dell'emigrazione italiana: Partenze* 213–236.
———. *Storia delle migrazioni internazionali*. Bari: Laterza, 2007. Print.
Crialese, Emanuele, dir. *Golden Door* [*Nuovomondo*]. Fabrizio Mosca Alexandre Mallet-Guy, 2006. Film.
———. *Once We Were Strangers*. Backpain Productions, 1997. Film.
———. *Terraferma*. Cattelaya, 2011. Film.
Cucchiarato, Claudia. *Vivo altrove. Giovani e senza radici: gli emigranti italiani di oggi*. Milan: Mondadori, 2010. Print.
Curcio, Renato. *Shish Mahal*. Postface by Clara Gallini. Rome: Sensibili alle foglie, 1991. Print.
Curti, Lidia. "Female literature of migration in Italy." *Feminist Review* 87 (2007): 60–75. Print.
Dadà, Adriana, ed. *Il lavoro di balia: Memoria e storia dell'emigrazione femminile da Ponte Buggianese nel '900*. Ospedaletto (Pisa): Pacini, 1999. Print.
Dal Lago, Alessandro. *Non-persone: L'esclusione dei migranti in una società globale*. Milan: Feltrinelli, 1999. Print.
D'Angelo, Pascal. *Son of Italy*. 1924. Toronto: Guernica Press, 2003. Print.
D'Apollonia, Ariane Chebel. "Immigration, Security, and Integration in the European Union." *Immigration, Integration, and Security: America and Europe in Comparative Perspective*. Ed. Ariane Chebel D'Apollonia and Simon Reich. Pittsburgh: University of Pittsburgh Press, 2008. 203–28. Print.
De Amicis, Edmondo. "From the Apennines to the Andes." *Heart*. Charleston, SC: CreateSpace, 2009. 145–65. Print.
———. *On Blue Water*. 1890. Amsterdam: Fredonia Books, 2003. Print. Trans. of *Sull'oceano*. 1889. Milan: Garzanti, 1996. Print.
de Certeau, Michel. *The Capture of Speech and Other Political Writings*. Minneapolis: University of Minnesota Press, 1997. Print.
———. "Idéologie et diversité culturelle." *Act du Colloque: État National, Diversité Culturelle, Société industrielle*. Paris: Editions L'Harmattan, 1984. 231–40. Print.

———. *The Practice of Everyday Life*. Berkeley: University of California Press, 1984. Print.
Degiuli, Francesca. "A Job with No Boundaries: Home Eldercare Work in Italy." *European Journal of Women Studies* 14 (2007): 193–207. Print.
———. "Laboring Lives: The Making of Home Eldercare Assistants in Italy." *Modern Italy* 16.3 (Aug. 2011): 345–61. Print.
De Gregori, Francesco, and Giovanna Marini. *Il fischio del vapore*. Sony, 2002. CD.
De La Torre, Lidia. *Buenos Aires: Del conventillo a la Villa Miseria (1869–1989)*. Buenos Aires: EDUCA, 2008. Print.
De Lazzaris, Greta. "Qualche storia senza immagini." *Prove d'orchestra*. Rome: Lucky Red, 2006. 18–27. Print.
De Luca, Erri. *Solo andata: Righe che vanno troppo spesso a capo*. Milan: Feltrinelli, 2005. Print.
Del Boca, Angelo. *Gli italiani in Africa orientale* (four volumes). Milan: Mondadori, 1992. Print.
———. *Gli italiani in Libia* (two volumes). Milan: Mondadori, 1993–94. Print.
———. *Italiani, brava gente?* Vicenza: Neri Pozza, 2005. Print.
———. *La guerra di Etiopia. L'ultima impresa del colonialismo*. Milan: Longanesi, 2010. Print.
Del Giudice, Luisa. "Mountains of Cheese and Rivers of Wine: Paesi di Cuccagna and Other Gastronomic Utopias." *Imagined States: Nationalism, Utopia, and Longing in Oral Cultures*. Ed. Luisa Del Giudice and Gerald Porter. Logan: Utah State University Press, 2001. 11–63. Print.
Del Grande, Gabriele. *Mamadou va a morire: La strage dei clandestini nel Mediterraneo*. Rev. ed. Castel Gandolfo, Italy: Infinito Edizioni, 2009. Print.
Del Pozzo, Diego. "L'universo di 'Gomorra' visto dagli immigrati." *Il Mattino*. December 30, 2010. 23. Print.
Del Pra', Alvise, and Maddalena Tirabassi. "L'America Latina: Motivazioni per il riacquisto della cittadinanza." *Rapporto Italiani nel mondo*. Fondazione Migrantes. Rome: Idos, 2007. 357–69. Print.
Dell'Oro, Erminia. *Asmara addio*. Milan: Baldini Castoldi Dalai Editore, 1997.
de Marco, Camillo. "The American Dream à la Fellini: Interview with Emanuele Crialese." *Cineuropa: The Site for European Cinema*. 14 March 2007. Web. August 1, 2016. http://tinyurl.com/cineuropa1.
Derobertis, Roberto. *Fuori centro. Percorsi postcoloniali nella letteratura italiana*. Rome: Aracne, 2010. Print.
Derrida, Jacques, and Anne Dufourmantelle. *Of Hospitality: Anne Dufourmantelle Invites Jacques Derrida to Respond*. 1997. Stanford, CA: Stanford University Press, 2000. Print.
Devoto, Fernando. "In Argentina." Bevilacqua, *Storia dell'emigrazione italiana: Arrivi* 25–54.
Diaconescu-Blumenfeld, R. "*Lamerica*: History in Diaspora." *Romance Languages Annual* 13:11: 167–73. Print.
Dickie, John. "Imagined Italies." *Italian Cultural Studies: An Introduction*. Ed. David Forgacs and Robert Lumley. Oxford: Oxford University Press, 1996. 19–33.
———. "The Notion of Italy." Baranski 17–33.
Di Comite, Luigi, and Anna Paterno, eds. *Quelli di fuori: Dall'emigrazione all'immigrazione: il caso italiano*. Milan: Franco Angeli, 2002. Print.
di Donato, Pietro. *Christ in Concrete*. 1939. New York: Signet Classics, 2004. Print.
Dinu, Rudolf. "Appunti per una storia dell'emigrazione italiana in Romania nel periodo 1878–1914." Popescu 246–51.
DiStasi, Lawrence, ed. *Una Storia Segreta: The Secret History of Italian American Evacuation and Internment during World War II*. Berkeley, CA: Heyday Books, 2001. Print.
Dolkart, Andrew S. *Biography of a Tenement House in New York City: An Architectural History of 97 Orchard Street*. Santa Fe, NM: The Center for American Places, 2006. Print.
Dossier Statistico Immigrazione 2011 Caritas-Migrantes: Oltre la crisi, insieme. "Scheda di sintesi." Rome: Edizioni Idos, 2011. Web. August 1, 2016. http://tinyurl.com/dossier2011.

Dossier Statistico Immigrazione 2012 Caritas-Migrantes: *Non sono numeri.* "Scheda di sintesi." Rome: Edizioni Idos, 2012. Web. August 1, 2016. http://tinyurl.com/dossier2012.

Dossier Statistico Immigrazione 2013 Caritas-Migrantes: Dalle discriminazioni ai diritti. "Scheda di sintesi." Rome: Edizioni Idos, 2013. Web. August 1, 2016. http://tinyurl.com/Dossier13.

Dossier Statistico Immigrazione 2014 UNAR—Scheda di sintesi. Rome: Edizioni Idos, 2014. Web. August 1, 2016. http://tinyurl.com/2015dossier.

Durante, Francesco. "L'emigrazione e le esperienze della canzone napoletana in USA." *Euros: Rassegna di vita europea* 1 (January/February 1994): 117–21. Print.

The Egyptian Community in Italy—Annual Report on the Presence of Immigrants 2013. Ministero del Lavoro e delle Politiche Sociali. November 28, 2014. Web. August 1, 2016. http://tinyurl.com/EgyptiansinItaly.

Ehrenreich, Barbara, and Arlie Russell Hochschild. *Global Woman: Nannies, Maids, and Sex Workers in the New Economy.* New York: Henry Holt, 2002.

Einaudi, Luca. *Le politiche dell'immigrazione in Italia dall'unità a oggi.* Rome: Laterza, 2007. Print.

Einaudi, Luigi. "L'emigrazione temporanea italiana." *Nuova antologia di lettere, scienze ed arti* 4.88 (1900): 528–39. Print.

Elkadi, Hiasham, and Katherine M. Forsyth. *Piazza Vittorio: La trasformazione urbanistica. Quale identità per i nuovi cittadini?/Identity and Meaningful Place Making.* Rome: Edup, 2009. Print.

Erbani, Francesco. "La vita culturale." *Storia di Roma dall'antichità a oggi. Roma del Duemila.* Ed. Luigi De Rosa. Bari: Laterza, 1999. 251–303. Print.

Fallaci, Oriana. *La rabbia e l'orgoglio.* Milan: Rizzoli, 2001. Print.

Faris, Stephan. "*Arrivederci, Italia*: Why Young Italians Are Leaving." *Time.com*, Time Magazine. October 18, 2010. Web. August 1, 2016.

Favero, Luigi, and Graziano Tassello. "Cent'anni di emigrazione italiana." Rosoli 9–64. Print.

Fellini, Federico, dir. *And the Ship Sails On.* Cristaldi, 1983. Film.

———. *Prova d'orchestra*. Composer Nino Rota. RAI, 1978. Film.

Ferraro, Evelyn. "Moving Thresholds: Liminal Writing in the Italian Diaspora." PhD dissertation, Brown University, 2010.

Ferraro, Thomas J. *Feeling Italian: The Art of Ethnicity in America.* New York: NYU Press, 2005. Print.

Ferrarotti, Franco. "Tendenze evolutive." *Storia di Roma dall'antichità a oggi. Roma del Duemila.* Ed. Luigi De Rosa. Bari: Laterza, 1999. 225–50. Print.

Ferrente, Agostino, dir. *L'orchestra di Piazza Vittorio.* Lucky Red, 2006. Film.

Fiore, Teresa. "Andata e ritorni. Storie di emigrazione nella letteratura siciliana tra Ottocento e Novecento (Capuana, Messina, Pirandello, Sciascia e Camilleri)." *Neos* (Journal of Sicilian Emigration History) II.1 (Dec. 2008). 265–75. Print.

———. "'Architextualizing' the Italian Immigration Experience in the U.S.: Bricklayers and Writers in John Fante's Works." Parati, *The Cultures* 109–26.

———. "Builders, Mermaids and the Bauhaus: New Visions of the Migrant Return in Andrea Camilleri's *Maruzza Musumeci*." *Studi Italiani* XXVII.2 (2015 *Special issue: Scrittori tra due mondi/Writers Between Two Worlds*, ed. Simone Magherini). 183–96. Print

———. "From Exclusion to Expression in Segre's Participatory Documentaries: Visualizing Undocumented Detention Centers along Italy-Bound Migrant Routes." *Journal of Italian Cinema and Media Studies*, special issue, *Documentary Film and Migration in Twentieth-Century Italy*. Guest editor Gaoheng Zhang (forthcoming 2017).

———. "Immigration from Italy since the 1990s." *The Routledge History of Italian Americans.* Ed. Stanislao Pugliese and William J. Connell. New York: Routledge, 2017 (forthcoming). Print.

———. "La Sicilia come metafora dell'emigrazione negli scritti di Leonardo Sciascia." *Il Giannone* VI.13–14 (Italian literary journal—Special issue "Leonardo Sciascia vent'anni dopo," ed. Antonio Motta) (January–December 2009): 49–68. Print.

———. "Lunghi viaggi verso 'Lamerica' a casa: Straniamento e identità nelle storie di migrazione italiana." *Annali d'Italianistica* 24 (2006): 87–106. Print.

———. "Migration Italian Style: Charting the Contemporary U.S.-Bound Exodus (1990–2012)." *New Italian Migrations to the United States, Vol. 2: Art and Culture Since 1945.* Ed. Laura Ruberto and Joseph Sciorra. Champaign: University of Illinois Press, 2017 (forthcoming). Print.

———. "Post-'Colonia:' Emigration, Colonialism, and Immigration in Contemporary Italy." Lombardi-Diop, *Postcolonial Italy* 71–82.

———. "The Ship as a Pre-occupied Space: A Theoretical and Applied Approach to Migrant Culture between Italy and the United States" in *Comparative Sites of Ethnicity: Europe and the Americas.* Ed. Carmen Birlkle, William Boelhower, and Rocio Davis. Heidelberg: Winter Verlag, 2004. 29–44. Print.

Focacci, Federico. "Italia e Romania. Migrazioni a confronto II." October 29, 2009. Web. August 1, 2016. http://tinyurl.com/ItaliaeRomania.

Fondazione Leone Moressa. "Quali badanti per quali famiglie?" *L'economia dell'immigrazione* 0.2 (Special topic: *Migrazione al femminile*). February 2012. Web. August 1, 2016. http://tinyurl.com/leonemoressa2.

Fornara, Bruno. "Mostra attraente." *Cineforum* 458.8 (2006): 3–7. Print.

Foucault, Michel. "Of Other Spaces." *Diacritics* 16.1 (Spring 1986): 22–27. Print.

Franzina, Emilio. "Le canzoni dell'emigrazione." Bevilacqua, *Storia dell'emigrazione italiana*: *Partenze* 537–62.

———. *Gli Italiani al Nuovo Mondo: L'emigrazione italiana in America 1492–1942.* Milan: Mondadori, 1995. Print.

———. *Merica! Merica!: Emigrazione e colonizzazione nelle lettere dei contadini veneti e friulani in America Latina (1876–1902).* 1979. Rev. ed. Venice: Cierre, 1994. Print.

———. *Traversate: Le grandi migrazioni transatlantiche e i racconti italiani del viaggio per mare.* Foligno (Perugia, Italy): Editoriale Umbra, 2003. Print.

Frasca, Simona. "La canzone napoletana negli anni dell'*emigrazione* di *massa*." *Altreitalie* 29 (2004): 34–51. Print.

Fuller, Mia. *Moderns Abroad: Italian Colonial Architecture and Urbanism.* New York: Routledge, 2006. Print.

Gabaccia, Donna R. *Italy's Many Diasporas.* Seattle: University of Washington Press, 2000. Print.

———. "Tenement Residential Patterns." *From Sicily to Elizabeth Street: Housing and Social Change Among Italian Immigrants 1880–1930.* Albany, NY: State University of New York Press, 1984. 65–85. Print.

Galossi, Emanuele. "I lavoratori stranieri nel settore delle costruzioni." VII Rapporto Fondazione Giuseppe Di Vittorio—FILLEA (2012). Web. August 1, 2016. http://tinyurl.com/fillea.

Gandolfi, Anna, and Pietro Tosca. "Calderoli insulta il ministro Kyenge: 'Non posso non pensare a un orango.'" *Corriere della sera.* corriere.it. July 14, 2013.

Gassman, Alessandro, dir. *Sola andata.* 2014. Web. August 1, 2016. http://tinyurl.com/soloandata.

Gatti, Fabrizio. *Bilal. Viaggiare, lavorare, morire da clandestini.* Milan: Rizzoli, 2008. Print.

Gerbitz, Sarah. "Quando la sera, ad Alexandria." Interview with Franco Però. *Fucinemute.* 11 July 2005. Web. August 1, 2016. http://tinyurl.com/seralexandria.

Germi, Pietro, dir. *Cammino della speranza.* 1950. Film.

Ghermandi, Gabriella. "The Story of Woizero Bekelech and Signor Antonio." *Queen of Flowers and Pearls.* Bloomington: Indiana University Press, 2015. 216–49. Print. Trans. of *Regina di fiori e di perle.* Rome: Donzelli, 2007. Print.

Gilroy, Paul. *The Black Atlantic: Modernity and Double* Consciousness. London: Verso, 1993. Print.

Giordana, Marco Tullio, dir. *Quando sei nato non puoi più nasconderti.* Cattaleya and RAI Cinema, 2005. Film.

Giunta, Edvige. "Figuring Race." Guglielmo and Salerno 224–33. Print.

Giunta, Edvige, and Kathleen Zamboni McCormick, eds. *Teaching Italian American Literature, Film, and Popular Culture*. New York: Modern Language Association of America, 2010. Print.

Giustiniani, Corrado. "Vivere insieme. La storia, le storie." Castronovo 19–43. Print.

Golini, Antonio. "La popolazione." *Storia di Roma dall'antichità a oggi. Roma del Duemila*. Ed. Luigi De Rosa. Bari: Laterza, 1999. 119–57. Print.

Golini, Antonio, and Flavia Amato. "Uno sguardo a un secolo e mezzo di emigrazione italiana." Bevilacqua, *Storie dell'emigrazione italiana: Partenze* 45–60.

Guccini, Francesco, and Loriano Macchiavelli. *Macaronì: Romanzo di santi e delinquenti*. Milan: Mondadori, 1997.

Gugelberger, Georg M. "Introduction. Institutionalization of Transgression: Testimonial Discourse and Beyond." *The Real Thing: Testimonial Discourse and Latina America*. Ed. Georg Gugelberger. Durham, NC: Duke University Press, 1996. 1–22. Print.

Guglielmo, Jennifer. "Introduction: White Lies, Dark Truths." Guglielmo and Salerno 1–14. Print.

Guglielmo, Jennifer, and Salvatore Salerno, ed. *Are Italians White? How Race is Made in America*. New York: Routledge, 2003. Print.

Guglielmo, Thomas. "No Color Barrier: Italians, Race, and Power in the United States." Guglielmo and Salerno 30–43. Print.

Haenni, Sabine. *The Immigrant Scene: Ethnic Amusements in New York 1880–1920*. Minneapolis: University of Minnesota Press, 2008. Print.

Hardt, Michael. "Introduction: Laboratory Italy." *Radical Thought in Italy: A Potential Politics*. Ed. Paolo Virno and Michael Hardt. Minneapolis: University of Minnesota Press, 1996. 1–9. Print.

Henshall Momsen, Janet. *Gender, Migration, and Domestic Service*. New York: Routledge, 1999.

Highmore, Ben. *Michel de Certeau: Analyzing Culture*. London: Continuum, 2006. Print.

Immigration and Refugee Board of Canada. *Eritrea: Military service, including age of recruitment, length of service, grounds for exemption, penalties for desertion from and evasion of military service and availability of alternative service (2005–2006), Refworld*, UNHCR The UN Refugee Agency. February 28, 2007. Web. August 1, 2016. http://tinyurl.com/unhcreritrea.

"Indagine sull'assistenza familiare in Italia: il contributo degli immigrati." Centro Studi e Ricerche Idos, 2013. Web. August 1, 2016. http://tinyurl.com/idos2013.

"Italy: 'Historic' European Court Judgment Upholds Migrants' Rights." *Amnesty International*. 23 February 2012. Web. August 1, 2016. http://tinyurl.com/EUCourt.

Jijon, Maria Rosa, dir. *Forte e Chiaro*. Suttvuess, 2006. Film.

Kazan, Elia, dir. *America America*. Warner Bros, 1963. Film.

Keating, Abigail. "All Roads Lead to Piazza Vittorio: Transnational Spaces in Agostino Ferrente's Documusical." Angelone 197–209.

Kenney, William Howland. "The Phonograph and the Evolution of 'Foreign' and 'Ethnic' Records." *Recorded Music in American Life: The Phonograph and Popular Memory, 1890–1945*. New York: Oxford University Press, 1999. 65–87. Print.

Komla-Ebri, Kossi. *Imbarazzismi: Quotidiani imbarazzi in bianco e nero*. Milan: Edizioni dell'Arco, 2002. Print.

Kubati, Ron. *Il buio del mare*. Milan: Giunti, 2007. Print.

Kuruvilla, Gabriella. *Questa non è una baby-sitter*. Milan: Terre di mezzo, 2010. Print.

Kuruvilla, Gabriella, Ingy Mubiayi, Igiaba Scego, and Laila Wadia. *Pecore nere. Racconti*. Ed. Flavia Capitani and Emanuele Coen. Rome: Laterza, 2005. Print.

Kuwornu, Fred, dir. *18 ius soli*. 2011. Film.

Labanca, Nicola. "History and Memory of Italian Colonialism Today." Ed. Jaqueline Andall and Derek Duncan. *Italian Colonialism: Legacy and Memory*. New York: Peter Lang, 2005. 29–46. Print.

———. "Nelle colonie." Bevilacqua, *Storie dell'emigrazione italiana: Arrivi* 193–204.
———. *Oltremare: Storia dell'espansione coloniale italiana.* Bologna: Il Mulino, 2007. Print.
La collettività indiana in Italia 2014—Scheda di sintesi. Centro Studi e Ricerche IDOS and Prime Time Promotions. Web. Aug. 1, 2016 http://tinyurl.com/dossierindia.
Lagumina, Salvatore J. *WOP!: A Documentary History of Anti-Italian Discrimination.* 1973. Toronto: Guernica Editions, 1999. Print.
Lakhous, Amara. *Clash of Civilizations Over an Elevator in Piazza Vittorio.* New York: Europa Editions, 2008. Print. Trans. of *Scontro di civiltà per un ascensore a Piazza Vittorio.* Rome: Edizioni e/o, 2006. Print.
———. *Dispute Over a Very Italian Piglet.* Trans. Ann Goldstein. New York: Europea Editions, 2014. Kindle file. Trans. of *Contesa per un maialino italianissimo a San Salvario.* Rome: Edizioni e/o, 2013.
———. *Divorce Islamic Style.* Trans. Ann Goldstein. New York: Europea Editions, 2012. Print. Trans. of *Divorzio all'islamica a viale Marconi.* Rome: Edizioni e/o, 2010. Print.
"La popolazione straniera residente in Italia—Bilancio demografico. Anno 2013." Statistics report ISTAT. July 26, 2013. Web. August 1, 2016. http://www.istat.it/it/archivio/96694.
La Ruina, Saverio, dir. *Italianesi.* Teatro India, Rome, 2011. Performance.
Ledgeway, Adam, and Anna Laura Lepschy, eds. *In and out of Italy: Lingua e cultura della migrazione italiana.* Perugia: Guerra Edizioni, 2010. Print.
Lefebvre, Henri. *The Urban Revolution.* 1970. Minneapolis: University of Minnesota Press, 2003. Print.
Lems, Annika, and Christine Moderbacher, dirs. *Harraga.* Austria, 2009. Film.
Liberti, Stefano. *A sud di Lampedusa: Cinque anni di viaggi sulle rotte dei migranti.* Rome: Minimum Fax, 2008. Print.
Liehm, Mira. *Passion and Defiance: Film in Italy from 1942 to the Present.* Berkeley: University of California Press, 1984. Print.
Lombardi-Diop, Cristina. "Ghost of Memories, Spirits of Ancestors: Slavery, the Mediterranean, and the Atlantic." Oboe and Scacchi. 162–80.
———. "Italophone Literature." Ben-Ghiat 293–96. Print.
———. "Postracial/Postcolonial Italy." Lombardi-Diop and Romeo, *Postcolonial* 175–90.
———. "Roma Residence." *Interventions* 11.3 (2009): 400–419. Print.
Lombardi-Diop, Cristina, and Caterina Romeo, eds. *Postcolonial Italy: The Colonial Past in Contemporary Italy.* New York: Palgrave, 2012. Print.
———. "The Italian Postcolonial: A Manifesto." *Italian Studies* 69.3 (November 2014): 425–33.
Lonni, Ada. "Protagoniste della propria storia. I movimenti migratori femminili nell'esperienza italiana." *Mélanges de l'Ecole française de Rome. Italie et Méditerranée* 112.1 (2000): 441–468.
Lonni, Ada, and Mara Tognetti, ed. *Balie e colf straniere. Catalogue of the Historical Documentary Exhibit.* Milan: Teti, 1997. Print.
Lowe, Lisa, and David Lloyd, eds. *The Politics of Culture in the Shadow of Capital.* Durham, NC: Duke University Press, 1997. Print.
Luatti, Lorenzo. *L'immigrazione raccontata ai ragazzi: Vent'anni di proposte dell'editoria per l'infanzia—catalogo della mostra bibliografica.* Pistoia: Nuove esperienze, 2011. Print.
Lupo, Giuseppe. "Bambini uccisi dall'orco e che restano inascoltati." *Stilos* XI: 14 (10 July 2007). 4. Web. August 1, 2016. http://www.stilos.it/files/100707lasicilia.pdf.
Lutz, Helma. *The New Maid: Transnational Women and the Care Economy.* New York: Zed Books, 2011
Makaping, Geneviève. *Traiettorie di sguardi: E se gli altri foste voi?* Soveria Mannelli (Catanzaro): Rubettino, 2001. Print.
Marazzi, Martino. *Voices of Italian America: A History of Early Italian American Literature with a Critical Anthology.* 2001. Teaneck, NJ: Farleigh Dickinson University Press, 2004. Print.
Marino, Pino. "L'orchestra stabile di musicisti instabili." *Prove d'orchestra.* Rome: Lucky Red, 2006. 3–4. Print.

Marra, Vincenzo, dir. *Sailing Home [Tornando a casa]*. 2001. Film.
Martellini, Amoreno. "Il commercio dell'emigrazione: intermediari e agenti." Bevilacqua, *Storia dell'emigrazione italiana: Partenze* 293–308.
Martinelli, Marco, dir. *Noise in the Waters [Rumore di Acque]*. Teatro Rasi, Ravenna, Italy, 2010. Performance.
Martellone, Anna Maria. "Italian Mass Emigration to the United States, 1876–1930: A Historical Survey." *Perspectives in American History* I.1 (new series 1984): 379–423. Print.
Masri, Muin, Ingy Mubiayi, Zhu Qifeng, and Igiaba Scego. *Amori bicolori: Racconti*. Ed. Flavia Capitani and Emanuele Coen. Rome: Laterza, 2008. Print.
Matvejević, Predrag. *Mediterranean: A Cultural Landscape*. 1987. Berkeley: University of California Press, 1999. Print.
Mauro, Max. *La mia casa è dove sono felice (Storie di emigrati e immigrati)*. Udine: KappaVu, 2005. Print.
Mazzucco, Melania. "Intervista con Melania Mazzucco." Interview with Franco Baldasso. 2007. Unpublished.
———. "Loro." *Patrie impure*. Ed. Benedetta Centovalli. Milan: Rizzoli, 2003. 107–19. Print.
———. "Melania e il mondo di ieri." Interview with Silvana Mazzocchi. *La Repubblica*. July 4, 2003. Web. August 1, 2016. http://tinyurl.com/IntervistaMazzucco.
———. "Melania G. Mazzucco: *Vita*, una storia di emigrazione vista dall'Italia." Interview with Maddalena Tirabassi. *Altreitalie* 26.1 (January–June 2003): 112–15. Print.
———. "Seval." *Nuovi Argomenti* 39 (July-Sept. 1991): 75–81. Print.
———. *Vita: A Novel*. Trans. Virginia Jewiss. New York: Picador, 2006. Trans. of *Vita*. Milan: Rizzoli, 2003. Print.
Melliti, Mohsen, dir. *Io, l'altro*. Italy, 2006. Film.
———. *Pantanella: Canto lungo la strada*. Ed. Isabella Camera D'Afflitto. Rome: Edizioni Lavoro, 1992. Print.
Meneghelli, Donata. "Finzioni dell''io' nella letteratura italiana dell'immigrazione." *Narrativa* 28 *Altri stranieri* (2006): 39–51. Print.
Messina, Anna. *Cronache del Nilo*. Rome: Edizioni Italiane, 1940. Print.
Messina, Maria. *Behind Closed Doors: Her Father's House and Other Stories of Sicily*. New York: Feminist Press, 2007. Print.
———. *Piccoli gorghi*. 1911. Palermo: Sellerio, 1988. Print.
Meyer, Gerald. *Vito Marcantonio Radical Politician 1902–1954*. Albany: SUNY Press, 1989. Print.
Mezzadra, Sandro. *Diritto di fuga. Migrazioni, cittadinanza, globalizzazione*. Verona: Ombre corte, 2006. Print.
Mignonette, Gilda. *Napoli-New York solo andata*. Naples: Phonotype Record, 2007. CD.
Milza, Pierre. *Voyage en Ritalie*. Paris: Plon, 1003. Print.
Moe, Nelson. *The View from Vesuvius: Italian Culture and the Southern Question*. Berkeley: University of California Press, 2002. Print.
Molinari, Augusta. "Porti, trasporti, compagnie." Bevilacqua, *Storia dell'emigrazione italiana: Partenze* 237–55.
Moretti, Nanni, dir. *Dear Diary [Caro diario]*. Sacher, 1994. Film.
Moya, José, "Italians in Buenos Aires's Anarchist Movement: Gender Ideology and Women's Participation, 1890–1910." *Women, Gender and Transnational Lives: Italian Workers of the World*. Ed. Donna R. Gabaccia and Franca Iacovetta. Toronto: University of Toronto Press, 2002. 189–216. Print.
Mubiayi, Ingy, and Igiaba Scego, eds. *Quando nasci è una roulette*. Milan: Terre di mezzo. 2007. Print.
Mudu, Pierpaolo. "L'immigrazione straniera a Roma: tra divisioni del lavoro e produzione degli spazi sociali." *Roma e gli immigrati: La formazione di un popolazione multiculturale*. Ed. Eugenio Sonnino. Milan: Franco Angeli, 2006. 115–64. Print.

Musco, Giuliana. *Piccole Italie, grandi schermi. Scambi cinematografici tra Italia e Stati Uniti 1895–1945*. Rome: Bulzoni, 2004. Print.
Natale, Luisa. "Vicini l'un l'altro: Condividere lo spazio all'interno di Roma." Sonnino 165–94.
Nava, Sergio. "Dalla fuga alla circolazione dei talenti. Sfide per l'Italia del futuro." *Le nuove mobilità* 73–77. Print.
———. *La fuga dei talenti*. Milan: San Paolo Edizioni, 2009. Print.
———. "La fuga dei talenti." "Centro Studi TF." Web. August 1, 2016. http://fugadeitalenti.wordpress.com/centro-studi-fdt.
Nicotra, Grazia. "Il 'mal d'Europa': Storie di esuli nella narrative di Melania Mazzucco." *Bollettino d'Italianistica: Rivista di critica, storia letteraria, filologia e linguistica* VIII.2 (2011): 359–80. Print.
Noce, Claudio, dir. *Good Morning, Aman*. DNA Cinematografica/RAI Cinema, 2009. Film.
Oboe, Annalisa. *Approaching Sea Changes: Metamorphoses and Migrations across the Atlantic*. Padua: Unipress, 2005. Print.
Oboe, Annalisa, and Anna Scacchi. *Recharting the Black Atlantic: Modern Cultures, Local Communities, Global Connections*. New York: Routledge, 2008. Print.
O'Healy, Áine. "Border Traffic: Reimagining the Voyage to Italy." *Transnational Feminism in Film and Media: Visibility, Representation, and Sexual Differences*. Ed. Katarzyna Marciniak, Anikó Imre, and Áine O'Healy. New York: Palgrave Macmillan, 2007. 37–52. Print.
———. "Lamerica, Gianni Amelio, Italy, 1994." *The Cinema of Italy*. Ed. Giorgio Bertellini. London: Wallflower Press, 2004. 245–53. Print.
Orchestra di Piazza Vittorio. *L'orchestra di Piazza Vittorio*. Apollo 11, 2004. CD.
Orsi, Roberti. *The Madonna of 115th Street: Faith and Community in Harlem, 1880–1950*. 1985. Second edition. New Haven, CT: Yale University Press, 1985. Print.
Ottaviano, Chiara. "Riprese coloniali." *Zapruder: Storie in movimento* 23 (September–December 2010: "Brava gente: Memoria e rappresentazioni del colonialismo italiano"). 9–23. Print.
"Papa: migranti non sono un pericolo, sono in pericolo." 28 May 2016. Ansa.it. Web. August 1, 2016. http://tinyurl.com/Papamigranti.
Paradisi, Umberto, dir. *Dagli Appennini alle Ande*. Film Artistica Gloria, 1916. Film.
Parati, Graziella. "The Legal Side of Culture: Notes on Immigration, Laws, and Literature in Contemporary Italy." *Annali d'Italianistica* 16 (1998): 297–313. Print.
———. *Mediterranean Crossroads: Migration Literature in Italy*. London: Associated University Press, 1999. Print.
———. *Migration Italy: The Art of Talking Back in a Destination Culture*. Toronto: University of Toronto Press, 2005. Print.
———. "Where Do Migrants Live? Amara Lakhous's *Scontro di civiltà per un ascensore a Piazza Vittorio*." *Annali d'Italianistica* 28 (*Capital City Rome 1870–1910*): 432–46. Print.
Parati, Graziella, and Anthony Tamburri, eds. *The Cultures of Italian Migration: Diverse Trajectories and Discrete Perspectives*. Madison, NJ: Farleigh Dickinson University Press, 2011. Print.
Pariani, Laura. *Dio non ama i bambini*. Turin: Einaudi, 2007. Print.
Pastorino, Gloria. "Death by Water? Constructing the "Other" in Melliti's *Io l'altro*." Bullaro 308–39.
Pell, Gregory. "Terroni di mezzo; Dangerous Physiognomies." Bullaro 178–218. Print.
Pellicani, Michela C. "Transizione demografica, invecchiamento della popolazione e migrazioni di sostituzione." Di Comite 224–40.
Pendola, Marinette. *Gli italiani di Tunisia. Storia di una comunità (XIX–XX secolo)*. Foligno: Editoriale Umbra, 2007. Print.
Perco, Daniela, ed. *Balie da latte, una forma peculiare di emigrazione temporanea*. Feltre: Comunità montana feltrina, 1984. Print.
Perec, Georges. *Ellis Island*. 1980. New York: New Press, 1995. Print.

Però, Franco, dir. *Alexandria*. By Renata Ciaravino. 2008. Performance.
Però, Franco, and Patrizia Vascotto, eds. *Le rotte di Alexandria*. Trieste: EUT, 2012. Print.
Petricioli, Marta. *Oltre il mito: L'Egitto degli italiani (1917–1947)*. Milan: Mondadori, 2007. Print.
Petrollo, Cetta. *Senza Permesso: Avventure di una badante rumena*. Viterbo: Nuovi Equilibri, 2007.
Piccolo, Francesco. "Noi che all'Esquilino ci viviamo." *Prove d'orchestra*. Rome: Lucky Red, 2006. 5–9. Print.
Pirandello, Luigi. "L'altro figlio" *Novelle per un anno* (vol. 6): *In Silenzio*. Florence: Bemporad, 1923. Print.
Pojmann, Wendy. "Adopt a Domestic Worker? The Response of Immigrant Associations to the Centre-Right." *Resisting the Tide: Cultures of Opposition in the Berlusconi Years*. Ed. Daniele Albertazzi, Clodagh Brook, Charlotte Ross, and Nina Rothenberg. New York: Continuum Books, 2009. 177–89. Print.
Popescu, Grigore Arbore. *Dall'Adriatico al Mare Nero: Veneziani e romeni, tracciati di storie comuni*. Rome: Consiglio Nazionale delle Ricerche, 2003. Print.
Portelli, Alessandro. "Fingertips Stained with Ink: Notes on New 'Migrant Writing' in Italy" *Interventions* 8.3 (2006): 472–83. Print.
———. "Mediterranean Passage: The Beginnings of an African Italian Literature and the African American Example." *Black Imagination and the Middle Passage*. Ed. Maria Diedric, Henry Louis Gates Jr., and Carl Pedersen. New York: Oxford University Press, 1999. 282–304. Print.
Pugliese, Enrico. "In Germania." Bevilacqua, *Storia dell'emigrazione italiana*: *Arrivi*. 121–32.
———. *L'Italia tra migrazioni internazionali e migrazioni interne*. 2002. Rev. ed. Bologna: Il Mulino, 2006. Print.
Ragusa, Kym, dir. *Fuori/Outside*. New York: Third World Newsreel, 1996. Film.
———. *Passing*. New York: Third World Newsreel, 1996. Film.
———. "Sangu du sangu meu: Growing up Black and Italian in a Time of White Flight." Guglielmo and Salerno 213–23. Print.
———. *The Skin Between Us: A Memoir of Race, Beauty and Belonging*. New York: Norton, 2006. Print.
Rapporto Italiani nel mondo 2012. Fondazione Migrantes/TAU Edizioni. "Sintesi." Web. August 1, 2016. http://tinyurl.com/Rapporto2012.
Renda, Francesco. "L'occupazione militare alleata (10 luglio 1943–10 febbraio 1944)." *Storia della Sicilia dalle origini ai nostri giorni*. Palermo: Sellerio, 2006. 3:1227–71. Print.
Renoir, Jean, dir. *Toni*. 1935. Film.
Rinauro, Sandro. *Il cammino della speranza. L'emigrazione clandestina degli italiani nel secondo dopoguerra*. Turin: Einaudi, 2009. Print.
Rodari, Gianni. *I cinque libri: Storie fantastiche, favole, filastrocche*. Turin: Einaudi, 1993. Print.
Romeo, Caterina. "Una capacità quasi acrobatica." *La pelle che ci separa*. By Kym Rgusa. Rome: Nutrimenti, 2008. 249–70. Print.
Romeyn, Esther. *Street Scenes: Staging the Self in Immigrant New York, 1880–1924*. Minneapolis: University of Minnesota Press, 2008. Print.
Rosi, Francesco, dir. *I magliari*. Titanus, 1959. Film.
Rosoli, Gianfausto, ed. *Un secolo di emigrazione italiana 1876–1976*. Rome: Centro Studi Emigrazione, 1978. Print.
Rosselli, Amalia. *Locomotrix: Selected Poetry and Prose of Amelia Rosselli*. Ed. and trans. Jennifer Scappettone. Chicago: University of Chicago Press, 2012.
Ruberto, Laura. E. *Gramsci, Migration, and the Representation of Women's Work in Italy and the U.S.* New York: Lexington Books, 2007. Print.
———. "Neorealism and Contemporary European Immigration." *Italian Neorealism and Global Cinema*. Ed. Laura Ruberto and Kristi M. Wilson. Detroit: Wayne State University Press, 2007. 242–58. Print.

Rumiz, Paolo. "L'antica rotta delle badanti italiane." 28 August 2005. LaRepubblica.it. Web. August 1, 2016. http://tinyurl.com/Rumizbadanti.

Russo, Giovanni. *I cugini di New York: Da Brooklyn a Ground Zero.* Milan: Scheiwiller, 2003.

Sanfilippo, Matteo. "Elementi caratteristici di un museo d'emigrazione." *Museo nazionale delle migrazioni: L'Italia nel Mondo. Il Mondo in Italia.* Ed. Norberto Lombardi and Lorenzo Prencipe. Rome: MAE, 2008. 131–37. Print.

Sassen, Saskia. "The De-Facto Transnationalizing of Immigration Policy." Florence: Jean Monnet Chair Papers/The Robert Schuman Centre at the European University Institute, 1996. Print.

Sayad, Abdelmalek. *La doppia assenza. Dalle illusioni dell'emigrato alle sofferenze dell'immigrato.* 1999. Milan: Cortina Raffaello, 2002. Print.

Scacchi, Anna, and Elisa Bordin, eds. *Transatlantic Memories of Slavery: Reimagining the Past, Changing the Future.* Amherst, NY: Cambria Press, 2015. Print.

Scatafassi, Michele, Marco Sciò, Costanza Ulissi, and Silvia Violati. "La Pantanella e l'urbanistica a Roma." *Mulino Pantanella: Il recupero di una archeologia industriale romana.* Ed. Francesco Amendolagine. Venice: Marsilio, 1996. 17–29. Print.

Scego, Igiaba, ed. *Italiani per vocazione.* Florence: Cadmo, 2005. Print.

Schrader, Sabine, and Daniel Winkler, eds. *The Cinemas of Italian Migration: European and Transatlantic Narratives.* Newcastle upon Tyne, UK: Cambridge Scholars Publishing, 2013. Print.

Schweitzer, Sylvie. "La mère de Cavanna. Des femmes étrangères au travail au XXe siècle." *La Découverte (Travail, genre et sociétés)* 2008/2.20: 29–45. Print.

Sciascia, Leonardo. "Il lungo viaggio." *Il mare colore del vino.* Turin: Einaudi, 2003. 21–27. Print.

Sciotti, Antonio. *Napoli-New York solo andata.* Naples: Magma, 2007. Print.

Scott, Michael. *Maria Meneghini Callas.* Boston: Northeastern University Press, 1992. Print.

Segre, Andrea, Dagmawi Yimer, and Riccardo Biadene, dirs. *Come un uomo sulla terra.* 2008. Film.

Serra, Ilaria. *The Imagined Immigrant: Images of Italian Emigration to the United States between 1890 and 1924.* Madison, NJ: Fairleigh Dickinson University Press, 2009. Print.

———. *The Value of Worthless Lives: Writing Italian American Immigrant Autobiographies.* New York: Fordham University Press, 2007. Print.

Shehu, Natasha. *L'ultima nave.* Molfetta: La Meridiana, 2001. Print.

Soja, Edward W. *Thirdspace: Journeys to Los Angeles and Other Real-and-Imagined Places.* Cambridge, MA: Blackwell, 1996. Print.

Sonnino, Eugenio. *Roma e gli immigrati: La formazione di una popolazione multiculturale.* Milan: Franco Angeli, 2006. Print.

Speciale, Alessandra, dir. *Ritratto di famiglia con badante.* 2009. Film.

Spivak, Gayatri. *Death of a Discipline.* New York: Columbia University Press, 2003.

Spottswood, Richard. *Ethnic Music on Records: A Discography of Ethnic Recordings Produced in the United States, 1893 to 1942.* Champaign: University of Illinois Press, 1990. Print.

Stella, Gian Antonio. *Odissei: Italiani sulle rotte del sogno e del dolore.* Milan: Rizzoli, 2004. Print.

———. *L'orda. Quando gli albanesi eravamo noi.* Milan: Rizzoli, 2003. Print.

———. *Il viaggio più lungo: L'odissea dei migranti italiani.* Milan: Rizzoli, 2010. Print with DVD.

Stella, Gian Antonio, and Emilio Franzina. "Brutta gente. Il razzismo anti-italiano." Bevilacqua, *Storia dell'emigrazione italiana: Arrivi* 283–311.

Stoler, Ann Laura and Karen Strassler. "Castings for the Colonial: Memory Work in 'New Order' Java." *Comparative Studies in Society and History* 42.1 (January 2000): 4–48. Print.

Surdich, Francesco. "Nel Levante." Bevilacqua, *Storia dell'emigrazione italiana: Arrivi* 184–191.

Talese, Gay. "Gay Talese: Father of the New Journalism." CUNY Lecture (Kingsborough Community College's Best-Selling Author Series). June 2007. http://tinyurl.com/TaleseBridge.

Taviani, Paolo and Vittorio, dirs. *Kaos*. Gaetano "Giuliani" De Negri, 1984. Film.

Tekle, Feven Abreha with Raffaele Masto. *Libera: L'odissea di una donna eritrea in fuga dalla guerra*. Milan: Sperling and Kupfer, 2005. Print.

Tenzer, Livia. "Documenting Race and Gender: Kym Ragusa Discusses *Passing* and *Fuori/Outside*." *Women's Studies Quarterly* 30.1/2 (Spring/Summer 2002): 213–20. Print.

ter Wal, Jessica. "The Social Representation of Immigrants: The Pantanella Issue on the Pages of *La Repubblica*." *Journal of Ethnic and Migration Studies* 22.1 (1996): 39–66. Print.

Testa, Gian Maria. *Da questa parte del mare*. 2006. CD.

Tintori, Guido. *Fardelli d'Italia*. Rome: Carocci, 2009. Print.

Tirabassi, Maddalena and Alvise Del Pra'. *La meglio Italia: Le mobilità italiane nel XXI secolo*. Turin: Centro Altreitalie/Accademia University Press, 2014. Print.

Tomasella, Paolo. "Angelo Viecelli (1897–1948) e l'architettura sanitaria in Romania tra le due guerre mondiali." Popescu 236–42.

Tornatore, Giuseppe, dir. *The Unknown Woman* [*La sconosciuta*]. Medusa, 2006. Film.

Toso, Isotta, dir. *Scontro di civiltà per un ascensore a Piazza Vittorio*. 2010. Film.

"Trovato morto per freddo: Sher Khan partecipò all'occupazione della Pantanella." *La Repubblica Bologna*. December 9, 2009. Web. August 1, 2016. http://tinyurl.com/KhanPantanella.

Ultan, Lloyd, and Barbara Unger, ed. *Bronx Accent: A Literary and Pictorial History of the Borough*. New Brunswick, NJ: Rutgers University Press, 2000. Print.

"Una 'tuttofare' italiana per Kate e William. Antonella Fresolone a Kensington Palace." *La Repubblica*. 5 May 2014. Web. August 1, 2016. http://tinyurl.com/tuttofare

Valerio, Roberta. "Badanti." Photo project. 2009. Web. August 1, 2016. http://tinyurl.com/ValerioBadanti.

Vecoli, Rudolph. "The Italian Diaspora, 1876–1976." *The Cambridge Survey of World Migration*. Ed. Robin Cohen. Cambridge, UK: Cambridge University Press, 1995. 114–22. Print.

Vegliante, Jean-Charles. "Les productions culturelles des Italiens en France dans l'entre-deux guerres: éléments de réflexion." *L'Italie vue d'ici*. Ed. Ada Tosatti and Jean-Charles Vegliante. Paris: L'Harmattan, 2012. 19–35. Print.

Verdicchio, Pasquale. *Bound by Distance: Rethinking Nationalism through the Italian Diaspora*. Madison, NJ: Farleigh Dickinson University Press, 1997. Print.

Vial, Eric. "In Francia." Bevilacqua *Storia dell'emigrazione italiana: Arrivi* 133–146.

Viscusi, Robert. *Astoria*. 1995. Toronto: Guernica Editions, 2003. Print.

———. *Ellis Island*. 2009. New York: Bordighera Press, 2013. Print.

———. *Ellis Island* (Random Sonnet generator). Web. August 1, 2016. http://ellisislandpoem.com/viscusi.php

Viviani, Raffaele. *Scalo Marittimo ('Nterr' 'a Mmaculatella)*. *Teatro*. v. 1. Ed. Guido Davico Bonino, Antonia Lezza, and Pasquale Scialò. Naples: Guida Editori, 1987. 204–40. Print.

INDEX

18 Ius Soli (Kuwornu), 185, 189–91; children of immigrants, 189, 225n4; colonialism and postcolonialism, 190–1; Italian citizenship law, 186–7, 189, 191; pre-occupation, 191

A sud di Lampedusa (Liberti), 51, 53
Adascalitei, Mariana, 218n11. *See also* "Il giorno di San Nicola"
aging population in Italy, 223n28. *See also* elders, acceptance of immigrants and
AIRE (Anagrafe Italiani Residenti all'Estero), 3, 11, 197n3
Alexandria, 164. See also *Alexandria*; Egypt
Alexandria (Ciaravino and Però), 17, 132, 162, 164–72; behavioral codes, 168–9; cultural discovery and social experimentation, 166–8; ethnic co-existence, 164; exploitation of women, 168; financial security of women, 169; loneliness of women, 169; migratory chain, 166, 171; preoccupation/pre-occupied, 172; sexual satisfaction of women, 168; wet nurses, 165–6; women's return home, 169–71. *See also* Egypt; Però, Franco
"All at One Point" (Calvino), 1–3; belonging, 85; co-existence,1; pasta metaphor, 116; pre-occupied spaces in, 1–2; racism/discrimination, 2
Amelio, Gianni: *Così ridevano*, 99, 210n3; *Lamerica*, 19, 32
And the Ship Sails On. See Fellini, Federico: *And the Ship Sails On*
Argentina: anarchism, 90–1, 212n17; in De Amicis' "Dagli Appennini alle Ande," 220n2; Italian influence on Spanish language, 89; Italian migration patterns, 4, 7, 86, 197n6; Italian neighborhoods and *conventillos*, 87–9, 211nn5,12; in *L'orchestra di Piazza Vittorio*, 78; and Mignonette, 39; and *Nuovomondo*, 47; and Pariani, 83; reception of Italians, 89, 211n7, 211n9; "tanos," 87

Bachelard, Gaston, *The Poetics of Space*, 125–6
badanti, 173–4, 182, 220n4, 223n30, 224nn34,38,39,40; in *Clash*, 105
Baily, Samuel. See *Immigrants in the Lands of Promise*
Bertelli, Gualtiero. See *L'orda: Storie, canti e immagini di emigranti*
Bhabha, Homi,13
boardinghouses, 117; children, 122–3; as domestic space/production space hybrid, 122–3; domestic workers, 121–2; habiting, 120–1; as microcosm in *Vita*, 119; transnationality, 117–28. *See also* tenement houses
Bonifazi, Corrado, geography of preoccupation, 12
Bordonaro, Tommaso, *La spartenza*, 31–2
Brotherhood of the Grape (Fante), 142
Buenos Aires, Italians in, 90, 211n5; residential patterns, 211n12. *See also* Argentina
Buti, Carlo, Mignonette and, 38

Callas, Maria Meneghini, 108
Calvino, Italo. *See* "All at One Point"
Camilleri, Andrea, books about immigration, 212nn2,24, 217n8
casa di ringhiera, 94–6
"Case e palazzi" (Rodari), 132–3; "homeless," 133; migrant construction labor, 132–3; transnational labor, 133
Cassano, Franco, 13, 184
Cavanna, François, 218n10. See *Les Ritals*
children of immigrants in Italy, citizenship and, 184–8, 225n4
children's literature, *Questa non è una baby-sitter* (Kuruvilla), 132. *See also* Rodari, Gianni
Christ in Concrete (di Donato), 138, 142, 216n26
Ciaramella, Roberto, 33–4
Ciaravino, Renata, 221n10. See also *Alexandria*

241

citizenship: children of immigrants, 225n4; law for immigrants, 184–8
Clash of Civilizations Over an Elevator in Piazza Vittorio (Lakhous), 16, 84, 93–105; Arabic version of, 212n26; *civiltà*, 212n22; coexistence, 78, 96; displacement/*spiazzamento*, 94, 97; elevator, 96–7; empathy, 96; internal migrations, 99; intradiegetic space, 101; Italian diaspora, 99; lock syndrome, 96; palazzos, 84, 94; passing, 97–8; piazza/*pazzia*, 103; postcolonial detective novel, 103; question of language, 101–3; racism, 100; Rome, 97, 99–100; the South, 100; translation, 101–2. *See also* de Certeau, Michel
coexistence, between locals and immigrants, 1; in *Alexandria*, 164, 172; in *Clash of Civilizations*, 96; in *Dio non ama i bambini*, 89; Italian migration experiences, 14–16; multiethnic and intercultural in *L'orchestra di Piazza Vittorio*, 78; slavery and Italian emigration, 50. *See also* empathy
colonialism: colonies and Empire, 7, 197n7; emigration overlap, 8; Eritrea, 66–7; Ethiopia, 175, 223n32; invasion of space, 183; Italian, geostatistics, 7–9; in *L'orchestra di Piazza Vittorio*, 79; Pantanella affair and, 111, 116; race relations and, 13; and the South, 54, 100; "The Story of Woizero Bekelech and Signor Antonio," 162, 175, 180–1; term use, 225n2. *See also* postcolonialism
Come un uomo sulla terra, 51, 66
Compagnia delle Acque. *See L'orda: Storie, canti e immagini di emigranti*
connectivity, 157, 184, 225n1
construction labor, 137–8; anonymity and, 134; bricklayer, 151; *caporalato*, 153–5; *Christ in Concrete* (di Donato), 138; construction sites, 140; Einaudi on, 140; exploitation, 153–5; "Il giorno di San Nicola" (Adascalitei), 151–5; invisibility of immigrants, 138; Italian companies in Romania, 158–9; Italians in France, 139–50; military service and, 208n31; padrone system, 151; Romanian, 151–2; Roverato, Jean-Francois, 140; site as sanctuary, 145; statistics, 150–1; symbolism in *Les Ritals*, 144–5; undocumented, 150; during war times, 140–1; women and, 154–5, 218n17
conventillos, 83, 210n1; composition, 89; *Dio non ama i bambini* and, 83–4, 87–91; entrapment metaphor, 88–9; photograph, Buenos Aires, 88
Corti, Paola, 19–20

Crialese, Emanuele, 40; *Once We Were Strangers*, 40; *questione meridionale*, 40; *Respiro/Grazia's Island*, 40; *Terraferma*, 204n25. *See also Nuovomondo*
Cultural-Shock project, 191–2; foreigner, 191–2; national identity as an approximation, 191
Curcio, Renato, *Shish Mahal*, 108–9, 117

"Dagli Appennini alle Ande." *See* De Amicis, Edmondo; Paradisi, Umberto
D'Angelo, Pascal, *Son of Italy*, 31
De Amicis, Edmondo: "Dagli Appennini alle Ande," 165, 220n2; *On Blue Water*, 29, 37–8, 205n34; and Paradisi, 32
de Certeau, Michel, 13; delinquent space, 84, 91; everyday life, 84, 93, 103; migration and migrants, 84, 93; theory of space, 84–5, 101; walk the city, 92
De Gregori, Francesco, 25
De Luca, Erri, 138; *Sola andata: Righe che vanno troppo spesso a capo*, 193–4
Del Grande, Gabriele, 68; *Mamadou va a morire: La strage dei clandestini nel Mediterraneo*, 24, 26, 42, 51
delinquent space, 13, 41, 84
di Donato, Pietro. *See Christ in Concrete*
dialects: in *Clash*, 102; in *Les Ritals*, 143
diaspora: exodus, 99; *Italy's Many Diasporas* (Gabaccia), 140; size, 4
Dio non ama i bambini (Pariani), 16, 85–93; anarchism, 90–1; anti-Italian sentiments, 87; children, 92; *conventillos*, 83–4, 87–91; detective/noir genre migrant style, 84, 93; gender roles, 90–1; Italians in Argentina, 86–7, 89; linguistic inventivess, 89–90; multimedia quality, 86; multi-regional/multinational coexistence, 89; photography in, 93; preoccupation, 88; themes, 85. *See also* Argentina; de Certeau, Michel
discrimination. *See* racism
dispersion of migration, 8–10, 197n6
dissemiNation, 13, 183
Dispute Over a Very Italian Piglet, 159, 189
Divorce Islamic Style (Lakhous), 102–3; dialect, 213n34; Egypt in, 222n21; Tunisia in, 213n34
Dolkart, Andrew, *Biography of a Tenement House in New York City*, 119–20
domestic workers: *badanti*, 173–4; in boardinghouses, 121–2; construction sites and, 154–5, 218n17; *Dossier Statistico Immigrazione*, 223n26; fear of, 223n3; gender and, 161–2, 218n17; invisibility and, 134, 161; Italians in Egypt, 162–72; postcolonialism and, 172–9; risk of perdition, 222n17;

stereotypes, 161; stigma, 221n8; "The Story of Woizero Bekelech," 132; tasks included, 161; transnational spaces and, 179–82. *See also badanti*; wet nurses
Dossier Statistico Immigrazione, 10, 158, 223nn26,28

Egypt: demographic colonialism in, 198n8; homogenization and, 169–70; Italian domestic workers, 162–72; Italian migration to, 17, 162–4, 221n12; Italians in, 164. *See also* Alexandria; *Alexandria*
Einaudi, Luigi, on construction laborers, 140
elderly caretakers. *See badanti*
elders, acceptance of immigrants and, 201n35. *See also* aging population in Italy
Ellis Island: *Nuovomondo*, 47–8; *Vita*, 118
emigration from Italy: colonialism overlap, 8; descendants, 9; and Fascism, 185, 198n8; and immigration, 11, 15, 17–19; patterns, 4, 7; and postcolonialism, 188–92; scholarly projects, 198n15; from Sicily, 205n28; and slavery, 58. *See also* Argentina; Buenos Aires; colonialism: Emilia; empathy; France; Friuli; Tunisia; United States
Emilia: anti-immigrant denigration in, 148; emigration from, 143; Piacenza dialect, 143
empathy, 193–4, 200n31; between locals and immigrants, 17–20; in *Clash of Civilizations*, 96; in "Il giorno di San Nicola," 159; in *Pantanella*, 114; in *Sailing Home*, 56
Eritrea: dictatorship, 65; immigration to Italy, 70, 173; Italian colonialism in, 7–8, 66–7, 197n7; push factors for emigration from, 66; war with Ethiopia, 66, 67, 70, 208n31. *See also Libera: L'odissea di una donna eritrea in fuga dalla guerra*
Ethiopia: in *Come un uomo sulla terra*, 66; dictatorship in, 175; immigration to Italy, 173; Italian colonialism in, 7–8, 177–8, 181, 197n7; oral storytelling, 175; resistance to Italian colonization, 175, 223n32; war with Eritrea, 66, 67, 70. *See also* "The Story of Woizero Bekelech and Signor Antonio"
EU (European Union), 4, 11, 28, 72, 209n36; "extra-community" versus people, 151–2, 158, 186–7; Fortress Europe, 4, 68
exclusion, self-recognition and, 148–9

Fallaci, Oriana, *La rabbia e l'orgoglio*, 18
Fante, John: *Brotherhood of the Grape*, 142; works on construction, 217n3
fascism: demographic colonialism, 198n8; emigrants' alleged affiliation with, 39, 140; "Faccetta nera," 38; racist laws in the colonies, 173; view of emigrants, 185
Fellini, Federico: *Prova d'orchestra*, 80–1; *And the Ship Sails On*, 107
Ferrente, Agostino, Fellini and, 80–1. *See also L'orchestra di Piazza Vittorio*
fertility rates in Italy, 223n29
Firstspace (Soja), 51, 55
foreign population: of Italy, 9–11; of Rome, 77
foreign students in Rome, 94, 100
Forte e Chiaro (Jijon), 184–5, 188–9, 190; *artivismo*, 226n13; G2, 188–9; impact of cizenship law, 188–9
Fortress Europe, 4, 68
Foucault, Michel, 13, 199n21; heterotopia and ship's culture, 46, 205n37
France: crossing the Alps to, 27, 203n3; Italian construction workers, 134, 139–40; Italian immigration patterns to, 7, 140, 144, 218n12; racism in, 140–50; *Ritals*, 142; wet nursing, 163; Vial, 140, 143, 144. *See also Les Ritals*
Friuli: emigration from, 134, 159, 163; return to, 222n20; wet nurses and maids from, 17, 221n7; women's lives in, 165
From Sicily to Elizabeth Street (Gabaccia), 119, 143

G2 (second generation immigrants in Italy), 186–7, 188–92
Gabaccia, Donna: *Italy's Many Diasporas*, 140; *From Sicily to Elizabeth Street*, 119, 143
Gallini, Clara: on anti-immigrant sentiments, 116; Pantanella and, 108
gender: *Dio non ama i bambini* (Pariani), 90–1; emigrants aboard ship, 45; Moya on, 90–1; occupations, 131; roles, domestic work and, 161–2; *The Skin Between Us: A Memoir of Race, Beauty and Belonging* (Ragusa), 57
geography of preoccupation, 12
Ghermandi, Gabriella, 223n33. *See also Queen of Flowers and Pearls*; "The Story of Woizero Bekelech and Signor Antonio"
Ginzburg, Carlo, 27
Giordana, Marco Tullio, *Quando sei nato non puoi più nasconderti*, 51, 206n2
Golden Door. See Nuovomondo
graffiti against immigrants, 75, 82, 102, 192

habiting, 105, 112; boardinghouses, 120–1
Hardt, Michael, Laboratory Italy, 193
Harraga (Lems), Tunisia, 207n7
Harraga, burning documents, 53
Harlem: growth of Italian presence, 207n20; *The Skin Between Us: A Memoir of Race, Beauty and Belonging* (Ragusa), 59–60

heterotopia, 13, 46, 205n37
homogeneity in multiethnic neighborhoods, 75–6
houses/residential places, 14, 75. See also *casa di ringhiera*; *conventillos*; *palazzos*; Pantanella pasta factory

I magliari (Rosi), 32–3; "'A Cartulina 'e Napule," 32
identity: *Sailing Home* (Marra), 55–6; *The Skin Between Us: A Memoir of Race, Beauty and Belonging* (Ragusa), 59–61; stories of return, 52–6
"Il giorno di San Nicola" (Adascalitei), 17, 131–2, 139, 151–8; *caporalato*, 153–4; construction business, 153; corruption, 156; cultural mediation, 157; empathy, 159; exploitation of migrants, 154–5; preoccupation and pre-occupied, 156, 158; translation and interpretation, 152, 153, 157; women in, 152–5, 157. *See also* Romania
"Il muratore della Valtellina" (Rodari), 133–4; entrapment on construction site, 133; migrant construction labor, 133; transnational labor, 133
imagination, Cassano, 13, 184
imagining planetarity, 13
immigrants in Italy: accounts of crossing, 51; aging population and, 201n35; burning documents, 53, 207n7; *casa di ringhiera* apartments, 95; citizenship law, 185–8; countries of origin, 3, 10; exploitation of, 153–5; and G2, 188–92; graffiti against, 75, 82, 102, 192; in the media, 214n14; mixed marriages, 9–10; postcolonial, 16–17. *See also* Eritrea; Ethiopia; India; Romania; Tunisia
Immigrants in the Lands of Promise (Baily), 89, 119, 209n1, 211nn2,5,6
"In Francia" (Vial), 140, 143, 144
India: Indian immigrants in Italy, 10, 217n9; immigrant musicians, 79; Pantanella occupation, 108, 215n16. See also *Questa non è una baby-sitter*
indirect postcolonialism, 17, 173
Io, l'altro (Melliti), 51
ISTAT data on migration, 3
Italian descendants, 3, 9; and citizenship law, 185–7; in France, 150
Italian emigration. *See* emigration from Italy
Italophone literature, 106
Italy's Many Diasporas (Gabaccia), 140
Ius sanguinis versus *ius soli*, 187, 226n14. See also *18 Ius Soli*

Jijon, Maria Rosa, 226n13. See also *Forte e Chiaro*

Koch, Gaetano, 77–8
Kuruvilla, Gabriella, 216n3. See also *Questa non è una baby-sitter*
Kuwornu, Fred, 226n15. See also *18 Ius Soli*
Kyenge, Cécile, 11

La Carusiana (Mignonette), 39
La leggenda del pianista sull'oceano (Tornatore), 32
La rabbia e l'orgoglio (Fallaci), 18
La spartenza (Bordonaro), 31–2
Laboratory Italy, 193
Lakhous, Amara, 83. See also *Clash of Civilizations Over an Elevator in Piazza Vittorio*; *Dispute Over a Very Italian Piglet*; *Divorce Islamic Style*
Lamerica. See Amelio, Gianni: *Lamerica*
language: and colonialism in "The Story of Woizero Bekelech and Signor Antonio," 177–9; and *Dio non ama i bambini*, 89–90; and emigration in *Les Ritals*, 146–7; and immigration in *Clash of Civilizations*, 101–2; and *Vita*, 184–6
Lefebvre, Henri: control and resistance in space, 105; critique of urban space, 13; habiting, 112, 117, 120, 123, 127; space trialectics, 50–1; spontaneous city, 109; *Urban Revolution*, 105; urban self-management, 107; u-topia, 115
L'emigrante (Mari), 32
Les Ritals (Cavanna), 17, 131, 139, 140–50; construction site as sanctuary, 145; dialects, 143; family area of origin, 143; empathy across generations, 159; Fascist era, 146; illiteracy, 142; interethnic solidarity, 149–50; language, 146–7; laughter, 145; linguistic pre-occupation, 143–4; racism, 148–9; relativism, 148; school system and, 146–7; setting, 140–1; stereotyping and, 148; symbolism of construction, 144–5; social discrimination, 144, 146. *See also* Emilia; Ritals
letté, 173
Libera: *L'odissea di una donna eritrea in fuga dalla guerra* (Tekle), 16, 50–1, 64–72; colonialism, 66–7; Firstspace, Secondspace and Thirdspace, 71–2; influence of native speaker, 71; life in Eritrea (Asmara), 64–6; migrant camps in Libya, 67; migration to Ethiopia, 66–7; Raffaele Masto, role of, 70–1; Mediterranean crossing, 65, 68–9; migrant trafficking, 67–8; preoccupation,

71–2; *refoulment*, 69, 208n33; *testimonio* genre, 70–2; Tunisia, 69; women, 66–7
Liberti, Stefano, 68; anti-European revolution, 68. See also *A sud di Lampedusa*
Libya: anti-immigrant racism, 67; colonial enterprise, 7, 197n7; Italians leaving Libya, 169
Lombardi-Diop, Cristina, 69; and Romeo, Caterina, 225n1. See also Roma Residence
L'orchestra di Piazza Vittorio (Ferrente), 16, 76, 78–82; "cinema of relation," 81; documusical genre, 78; multiculturalism in end credits, 78–9; postcolonial immigrants, 78; pre-occupation/preoccupation, 81; regional perspectives, 80; Rome, 76–8; routes of the Italian diaspora, 79; Tower of Babel, 80–1; transnationalization of Italian space, 76. See also Piazza Vittorio; *Prove d'orchestra*
L'orda: Storie, canti e immagini di emigranti (Stella, Bertelli, Compagnia delle Acque), 15, 18–19, 23–9; book *L'orda*, 24; businessmen of emigration, 26; death in "Figlia benedetta," 25; emigrant ships in "Le Navi," 28–9; Italian emigration to Brazil, 24; multicultural call in "Noi," 27–8; preoccupied space, 29; Sirio shipwreck, 25; transnational identity, 27. See also *Odisee*; *On Blue Water*; Sciascia, Leonardo

madamismo, 173
Mamadou va a morire: La strage dei clandestini nel Mediterraneo (Del Grande), 24, 26, 42, 51
Mari, Febo, *L'emigrante*, 32
Marini, Giovanna, 24
Mario, E. A., 35
Marra, Vincenzo, 55. See also *Sailing Home*
Masto, Raffaele. See *Libera*
Matvejević, Predrag, 23
Mazzucco, Melania, 213n1. See also *Vita*
Mediterranean Sea: Channel of Sicily, 50; as Golden Door to Europe, 69; immigrants crossing and rescued, 56, 65; as life opportunity, 72; as Secondspace, 55; as Thirdspace, 55; written accounts of crossing, 51
Melliti, Mohsen, 213n1, *Io, l'altro*, 51. See also *Pantanella: Canto lungo la strada*
Mignonette, Gilda, 15, 32–9; Acierno, Feliciano, 34; "'A Cartulina 'e Napule," 32, 34; Ciaramella, Roberto, 33–4; death, 39; endurance in songs, 37; established songs, 34; fatalism in songs, 37; healing capabilities of, 33; "Il festoso arrivo," 35; La Carusiana, 39; "La dura traversata," 34, 36–7; lyrics, recycling, 37; migrants in songs, 36; New York and, 33–4; "Partenza degli emigranti per l'America," 34–6; political affiliations, 39; Queen of Emigrants, 39; "Rimpatrio dei napoletani," 35; songs about colonial enterprises, 38–9; songs about Italian emigration, 32–7; transnational career, 33–4; Viviani, Raffaele, 33
migrations: de Certeau, 84–5; the departure, 43–4; dispersion, 8–10; geostatistics, 3–12; globalization, 13; invasion myths, 11; Italian immigration peak years, 86–7; migrant terminology, 199n23; militarization and, 202n18; Rome as migratory site, 76–7; space, 13–14; *transmigratori*, 185
Moya, José, 90–1, 212n17

national space, pasta factory and, 105–17; Piazza Vittorio as, 75–82. See also transnationality
neighborhoods, ethnic, 16; Italians in Buenos Aires, 85, 211n4; multi-ethnicity in Italy, 62; multi-ethnicity in Rome, 75–8; pre-occupation, 209n2; as religious sites, 62
Neopolitan songs: "'A Canzona 'e Pusilleco" (Mario), 35; "'A Cartulina 'e Napule" (Mignonette), 32, 34; "Il festoso arrivo" (Mignonette), 35; "La dura traversata" (Mignonette), 34, 36–7; "Partenza degli emigranti per l'America" (Mignonette), 34–6; "Rimpatrio dei napoletani" (Mignonette), 35; "Santa Lucia luntana" (Mario), 34, 35; "Torna a Marechiaro" (Mario), 35
New York, immigration patterns from Italy, 197n6. See also boardinghouses; Ellis Island; Mignonette, Gilda; *Nuovomondo*; tenement houses
Nuovomondo (Crialese), 15–16, 32, 40–9; America as El Dorado, 41; creation of Italians outside of Italy, 44–5, 72; Ellis Island, 47–8; emigration voyages, 44–6; encounter with the ocean, 45; gender roles aboard ship, 45; magic realism, 48–9; Mancuso family, 40–2; ship as heterotopia (Foucault), 46, 205n37; ship as preoccupied space, 41–2; Sicily, 40; transnationality, 40, 48

occupation, 12. See also Pantanella occupation; workplaces
oceans/seas, 14, 24
Odissee (Stella), 19, 24, 201n7, 202n8
On Blue Water (De Amicis), 37–8, 43, 205n34
Once We Were Strangers (Crialese), 40
"The Other Son" (Pirandello), 40

padrone system in construction labor, 151
palazzos, 210n2; *Clash of Civilization Over an Elevator in Piazza Vittorio* (Lakhous), 84, 94
Pantanella: Canto lungo la strada (Melliti), 16–17, 105–17; Boudjedra, Rachid, 106; "city," 114–16; denationalizing, 106–7, 114; empathy, 114; exploitation of immigrants, 112; First World shortcomings, 113; habiting, 105, 112; invasion of city by the police, 116; Italian internal and international migration, 113; Italophone literature/translation, 106; pre-occupation/preoccupation and pre-occupied, 111, 113; post/colonial, 111–12; Rome, 107. *See also* Lefebvre, Henri; Pantanella pasta factory; Pantanella occupation
Pantanella pasta factory, 107–8; buildings, 107; Callas, Maria Meneghini, 108; current state, 214n8; Fellini, Federico, 107
Pantanella occupation, 108; Curcio's *Shish Mahal*, 108–9; data in Caritas study, 213n2, 214n12, 215n16; evacuation of immigrants, 109–10; inhabitants' differences, 115; Martelli Law Amnesty, 215n19; Montesi's photos of, 214n10; role-playing game, 215n23; transnationalism, 106–7, 116–17. *See also* Gallini, Clara; Lefebvre, Henri
Paradisi, Umberto, *Dagli Appennini alle Ande*, 32
Parati, Graziella: *The Cultures of Italian Migration*, 19; elevator in *Clash*, 96–7; *Mediterranean Crossroads*, 71; *Migration Italy*, 19, 181
Pariani, Laura, 83, 210n3. *See also Dio non ama i bambini*
Però, Franco, 221n10, *Alexandria* director, 132, 162; collaboration with Ciaravino, 171–2
Persephone myth, *The Skin Between Us*, 59, 63–4
Piazza Vittorio: architecture, 77–8, 210n8; *L'orchestra di Piazza Vittorio*, 76; market of, 210n9; Santa Maria Maggiore, 77; Stazione Termini, 77
The Poetics of Space (Bachelard), 125–6
Polezzi, *Borderlines: Migrazioni e identità nel Novecento*, 19
postcolonialism: domestic workers and, 172–9; emigration in G2 cultural production, 188–92; immigration in G2 cultural production, 188–92; indirect, 17, 173; reversed repossession, 183; *terrone* and, 54
pre-occupation/preoccupation: definition, 12–13; pre-occupied/preoccupied spaces, 14–18
Prova d'orchestra (Fellini), 80–1

Quando la sera ad Alexandria (Ciaravino). See Alexandria
Quando sei nato non puoi più nasconderti (Giordana), 51
Queen of Flowers and Pearls (Ghermandi), 17, 134, 162, 175
Questa non è una baby-sitter (Kuruvilla), 17, 132, 134–6; exclusion, 135; experience of Indian-Italian woman, 136; pre-occupied, 135; racism and embarassment, 136. *See also* India

racism: anti-African in Italy, 53, 177, 181; anti-African American in *The Skin Between Us*, 60–1; anti-Arab in *Les Ritals*, 148–9; anti-immigrant, 1–2, 173; anti-Italian in France, 144–6, 148, 218n15; Calderoli, 198n13; in the colonies, 224n33; Fascist laws, 173; irony about, 136; myths of invasion, 11; recycled grammar of, 24, 201n4; reversal of/action against, 175, 184, 215n21
Ragusa, Kym, 208n25. *See also The Skin Between Us: A Memoir of Race, Beauty and Belonging*
regions of Italy: affiliation, 4, 31; dialects, 75, 187; in the diaspora and inter/transational space, 40, 43–6, 119, 124; diversity/variety, 4, 80, 119; emigration museums, 206; fragmentation, 8; friction, 87; homogeneous settlements in France, 143; interregional migrations, 99; labels, 48; matrix, 34; and national, 48, 72; neighborhoods, 207n20; regional diversity and coexistence, 77, 79, 89; regionalist and regionalism, 11, 99; separation, 40. *See also* Emilia; Friuli; Sicily
remapping, 14, 82, 181, 184–5, 194
Renoir, Jean. See *Toni*
Respiro/Grazia's Island (Crialese), 40
return: to ancestors' place, 78; departure and, in *Sailing Home*, 52–6; migratory loops in Marra, 52–6; rate of, for Italian emigrants, 4; statistics, 197n4; stories of, 51; temporary for wet nurses, 163
Ritals, 142; in Testa, 219n22
Rodari, Gianni, 216n2; "Case e palazzi," 132; *Favole al telefono*, 17; "Il muratore della Valtellina," 132–3
Roma Residence, 109, 124, 214n15
Romania: immigration patterns from, 10, 159; Italian presence in, 158–9; reception of immigrants from, 158; Romanian workers, 151–2. *See also* "Il giorno di San Nicola"

Rome: basin of languages, 102; foreign students, 100; as exotic South, 100; as migratory site, 76–7, 99–100, 219n24, 222n21; population, 209n4; Rome effect, 100; Urbs, 76; Vatican effect, 100. See also *L'orchestra di Piazza Vittorio*; *Pantanella: Canto lungo la strada*; Piazza Vittorio
Rosi, Francesco. See *I magliari*
Rosolen, Bortolo, 24
Roverato, Jean-Francois, 140

Sailing Home (Marra), 16, 50–6; anti-Maghrebi racism, 53; emigration to the U.S., 52; empathy, 56; Firstspace, Secondspace, and Thirdspace, 55; fishing industry, 52–3; Italian identity, 55–6; immigration to Italy, 53; preoccupation, 54–5; repatriation, 53; Tunisia, 16, 52–4, 56
Sayad, Abdelmalek: double absence of migrants, 49; emigrants/immigrants, 15
Scalo Marittimo (Viviani), 33
Sciascia, Leonardo, "The Long Crossing," 25–6
Secondspace (Soja), 51, 55, 59, 71
self-recognition by exclusion, 148–9
ships, 31; gender roles among emigrants, 45; heterotopia (Foucault), 46, 205n37; as laboratory of culture, 46; Mignonette's songs, 32–40; migrant as floating identity, 32; *Nuovomondo*, 42–6; as preoccupied spaces, 41–2; slave traffic ships, 58, 69
Shish Mahal (Curcio), 108
Sicily: emigrants, 205n28; *Nuovomondo*, 40–2; Ragusa and, 44, 58–9, 62–3; ship leaving dock, 44; *From Sicily to Elizabeth Street* (Gabaccia), 119, 143; Tunisians in, 9
The Skin Between Us: A Memoir of Race, Beauty and Belonging (Ragusa), 16, 50–1, 57–64; the Bronx, 60; Firstspace, Secondspace, and Thirdspace, 58–9; foreign immigration in Palermo, 62–3; gender in, 57; gyno-genealogy, 59–60; Harlem, 59–60; Madonna of Mt. Carmel, 62; Persephone myth, 63–4; preoccupation and preoccupied, 62; slavery and Italian emigration, 50, 58; the Strait, 58–9; white flight, 57
slave traffic ships used for emigrants, in *Libera*, 69; in *The Skin*, 58
Soja, Edward, 13. See also Firstspace; Secondspace; Thirdspace
Sola andata: Righe che vanno troppo spesso a capo (De Luca), 193–4
Son of Italy (D'Angelo), 31

songs: "Faccetta nera" (Micheli), 38; "Figlia benedetta" (Bertelli), 25; "Il naufragio della nave Sirio" (De Gregori and Marini); 25; "Navi" (Bertelli), 28–9; "Noi" (Bertelli), 27. See also Neapolitan songs; *Sola andata: Righe che vanno troppo spesso a capo*; Testa, Gian Maria
Southern Question, *Sailing Home* (Marra) and, 53–4
space: concepts, 13–14, 17; displacement/*spiazzamento* in *Clash of Civilizations*, 94, 97; de Certeau's theory, 84–5; heterotopia (Foucault), 13; juridical, 184–5; migration and, 13–14; oceans/seas, 14, 24; u-topia (Lefebvre), 115. See also houses; remapping; Soja, Edward; workplaces
Spivak, Gayatri, 13, 194
Stella, Gian Antonio. See *L'orda: Storie, canti e immagini di emigranti* and *Odissee*
"The Story of Woizero Bekelech and Signor Antonio" (Ghermandi), 17, 132, 162, 175–9; colonial history, 175–6, 178–9; domestic worker, 176–9; letter writing, 177–8; pre-occupation/pre-occupied, 15, 176, 179; racist abuse, 176–7; transcription and translation, 177–9. See also Ethiopia
students, foreign, 94, 100

Talese, Gay, 138
tano: *papolitano*, 211n8, *napoletano*, 211n8
Tekle, Feven Abreha. See *Libera: L'odissea di una donna eritrea in fuga dalla guerra*
tenement houses, 83, 122, 124, 127, 209n1; *Biography of a Tenement House in New York City* (Dolkart), 119–21. See also boardinghouses; *conventillos*
Terraferma (Crialese), 204n25
Testa, Gian Maria, 206n1; "Il passo e l'incanto," 51, 59, 206n4; "Ritals," 50–1; "Rock," 64, 208n28
testimonio, 65, 70–1, 208n30, 209n34, 219n25
Thirdspace, 50–1, 55; Mediterranean as, 55; the Strait, 58–9
Toni (Renoir), 144
Tornatore, Giuseppe: *La leggenda del pianista sull'oceano*, 32; *The Unknown Woman*, 220n3
transnational labor, 133–4; in construction, 139–50; for domestic work, 162–72
transnationality: boardinghouses, 117–28; intimate spaces, 179–82; *L'orchestra di Piazza Vittorio*, 76; Mediterranean Sea, 52; Mignonette and, 33–4; migrant trafficking, 67; Pantanella occupation, 106–7; and regional identity, 40, 48

Tunisia: in *Clash of Civilizations*, 79, 81; demographic colonialism, 198n8; destination for Italian emigrants, 15, 54; in *Divorce Islamic Style*, 213n34; in *Harraga*, 207n7; in *Libera*, 69; in Pendola, 207n10; in *Sailing Home*, 16, 52–4, 56; Tunisian immigrants in Italy, 9, 15, 198n11

unification process in Italy, 4–5
United States of America: discrimination against Italians, 98; dual citizenship, 187; Ellis Island, 47–8, 118; emigration from Italy, 52–3; immigrant neighborhoods, 119–21; Italian immigration patterns, 4, 7, 205n28, 226n17; Italians and African Americans, 61; slavery to, 16. *See also* Mignonette, Gilda; *Nuovomondo: The Skin Between Us*; *Vita*
Urban Revolution (Lefebvre), 105

Vial, Eric, "In Francia," 140
Viscusi, Robert, 32, 37, 40, 43, 47, 203n4

Vita (Mazzucco), 16, 104, 117–28; Bachelard, Gaston, 126–7; boardinghouses, 117–22; Ellis Island, 118; gramophone, 123–4; Italian newspapers, 124–5; language and education, 124–6; legacy of emigration, 127; Little Italy, 119; plot origins, 118; preoccupation/pre-occupation, 127–8; Prince Street building, 120; reproduction, 122–3; romance, 125–6; spatialization, 118–19; tenements, 119–20; women's lives, 121–2. *See also* Lefebvre, Henri
Viviani, Raffaele: and Mignonette, 33; *Scalo Marittimo*, 33, 49

wet nurses, 162–5; *Alexandria* (Ciaravino), 165–6; financial security, 169; personal care and, 166; postcolonialism and, 172–9; risk of perdition, 168, 222n17
workplaces, 14, 17, 131; anonymity of workers, 134. *See also* construction labor; domestic workers

IMAGE CREDITS

Figure 1. *The Cambridge Companion to Modern Italian Culture*, ed. Zygmunt G. Baranski and Rebecca J. West. New York: Cambridge University Press, 2011, xx.

Figure 2. *The Cambridge Companion to Modern Italian Culture*, ed. Zygmunt G. Baranski and Rebecca J. West. New York: Cambridge University Press, 2011, xxi.

Figure 3. Map developed by Antonio Bevacqua, Center for Mapping and GeoSpatial Analysis, Montclair State University, New Jersey. Data source: "Cent'anni di emigrazione italiana" by Luigi Favero and Graziano Tassello in *Un secolo di emigrazione italiana 1876–1976*, ed. Gianfausto Rosoli. Rome: Centro Studi Emigrazione, 1978, 9–64.

Figure 4. Map developed by Antonio Bevacqua, Center for Mapping and GeoSpatial Analysis, Montclair State University, New Jersey.

Figure 5. Map developed by Antonio Bevacqua, Center for Mapping and GeoSpatial Analysis, Montclair State University, New Jersey. Data source: Italian Ministry Foreign Affairs/Migrant Press (1994) in *Storia dell'emigrazione italiana: Partenze*, ed. Piero Bevilacqua, Andreina De Clementi, and Emilio Franzina. Rome: Donzelli, 2001.

Figure 6. Map developed by Antonio Bevacqua, Center for Mapping and GeoSpatial Analysis, Montclair State University, New Jersey. Data source: *Dossier Statistico Immigrazione 2014 UNAR—Scheda di sintesi*. Rome: Edizioni Idos, 2014.

Figure 7. *Golden Door* [*Nuovomondo*]. Dir. Emanuele Crialese. Fabrizio Mosca Alexandre Mallet-Guy, 2006. Film.

Figure 8. *Golden Door* [*Nuovomondo*]. Dir. Emanuele Crialese. Fabrizio Mosca Alexandre Mallet-Guy, 2006. Film.

Figure 9. Photo by Francesco Cocco—"Nero" series, 2003–7.

Figure 10. Photo by Paolo Pellegrin/Magnum Photos.

Figure 11. Conventillos (Classification: 445). Translation of full text on the back of the photo: "Housing for workers. How workers actually live. A tenement house in a central neighborhood of Buenos Aires where hundreds of workers live." Source: Archivo General de la Nación Dpto. Doc. Fotográficos, Buenos Aires, Argentina.

Figure 12. Photo by Rosy Schirer/Tam Tam. Source: *Album italiano Vivere insieme: Verso una società multiethnic*, ed. Valerio Castronovo. Bari: Editori Laterza, 2006, 137.

Figure 13. "Pantanella Shish-Mahal" photography series by Stefano Montesi.

Figure 14. "Pantanella Shish-Mahal" photography series by Stefano Montesi.

Figure 15. Public domain image.

Figure 16. Full caption: "Mortaria family, 8 Downing St., N.Y., making flowers wreaths. The Little three-year-old on left was actually helping, putting the center of the flower into the petal, and the family said she often works irregularly until 8:00 P.M. The other children, 9, 11, and 14 yrs. old[,] work much later (until 10:00 P.M.) The oldest girl told me her father is a soap-maker and has been making $3.00 a day steady [sic] for three years. They told the same to the other investigator." Source: The Records of the National Child Labor Committee (U.S.).

Figure 17. Photo by Uliano Lucas from the Alinari Archives, Florence, Italy.

Figure 18. Photo from a private collection published in "L'emigrazione femminile in Egitto da un comune del Friuli occidentale, Fontanafredda, nel Novecento: Un caso di studio" by Nadia Boz in *Le rotte di Alexandria*, ed. Franco Però and Patrizia Vascotto. Trieste, Italy: EUT, 2012, 249–64.

Figure 19. Photo by Patrizia Pulga in *Verso una società multiculturale: Immagini di un nuovo paese*, ed. Zeffiro Ciuffoletti. Florence: Alinari, 2007, 53.

Figure 20. *Queen of Flowers and Pearls: A Novel* by Gabriella Ghermandi. Tr. Giovanna Bellesia-Contuzzi and Victoria Offredi Poletto. Bloomington: Indiana University Press, 2015, 230.

Figure 21. Photo by Roberto Cavallini in *Album italiano Vivere insieme: Verso una società multietnica*, ed. Valerio Castronovo. Bari: Editori Laterza, 2006, 196.

Figure 22. Image from the Internet with no related information available.

Critical Studies in Italian America
Nancy C. Carnevale and Laura E. Ruberto, *series editors*

Joseph Sciorra, ed., *Italian Folk: Vernacular Culture in Italian-American Lives*
Loretta Baldassar and Donna R. Gabaccia, eds., *Intimacy and Italian Migration: Gender and Domestic Lives in a Mobile World*
Simone Cinotto, ed., *Making Italian America: Consumer Culture and the Production of Ethnic Identities*
Luisa Del Giudice, ed., *Sabato Rodia's Towers in Watts: Art, Migrations, Development*
Teresa Fiore, *Pre-Occupied Spaces: Remapping Italy's Transnational Migrations and Colonial Legacies*

www.ingramcontent.com/pod-product-compliance
Lightning Source LLC
Chambersburg PA
CBHW080119020526
44112CB00037B/2781